# PRIMA Official Game Guide

D0992837

# GHOST RECON
# FUTURE SOLDIER

Written by
David Knight
& Sam Bishop

Prima Games // 3000 Lava Ridge Road, Suite 100 // Roseville, CA // 95661

# CONTENTS

## FOREWORD BY XAVIER MARQUIS, ART DIRECTOR

*Ghost Recon Future Soldier* is designed as a modern military experience featuring the technology of tomorrow. Staying true to the values of the Tom Clancy universe, Ghost Recon puts a high priority on authenticity and believability. Virtually all of the equipment seen in the game is inspired by authentic real-world technology, scientific prototypes or research projects. We're not creating science fiction; we are just putting forward our view of how the battlefield of tomorrow can be changed through the combination of the US Warfighter's abilities and the most cutting-edge tools for combating the enemy.

The Ghosts are part of a unique special force in the world. Since the Ghost team is an elite team acting in full discretion and secrecy, we needed to define their visual appearance accordingly. I wanted to add scarves to give them their own identity and make them look like executioners, bandits...ghosts. You don't belong to the Ghosts by chance.

But it's not just about their look, their actions speak louder. We think the "Ghost" name is perfect for this type of soldier's approach, as they would prefer that their mission is completed with nobody noticing. Only the best of the best, soldiers with a unique mix of skills on and off the battlefield, ever get to wear the coveted Ghost

insignia. Equipped with the most advanced combat technology, the Ghosts track down the highest-value targets in the highest-risk conflict areas around the world, fighting from the shadows in any climate or terrain. Generally, this elite group of soldiers likes to blend in, quietly take in their surroundings and learn about the people and situations they have come into contact with. They are soldiers with a well-developed sense of proportionality, knowing just how much energy to apply to a given situation, and exactly when to do so.

Ghost Recon Future Soldier is a journey. A believable journey that takes place in a realistic world. Our creative team travelled to many places around the World such as India, Africa, Russia, Eastern Europe and the U.S.A. in order to recreate the most accurate environments in the game. We needed to remain faithful to both the settings and the culture, repre-

senting the local customs, fashion, buildings and natural surroundings. We even created advertising spots in the game reflecting each culture to give the player deeper immersion into the world.

Among all Special Forces in the world, there is only one that wears the mask of death: the Ghosts.

*In traditional belief, a ghost is a scary manifestation of the dead. They remain in the physical realm to avenge, help, or punish the living.*

When you choose to embrace the title, you do what you have to do to complete your mission. Only the dead fight fair.

# 1

# INTRODUCTION

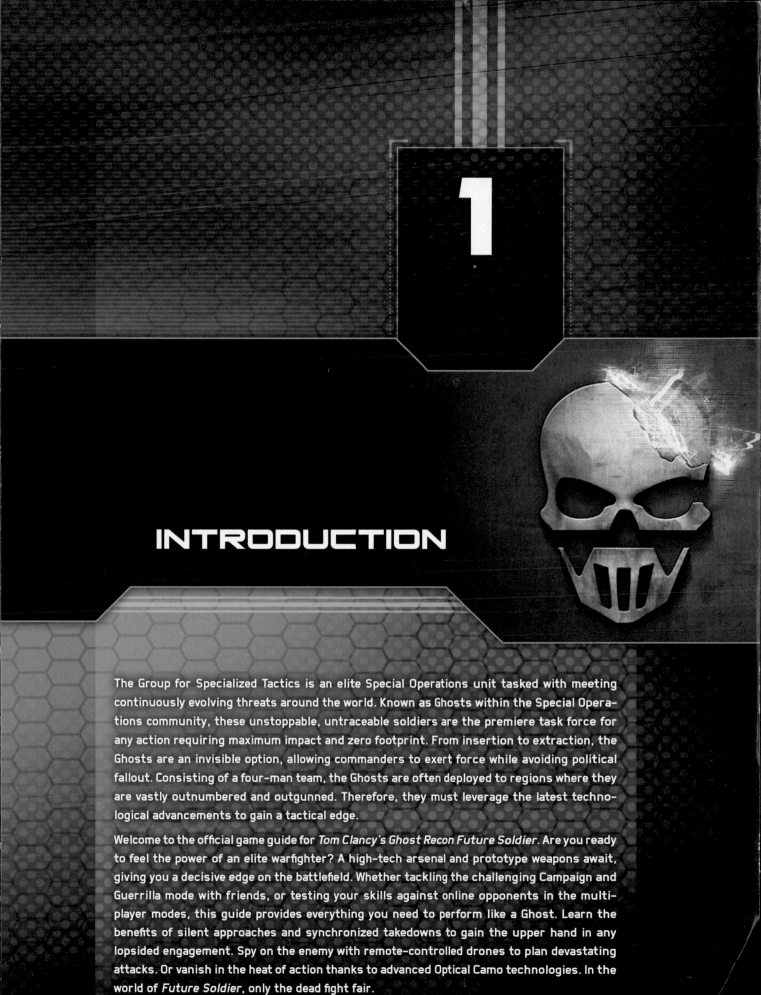

The Group for Specialized Tactics is an elite Special Operations unit tasked with meeting continuously evolving threats around the world. Known as Ghosts within the Special Operations community, these unstoppable, untraceable soldiers are the premiere task force for any action requiring maximum impact and zero footprint. From insertion to extraction, the Ghosts are an invisible option, allowing commanders to exert force while avoiding political fallout. Consisting of a four-man team, the Ghosts are often deployed to regions where they are vastly outnumbered and outgunned. Therefore, they must leverage the latest technological advancements to gain a tactical edge.

Welcome to the official game guide for *Tom Clancy's Ghost Recon Future Soldier*. Are you ready to feel the power of an elite warfighter? A high-tech arsenal and prototype weapons await, giving you a decisive edge on the battlefield. Whether tackling the challenging Campaign and Guerrilla mode with friends, or testing your skills against online opponents in the multiplayer modes, this guide provides everything you need to perform like a Ghost. Learn the benefits of silent approaches and synchronized takedowns to gain the upper hand in any lopsided engagement. Spy on the enemy with remote-controlled drones to plan devastating attacks. Or vanish in the heat of action thanks to advanced Optical Camo technologies. In the world of *Future Soldier*, only the dead fight fair.

OPT-CAMO
OPERATIONAL
∨

## // DRESSED FOR SUCCESS

In the world of *Future Soldier*, knowledge is power. While the Ghost operatives are armed with a variety of lethal weapons, they gain their greatest tactical advantage from their state-of-the-art communications and reconnaissance equipment. As eyes on the ground, it's up to the Ghosts to observe and report while commanders and politicians mull over decisions with potentially dire repercussions.

5° 37' 59" E
6° 19' 59" N
Alt. 80

## // CQC SPECIALISTS

Many missions take the Ghosts to urban environments where they must rely on their Close Quarter Combat (CQC) training to safely navigate cramped alleys and streets while avoiding detection and collateral damage. Retrieval of VIPS often requires precise room-clearing techniques, where speed, expert marksmanship, and the element of surprise are leveraged to overwhelm hostile forces.

## // STEELY RESOLVE

The Ghosts are revered in the Special Operations community for their composure while under fire. These operators are often sent to extremely dangerous locations controlled by hostile forces intent on keeping their secrets from getting out. When all hell breaks loose, the Ghosts are more than capable of defending themselves and extracting successfully with intel critical in forming policy decisions and future military actions.

// ON THE SCENE

Wherever there's a crisis, the Ghosts are available for immediate deployment. Operating out of Fort Bragg, North Carolina, the Ghosts can be deployed anywhere in the world within an 18-hour window. When a helicopter insertion is not an option, the Ghosts are trained to enter hostile territory by other methods, including High Altitude-Low Opening (HALO) jumps.

INFILTRATE
СЕВМОРПУТЬ
*46m*

## // WITHOUT A TRACE

In most cases, the Ghosts have the choice to engage hostile forces or simply sneak past them. One such incident occurs at the beginning of Deep Fire, when the Ghosts are tasked with sneaking aboard a heavily guarded oil drilling ship in the Norwegian Sea.

## // CROSS-COMS ACTIVE

The Cross-coms system deployed by the Ghosts gives each team member the ability to stay in touch with one another and relay crucial intel and targeting information. All data is displayed on an eyepiece, allowing each operative keep their eyes on the action while staying informed.

## // EXPANSIVE ENVIRONMENTS

The Russian airport in Firefly Rain is one of the largest open environments in the campaign. It forces the Ghosts to rely on sparse cover and their Optical Camo to avoid detection while crossing large spans of tarmac. Watch out for enemy snipers!

## // THE INVISIBLE OPTION

The inclusion of Optical Camo adds a whole new gameplay dynamic, allowing the Ghosts to slip through enemy defenses without firing a shot. Because they are often outnumbered and outgunned, the Ghosts are better off avoiding firefights. But Optical Camo has its limitations, functioning only while the operative is moving slowly.

OPTICAL CAMO INITIALISATION

## // EPIC ACTION

While stealth is an important element of *Future Soldier*, in some instances the Ghosts must leverage their vast firepower and unparalleled training to get out of tight spots. One such incident in Firefly Rain involves an intense vehicle chase and a massive cargo aircraft.

## // UNIQUE SETTINGS

Set on an enormous oil drilling ship in the Norwegian Sea, Deep Fire is just one of many original settings featured in the campaign. As the Ghosts fight to reach the ship's control room, there's no time for a sneaky approach. The ship's drilling room features a vertical layout, forcing the Ghosts to traverse a series of catwalks and stairways while battling hostiles and an unforgiving objective time limit.

## // FREEDOM OF MOVEMENT

Each member of the Ghost team is equipped with the latest high-tech weaponry and communications equipment. All gear is designed to be lightweight, significantly reducing encumbrance. This allows each operative to move through a variety of environments at a speed of their own choosing.

Cargo Segment

GPS coordinates confirmed
26°N 43°E

backup data in progress

## // OBSERVE, PLAN, EXECUTE

Frequently outnumbered by hostile forces, Ghosts never rush into a dangerous situation without first observing and planning. If lethal action is necessary, the Ghosts can get the upper hand in most engagements by marking targets and initiating synchronized shots to simultaneously neutralize multiple targets.

## // NO VISIBILITY. NO PROBLEM

By utilizing a variety of intel-gathering devices and advanced optics, Ghosts don't have to physically see their enemies to engage them. By deploying Sensors or a UAV drone, Ghost teams can keep tabs on enemy movements during firefights; enemies are displayed as silhouettes on the Ghosts' heads-up displays. Night Vision Goggles and metal-detecting optical devices allow the Ghosts to spot enemies through dense smoke and even thick pieces of cover.

## // INTIMIDATED BY NOTHING

Each Ghost team member is trained in weaponry ranging from standard-issue firearms to the latest high-tech prototypes. Whether engaging hostile infantry or armored vehicles, the Ghosts are capable of neutralizing a variety of threats.

ANTI-TANK AMMO ON

>WEAK POINT

xx 00;00;05;06;15
SYSTEM DATA

xx 00;00;05;06;15
SYSTEM DATA

xx 00;00;05;06;15
SYSTEM DATA

xx 00;00;05;06;15
SYSTEM DATA

## // WELL TRAVELED

The *Future Solider* campaign takes the Ghosts all over the world while they track down an elusive group responsible for trafficking high-grade military arms. Their journey spans four continents as well as a number of unique environments, including the streets of Moscow.

## // TACTICAL FLEXIBILITY

Even for the Ghosts, not everything goes as planned. With the gathering of fresh intel comes new objectives that require the Ghosts to adjust on the fly. During Subtle Arrow, a fleeing cargo aircraft forces the Ghosts to take aggressive actions, leading to a whole new set of challenges.

## // AMERICA'S SILENT WARRIORS

Only the most elite operators are invited to become Ghosts, having already proved themselves in combat during previous deployments. While all Ghosts serve with a strong sense of honor and duty, they understand their successes will never be publicly acknowledged by politicians or broadcast on the evening news.

WAYPOINT
`LOCK` `INF` `DEL`

The Cross-coms system deployed by the Ghosts utilizes augmented reality to overlay critical mission intel onto each team member's eyepiece. The displayed intel keeps each team member informed of adjustments to objectives as well as updates to navigational data, such as the team's current waypoint. Waypoints are used to guide the team through the area of operations, leading them from one objective to the next like a trail of digital breadcrumbs.

WAYPOINT
`LOCK` `INF` `DEL`

WAYPOINT
`LOCK` `INF` `DEL`

WAYPOINT

## // BROTHERS IN ARMS

Each Ghost team must function in unison under a variety of high-stress situations. Psychological profiles and other personal characteristics are taken into account when forming each four-man team. But no amount of data can predict how each unit will perform under pressure. Compatibility is truly tested on the battlefield, where Ghosts form tight bonds with their teammates.

## // ENHANCED FIREPOWER

The Cross-coms system can interface with a number of heavy weapon systems, such as the Warhound, which is available in Silent Talon. While the Ghosts have the capability to neutralize Infantry and most vehicles, they must seek out heavier firepower when it comes to taking out Main Battle Tanks (MBTs) and helicopters. When close air support is available, Ghost operatives can even take control of guided missiles fired by Allied aircraft.

# GHOST RECON: LEGACY

The *Ghost Recon* series has been going strong since 2001, providing gamers with a steady mix of intense, tactical gameplay and intriguing storytelling. Here's a brief look back at the previous entries in the series.

## 2001 TOM CLANCY'S GHOST RECON

**RELEASE DATE: NOVEMBER 13, 2001**
**PLATFORMS: PC, XBOX, PS2, GAMECUBE**

Eastern Europe, 2008. Russia has fallen under the control of ultranationalistic politicians intent on rebuilding the iron curtain. This leads to conflict with NATO as Russia attempts to reclaim the breakaway Republic of Georgia and the Baltic states of Estonia, Latvia, and Lithuania. As the regional wars escalate out of control, the casualties mount and the Ghosts are sent in. Their mission: Spearhead the way for a NATO peacekeeping force and keep the lid on the conflict before it mushrooms ... literally.

## 2004 TOM CLANCY'S GHOST RECON: JUNGLE STORM

**RELEASE DATE: MARCH 16, 2004**
**PLATFORMS: PS2**

Havana, 2009: Deep in the sweltering jungles of Cuba, a deadly revolution is brewing. Led by a drug-funded warlord, its aim is to take advantage of the post-Castro power vacuum and seize control of the island republic. Enter the Ghosts. Sent to Cuba as part of a UN peacekeeping force, their mission is to destroy the warlord and his mercenary forces, and secure the elections for a free Cuba.

2000 2001 2002 2003 2004 2005

## 2002 EXPANSION PACK TOM CLANCY'S GHOST RECON: DESERT SIEGE

**RELEASE DATE: MARCH 27, 2002**
**PLATFORMS: PC**

East Africa, 2009. A 60-year conflict boils over as Ethiopia invades its smaller neighbor Eritrea, threatening the world's most vital shipping lanes in the Red Sea. An elite team, known as the Ghosts, moves in to safeguard the seas and free Eritrea. As the war rages on, the Ghosts are drawn from Eritrea's shores to the heart of Ethiopia in their deadliest battles yet.

## 2002 EXPANSION PACK TOM CLANCY'S GHOST RECON: ISLAND THUNDER

**RELEASE DATE: SEPTEMBER 25, 2002**
**PLATFORMS: PC, XBOX**

Cuba, 2009: Castro is dead, and the first free Cuban elections in decades are thrown into turmoil by a drug-funded warlord. The Ghosts are sent to Cuba as part of a UN peacekeeping force to destroy the rebel forces and their mercenary leaders and secure the elections for a free Cuba.

## 2004 TOM CLANCY'S GHOST RECON 2

**RELEASE DATE: NOVEMBER 16, 2004**
**PLATFORMS: XBOX, PS2, GAMECUBE**

Korean Peninsula, 2007. North Korea is experiencing a terrible famine, while a corrupt general diverts food supplies to his private army. His goal is to strengthen them until they can conquer a weakened, hungry populace. As food riots worsen and diplomacy breaks down, China and Korea are on the verge of launching nuclear missiles. The Ghosts are being sent in to safeguard the China/North Korea border and depose the rogue general.

## 2005 TOM CLANCY'S GHOST RECON 2: SUMMIT STRIKE

RELEASE DATE: AUGUST 3, 2005
PLATFORMS: XBOX

Kazakhstan, 2012. A Pakistani warlord attempting to take control of the country has assassinated the Kazakh president. Follow the Ghosts as they work in concert with UN forces to track him and his military across Kazakhstan. The Ghosts are the only chance to thwart his attacks against high-profile targets and to prevent national devastation.

## 2010 TOM CLANCY'S GHOST RECON PREDATOR

RELEASE DATE: NOVEMBER 16, 2010
PLATFORMS: PSP

Lead your elite squad on the hunt for terrorists in the jungles of Sri Lanka. Deep behind enemy lines, you have a mission to accomplish: Take out the insurgents before the situation gets out of hand. You'll encounter the enemy on his own ground. He knows the terrain better, has more allies, knows where to hide and where to attack. Surprise is on his side—he can be anywhere, he can be anyone.

## 2010 TOM CLANCY'S GHOST RECON WII

RELEASE DATE: NOVEMBER 16, 2010
PLATFORMS: WII

After being recruited by the Ghosts in Norway, Hibbard and Booth are inserted in Moscow with the Bravo team. When events don't go as planned, Bravo team is ambushed and separated from the rest of their team. Operating as a two-man team and relying on the intel of the local militia, Hibbard and Booth must fight their way to their target in a city infested with enemies. With the numbers clearly not in their favor, they will have to use their advanced weaponry and training to ensure to gain the upper hand.

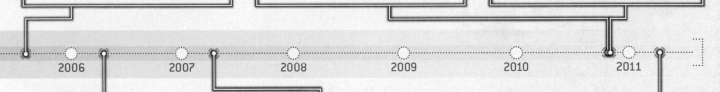

2006  2007  2008  2009  2010  2011

## 2006 TOM CLANCY'S GHOST RECON ADVANCED WARFIGHTER

RELEASE DATE: MARCH 9, 2006
PLATFORMS: PC, XBOX, PS2, XBOX 360, PS3

Mexico, 2013. Following an insurgence in the heart of Mexico City, the U.S. Army's most elite Special Forces team is deployed to the center of the conflict to regain control of the city. Greatly outnumbered but fully equipped with the IWS (Integrated Warfighter System), this elite team is the first and last line of defense on the battlefield. They are the "quiet" professionals. They are the Ghosts.

## 2007 TOM CLANCY'S GHOST RECON ADVANCED WARFIGHTER 2

RELEASE DATE: MARCH 6, 2007
PLATFORMS: PC, XBOX 360, PS3, PSP

Mexico, 2013. The rising conflict between Mexican loyalists and insurgent rebel forces has thrown Mexico into full-scale civil war. Under the command of Captain Scott Mitchell, the Ghosts are called upon to face an imminent threat to the United States. The fate of two countries now lies in the hands of the Ghosts as they fend off an attack on US soil. Equipped with the most cutting-edge weaponry and technology, the Ghosts must battle on both sides of the border to neutralize the escalating rebel threat.

## 2011 TOM CLANCY'S GHOST RECON: SHADOW WARS

RELEASE DATE: MARCH 27, 2011
PLATFORMS: 3DS

As the commander of the Ghosts, your mission is to stop the Russian ultranationalist Yuri Treskayev from coming to power. From the hot deserts of Kazakhstan to the towns and villages of Ukraine and the frozen lands of Siberia, you must discover and disable the secret Soviet-era "Dead Hand" bases that Treskayev is using to build an army of drones to seize power. You have access to full resources to build, train, and equip your team, using increasingly high-tech weapons and armor.

## GHOST TEAM: HUNTER

- Based out of Fort Bragg, North Carolina
- All personnel assigned to the group (soldiers and dedicated support staff) work in a closed and secure compound within Ft. Bragg. Everything they need to complete their mission, from weapon testing ranges, to training 'kill houses' to dining facilities and research and development areas are housed within the compound.
- Can be deployed anywhere in the world within 18 hours

Created as a Special Mission Unit (and initially formed from the members of the 5th Special Forces Group, D Company) this specialized force has unique authority and ability to deploy anywhere in the world, in order to protect US and Allied interests. The unit's reputation for getting the job done and leaving no trace followed them from 5th SFG, as did their nickname …"The Ghosts."

## TEAM DYNAMIC

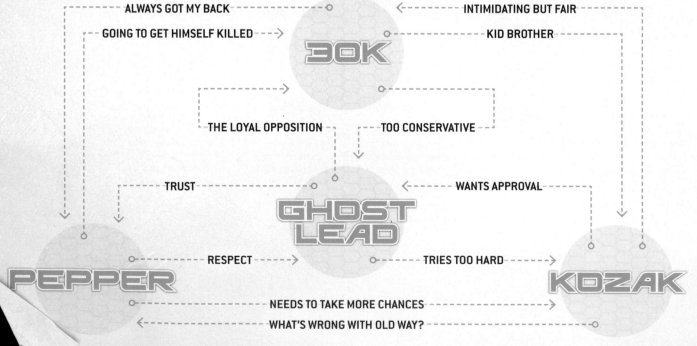

ALWAYS GOT MY BACK        INTIMIDATING BUT FAIR

GOING TO GET HIMSELF KILLED        KID BROTHER

### 30K

THE LOYAL OPPOSITION        TOO CONSERVATIVE

TRUST        WANTS APPROVAL

### GHOST LEAD

RESPECT        TRIES TOO HARD

### PEPPER        ### KOZAK

NEEDS TO TAKE MORE CHANCES

WHAT'S WRONG WITH OLD WAY?

# GHOST LEAD

RANK: Captain
NAME: Cedrick Ferguson
AGE: 38
HEIGHT: 6' 2"
WEIGHT: 185 lbs
BUILD: Long and lanky
HAIR COLOR: Black
EYE COLOR: Brown
BIRTHPLACE: Minneapolis, MN
ETHNICITY: African-American
ACCENT: Slight Midwestern
LANGUAGES SPOKEN: Arabic, Some Farsi

**REASON FOR JOINING THE MILITARY:**
Father and uncles all served; it was the expected career in his family.

**REASON FOR JOINING THE GHOSTS:**
Exemplary service record and skills led him naturally to Special Forces; it's where he feels he can do the most good.

**ATTITUDE TOWARD THE ENEMY:**
Everything the Ghosts do is part of a larger whole. Fight the right battle today and you might not have to fight one tomorrow.

Captain Ferguson is the kind of leader that every team wants, the one who keeps a clear head even in the midst of chaos. He's decisive, executes with precision, and has a long record of doing just the right thing at just the right time. His cool under fire inspires the utmost confidence in his team. He knows when to push and when to push back, and ultimately commands the respect of all those around him, whether friend or foe.

# 30K

| | |
|---|---|
| RANK: | Sergeant First Class |
| NAME: | James "Jimmy" Grant Ellison |
| AGE: | 28 |
| HEIGHT: | 5' 9" |
| WEIGHT: | 190 lbs |
| BUILD: | Stocky |
| HAIR COLOR: | Dirty blond |
| EYE COLOR: | Blue |
| BIRTHPLACE: | Alma, AR |
| ETHNICITY: | Caucasian |
| ACCENT: | Southern |
| LANGUAGES SPOKEN: | English, enough Spanish to get by |

## REASON FOR JOINING THE MILITARY:

It was that or work at the feed lot, and the pay in the Army was a hell of a lot better.

## REASON FOR JOINING THE GHOSTS:

"Big Army" pay wasn't as good as he'd been told, and damned if he was going to let some precious city kids outdo him during selection. The challenge of training earned his respect, and now he's genuinely proud of the unit and its accomplishments.

## ATTITUDE TOWARD THE ENEMY:

They must've done something wrong, or else he wouldn't have to be out in Godforsakenstan killing them.

Ellison head butts what he doesn't understand. He's always been an up-front-in-your-face guy whose only interest is getting done whatever it is that needs doing. He's the rowdy best friend you don't want in the bar, but you rely on in the bar fight. He's fearless in offering opinions, regardless of rank or etiquette. Although he tends to be one of the most aggressive Ghosts, he's not reckless, and his willingness to stand up and go toe-to-toe with the enemy has gotten the team out of enough tough spots that they forgive him the few he got them into.

# PEPPER

| | |
|---|---|
| RANK: | Master Sergeant |
| NAME: | Robert Bonifacio |
| AGE: | 39 |
| HEIGHT: | 6' 0" |
| WEIGHT: | 195 lbs |
| BUILD: | Average |
| HAIR COLOR: | Salt-and-pepper |
| EYE COLOR: | Hazel |
| BIRTHPLACE: | Stephenville, TX |
| ETHNICITY: | Half-Latino |
| ACCENT: | None |
| LANGUAGES SPOKEN: | Fluent in Spanish |

**REASON FOR JOINING THE MILITARY:**

Thought he'd do a hitch and use the GI Bill to go to college; instead became a lifer.

**REASON FOR JOINING THE GHOSTS:**

Had no particular ambition toward going Special Forces but was approached about it so many times he finally went for it; never looked back.

**ATTITUDE TOWARD THE ENEMY:**

They're just people who've made some poor choices in life, the worst of which was trying to kill him.

Bonifacio has been there, put holes in that. Whatever just happened, he's seen it before and the other time was worse. Pepper is the Old Man, and everyone treats him accordingly. His advice is valuable, even if you have to endure the story that goes with it, and his marksmanship is legendary. His team leads rely on him to give the worst-case breakdown of any of their plans, and he has a good eye for where things can (and will) go wrong. Jokes are rare, except for the one about being "two days from retirement" whenever a mission starts going south.

# KOZAK

| | |
|---|---|
| RANK: | Staff Sergeant |
| NAME: | John Dmitri Kozak |
| AGE: | 26 |
| HEIGHT: | 6' 1" |
| WEIGHT: | 180 lbs |
| BUILD: | Slightly thin |
| HAIR COLOR: | Shaved |
| EYE COLOR: | Blue |
| BIRTHPLACE: | Brooklyn, NY (Little Odessa) |
| ETHNICITY: | Russian-American |
| ACCENT: | A little Russian, a little Brooklyn |
| LANGUAGES SPOKEN: | Russian, Spanish |

**REASON FOR JOINING THE MILITARY:**

First generation Russian-American, extremely patriotic and has a keen sense of "being American."

**REASON FOR JOINING THE GHOSTS:**

Wants to be the best of the best. The Ghosts are the best unit, so he wants to be a part of it—and someday lead it.

**ATTITUDE TOWARD THE ENEMY:**

The thing to remember is that the other guy thinks he's the hero, too.

Kozak hacks security faster than you text. He's either the most badass nerd, or nerdiest badass you've ever met. He's got two loves: technology and the USA. Like most young bucks, he's eager to prove that he belongs on the team, and though he sometimes seems to be making it up as he goes along, he's pulled it off too many times to just be lucky. His unorthodox nature and willingness to improvise sometimes rub his more conservative teammates the wrong way, but there's no doubt he brings a unique skill set to the team. He tends to talk more than he should, and sometimes argues points into oblivion. For the most part, the other Ghosts look out for him like a kid brother ... unless he's brought something on himself, in which case he gets to learn things the hard way.

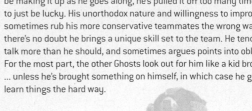

# INTERFACE: THE GHOST HUD

### // KEY LOCATION

Some key locations are marked on the HUD through augmented reality, highlighting objectives and other points of interest within the area of operations.

### // WAYPOINT MARKER

This icon represents the current waypoint, along with the distance to the waypoint, measured in meters. Follow waypoints to navigate the area of operations, moving from one objective to the next.

### // MAGAZINE AMMO

This number represents how much ammo is remaining in your selected weapon's magazine. Reloading automatically occurs when a magazine is empty.

### // ENEMY CONTACTS

Detected enemies appear on the HUD marked with orange diamond icons. Detected enemies obscured by cover show up on the HUD as colored silhouettes. The color of each silhouette represents the alertness of each enemy. If the silhouette is yellow, the enemy is at ease and unaware of the Ghosts' presence. A red silhouette represents an alert enemy who will actively engage the Ghosts. When an enemy is killed, the silhouette turns white.

### // TEAMMATES

Like the enemies, all teammates within your field of view also appear on the HUD marked with blue diamond icons. If a teammate is obscured by cover, the man's position is shown by a blue silhouette.

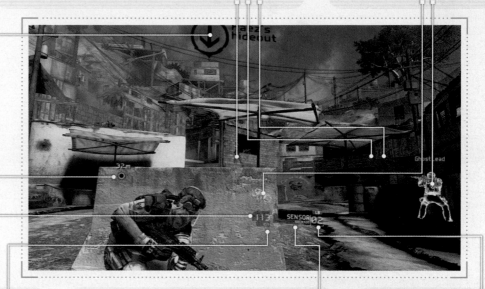

### // RESERVE AMMO

This number indicates the total number of rounds you're carrying around in spare magazines.

### // SELECTED ITEM/DRONE

The name of the currently selected item or drone appears here. Items include a variety of grenades and Sensors. Available drones include the UAV or the Warhound.

### // ITEM COUNT

When an item is selected, the quantity of each item is shown here.

# CONTROLS

## PLAYSTATION 3 CONTROLS

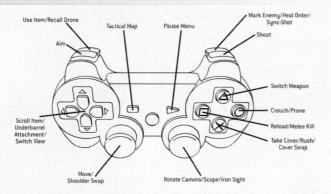

## XBOX 360 CONTROLS

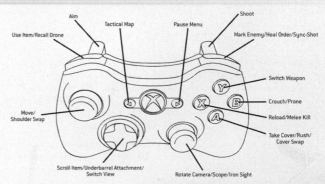

### // Kinect Controls

Kinect functionality is exclusive to the Xbox 360 version, allowing for a controller-free experience while in the Gunsmith interface. Use hand motions to rotate each weapon and apply different attachments. Kinect also recognizes voice commands, allowing you to select weapon modification points by saying words like "Optics" or "Magazine." You can also optimize weapons entirely with your voice by saying phrases, such as, "Optimize for Range." Once you've created a weapon, take it onto the Firing Range and try it out, using only your hands to aim and fire the weapon.

# PC CONTROLS

## PC CONTROLS

| Action | Keystroke |
|---|---|
| Forward | w |
| Back | s |
| Left | a |
| Right | d |
| Reload | r |
| Sprint | Shift |
| Take cover | Sprint or Space |
| Jump over | Space (near object) |
| Crouch | Ctrl |
| Prone | Alt |
| Interact / Melee | e |
| Shoot | Left Mouse Button |
| Aim | Right Mouse Button |
| Iron Sight | Click Mouse Wheel |

## PC CONTROLS

| Action | Keystroke |
|---|---|
| Primary Weapon | 1 |
| Secondary Weapon | 2 |
| Underbarrel Attachment | 3 |
| Inventory Item 1 | 4 |
| Inventory Item 2 | 5 |
| Launch Drone / Switch to Drone | 6 |
| Use Selected Item | f |
| Camera swap | c |
| Mark Enemy / Coordination / Wave Streaks Menu | q |
| Night / Magnetic Vision | v |

## PC CONTROLS

| Action | Keystroke |
|---|---|
| Drone Up | Mouse Wheel up or Up Arrow |
| Drone Down | Mouse Wheel down or Down Arrow |
| Land Drone (when using drone) | Ctrl |
| Call for Help | h |
| Tactical Map / Skip inter Wave | Tab |
| Scoreboard | ~ |
| Next Spectator Camera Target | Right Mouse Button |
| Previous Spectator Camera Target | Left Mouse Button |
| Pause Menu | Esc |

# CAMPAIGN SCORING AND CHALLENGES

Before jumping into the campaign, take a moment to review the Ghost score system as well as the various challenges that await. Understanding the Ghost score system will help you better understand what's expected of an elite operative. The campaign and individual missions also feature a variety of challenges that allow you to unlock new weapons, attachments, and camouflage patterns.

# GHOST SCORE

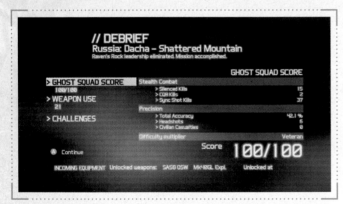

*The scoring system rewards players who perform like a Ghost. Step lightly, kill quietly, and leave no trace behind.*

Do you have what it takes to be a Ghost? During the campaign's missions, your team is awarded points for performing a variety of stealthy and skill-specific actions characterized by Ghost tactics. At the end of each mission, these points, along with the difficulty setting, are calculated to determine your Ghost score. The Ghost score is a percentage, ranging from 0 to 100 percent. See the accompanying table for a rundown of the various actions that earn you points.

Each mission has a predetermined max score representing the score that must be reached to obtain 100 percent in the mission. This max score is based on how many enemies can be killed silently during the mission, and what's expected from you. At the end of the mission, your total points are added, then divided by the mission's max score. This value is then multiplied by 100 to determine your final Ghost score. Here's the formula: **Ghost score = (Total Points / Mission Max Score) × 100**

## ACTIONS AND POINTS

| Action | Description | Points |
|---|---|---|
| Silenced Kill | Kill an unalerted enemy with a suppressed weapon | 2 |
| CQB Kill | Kill an enemy with your bare hands | 3 |
| Sync-Shot | Simultaneously kill a group of enemies with your teammates | 2 (per enemy) |
| Accuracy | Percentage of bullets fired by the whole squad that hit a target | 1 (per percent) |
| Headshot | Shoot an enemy in the head (alerted or not) | 1 |
| Civilian Casualty | Kill an innocent civilian | -20 |
| Trainee Bonus | Complete the mission on Trainee difficulty | 50 |
| Veteran Bonus | Complete the mission on Veteran difficulty | 75 |
| Elite Bonus | Complete the mission on Elite difficulty | 100 |

## MISSION MAX SCORES

| Mission | Max Score |
|---|---|
| Nimble Guardian | 220 |
| Subtle Arrow | 330 |
| Noble Tempest | 290 |
| Tiger Dust | 240 |
| Silent Talon | 200 |
| Firefly Rain | 280 |
| Ember Hunt | 260 |
| Deep Fire | 250 |
| Valiant Hammer | 225 |
| Gallant Thief | 260 |
| Invisible Bear | 200 |
| Shattered Mountain | 225 |

# CHALLENGES

*Weapon and tactical challenges are completed during missions. A notification box appears on the HUD when a challenge has been completed.*

During the course of the campaign, you can complete a variety of optional challenges to unlock new weapons and gear. There are four different types of challenges. Weapon challenges usually require you to perform a specific feat with a certain type of weapon. If you manage to complete a mission's weapon challenge, you're awarded with a new weapon. Tactical challenges are split up into three separate tasks. If you complete all three tasks within a tactical challenge, you'll unlock a new weapon attachment. The Ghost challenges require you to complete a number of missions with a specific Ghost score, thereby unlocking new weapons and camouflage patterns. Finally, there's the Elite challenge, which requires you to complete all missions on Elite difficulty to unlock the G106 Explosive grenade launcher. Before starting a mission, always take into account the challenges and select your gear accordingly.

## ELITE CHALLENGE

**DIFFICULTY:** ★★★★★
**UNLOCK:** G106 GRENADE LAUNCHER

- **Complete all missions on Elite difficulty**

## // NOTE

*All weapon and tactical challenges are covered in the campaign walkthrough. For a complete listing of all challenges, flip to the Compendium at the back of the guide.*

### GHOST CHALLENGES

| Challenge | Reward |
|---|---|
| Perform a Ghost Score of 60% in one mission | Iranian Special Forces weapon paint |
| Perform a Ghost Score of 60% in two missions | Sri Lankan Separatist weapon paint |
| Perform a Ghost Score of 60% in three missions | OTs-33 pistol |
| Perform a Ghost Score of 60% in four missions | Chinese Type 07 Desert weapon paint |
| Perform a Ghost Score of 60% in five missions | Finnish M05 weapon paint |
| Perform a Ghost Score of 60% in six missions | AKS-74U PDR |
| Perform a Ghost Score of 60% in seven missions | Greek weapon paint |
| Perform a Ghost Score of 60% in eight missions | Kuwaiti Special Forces weapon paint |
| Perform a Ghost Score of 60% in nine missions | Ultimax Mk.5 LMG |
| Perform a Ghost Score of 60% in ten missions | Indian Vertical Lizard weapon paint |
| Perform a Ghost Score of 60% in eleven missions | USSR TTsKO weapon paint |
| Perform a Ghost Score of 60% in twelve missions | MK40GL grenade launcher |

# 2

## CAMPAIGN

First into any conflict and last to retreat, the Ghosts handle the missions that no one else can. Inserted deep behind enemy lines, they strike swiftly and then vanish. When a stolen military grade bomb takes out a Ghost squad, a new Ghost Unit must track down the source of the weapons. But the trail Kozak, Ghost Lead, Pepper, and 30K follow leads around the world, into the corridors of power where rebellion and war are brewing. Soon, the Ghosts are all that stands between the world and a devastating global conflict.

NICARAGUA

# GHOST

In traditional belief, a ghost is a scary manifestation of the dead. They remain in the physical realm to avenge, help, or punish the living.

Somewhere in Nicaragua a suspicious military convoy rolls north. The convoy's cargo and destination remain unknown, piquing the interest and concern of US high command. The four-man Ghost team of Ramirez, Allen, McGann, and Haynes are tasked with stopping the convoy and inspecting the cargo. Facing stiff opposition from the convoy's security personnel, the Ghosts have setup an ambush along a remote dirt road carved alongside a steep cliff. They start by eliminating a few of the convoy's drivers, resulting in chaos on the road as trucks crash and overturn.

Before inspecting the convoy's cargo, it's important to eliminate any survivors. Start by picking off one of the confused soldiers inspecting the crash, as viewed from the scope of one of the Ghost's weapons. During this sequence, all you have to do is pull the trigger to initiate the assault—the aim is automatically established and stabilized. Your shot triggers a salvo of automatic fire from your teammates, causing more enemy soldiers to drop dead while others scramble for cover.

Now it's time to identify and capture the target. In an effort to cover their advance, the Ghosts deploy smoke on the wrecked convoy. After rappelling down to the road from their cliffside perch, the Ghosts advance toward the devastated convoy. You can now control one of the Ghost operatives. Move the left control stick to begin moving toward the convoy. Let your teammates take the lead and watch as they engage enemies in the smoke screen ahead. While you may spot muzzle flashes and incoming tracers, the smoke makes it difficult to spot enemies hiding among the wrecked convoy.

Instead of stopping, keep moving into the smoke screen until your thermal vision is activated. The HUD is suddenly filled with bright greens, reds, and yellows. Thermal vision highlights heat given off by your immediate surroundings. This makes it possible to view the heat signatures of yourself, teammates, and enemies. Detected enemies are also highlighted in red, making them easier to spot. When you see an enemy, hold down the aim button and move your weapon's aiming reticle over your target

before firing. Your weapon is automatic and will continue firing as long as you hold down the trigger. But it only takes a few shots to drop each hostile, so fire short bursts when engaging enemies. If you let your teammates lead the way, they'll automatically engage and neutralize most enemy contacts. But be ready to support them, scanning the convoy wreckage for survivors.

After clearing the convoy of hostiles, a cinematic shows the Ghosts inspecting the contents of one of the trucks. Inside, they find a crate containing a large warhead, perhaps from a missile. Suddenly the ringing of a cell phone gets the team's attention—the warhead is rigged to explode within seconds! Realizing the danger, the Ghosts scramble, sprinting away from the truck. But it's too late. Ramirez, Allen, McGann, and Haynes are all caught within the warhead's massive blast radius. While they managed to stop the convoy from reaching the US, they sacrificed their lives in the process.

Where did this weapon come from? Who is behind this? What other threats can be expected? These are just some of the questions lingering in the moments following the incident in Nicaragua. It will be the task of another team of Ghosts to uncover answers to these questions ... and avenge the deaths of their brothers.

## PROLOGUE: COMPLETION UNLOCKS

| Type | Category | Item |
|------|----------|------|
| Weapon | PDR | Goblin |
| Weapon | LMG | Mk48 |
| Weapon | Sidearm | 45T |
| Attachment | Optics | Iron Sight |
| Attachment | Optics | Red Dot |
| Attachment | Underbarrel | Vertical Foregrip |
| Attachment | Underbarrel | Rail Cover |
| Attachment | Magazine | Standard |
| Attachment | Stock | Standard |
| Attachment | Muzzle | Suppressor |
| Items | Grenades | Frag Grenades |
| Items | Grenades | Sensors |
| Paint | Weapon paint | Solid Black |
| Paint | Weapon paint | Solid Green |
| Paint | Weapon paint | Solid Tan |
| Paint | Weapon paint | Multicam |

# NIMBLE GUARDIAN

## BRIEFING

LOCATION: BOLIVIA
OBJECTIVES: EXTRACT GABRIEL PAEZ
CURRENT CONTACT: SENIOR MASTER SERGEANT MARCUS KELSO

_MID-LEVEL DRUG RUNNE

_GABRIEL PAEZ

INSERTION

EXTRACTION

The bomb that killed our men was headed for our southern border. They paid a steep personal price to stop it. But that's the cost we choose to bear for our nation. The cost that Ramirez, Allen, McGann, and Haynes chose to pay, on our behalf. Their sacrifice was not in vain. Let's just hope we don't have to make the same one again.

That bomb had to pass through a lot of hands to end up where it did. One of the men in the chain, Gabriel Paez, wants to come in. Paez is a mid-level drug runner and a new kid on the block in gun running. Sounds like he bit off more than he can chew and now he wants out. He claims he didn't know the bomb's target. Paez is a loose thread: time to pull.

## MISSION CHALLENGES

### WEAPON CHALLENGE: FIELD OF FIRE

DIFFICULTY: ★★★☆☆
UNLOCK: PKP

- Kill five or more enemies with a single burst from a LMG.

### TACTICAL CHALLENGES

DIFFICULTY: ★☆☆☆☆
UNLOCK: UBSG

- Express Train: During the ambush at the cog rail station, kill all soldiers in 60 seconds
- No Witnesses: Don't leave any witnesses in Paez's HQ
- Ace of Diamonds: Execute 10 headshots while in diamond formation

## GEAR SELECTION

| Equipment Slot | Default | | Recommended | |
|---|---|---|---|---|
| **PRIMARY** | **GOBLIN PDR**  | | **MK48 LMG** | |
| | POWER 👊 | | POWER 👊 | |
| | RANGE ➡ | | RANGE ➡ | |
| | CONTROL ⊙ | | CONTROL ⊙ | |
| | MANEUVERABILITY ✛ | | MANEUVERABILITY ✛ | |
| | RATE OF FIRE ⏱ 720 RPM | | RATE OF FIRE ⏱ 702 RPM | |
| | MAGAZINE CAPACITY ≣ 30 | | MAGAZINE CAPACITY ≣ 150 | |
| | **CONFIGURATION SUMMARY** | | **CONFIGURATION SUMMARY** | |
| | Muzzle: Standard | | Muzzle: Standard | |
| | Scope: Red Dot | | Scope: Red Dot | |
| | Underbarrel: Vertical Foregrip | | Underbarrel: Vertical Foregrip | |
| **SECONDARY** | **45T SIDEARM** | | **GOBLIN PDR** | |
| | POWER 👊 | | POWER 👊 | |
| | RANGE ➡ | | RANGE ➡ | |
| | CONTROL ⊙ | | CONTROL ⊙ | |
| | MANEUVERABILITY ✛ | | MANEUVERABILITY ✛ | |
| | RATE OF FIRE ⏱ 600 RPM | | RATE OF FIRE ⏱ 648 RPM | |
| | MAGAZINE CAPACITY ≣ 15 | | MAGAZINE CAPACITY ≣ 30 | |
| | **CONFIGURATION SUMMARY** | | **CONFIGURATION SUMMARY** | |
| | Muzzle: Standard | | Muzzle: Suppressor | |
| | Scope: Iron Sights | | Scope: Red Dot | |
| | Underbarrel: None | | Underbarrel: Vertical Foregrip | |
| **ITEM 1** | **SENSOR** QUANTITY: 5 | | **SENSOR** QUANTITY: 5 | |
| | Detects nearby enemies, highlighting them on the HUD | | Detects nearby enemies, highlighting them on the HUD | |
| **ITEM 2** | **FRAG** QUANTITY: 3 | | **FRAG** QUANTITY: 3 | |
| | High-explosive grenade intended to kill or wound | | High-explosive grenade intended to kill or wound | |

# SECURE GABRIEL PAEZ

◇ Start    ◉ Objective    ▥ Ammo Crate
◈ End      ⌐ Weapon Box   ✓ Challenge

Tactical Challenge:
Express Train

Protect Paez/
Hold For Extraction

Weapon Challenge:
Field of Fire

Secure Gabriel Paez

The Ghost team, designated Hunter, is on the ground in Bolivia, ready to bring in Paez. Ghost Lead, 30K, Pepper, and Kozak gather in a small home on the outskirts of the favela while consulting with Paez on his whereabouts. Paez has agreed to rendezvous with the Ghosts in a nearby market. But the neighborhood is far from friendly. Paez's associates won't take kindly to armed strangers poking around their lucrative business. However, not every contact is hostile. In addition to a few gun-toting thugs, the streets and alleys of this favela are also filled with civilians. Bystanders respond as expected when spotting your team—they run and scramble to safety. But they won't alert the hostiles, so don't worry about hiding from civilians.

As your team advances down the alley, follow them. Along the way take note of the round waypoint marker on the HUD. This icon shows you where you need to go to reach the current objective. The number beneath the icon represents your distance to the waypoint, measured in meters. If you ever get lost, look for one of these waypoint markers to get your bearings. From insertion to extraction, waypoints will get you where you need to go. In most instances, reaching a waypoint simply causes a new waypoint to appear on the HUD, acting like a trail of virtual bread crumbs guiding you through the mission. But certain events (or cutscenes) can also be triggered by reaching a waypoint. So don't get too far ahead of your team. Either let them lead the way or make sure they're close behind you.

While moving through the alley, the word "Contact" appears at the top of the HUD, indicating that hostile units are nearby. By default, your Ghost operative moves in a upright position. While upright you can move quickly, but you also increase your chances of being spotted. Drop down to a crouched stance to reduce your visible profile. While crouched, your movement is slower, but also quiet, making it easier to sneak up on unsuspecting hostiles. When an enemy contact has been detected, make a habit of dropping into a crouched stance. This is the best way to maintain the element of surprise.

## // NOTE

*At any time during the mission you can bring up the Tactical Map by pressing the Tac Map button. This brings up a helpful overlay on the HUD showing your current objective as well as a small map of the area. Along the right side of this*

*screen is a list of all the weapon and tactical challenges. So reference this screen regularly to check up on challenges and objectives. But note that the game isn't paused while the Tactical Map is open.*

The alley opens into a small courtyard occupied by several armed men. There is no way to slip past these guys undetected. But before you plan your attack, find a suitable piece of cover. Your team has taken cover near a row of crates and ice cream carts. Move next to one of the ice cream carts and press the cover button (as shown on-screen) to automatically transition into a covered position. Cover not only increases your concealment, but it also offers protection once the bullets start flying. However, not all cover is equal. For instance, the wooden crates on the right will splinter and fall to pieces quickly. The metal ice cream carts offer the best protection here. While in cover, you can take aim and deploy items such as Sensors or grenades.

Once behind cover, you're prompted to toss a Sensor toward the group of armed men in the courtyard. This baseball-sized device is tossed by hand and can detect all enemy contacts within a 20 meter radius. The data is automatically relayed to each Ghost's HUD through the use of augmented reality. This allows each member of the Ghosts to see all detected threats, even if they're hidden behind cover or within buildings. Threats outside your line of sight are shown as a silhouette on the HUD. Enemies outlined in yellow are unaware of the Ghosts' presence and will not attack. However, enemies outlined in red are on alert and will return fire.

In this case, deploying the Sensor reveals two hidden enemies armed with rifles on the left side of the courtyard, standing behind a stall. If you hadn't deployed the Sensor, you'd have no idea these enemies were there. So now instead of the three visible enemies in the courtyard, you're tasked with taking out five enemies total. Take aim at one of the two enemies hiding behind the stall. As you aim at the silhouetted figure, notice the small pop-up box that appears, displaying what type of weapon the enemy is carrying as well as their distance from you. Quickly pan your aim across all enemies to reveal what type of weapon each is carrying. In this case, all the hostiles are carrying rifles. But sometimes enemies may be carrying more powerful weapons such as shotguns, sniper rifles, or light machine guns (LMGs). Before attacking, always aim at each enemy to determine the threat level and prioritize your targets accordingly.

## ENEMY PROFILE: RIFLEMAN

*The rifleman is a medium-range threat (armed with an assault rifle) and the most common enemy in the campaign. Riflemen aren't a big threat when alone, but they become increasingly dangerous when attacking in numbers. Riflemen are like the counterpart of the Ghosts—they fight intelligently, moving from cover to cover, encouraging your team to use all the cover fighting techniques they know to neutralize them.*

Once you have an enemy in your sights, open fire. Even the two enemies behind the stall are not safe, as your bullets slice through the flimsy wooden stall. Your team follows your lead and opens fire on the enemy units. If you start taking incoming fire, release the aim button to drop back down behind cover. If you take too much damage, you may become incapacitated, requiring a teammate to heal you before you can get back up on your feet. This is why cover is so important. When engaged in a firefight, only peek out of cover momentarily to fire a few shots, then release the aim button to slip back behind protection. In this fight, after shooting the first target, drop behind cover and locate a second target before taking aim. Continue peeking out of cover and firing until all hostiles are eliminated. The word "Clear" appears at the top of the HUD when all the enemies are down.

## WEAPON CHALLENGE: FIELD OF FIRE

**CRITERIA: KILL FIVE OR MORE ENEMIES WITH A SINGLE BURST FROM A LMG.**

If you brought along a light machine gun, you can complete this weapon challenge during the first firefight. Start by taking aim at the enemy hiding behind the stall on the far left side of the courtyard. Open fire and hold down the trigger as you pan your aim from left to right across the courtyard, engaging all five enemies. You must hold down the trigger until all the enemies are dead. The recoil can make your LMG tough to aim, so apply some downward pressure on the right control stick to fight the muzzle climb. This is the easiest spot in the mission to complete the challenge. If you fail to kill all five enemies with one burst, consider reloading from the previous checkpoint and trying again. Completing this challenge unlocks the PKP light machine gun, which is available from the Gunsmith interface.

After eliminating all the enemies in the courtyard, stay behind your cover and press the cover button while pushing up on the left control stick. This causes your operative to hop over your cover. This is the only way to jump over low obstacles such as crates or the ice cream cart you were hiding behind. But remember, you must first take cover behind an obstacle before you can jump over it.

Follow your team toward the next waypoint marker. Along the way, stop and interact with a ammo crate on the right side of the path. Ammo crates allow you to top off your ammo as well as replenish all Sensors or grenades. Stand next to the ammo crate and hold down the button shown on the HUD to stock up. You can only carry five Sensors at a time, so ammo crates are essential for replenishing these effective, intel-gathering devices.

## // NOTE

*Don't wander too far from your teammates. If you move into an area of the map that is off-limits, you'll get a "Losing Signal" warning and the screen will become pixelated. Move toward your teammates or the nearest waypoint to clear the screen.*

Paez is supposed to be somewhere ahead, in the market. Take a covered position behind the low wall straight ahead. From here, you can monitor activity in the street below. Paez is hidden somewhere among the crowd of civilians in the market. Cut through the clutter by deploying a Sensor. While still behind cover, lob a Sensor as far as you can, tossing it toward the parked pickup truck on the left side of the street. When the fight starts, this will help identify enemies in the adjoining building.

## PROTECT PAEZ

Once the Sensor is deployed, a cutscene plays, showing Paez in the street below—he looks nervous. The Sensor also identifies a few gunmen patrolling nearby. While still behind cover, take aim at one of the patrolling enemies. At this range, it's best to use the scope view. While aiming, click down on the right control stick to enter a first-person view, aiming through your weapon's sight or scope. The scope view allows more precise targeting, which is ideal for scoring lethal headshots. So, center you scope on an enemy's head and squeeze the trigger. As soon as you open fire, your team joins in. After dropping your first target, release the aim button and duck behind cover while scouting for a new target. As chaos erupts in the street, Paez seeks cover. Don't worry too much about protecting Paez—he'll be fine. Instead, focus your attention (and firepower) on the hostiles scattering for cover.

The sound of gunfire attracts more enemies to your location; some take up positions in the three-story building across the street. The Sensor you deployed earlier may not detect these enemies, as Sensors can detect enemies for only a limited time after being deployed. So toss a second Sensor toward this building to identify new contacts. If you're having trouble getting a clear shot at these enemies, follow your team to the right while remaining crouched. Take cover directly across from the building and engage the hostiles inside. Remember, your bullets can pass through light cover, so don't let the enemies hide. When they duck behind cover, simply take aim at their silhouette on the HUD and open fire. There may be a few enemies on the building's rooftop. Take out enemies on the rooftop as soon as they appear. Their height advantage may allow them to see over your cover and score hits.

## // CAUTION

*If your cover has been compromised or flanked, you can sustain damage and become incapacitated. If this happens, you must wait for a teammate to heal you. You can heal downed teammates yourself by approaching them and holding down the button shown on-screen. You can also order your teammates to heal a downed squadmate, by aiming at the wounded Ghost and pressing the focus fire button.*

# HOLD FOR EXTRACTION

After clearing out all the gunmen in the area, you're issued an objective update ordering you to hold your current position while awaiting extraction. On cue, a Blackhawk arrives overhead and prepares to extract Paez. But an incoming RPG round forces the chopper to take evasive action. The area is still hot! You need to secure the street ahead before Paez can be extracted.

As Paez races down the street, keep up with him, advancing along the high ground. Paez seeks cover near a cog rail station. But the area is surrounded by gunmen. Immediately deploy another Sensor to identify all contacts, then help your team clear out the resistance. During the middle of the fight, a cinematic shows Paez racing toward the train—he says he's been shot and is bugging out. Apparently the deal is off. Paez is no longer willing to turn himself in. He ignores the Ghosts' orders, racing to safety aboard the train.

## // TIP

*While engaging hostiles at the cog rail station, notice the ammo crate nearby. Use this to stock up on Sensors and ammo.*

Immediately after the cutscene, a pickup truck equipped with a mounted machine gun appears in the street below and opens fire on your team. Make sure you're behind cover and wait for the opportunity to peek out and take aim at the gunner. The gunner is partially protected by a steel plate fitted to the machine gun. But this steel plate doesn't protect his whole body. Hit the gunner anywhere you can, even it means hitting him in the shoulder or foot. Inflict as much damage as possible to neutralize the gunner and silence the machine gun. Alternatively, you can focus your fire on the vehicle itself—destroying the pickup truck kills the gunner.

## TACTICAL CHALLENGE: EXPRESS TRAIN

### CRITERIA: DURING THE AMBUSH AT THE COG RAIL STATION, KILL ALL SOLDIERS IN 60 SECONDS

When Paez runs toward the cog rail station, you have exactly one minute to eliminate all enemies to complete this tactical challenge. Use a Sensor to identify all the threats, then methodically pick off all the gunmen, including those gathered on the right side of the station. When the pickup truck arrives, immediately take aim at the gunner before he can swing his weapon in your direction. Don't worry about accuracy. Fire an aggressive automatic burst in his direction to take him down. This is the first of three tactical challenges you can complete in this mission. Complete all three to unlock UBSG underbarrel shotgun attachment.

## ENEMY PROFILE: MOUNTED MACHINE GUN

*Mounted machine guns are heavy, suppressing, medium-range threats. These miniguns are sometimes found in fixed positions, but they're usually mounted on vehicles. Mounted machine guns should be taken seriously whenever encountered. When the gunner isn't firing at you, peek out of cover and fire a burst in his direction. Some of these weapons have a front shield, preventing a frontal assault. In that case, try to get around the machine gunner to get a good shot at him, where there is no shield protecting him. Explosive weapons, like grenades, are also effective when engaging these enemies.*

# REACH PAEZ'S HIDEOUT

Just ahead is a small structure with two doorways. Before moving toward one of the doors, toss a Sensor near the structure to reveal four enemies hiding inside—you can top off your Sensors at the nearby ammo crate before proceeding with the entry. While your team prepares to make entry, move into the white circle next to one of the doors. Your operative automatically stacks up on the door and prepares for entry. Before giving the breach order, get an idea of what enemies you'll target as soon as you enter.

When you're ready to enter the structure, give the breach order. At this point the action slows, giving you ample time to take aim at the enemies as your team performs a dynamic entry. Sweep your weapon across the room from left to right, gunning down any hostiles that are in your direct line of sight. This gives you the chance to hit any targets missed by your teammates. If all goes well, all enemies will be dead within a second, demonstrating the expertise of the Ghosts. Follow your team upstairs and prepare to pass through another sliding door.

The extraction of Paez was a failure. It is believed he has taken refuge at his hideout. Your team must now reach his hideout and extract him as initially planned. Regroup with your team by the sliding door. This is a point where your four-man team must be together before proceeding. There's a white circle on the floor in front of the door. Move into this white circle to initiate entry. When playing co-op, all non-AI players must move into this area before proceeding. Beyond the door is a ladder. Hold down the button shown on the HUD to interact with the ladder, then climb to the top.

## FAVELA STREETS

LEGEND ◇ Start   ⊙ Objective   ▓ Ammo Crate
◈ End   ▤ Weapon Box   ✓ Challenge

Reach Paez's Hideout

As you advance down the adjoining alley, a pickup truck equipped with a mounted machine gun moves into view ahead and spews automatic fire in your direction. Immediately take cover along the left side of the alley. There's no way to get a good shot at the gunner from this position so you'll need to maneuver and flank from a different direction. Start by swapping cover to the right side of the alley. Move the camera view until a blue ring icon appears at the base of the wall on the right side of the alley—these blue markers show all possible cover swap opportunities. Once you've located a spot to move to, hold down the button shown on screen to swap cover. Hold down the button until the move is complete. Your operative dashes across the alley and assumes a covered position.

From your new position on the right side of the alley, peek out to the left and spot a new covered position at the base of the wall just beneath the pickup truck. Swap cover to this position to escape the machine gun's field of fire. Once you reach the wall, turn to the right and climb the nearby steps. Take cover behind the crates on the left side of the path to spot the gunner in the pickup. Peek over the crates and neutralize the gunner with a single shot to the head. As you can see, swapping cover is a quick and effective way to maneuver, even if you're under heavy fire.

### // TIP

It's possible to destroy the pickup truck with a grenade. However, you must wait until the gunner stops firing to avoid being hit while tossing the grenade in the direction of the vehicle. It's much safer to advance to a flanking position.

Once the gunner in the pickup truck is down for the count, turn toward the next waypoint marker and advance up the street—but don't move too far. Take cover behind the car in the street and lob a Sensor ahead to spot multiple enemies waiting to ambush your team. Using the intel from the Sensor, methodically pick off each gunman, one by one. If necessary, push forward using cover swaps until you can engage all the contacts. Grenades are great for taking out the enemies hiding behind windows. Once all the threats are eliminated, visit the ammo crate on the left side of the street to stock up on Sensors and grenades.

Your team emerges onto a cramped city street. There isn't much time for sneaking around now. Anyway, the enemy already knows you're here. This becomes clear when the word "Engaged" flashes across the top of the HUD, indicating that your team has been spotted. Immediately dash into cover wherever you can find it and toss a Sensor toward the muzzle flashes at the end of the street.

Multiple enemies have taken up positions on the raised walkway at the end of the street. This is a good opportunity to deploy a frag grenade. Follow the on-screen instructions to select a frag grenade, then initiate a throw. Make note of the white arc that appears; it represents the trajectory of your grenade—this works just like throwing a Sensor. Adjust the trajectory so the grenade lands next to at least two enemies. The arc that appears makes it easy to toss grenades with great accuracy. The arc even accounts for bouncing the grenade off surfaces such as walls, showing you where the grenade will ultimately land. Experiment with different grenade tosses to eliminate these enemies. Finish off any survivors by firing through cover. Move out as soon as all the enemy contacts have been eliminated.

Follow the waypoint markers deeper into the favela as a crowd of civilians comes rushing in your direction. There are no hostiles in this group, so hold your fire and rush up the slope, pressing the button shown on-screen. The rush function causes your operative to sprint. While rushing, you cannot fire and lateral movement is reduced. As a result, rushing is best used when you need to move quickly in a straight line. At the end of the street, turn left and crouch beneath an obstacle in the path by pressing the button shown on-screen. Drop off the nearby ledge and turn left to continue your advance toward Paez's hideout.

When your reach the next intersection, a cutscene shows two vehicles exploding due to an impact from an rocket-propelled grenade (RPG). When you resume control, your operative is already behind cover on the left side of the street. Peek out of cover long enough to toss a Sensor as far as you can. This reveals the locations of all hostiles, including two enemies carrying RPGs positioned on rooftops on the left and right sides of the street. Incoming RPGs are deadly, so you need to eliminate these threats quickly. Start by picking off the RPG soldier on the right side of the street. Peek out of cover and take aim—at this range, the scope view is helpful for hitting your target.

// TIP

*If you're having a tough time spotting the RPG soldiers, follow the smoke trail from their rockets to identify each shooter's location.*

Once the first RPG soldier is down, swap cover to the right side of the street. From here you can spot and engage the second RPG soldier in the distance. Once again, take aim using the scope view to end the incoming barrage of rockets. Mop up the remaining hostiles, then rush toward Paez's hideout before time runs out. Regroup with your team at the next waypoint and watch as the Ghosts help each other over the wall. If your entire team doesn't reach this wall within the allotted six minutes, you must restart from the previous checkpoint and try again.

# HIDEOUT ENTRANCE

LEGEND
- ◇ Start
- ◇ End
- ⊙ Objective
- Weapon Box
- ⫼ Ammo Crate
- ✓ Challenge

On the other side of the wall, there's a weapon box, which allows you to select a weapon with a suppressor. Before interacting with the crate, switch to your secondary weapon. When interacting with a weapon box, your currently selected weapon is exchanged for a weapon pulled from the box. So always equip the weapon you want to ditch before interacting with the box. A weapon box can hold up to five different weapons. By selecting the options in the radial menu, you can view each weapon's stats and attachments. In this instance, you can choose a suppressed SR-3M PDR from the box. If you already have a suppressed weapon, you do not need to take the SR-3M. But make sure you have a suppressed weapon before moving into Paez's hideout. After checking over your weapons, regroup with your team at the entrance to Paez's hideout.

## // NOTE

*Interacting with weapon boxes replenishes ammo and items such as Sensors and grenades.*

## ENEMY PROFILE: RPG SOLDIER

*The RPG soldier is a medium- to long-range static threat that fires a high-explosive rocket. These are very dangerous units as they're the only ones capable of inflicting area damage, due to the rocket's large blast radius. While an RPG soldier's firing and reload rate is slow, once he shoots, the destruction is massive. To take him down, shoot him when he is acquiring a target. If the RPG soldier shoots at you, run away from your current position to escape the blast radius. Smoke grenades can hinder an RPG soldier's sight, making it more difficult for this unit to acquire targets.*

# RESCUE PAEZ

Apparently Paez's associates aren't thrilled with his decision to share information. He's being held in a small structure at the back of his hideout. You need to move in quietly and secure Paez without raising any alerts. If the enemy detects your presence, Paez will be executed and you'll have to restart from the previous checkpoint. If that isn't pressure enough, you have only six minutes to reach Paez. A large courtyard dominates the center of the compound. Stay low and creep toward a piece of cover to get a better view of the surroundings. There are multiple enemies in the courtyard as well as a few patrolling the perimeter. Toss at least two Sensors into the courtyard to identify all hostiles.

## // CAUTION

*Remain crouched and use cover while moving around the courtyard. If you stand out in the open, there's a good chance you'll be spotted. If you're within an enemy's line of sight, a white arc appears on the HUD, indicating what*

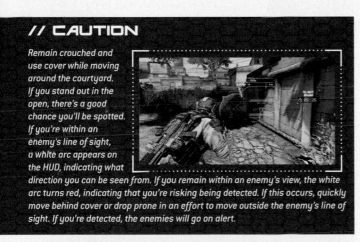

*direction you can be seen from. If you remain within an enemy's view, the white arc turns red, indicating that you're risking being detected. If this occurs, quickly move behind cover or drop prone in an effort to move outside the enemy's line of sight. If you're detected, the enemies will go on alert.*

| LEGEND | | |
|---|---|---|
| ◇ Start | ⊕ Objective | ⫼ Ammo Crate |
| ◇ End | 🔫 Weapon Box | ✓ Challenge |

Tactical Challenge: No Witnesses

Escort Paez to Extraction

Rescue Paez

Tactical Challenge: Ace of Diamonds

To rescue Paez you do not need to kill every enemy in this courtyard. Instead, sneak up along the right side of the courtyard, where one enemy soldier has his back turned. When you're close enough, you can perform a stealth kill by pressing the button shown on-screen. This lethal melee attack is the best way to eliminate threats at close range.

After taking out the first soldier, toss another Sensor toward the top of the stairs, in the direction of the next waypoint. One more soldier is patrolling here, preventing your team from reaching the waypoint without being detected. Monitor his patrol and when he turns away, creep up the stairs and turn right to enter the small structure. Hide in this structure until the soldier turns away from you, then sneak up behind him and perform another stealth kill. Alternately, you can simply shoot him the back of the head with your suppressed weapon. The path to Paez is now clear. You can proceed with the rescue without killing the rest of the enemies in the courtyard. However, leaving witnesses prevents you from completing the No Witnesses tactical challenge.

## TACTICAL CHALLENGE: NO WITNESSES

### CRITERIA: DON'T LEAVE ANY WITNESSES IN PAEZ'S HQ

While you need to kill only two enemies to reach Paez, you must kill all the enemies in the courtyard to complete this challenge. After eliminating the first two, locate the lone enemy patrolling the high ground on the left side of the courtyard. If necessary, deploy another Sensor to locate him. This hostile is isolated from the main group in the courtyard, which makes it easy to pick him off without anyone noticing. Take careful aim and neutralize him with a shot to the head from your suppressed weapon. Alternately, you can sneak up behind him and take him out with a stealth kill.

Now comes the hard part. The remaining enemies in the middle of the courtyard are all within view of each other, making it difficult to take them out one by one. Load a fresh magazine in your suppressed weapon and mow them all down before they can trigger an alert. If you're playing the mission with friends, you can attempt a sync-shot of your own by calling out targets and simultaneously engaging the hostiles. In either case, if you act quickly you can eliminate all the hostiles without raising an alert. The key is to find the right angle so that the enemies are closely aligned within your sight, allowing you to take all of them out with a prolonged burst. The cover by the alley (near the ammo crate) offers a good line of sight on all the enemies in the courtyard.

Once you've made it past the courtyard, stock up on ammo, Sensors, and grenades from the nearby ammo crate before heading toward the structure where Paez is being held. You don't have much time before Paez's captors lose patience. A timer appears, giving you just under four minutes to rescue Paez before he's executed. Before stacking up for a dynamic entry, toss a Sensor outside the structure to gather intel on the occupants. There are four armed men in the room with Paez. You'll need to act (and shoot) fast to maintain the element of surprise. When you're ready to enter, move to the white circle at the base of a small window and prepare to breach.

Upon the breach, take aim at the soldier standing over Paez and mow him down. Your teammates will handle the other hostiles in the room. If everything goes well, the room will be clear in mere seconds. Now that Paez has been secured, it's time to get him out of here. Unfortunately, the extraction helicopter can't land at Paez's hideout. You must get him out on foot.

# ESCORT GABRIEL PAEZ TO EXTRACTION

During this sequence, it's your job to keep Paez alive while escorting him through the streets. The Ghosts arrange themselves in a diamond formation, a formation designed to protect VIPs while moving through hostile environments. Paez may be little more than a low-level gun runner, but his intel is critical to the mission, so his survival is paramount. With one hand on Paez at all times, your other hand is free to carry only a pistol. As you exit the structure where Paez was being held, a pickup equipped with a machine gun pulls up outside and begins firing. Immediately fire your pistol at the gunner, then eliminate the driver and any other hostiles that move into view.

## TACTICAL CHALLENGE: ACE OF DIAMONDS

### CRITERIA: EXECUTE 10 HEADSHOTS WHILE IN DIAMOND FORMATION

This is the toughest of the tactical challenges in this mission, requiring you to score ten headshots during this sequence. While in the diamond formation, you can still aim your pistol, but it zooms in only slightly. Still, always aim and take your time with each shot to guarantee a headshot. Unfortunately, if you clip an enemy in the arm or shoulder, they will die, preventing you from getting the headshot kill. Completing this challenge comes down to skill and technique.

After eliminating the first wave of enemies, the team moves toward the disabled pickup truck for cover. During this sequence, you don't need to worry about movement—the team moves for you. All you have to do is worry about aiming and shooting. When you take cover near the pickup truck, an enemy opens fire with a mounted machine gun positioned on the nearby building. Don't worry too much about accuracy here. Fire multiple rounds at the machine gunner, then carefully take aim at his friends in an effort to score more headshots.

The Ghosts continue advancing in the diamond formation, encountering a steady stream of resistance along the way. As the team moves, take aim and open fire on the hostiles that move into view. Numerous civilians are mixed into the crowds, so watch your fire. Enemy contacts are marked with an orange diamond icon that makes them easier to spot. Continue firing your pistol throughout the advance, scoring as many headshots as possible. The Ghosts eventually find safety after passing through a shed, ending the diamond-formation sequence and the mission. Hopefully Paez was worth the trouble.

 **// Loose Thread**

achievement trophy

Loose Thread is earned upon the completion of the Nimble Guardian mission.

## NIMBLE GUARDIAN: COMPLETION UNLOCKS

| Type | Category | Item |
|------|----------|------|
| Weapon | Assault Rifle | 417 |
| Weapon | SMG | MP7 |
| Weapon | Shotgun | M590A1 |
| Attachment | Optic | Tac Scope |
| Attachment | Underbarrel | Angled Foregrip |
| Attachment | Side Rail | Aiming Laser |
| Attachment | Stock | Folded |
| Items | Camo | Optical Camo |
| Items | View | Magnetic |
| Paint | Weapon paint | USSR TTsKO North Africa |
| Paint | Weapon paint | French Daguet |

# SUBTLE ARROW

## BRIEFING

LOCATION: ZAMBIA
OBJECTIVES: LOCATE AND ASSESS WARLORD DEDE MACABA. RECOVER INTEL ON ARMS SHIPMENT.
CURRENT CONTACT: CSENIOR MASTER SERGEANT MARCUS KELSO

// ANGOLAN WARLORD_

// W

INSERTION

EXTRACTION

// FIND_MACABA_
// FIND_SHIPMENT_
// FIND_SOURCE_

ZAMBIA_

The man you brought in, Paez, coughed up about a hundred names. Most of them are small- to mid-time players in South America, but we did dig out one unusual connection. Gentlemen, we're heading to Africa. Paez's gear was only part of a larger shipment. Another part went into Zambia, to a man named Dede Macaba. Macaba's an Angolan warlord and war criminal. He fled Angola and crossed the border into Zambia, where he set up shop right in the middle of a refugee camp. He's got a fresh shipment en route. Macaba's just a means to an end.

Your priority is intel on the source of that shipment. Our window's tight on this, so it's gonna have to be a daylight raid. A local contact will get you into the camp. Find Macaba, find his shipment, and find his source.

## MISSION CHALLENGES

### WEAPON CHALLENGE: OVERWATCH

DIFFICULTY: ★★★★☆
UNLOCK: PSL-54C

- Eliminate 10 enemies using a sniper rifle without moving

### TACTICAL CHALLENGES

DIFFICULTY: ★★☆☆☆
UNLOCK: FLASH HIDER

- Protector: Complete the mission without any civilian casualties
- Secure the Camp: Eliminate all of the soldiers who have taken control of the refugee camp
- Steely Gaze: Kill ten enemies while in Magnetic view

ZAMBIA

## GEAR SELECTION

| Equipment Slot | Default | Recommended |
|---|---|---|
| **PRIMARY** | **417 ASSAULT** 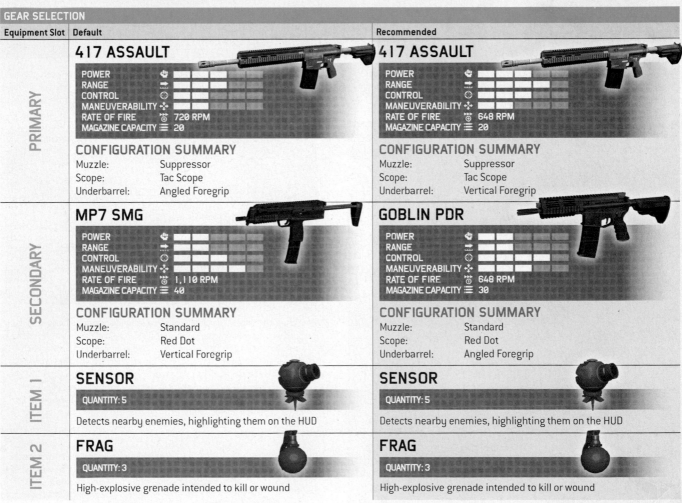<br>POWER<br>RANGE<br>CONTROL<br>MANEUVERABILITY<br>RATE OF FIRE: 720 RPM<br>MAGAZINE CAPACITY: 20<br><br>**CONFIGURATION SUMMARY**<br>Muzzle: Suppressor<br>Scope: Tac Scope<br>Underbarrel: Angled Foregrip | **417 ASSAULT**<br>POWER<br>RANGE<br>CONTROL<br>MANEUVERABILITY<br>RATE OF FIRE: 648 RPM<br>MAGAZINE CAPACITY: 20<br><br>**CONFIGURATION SUMMARY**<br>Muzzle: Suppressor<br>Scope: Tac Scope<br>Underbarrel: Vertical Foregrip |
| **SECONDARY** | **MP7 SMG**<br>POWER<br>RANGE<br>CONTROL<br>MANEUVERABILITY<br>RATE OF FIRE: 1,110 RPM<br>MAGAZINE CAPACITY: 40<br><br>**CONFIGURATION SUMMARY**<br>Muzzle: Standard<br>Scope: Red Dot<br>Underbarrel: Vertical Foregrip | **GOBLIN PDR**<br>POWER<br>RANGE<br>CONTROL<br>MANEUVERABILITY<br>RATE OF FIRE: 648 RPM<br>MAGAZINE CAPACITY: 30<br><br>**CONFIGURATION SUMMARY**<br>Muzzle: Standard<br>Scope: Red Dot<br>Underbarrel: Angled Foregrip |
| **ITEM 1** | **SENSOR**<br>QUANTITY: 5<br>Detects nearby enemies, highlighting them on the HUD | **SENSOR**<br>QUANTITY: 5<br>Detects nearby enemies, highlighting them on the HUD |
| **ITEM 2** | **FRAG**<br>QUANTITY: 3<br>High-explosive grenade intended to kill or wound | **FRAG**<br>QUANTITY: 3<br>High-explosive grenade intended to kill or wound |

# REACH OBSERVATION POINT

The Ghost team is on the ground in Zambia, not far from the refugee camp where warlord Dede Macaba has been spotted. Macaba's men are little more than opportunistic thugs, preying on the weak for their own gain and amusement. One such incident plays out in front of the Ghosts, not far from the insertion point. A thug singles out a refugee woman and begins harassing her. But when she fights back and runs away, the thug takes aim with his assault rifle. Fortunately for the woman, she has guardians nearby....

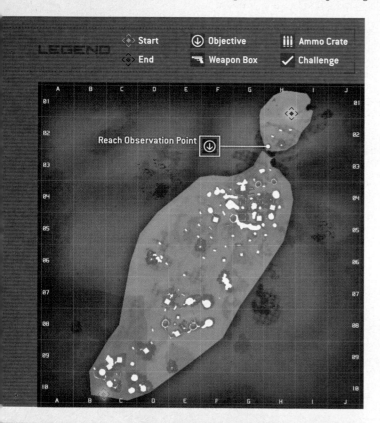

LEGEND

| | | |
|---|---|---|
| ◈ Start | ⊕ Objective | ⫼ Ammo Crate |
| ◈ End | 🔲 Weapon Box | ✓ Challenge |

Reach Observation Point ⊕

Sporting the new Optical Camouflage, you blend into your surroundings, remaining unnoticed while monitoring the situation. Sneak up behind the thug as he attempts to clear his jammed assault rifle. When you're close enough, perform a stealth kill, pressing the button shown on-screen. You can also perform a stealth shot by pressing the fire button when you are close to an enemy. Having averted a tragedy, it's time to focus on the mission. You must reach an observation point several hundred meters away. From there, you can monitor the refugee camp and locate your contact tasked with driving you in.

After eliminating the first thug, move out with your team. Several enemy contacts are detected in the village ahead. Follow your team's lead by assuming a crouched stance. While crouched, the Optical Camo is activated, making you difficult to spot. Optical Camo allows the Ghosts to live up to their namesake, causing them to virtually disappear into the background and significantly reducing their visual signatures. While Optical Camo doesn't make you invisible, it decreases the range at which enemies can detect you—if you get too close, they'll spot you! When equipped, Optical Camo is automatically activated whenever you crouch or drop prone. This makes it easy to sneak up on hostile units and perform stealth kills. However, if you stand up, start moving quickly, or are hit by a bullet, the Optical Camo is deactivated.

## // TIP

*The first part of this mission is wide open. The Ghosts' sole purpose is to reach the observation point to get a clear view on the refugee camp. You can interfere with the enemy activities you witness along the way, or you can simply proceed to the observation point.*

As long as you remain crouched, with the Optical Camo active you can move close to the village without being spotted. Find some cover on the outskirts of the village and activate the Magnetic Goggles—another piece of new technology available during this mission. Like the hand-thrown Sensor, the Magnetic Goggles are another way to identify gun-toting hostiles in a crowd. Think of this optical device as X-ray vision that is capable of detecting magnetic objects such as firearms, regardless of line of sight. The ability to see through walls and other solid objects makes this device extremely useful in close-quarter situations. However, the Magnetic Goggles have an effective range of only 30 meters, so limit their use when operating in larger, open environments where your own eyesight is more effective.

In this situation the Magnetic Goggles view identifies five hostiles, each carrying rifles. If you can take out one of these guys quietly, you can eliminate the other four with a sync-shot. Sneak up behind the gunman standing by the well and perform a stealth kill—one down, four to go.

Now it's time to drop the other four hostiles in the village. Sometimes it's necessary to neutralize multiple enemies simultaneously—this is where the sync-shot comes in. Sync-shots are best used in situations where your team must remain undetected to avoid jeopardizing a mission's objectives. The stakes aren't so high here, but this is a good opportunity to practice this effective tactic. Before you can pull off a sync-shot, you must first mark all four of the enemies in the village. If you made a mistake in marking your enemies, you can un-mark them by pressing the same button you used to mark the targets. As you mark targets, your teammates take up positions around the village to ensure they can hit each marked target. Every target with a blue icon above his head indicates that a teammate has established a line of sight and is ready to fire. Since four targets are marked and you only have three teammates, you must take out the fourth enemy yourself. Locate the target with a white icon above his head—this icon indicates he hasn't been targeted by a teammate. Alternately, you can target any of the marked enemies and your teammates will adjust their aim so that all four targets are covered. When you're ready to perform the sync-shot, aim at your target and squeeze the trigger. Your teammates automatically follow your lead, neutralizing all four enemies simultaneously.

// TIP

*Immediately following a sync-shot, time is slowed. You can use this to your advantage if there are more than four enemies in an area. After your team kills the four marked targets, quickly engage other enemies in the area, while time is still slowed. This technique is useful for silently eliminating large groups of hostiles without triggering an alert.*

Following the sync-shot, resume the advance to the observation point. Along the way, a convoy of three hostile pickup trucks moving in your direction appears near a small cluster of huts. Do not engage these enemies. Instead, drop prone to reduce your visible profile and continue crawling toward the waypoint. The Optical Camo remains active while you're prone, making you extremely difficult to detect. As long as you stay low, the three trucks will pass your position without stopping. When your teammates raise to a crouched stance, follow suit and resume the advance toward the huts ahead.

As you near the huts, a couple of enemy rifleman come into view. One is standing near the dirt road leading into the cluster of huts. The other rifleman is patrolling the hill in the distance. Mark both enemies, then order your team to perform a sync-shot. You don't have to target four enemies to perform a sync-shot. In fact, it's often faster to eliminate enemies in smaller groups. However, make sure the bodies fall in a position where they can't be spotted by other hostiles. If dead bodies are discovered, enemies will go on alert and you're likely to have a firefight on your hands.

There are five more hostiles located in this small village near the observation point. While you can sneak past them without being seen, this is a good opportunity to practice another sync-shot. Four of the hostiles are gathered near a village courtyard while the fifth patrols around the perimeter. Deal with the patrolling rifleman first. You can either drop him yourself or mark him for a teammate. Just make sure his body falls outside the line of sight of his friends. Next, deal with the four hostiles in the courtyard. Mark all four targets, take aim at one, then drop all four with a sync-shot. The village is now clear of threats. You can now proceed to the observation point without being spotted. Regroup with your teammates on the hill overlooking the refugee camp to receive an intel update from Overlord.

## OVERLORD INTEL UPDATE: NEW LUENDA REFUGEE CAMP

It's a powder keg down there, gentlemen. "Humanitarian crisis" doesn't even begin to cover it. Macaba's thugs control everything: food, water, supplies. And what they can't control through possession, they control by fear. Once you're inside, track Macaba down and he should lead you to the shipment. Macaba controls everything, one way or another. Everything begins and ends with Macaba. He's your top priority there. Your contact's already on site. He'll have to keep a low profile. Just try not to draw any attention to him. He's putting a lot on the line to get us in.

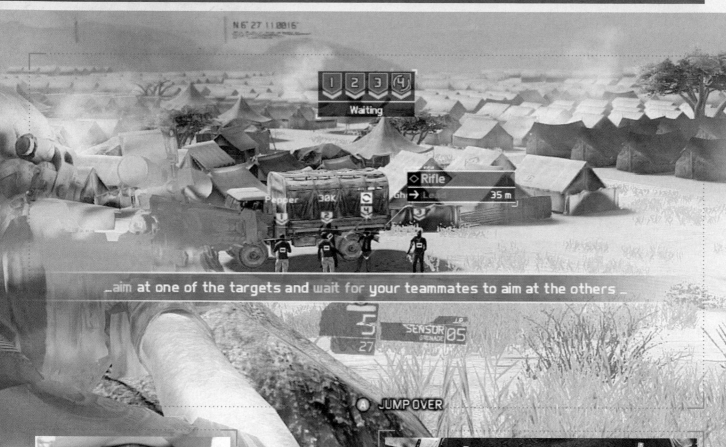

Your contact is located at the next waypoint, sitting in a truck outside the refugee camp. But there's a problem. Your contact is being harassed by four of Macaba's thugs—time for another sync-shot. Creep down the hillside until you have a clear view of the truck and all four enemy riflemen. This is the perfect opportunity for a sync-shot; you can kill all threats in an instant, minimizing the danger to your contact. Take cover behind a rock along the hillside and begin marking targets for your team. Once you have all four hostiles marked, take aim at one of them and perform the sync-shot—at this range you may want to use the scope view. All four riflemen drop to the ground in an instant, prompting your contact to hop in his truck and prepare for your arrival.

Follow your team toward the waypoint marker by the truck. As you near the truck, the driver urges you to hop in the back—this is your ride inside the camp. During the ride, Ghost Lead briefs the team on the tricky rules of engagement. Your team is clear to engage hostiles, but you can't afford to set off any alarms. He advises to get in close and make each shot count. You'll also want to make use of sync-shots when engaging multiple targets. Your Optical Camo will help you avoid detection, so you can get close to Macaba without spooking him. Overlord advises that a storm is heading toward the camp. It's best to take care of business before the storm hits.

# LOCATE DEDE MACABA

Your contact drops you near the entrance to the refugee camp. Hostiles are detected nearby so immediately assume a crouched stance to activate your Optical Camo. Move parallel with the dirt road toward a large tree. Here, you can take cover near a rock and spot four rifleman. Three are standing in a tight group while a fourth patrols a nearby rooftop. Mark all four hostiles, then take aim at the hostile on the rooftop. Wait until he stops his patrol, then put a bullet in his head to initiate the sync-shot. Once the four riflemen are down, follow your team into the refugee camp.

## TACTICAL CHALLENGE: STEELY GAZE

### CRITERIA: KILL 10 ENEMIES WHILE IN MAGNETIC VIEW

This challenge is simple to complete as long as you remember to activate the Magnetic view before you pull the trigger. As long as you eliminate a hostile while the Magnetic view is active, the kill will count toward the challenge's criteria. This challenge can

be done at the same time as the sniper kills required for the Overwatch weapon challenge later in the mission. Bring up the Tactical Map to view your progress toward each challenge.

The refugee camp is a maze of tents and other temporary shelters. Although the tents offer decent concealment while moving around the camp, they make it difficult to see farther than a few meters. Given the poor visibility, rely on Magnetic view to see through the tents and spot hostiles carrying weapons. This makes it easier to navigate and plan your attacks. Start by sneaking up behind a lone gunman stealing a bag of food from a refugee woman. He's isolated from his cronies and among civilians, so there's no reason to open fire and put bystanders at risk. Simply sneak up behind him and perform a stealth kill—the civilians don't seem to mind your intervention.

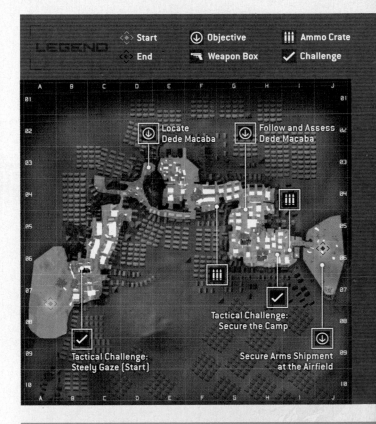

**LEGEND**
◇ Start    ⊻ Objective    ⦀ Ammo Crate
◇ End    🔫 Weapon Box    ✓ Challenge

Locate Dede Macaba
Follow and Assess Dede Macaba

Tactical Challenge: Secure the Camp

Tactical Challenge: Steely Gaze (Start)

Secure Arms Shipment at the Airfield

## // TIP

*Using Magnetic view, you can spot and engage targets that would otherwise be outside your line of sight. The tents in the refugee camp offer concealment, but they make lousy cover. Use this to your advantage by firing through the tents to kill enemies on the other side. They'll never see it coming.*

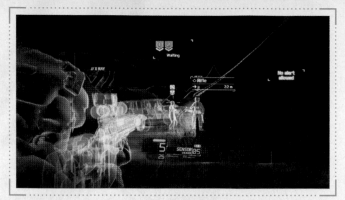

Next, locate a pair of thugs standing next to a white SUV. Mark both targets and take aim at one of them. There's a chance your teammates won't be able to get a line of sight on one of the targets, so be ready to pick off whichever target your teammates can't. When both targets are within view and ready to drop, squeeze the trigger to perform another sync-shot. Remember, try to take out targets with the Magnetic view on in order to complete the tactical challenge.

Move past the white SUV and approach another rifleman harassing refugees near a well. Mark the hostile, but hold off on giving the shoot order. Instead, try to sneak up behind him to perform a stealth kill. However, if the hostile turns in your direction, you may be spotted, even with your Optical Camo deployed. So as you near the rifleman by the well, be ready to give the shoot order to your team, just in case the enemy turns around. Even if you think you have a clear path for a stealth kill, always make sure a teammate watches your back during the approach. Your Ghost teammate may have to shoot the hostile before you're within range to perform the stealth kill.

After clearing out the rifleman by the well, follow your team to a small market area filled with a few stalls covered by a mix of thatch and cloth awnings. Several civilians and two rifleman are in the adjoining courtyard beyond the market. Use Magnetic view to identify the two gunmen in the crowd and mark them both. This time, let your team take out both hostiles. Once your team is in position, give them the shoot order.

## TACTICAL CHALLENGE: PROTECTOR

### CRITERIA: COMPLETE THE MISSION WITHOUT ANY CIVILIAN CASUALTIES

As you can see, the combination of Magnetic view and the sync-shot is perfect for picking off hostiles in a crowd. This is the best way to complete this challenge. Stealth kills and sync-shots greatly minimize the amount of bullets flying through the air. So use

these tactics to avoid collateral damage. As long as the enemy is unaware of your presence, you can avoid heated firefights in which bystanders might be caught in the crossfire. To complete this challenge, no civilians can be killed. If you accidentally kill a civilian, immediately restart from the last save checkpoint. Otherwise you'll have to replay the entire mission.

## FOLLOW AND ASSESS DEDE MACABA

Not far beyond the market is makeshift supply area where Macaba's men are hoarding humanitarian aid. As promised, Macaba is on site overseeing the arrival of new supplies. Overlord advises following Macaba to his HQ. Chances are, he'll lead you straight to the shipment of weapons. But you need to do this quietly. You can't afford to scare him off. Shortly after the update from Overlord, Macaba wanders off on his own, heading back to his HQ. You need to keep up with him, but you'll need to deal with a few of his men along the way. Start by sneaking up behind the lone rifleman patrolling near the tents and take him down with a stealth kill.

Next, toss a Sensor toward the supply area to identify three more of Macaba's men. Mark the three, then search for a fourth rifleman standing on a rooftop in the distance—mark him, too. While your teammates target the nearby hostiles, take aim at the rifleman on the rooftop by peering through your scope. When you have the rooftop hostile in sight, squeeze the trigger to initiate the sync-shot.

Macaba is still on the move, so don't fall too far behind. His position appears on the HUD as a moving waypoint marker. This allows you to keep tabs on him. But if he gets too far ahead, you'll lose him and have to restart from the last save checkpoint. The next hostile has his back turned, making it easy to sneak up behind him and perform a stealth kill.

## // TIP

*Before reaching Macaba's guards near the white SUV, a vehicle passes along the road nearby. You don't need to kill the vehicle's driver to progress. But if you want to complete the Secure the Camp challenge, mark the driver. Wait for the vehicle to turn behind the tents and perform the sync-shot.*

Just ahead, Macaba walks past two riflemen standing next to a white SUV. Do not kill these guys while Macaba is nearby. Instead, hold back and watch. After Macaba passes, one of the rifleman turns to the left, walking along the passenger side of the SUV. When he pauses to smoke, sneak up behind him and perform a stealth kill. Now locate the second rifleman. He walks alongside Macaba for a few paces, then turns right into a side alley. Creep up behind him and take him out, too. In this alley, you can stock up on ammo, Sensors, and grenades from an ammo crate.

Just ahead, two riflemen come walking toward Macaba. Take cover alongside one of the tents and watch the two patrolling riflemen as they move toward you—mark both of them, but don't shoot until Macaba is out of the area. When Macaba turns down an alley to the right, give the shoot order. Depending on your teammates' positions, you may need to shoot one of these riflemen before he gets close enough to spot you. The path to Macaba is now clear. Follow him to small warehouse where he conducts a call. It sounds like the weapons haven't arrived yet. They're scheduled to arrive by air at a nearby airstrip. Now that you know where the weapons are, Overlord gives permission to take out Macaba.

There are three riflemen within view of Macaba. You'll need to set up a sync-shot if you want to take out Macaba without setting off a small war. Mark the two riflemen on the path near Macaba, then mark the rifleman on the rooftop in the distance. Finally, mark Macaba. Wait for your team to line up their shots while you take aim at the back of Macaba's head. When everyone is in position, squeeze the trigger. Now it's time to get out of the refugee camp and take possession of that incoming arms shipment at the airstrip.

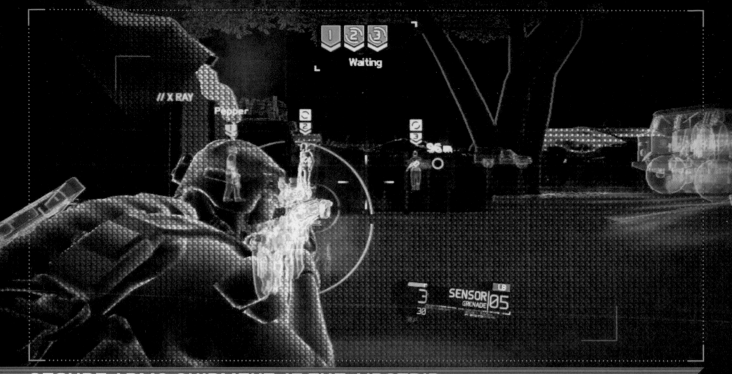

# SECURE ARMS SHIPMENT AT THE AIRSTRIP

You're free to make as much noise as you want now. But it's safest to proceed quietly, stealthily picking off the remainder of Macaba's men as you make your way to the outskirts of the refugee camp. Activate the Magnetic view to spot a small group of enemies loitering nearby. Mark all three, then peer off to the right to spot a hostile carrying a LMG on a distant rooftop. Mark him, too. Wait for your team to line up their shots while you take aim at the guy with the LMG. When you have your target in sight, squeeze the trigger to initiate the sync-shot, eliminating all four hostiles in an instant.

## ENEMY PROFILE: LMG SOLDIER

LMG soldiers are heavy, suppressing, medium-range threats. These enemies are mobile, but once they are positioned properly to shoot at your team, they won't move. When fired at by one of these enemies you may become suppressed, which means you're prevented from aiming properly for a few seconds, even if you're behind cover. So always make note of LMG soldiers and take steps to eliminate them before they become aware of your team's presence. If you come under attack by one of these enemies, stay behind cover and issue a focus fire order on the target. You can also cover swap to avoid getting suppressed, but always wait for the LMG soldier to stop firing before moving. Smoke grenades can block an LMG soldier's line of sight, giving you and your team a chance to engage him through the smoke using the Magnetic view.

Two more riflemen are blocking your path to the refugee camp's exit. Using Magnetic view, get a bearing on their positions and mark them. Although there are only two, it's easiest to perform a sync-shot. When your teammates have a line of sight on both targets, give the shoot order. The refugee camp is now clear. Proceed to the waypoint to reach the rendezvous point with your driver—he'll take you to the airstrip. Overlord reports that Macaba's shipment has arrived and is already being unloaded. The plan now is to recover the data recorder from the aircraft to try to determine where it's been. This the best shot at tracking the shipment back to where it originated. But you need to move fast. That storm is still inbound and the aircraft's flight crew will probably try to get airborne before it hits.

## TACTICAL CHALLENGE: SECURE THE CAMP

### CRITERIA: ELIMINATE ALL OF THE SOLDIERS WHO HAVE TAKEN CONTROL OF THE REFUGEE CAMP

If you eliminated every enemy described in the walkthrough, you will complete this challenge just before reaching the rendezvous point outside the refugee camp. If you haven't completed this challenge yet, consider circling back and scouring the camp for any stragglers—you must do this before you board the truck.

### // TIP

*You often have the possibility to avoid enemy reinforcements if you pass through a situation without triggering an alert. If the current objective is not stated as "Secure", you don't have to kill all enemies to proceed. Simply sneak past the enemies to reach the next objective.*

# RECOVER THE BLACK BOX

ZAMBIA

After a brief ride in the truck, the Ghosts are deployed a few hundred meters away from the airstrip. Before you can make your way to the aircraft, you'll need to take out the airstrip's security detail. Creep toward the large hangars until you spot two rifleman walking along a dirt road. Mark both enemies and wait until they walk behind a set of crates before giving the shoot order. As they fall to the ground, the crates hide their bodies from the other hostiles near the hangars.

Now it's time to deal with the riflemen near the hangars. Creep toward the hangars using the crates and concrete barriers for cover. Getting close allows you to get a better view of the enemies. Tossing a Sensor in between the two hangars makes it easier to identify the locations of these hostiles. There are four riflemen in this area. Two are standing in between the two hangars. The third is located in the hangar on the left and the fourth patrols a catwalk between the two hangars. Mark all four targets and keep an eye on the patrolling rifleman on the catwalk. When he enters the hangar on the right, take aim at any of the targets and give the shoot order. It's important the enemy on the catwalk is killed within the hangar. Otherwise enemies in the guard towers by the airstrip may see him fall and raise an alert. Shortly after dropping these four enemies, the engines of the cargo plane can be heard starting up—you need to reach the plane before it can take off!

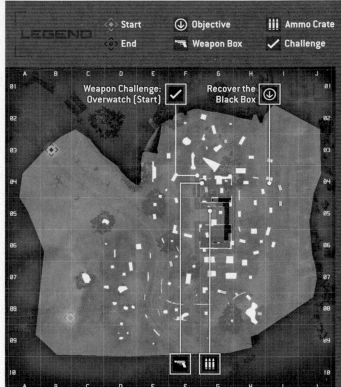

LEGEND

◇ Start  ⊕ Objective  ⫼ Ammo Crate
◉ End  🔫 Weapon Box  ✓ Challenge

Weapon Challenge: Overwatch (Start) ✓   Recover the Black Box ⊕

However, don't let the sound of the plane's engines make you rush. You still need to neutralize a few more enemies near the airstrip. Move to a position where you can spot both guard towers. There's a hostile armed with an LMG in each guard tower. Take them out yourself by firing a bullet through each hostile's head. Otherwise, set up a sync-shot and order your team to clear the two guard towers. With the enemies in the guard towers out of the picture, you can now mop up the remaining hostiles guarding the airstrip.

# WEAPON CHALLENGE: OVERWATCH

## CRITERIA: ELIMINATE TEN ENEMIES USING A SNIPER RIFLE WITHOUT MOVING

At the start of this mission, no sniper rifles are available. However, you can find a VSS sniper rifle in the weapon box within the left hangar. Acquiring this weapon allows you to complete the weapon challenge. To complete the challenge, you must kill ten enemies with a sniper rifle. But the key is that you can't move after taking the first shot. This means you must kill ten enemies from a fixed position. The crash site is the best place to get these kills. When you reach the crash site, don't kill the first five enemies. Instead, sneak into the crash site by moving around the aircraft's tail

section, taking cover in the trench. From this fixed position you can start racking-up sniper rifle kills as enemy reinforcements arrive. But once you've started killing, you can't move. Otherwise the kill counter resets.

Creep between the two hangars and interact with the ammo crate to stock up on ammo and Sensors. Next, toss a few Sensors in the direction of the airstrip to locate the four remaining hostiles. Mark all four enemies and take them out with a sync-shot. Suddenly, the cargo plane begins moving down the runway. You have no other option—you need to destroy the plane's engine to prevent it from getting away. Equip your secondary weapon and open fire on the starboard engine. You have exactly 20 seconds to destroy the engine, so don't waste any time. Keep firing at the engine as the plane moves down the runway. You'll know you've succeeded when the engine erupts in flames. The plane still manages to take off, but it won't get far. Shortly after takeoff, the plane is seen falling out of the sky. It's not too late. You can still recover the plane's black box. Before leaving the airstrip, visit the ammo crate between the two hangars and stock up on ammo and Sensors.

**// What Goes Up ...**
*achievement trophy*

This achievement/trophy is unlocked after successfully shooting down the cargo plane.

# RECOVER THE BLACK BOX AT THE CRASH SITE

Your team must now reach the crash site to recover the cargo plane's black box. As you follow your team toward the next waypoint marker, a pickup truck armed with a mounted machine gun comes racing down the road toward you. Immediately take cover behind a rock and mark the machine gunner. When you mark an enemy during a firefight, an orange icon appears above his head. This instructs your team to focus their fire on the target. Issuing focus-fire orders is a good way to quickly eliminate dangerous threats such as this gunner. Once the gunner is down, track down the two riflemen that scrambled out of the truck. Once the area is clear, resume your advance toward the crash site.

## // CAUTION

*While advancing through the sandstorm toward the crash site, you must pass through the refugee camp. Along the way, you encounter two enemy vehicles crossing directly in front of your team's path. Do not engage them. There's no need to start a firefight in the middle of the desert, where you have minimal cover. Engaging the vehicles will also trigger an alert in the camp, making it much more difficult to reach the crash site. Let the vehicles pass. You'll deal with the occupants soon enough.*

## CAMP/CRASH SITE

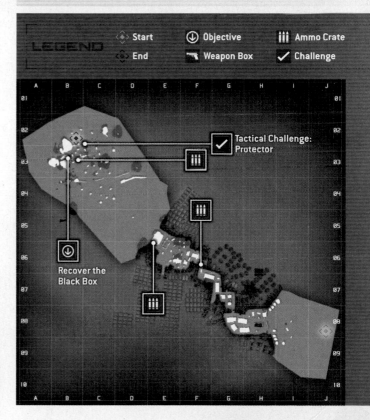

By now, the sandstorm is upon you. But there's no time to hunker down and ride it out. You must continue moving toward the crash site. Activate Magnetic view and stay close to your teammates. Before you can reach the crash site, you must pass through the refugee camp, which has been reinforced by more gunmen. When you come to the outskirts of the refugee camp, there are five hostiles you need to take out. Start by picking off the rifleman patrolling the rooftop. The wind can make it difficult to stabilize your shot. But the sandstorm also works in your favor by reducing visibility for your enemies. This allows you to get relatively close to your targets without being detected. So creep up toward the building where the rifleman is patrolling and take him out with your suppressed weapon of choice.

Now set up a sync-shot to eliminate the remaining hostiles, including a machine gunner in a pickup truck. If you're having trouble spotting all four hostiles in this area, deploy a Sensor. When you've located all four enemies near the pickup truck, mark them all. Now pick a target from the four, take aim, and squeeze the trigger to initiate the sync-shot. You can now infiltrate the refugee camp. If you need to restock ammo or Sensors, there's an ammo crate on the rooftop of the building where you dropped the first rifleman.

Keep the Magnetic view active while advancing through the refugee camp. This makes it easy to spot the rifleman patrolling around the nearby tents. Due to the poor visibility, you can pick off these threats with little difficulty. Either take them out yourself, or mark them for your team and drop them with sync-shots. Continue advancing through the refugee camp, picking off enemies as you encounter them. The sandstorm helps hide the bodies so you don't worry too much about raising an alert.

As you near the exit to the refugee camp, a large truck pulls up in the distance and two riflemen get out. They join a group of four other hostiles, making a total of six targets. You need to approach this situation delicately to avoid setting off a firefight. Start by marking the hostile in the building ahead—he's armed with an LMG. Since this guy is inside a building, none of his friends will notice he's gone when you give the shoot order. One down, five to go.

The next five enemies can be taken out with two separate sync-shots. First, identify the three enemies closest to your position and mark them. Before giving the shoot order, make sure all three targets are a reasonable distance away from the other two hostiles near the truck. The sandstorm helps to hide the bodies, so you can drop the first three targets without raising an alert. Finally, mark the last two hostiles near the truck and take them out with another sync-shot. The refugee camp is now clear. You can proceed to the crash site. Be sure to visit the ammo crate near the camp's exit to stock up on ammo and Sensors.

# ZAMBIA

# SECURE CRASH SITE

## // CAUTION

*During the fight at the crash site, watch out for incoming grenades. Grenades are highlighted by an orange hexagonal icon on the HUD, making them relatively easy to spot as they fly through the air. If a grenade comes your way, immediately move, preferably by using the cover swap method. Grenades have a timed fuse, so you have a few seconds to get away before they detonate.*

The crash site is located approximately 200 meters beyond the refugee camp. Overlord chimes in with news that hostiles have closed in on the site. Fortunately, enemy activity at the site is currently light. At this point, you're given 90 seconds to secure the crash site before reinforcements arrive. Drop to a crouched stance and approach the crash site with your Optical Camo active. By now, the dust storm has subsided, greatly improving visibility. So make sure you utilize cover and the Optical Camo to avoid being detected. There are a total of five enemies at the crash site—deploy a Sensor near the crash site to spot them. Start by marking the two riflemen near the truck and order your team to take them out with a sync-shot. The remaining three riflemen standing near the airplane wreckage can also be eliminated with a second sync-shot. If you act quickly, you can easily eliminate all five threats without triggering a firefight.

Time to move in on the crash site. Regroup with your team at the waypoint in the middle of the aircraft wreckage. Overlord reports that a Quick Reaction Force (QRF) is inbound and will establish a perimeter upon arrival. Until then, it's up to your team to defend the area against approaching hostile forces. Not long after the report from Overlord, a pickup truck filled with hostiles arrives on the scene. Immediately mark the machine gunner in the back of truck with a focus-fire order. This instructs your team to focus their fire on the gunner, eliminating this threat before he can dish out too much damage. Toss a Sensor toward the truck to highlight the positions of other hostiles that may be concealed behind the high grass. Once they are revealed, you can fire through the grass to hit these obscured enemies. You can acquire more Sensors from the ammo crate near the plane's fuselage.

During this defensive action, more reinforcements arrive in pickup trucks armed with mounted machine guns. Fortunately, there's plenty of cover among the wreckage, including several steel crates. So monitor the arrival of new threats and make sure you put a solid piece of cover between yourself and the attackers. You will need to constantly move around and seek new cover as new threats arrive from different directions. Continue deploying Sensors around the perimeter of the crash site to reveal the positions of enemies hiding behind trees, rocks, or high grass.

Continue engaging the attackers while seeking cover among the wreckage. The QRF eventually arrives in two Blackhawks, raining down automatic fire from their door-mounted miniguns. Help the Blackhawks mop up any resistance at the crash site and wait for a report from Overlord. Your work here is complete. The QRF will establish a perimeter and recover the black box. Hopefully the black box will reveal where Macaba's weapons shipment originated.

| SUBTLE ARROW: COMPLETION UNLOCKS | | |
|---|---|---|
| Type | Category | Item |
| Weapon | PDR | L22A2 |
| Weapon | LMG | Stoner 96 |
| Attachment | Muzzle | Compensator |
| Attachment | Underbarrel | Bipod |
| Items | Drone | UAV |
| Paint | Weapon paint | Libyan |

# TOM CLANCY'S GHOST RECON FUTURE SOLDIER

# NOBLE TEMPEST

NIGERIA

## BRIEFING

LOCATION: NIGERIA
OBJECTIVES: LOCATE, SECURE, AND EXTRACT CIA OFFICER DANIEL SYKES.
CURRENT CONTACT: SENIOR MASTER SERGEANT MARCUS KELSO

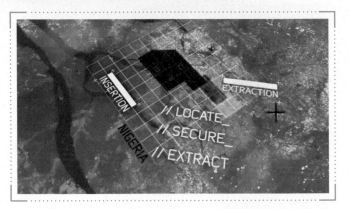

The black box you recovered in Zambia was well traveled. The Defense Intelligence Agency (DIA) managed to pull the nav data from it, and came back with hits in Nigeria. There's been a lot of activity in the Niger Delta recently. Turns out the CIA already had an asset in-country to monitor a Private Military Company (PMC) operating in the region. Watchgate says they're providing security for oil companies, but it looks like that's not all they're up to. These guys are muscling in on refineries, running ops into local villages. They're destabilizing an already shaky area. We want to know why.

CIA's agent, Officer Daniel Sykes, delivered an intel package on the situation and then went dark. Langley's tried to reestablish contact. So far, no luck. They're assuming the worst. We're going in to locate, secure, and extract Officer Sykes, whatever his condition.

## MISSION CHALLENGES

### WEAPON CHALLENGE: FIVE SHOT

| DIFFICULTY: | ★☆☆☆☆ |
| --- | --- |
| UNLOCK: | SR-3M |

- Make five consecutive kills on unalerted enemies using a PDR.

### TACTICAL CHALLENGES

| DIFFICULTY: | ★★★★☆ |
| --- | --- |
| UNLOCK: | DRUM MAGAZINE |

- Fast Mover: Go through the village in under 60 seconds without any civilians dying
- Clear the Pitch: Eliminate all the mercs playing soccer without raising the alarm
- No Blood No Foul: Infiltrate the outpost, retrieve the data, and extract without raising the alarm

## GEAR SELECTION

| Equipment Slot | Default | | Recommended | |
|---|---|---|---|---|

### PRIMARY

**STONER 96 LMG**

| | Default | Recommended |
|---|---|---|
| POWER | | |
| RANGE | | |
| CONTROL | | |
| MANEUVERABILITY | | |
| RATE OF FIRE | 960 RPM | 864 RPM |
| MAGAZINE CAPACITY | 150 | 150 |

**CONFIGURATION SUMMARY**

| | Default | Recommended |
|---|---|---|
| Muzzle: | Suppressor | Compensator |
| Scope: | Tac Scope | Red Dot |
| Underbarrel: | Bipod | Bipod |

### SECONDARY

**L22A2 PDR**

| | Default | Recommended |
|---|---|---|
| POWER | | |
| RANGE | | |
| CONTROL | | |
| MANEUVERABILITY | | |
| RATE OF FIRE | 1,020 RPM | 918 RPM |
| MAGAZINE CAPACITY | 30 | 30 |

**CONFIGURATION SUMMARY**

| | Default | Recommended |
|---|---|---|
| Muzzle: | Suppressor | Suppressor |
| Scope: | Red Dot | Tac Scope |
| Underbarrel: | Vertical Foregrip | Vertical Foregrip |

### ITEM 1

**SENSOR**

QUANTITY: 5 | QUANTITY: 5

Detects nearby enemies, highlighting them on the HUD

Detects nearby enemies, highlighting them on the HUD

### ITEM 2

**FRAG**

QUANTITY: 3 | QUANTITY: 3

High-explosive grenade intended to kill or wound

High-explosive grenade intended to kill or wound

# LOCATE CIA OFFICER SYKES

The nav data from the cargo plane has lead the Ghost team to Nigeria. It's unclear how this region ties into the weapons obtained by Paez and Macaba. But there's a good chance Watchgate is involved. Watchgate is a Private Military Company (PMC) operating in the region, officially serving as security consultants for oil companies. The CIA's man on the ground, Officer Daniel Sykes, will likely know more of Watchgate's involvement. But Sykes has gone missing and nearby Yakoromor village was his last known location. As the Ghost team sneaks toward the village along a shallow waterway, they witness a few Watchgate mercs gun down a couple of locals for no apparent reason. These guys don't play fair. It's time to give them a taste of their own medicine.

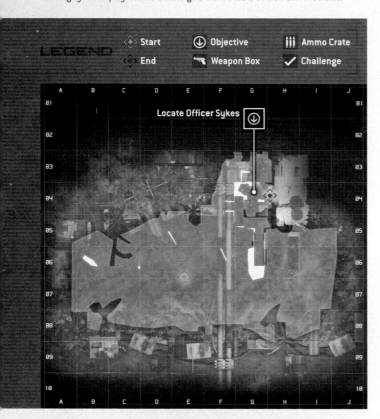

| LEGEND | | | | |
|---|---|---|---|---|
| | ◇ Start | ⬇ Objective | ⫼ Ammo Crate | |
| | ◇ End | 🔫 Weapon Box | ✓ Challenge | |

Locate Officer Sykes

In this mission, you have access to a new piece of equipment: the UAV. This miniaturized, unmanned aerial vehicle (UAV) is small enough to take off and land from the operator's palm. But don't let its small size fool you. The UAV is one of the most effective reconnaissance tools available, allowing the Ghosts to receive real-time encrypted intelligence from up to 50 meters above the area of operations. The UAV is equipped with a high-resolution infrared camera complete with a zoom lens and two vision modes perfect for identifying the heat signatures (and weapons) of hostile contacts. However, the camera cannot penetrate through solid objects such as walls and rooftops, where devices like the Sensor or Magnetic view prove more effective. Still, the UAV's ability to take to the sky and scout ahead should never be overlooked.

Follow the on-screen prompts to launch the UAV and pilot it toward the nearby shack, which is marked with a waypoint. Fly the UAV just above the shack where it can peer through a hole in the rooftop. The UAV identifies four hostiles inside the shack, three armed with assault rifles. The fourth merc sits at a table and is unarmed—you need to interrogate this guy to find Officer Sykes's whereabouts. Exit the UAV view and prepare to assault the shack.

While Ghost Lead and 30K stack up on one of the shack's doorways, follow Pepper to the doorway on the opposite side of the shack. As you approach the door, Magnetic view is automatically activated, providing a better view of the four hostiles inside. From your entry point, the merc on the left side of the shack, nearest your door, is the best target to focus on. When you're ready to attack, give the breach order. During entry, pan your aim to the left side of the room and open fire on the merc by the window. Within a couple of seconds, all hostiles are down. Once the room is clear, Kozak grabs the unarmed merc in the center of the room and shoves him to the floor while jamming a pistol to the back of his head. It's not long before he coughs up the intel you've been hoping for—Sykes is being held at the nearby refinery, within a shipping container.

GhostLead

DRONE AVAILABLE ↑ 150

## SECURE OFFICER SYKES

Before you can reach the refinery, you must first pass through the Yakoromor village, which is occupied by Watchgate mercs. You can't pass through the village undetected so prepare for an intense firefight. Just ahead, three mercs are harassing some villagers. Toss a Sensor toward the mercs to highlight them amongst the crowd, then open fire with your LMG, being careful not to hit any civilians as they scramble for cover. During this sequence, let your team lead the way through the village while you provide fire support (and deploy Sensors) from the rear. Don't be stingy with the Sensors. They're the best way to reveal the positions of mercs hiding behind objects like vehicles and structures. Avoid using the UAV here, as it pulls your view away from the action, potentially leaving you vulnerable to attack. As your Sensors detect enemies, issue focus-fire orders to overwhelm the hostiles with firepower. Continue the advance until the village is clear of threats. Shortly after downing the last enemies, you can stock-up on ammo and Sensors by interacting with an ammo crate near the village's exit.

## TACTICAL CHALLENGE: FAST MOVER

### CRITERIA: GO THROUGH THE VILLAGE IN UNDER 60 SECONDS WITHOUT ANY CIVILIANS DYING

The strict time constraint makes this challenge very difficult. From the moment you exit the shack (where you interrogated the merc) the clock is ticking. You need to rush through the entire village in less than 60 seconds, while avoiding any civilian casualties.

To pull this off, you need to keep moving the whole time, even while firing. When you're not engaging enemies, sprint. You can view the challenge timer by accessing the Tactical Map. If you're running low on time, restart from the last save checkpoint (at the shack) and try again. It may take several attempts to complete this challenge, so don't get discouraged. Once you know where the enemies appear in the village, it becomes much easier to move and shoot.

LEGEND

◇ Start  ⊘ Objective  ⦙⦙⦙ Ammo Crate
◇ End  ▭ Weapon Box  ✓ Challenge

✓ Tactical Challenge: Fast Mover (Start)

With your Optical Camo active, drop off the left side of the bridge to drop into the shallow ravine below. Once out of the water, assume a crouched stance and creep along the left side of the facility. The mercs playing soccer and the other hostiles won't see you thanks to your Optical Camo. However, make a habit of utilizing cover as you advance into the facility. A lone guard patrols on the left side of the refinery. Unlike the other mercs, this guy is completely isolated so he is easy to take out. Instead of shooting him with a suppressed weapon, simply sneak up behind him and perform a stealth kill—his body won't be spotted by any of the mercs.

Continue advancing along the left side of the facility and assume a position on the raised platform outside the hangar-like structure. From here, you have a clear view of the facility, including all hostiles. Take cover along one of the low walls on the perimeter of the platform. Peek over the wall and begin marking targets. Mark the four hostiles at the back of the facility, including the merc with the LMG on the central platform. When your team has established lines of sight on their targets, take aim at the fourth merc and line up your shot using the weapon of your choice. A suppressed weapon doesn't make a difference here since the four targeted mercs will be spotted by their comrades when they drop to the ground, resulting in an alert. So initiate the sync-shot to trigger the firefight.

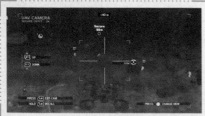

After dropping the first four mercs, take cover and issue focus-fire orders for your team. Given your position at the rear of the facility, you can catch the remaining mercs in a crossfire. If you can't get a line of sight on the enemies, return to the UAV view and orchestrate the attack from the air. From the UAV view you can watch the fight from above and issue focus-fire orders for your teammates. Although outnumbered, thanks to some careful planning and maneuvering, your team can secure the refinery within a matter of seconds.

## TACTICAL CHALLENGE: CLEAR THE PITCH

**CRITERIA: ELIMINATE ALL THE MERCS PLAYING SOCCER WITHOUT RAISING THE ALARM**

This challenge is much easier than it sounds. Before attacking the refinery, locate the four mercs playing soccer, not far from the bridge. Deploy the UAV and mark all four targets. With the targets marked, perform a sync-shot to take out the soccer-playing mercs. Of course, killing these mercs causes the other hostiles to go on alert, triggering the firefight at the refinery. But as long as the mercs playing soccer are the first victims, you'll complete the challenge. This isn't the best method of attack, as it leaves the merc armed with the LMG still standing on the platform in the distance. So be sure to issue a focus-fire order on the guy with the LMG shortly after performing the sync-shot.

Following the assault on the refinery, regroup with your team at the shipping container marked with a waypoint—Officer Sykes is inside. Once your team is in position, open the container and rescue Sykes. He isn't in great condition, but at least he can walk. While you're inside the container securing Sykes, all hell breaks loose outside as two Mi-24 Hind attack choppers arrive at the refinery and drop off merc reinforcements—these are the same choppers that Overlord warned you about earlier. Ghost Lead orders the team to assume a diamond formation in an effort to protect the VIP.

As the diamond formation sequence begins, take aim with your pistol and start drilling mercs as fast as you can. This sequence plays out much like the one in Bolivia, when you were escorting Paez. You don't need to worry about moving. Simply aim and shoot. All it takes is a single hit to kill each merc, so conserve your ammo to prevent frequent reloads. Simply pan the aiming reticle over a target and squeeze the trigger. Prioritize enemies who are stationary and shooting at you. Mercs who are running around pose less of an immediate threat.

**MISSILE CAMERA**
#045-373 AKM

# OIL HARBOR

## ENEMY PROFILE: MI-24 HIND

*Also known as "the flying tank," this large attack helicopter is armed to the teeth with a variety of weapons and a mean four-barrel chin turret. The two-person crew makes this helicopter very reactive, able to maneuver or deploy troops while at the same time shoot with deadly accuracy. The heavy armor and titanium rotor blades on this beast can take most of what you can carry with no problems. If you're faced with one, take cover at once and try to locate heavier guns.*

It soon becomes clear that you're not going to get out of this mess without help. Overlord reports that an air strike package is available for close support. When Kozak huddles next to crate with Sykes, press the button shown on-screen to initiate the air strike. Your view suddenly changes to a camera fixed to the nose of an incoming missile. Using the right control stick, guide the missile toward the refinery, aiming it between the two choppers. The missile explodes just above the choppers. The powerful air-burst warhead flings the choppers around like toys, causing them to crash. The explosion also wipes out the remaining merc reinforcements.

# EXTRACT OFFICER SYKES

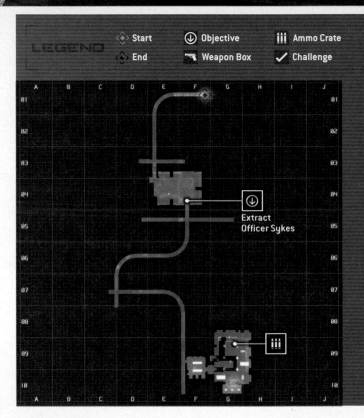

LEGEND

|  |  |
|--------|-------|
| ◆ Start | ⊕ Objective |
| ◇ End | Weapon Box |
| ⫶⫶⫶ Ammo Crate | ✓ Challenge |

Extract
Officer Sykes

Sykes and the Ghost team survive the air strike with only temporary hearing damage. Ghost Lead orders the team to take cover in the nearby hangar—it's time to get Sykes out of here. Overlord reports that there's a subterranean passage underneath the hangar. You can use this passage to reach Sykes's extraction point. Before entering the passage, visit the ammo crate in the hangar to stock up on ammo and Sensors. With the exception of some rats, the underground passage is clear of hostiles, so you don't need to worry about encountering any threats. As you move through the tunnels, Sykes reports that the Watchgate mercs are involved in something big. He suspects even the mercs don't realize what they've gotten themselves into. Sykes had to ditched his intel inside a car at an abandoned gas station before the mercs captured him. Proceed to the end of the tunnel system, where a Blackhawk is waiting overhead to extract Sykes. His mission is over, but the Ghosts need to track down that intel before they can extract.

## // Precious Cargo

achievement
trophy

This achievement/trophy is unlocked after transferring Officer Sykes to the exfiltration team.

# RECOVER SYKES'S DATA

Follow a waypoint marker through another drainage tunnel leading toward a shantytown. As you near the exit of the tunnel, drop to a crouched stance to activate your Optical Camo—there are hostiles patrolling the shantytown. Creep out of the tunnel and deploy your UAV to take a look around. Near the exit of the tunnel are four mercs patrolling. Some are equipped with shotguns. Instead of trying to take out all four mercs with one sync-shot, mark only two mercs at a time, preferably when they're isolated and out of sight from any nearby hostiles. By setting up two separate sync-shots, you can easily clear this part of the shantytown without triggering an alarm.

## ENEMY PROFILE: SHOTGUNNER

The shotgunner is a close-range threat, and should be avoided in close quarters. These enemies are only dangerous at close range. As a result, they often advance, closing in on their targets to inflict maximum damage. The goal is to kill these enemies before they get too close and too dangerous. When possible, issue focus fire orders on these guys so you team can overwhelm them with concentrated firepower. If you fail to deal with these threats quickly, they'll often move to flanking positions, taking you by surprise.

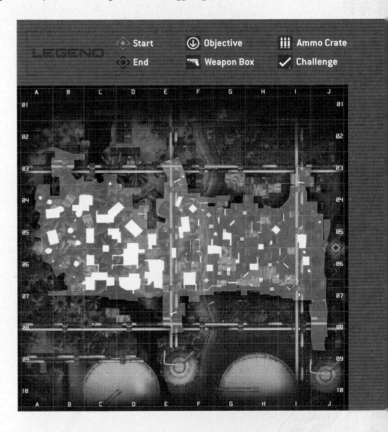

LEGEND

◇ Start  ⊙ Objective  ⦀ Ammo Crate
◈ End  ⊐ Weapon Box  ✓ Challenge

After taking out the first four mercs, do not move from your current position by the drainage tunnel. Instead, fly the UAV toward the road that cuts through the shantytown. Four more mercs are patrolling this area. Once again, don't worry about taking out all of these mercs simultaneously. Instead, mark two or three at a time and pick them off with sync-shots as they become isolated from each other.

With the area near the road secure, move forward through the shantytown. As you move out, two enemy choppers fly overhead and drop off more reinforcements in the distance. Keep pushing forward and seek cover near one of the shacks by the road. Once again, deploy your UAV to locate the nearest group of reinforcements. Monitor the nearby group of four mercs from the air and wait for them to spread out as they begin patrolling. As they separate from each other, begin marking and picking them off with sync-shots.

Just ahead, there is a large group of eight mercs gathered around a light vehicle. These guys are stationary and don't move around, making it impossible to isolate them and whittle their numbers down with sync-shots. But since they're stationary, you can slip right past them without being spotted. While crouched, sneak along the right side of the shantytown while making your way toward the waypoint. At the waypoint, you come to a set of double doors. Move into the white ring icon in front of the door and wait for your team to catch up. You team will follow your lead, slipping right past the large group of mercs undetected.

# VILLA

LEGEND
◇ Start   ◉ Objective   ▥ Ammo Crate
◈ End   🔫 Weapon Box   ✓ Challenge

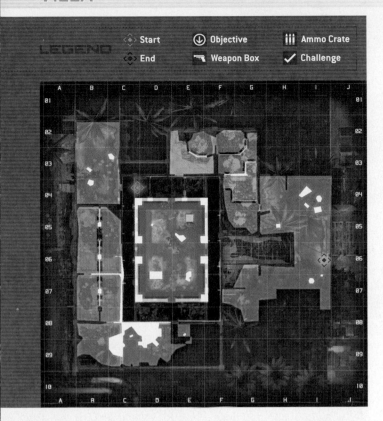

Once inside the villa-like structure, you don't need to worry about running into any mercs. However, the enemy chopper overhead is a sign that your team isn't out of danger just yet. A series of waypoint markers guides you through the villa. In multiple areas, you must hop over low walls to proceed through the debris-filled structure. To hop over these walls, take cover at the base of the wall by pressing the cover button. While in cover, press the cover button again to hop over the wall. On the upper level, wait for your team at a set of double doors that lead out onto a promenade overlooking a courtyard. It looks like some machete-wielding locals are taking revenge on a merc below—too bad for him. Climb over the low walls on the left side of the promenade and make your way to the villa's exit.

# COASTAL TOWN

LEGEND
◇ Start   ◉ Objective   ▥ Ammo Crate
◈ End   🔫 Weapon Box   ✓ Challenge

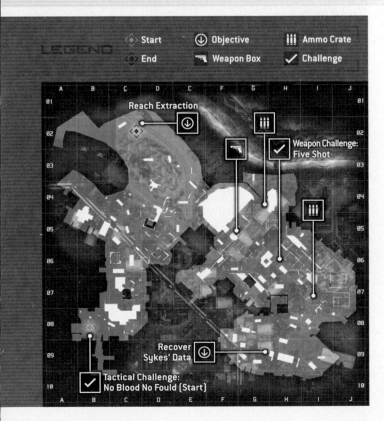

**Reach Extraction** ◉

▥

✓ **Weapon Challenge: Five Shot**

🔫

▥

**Recover Sykes' Data** ◉

✓ **Tactical Challenge: No Blood No Foul (Start)**

The villa exits onto a coastal town filled with a few civilians—so hold your fire. Cautiously advance through the town while moving toward the next waypoint marker. When enemy contacts are detected, drop to a crouched stance to activate your Optical Camo and creep toward a large guard tower near the shore. Take cover near the guard tower and deploy your UAV. One rifleman is in the guard tower and seven other hostiles are patrolling nearby. Mark the rifleman in the guard tower first and order one of your teammates to take him out. Next, set up sync-shots to eliminate the remaining hostiles on the ground. With the exception of one merc standing next to the guard tower, all of the hostiles conduct patrols in pairs. During the patrols, each pair of hostiles is frequently outside the line of sight of one another. This makes them easy to pick off, two at a time, using sync-shots. You must eliminate all of these enemies before advancing deeper into the town. When the area is clear, recall your UAV.

## // CAUTION

*If you fail to kill the enemies by the guard tower silently, a GAZ-2330 light vehicle (with a mounted machine gun) will arrive, unloading more troops. Triggering such an alert causes you to fail the No Blood No Foul tactical challenge.*

After clearing the area along the shore, follow your team up a nearby set of steps to enter a building containing a weapon box. If things go well, you won't need any of the weapons offered in this box. However, take cover beneath the window next to the box and begin scouting the area outside for more hostiles. This part of town is patrolled by multiple mercs as well as an attack chopper flying overhead. Deploy your UAV and focus on eliminating the hostiles in elevated positions first. Taking out these guys is important because they have a clear view of the area and may spot dead bodies on the ground. Mark the merc in the guard tower, then mark the two riflemen standing on a rooftop next to a mounted machine gun. Wait for your team to get into position, then use a sync-shot to eliminate all three threats in an instant.

Before you start picking off the mercs on the ground, there are two more hostiles you need to eliminate on a distant rooftop. Fly the UAV past the guard tower and veer left to spot these two riflemen. Mark both of them and take them out with another sync-shot. Now that the you've eliminated all of the hostiles in elevated positions, you'll have an easier time of clearing out the town without raising an alert. There are five mercs on the ground. Monitor their positions and patrols and set up sync-shots to pick them off in groups of two or three.

## // CAUTION

The UAV cannot see through solid objects such as rooftops. As a result, one of the mercs in the town may not be visible from your eye in the sky. Instead, use your Magnetic view or Sensors to locate this rifleman—he's in one of the nearby structures doing push-ups. Once you've located him, you can mark him for one of your teammates or simply take him out yourself.

## WEAPON CHALLENGE: FIVE SHOT

### CRITERIA: MAKE FIVE CONSECUTIVE KILLS ON UNALERTED ENEMIES USING A PDR.

Instead of relying on sync-shots to eliminate the enemies in town, consider hunting them down yourself using a suppressed PDR. To complete this challenge you must kill five unalerted enemies in a row using a PDR. Given the relatively isolated nature of the mercs on the ground, it is relatively easy to sneak around and pick off each merc, one at time. Utilize Optical Camo and cover to approach each threat to close range and then eliminate him with a single shot to the head. Once you've eliminate five consecutive mercs in this fashion, the challenge is complete.

After clearing out the mercs in the town, don't let your guard down. There's still that enemy chopper flying overhead to worry about. Remain in a crouched stance to keep your Optical Camo active. As long as your Optical Camo is active, the chopper can't see you. The path to the gas station is now clear. Just as Sykes described, an SUV is parked at the gas station. Make your way to the back of the SUV and retrieve the data from the trunk. It's time to get out of here.

**// TIP**

*If you're spotted by the chopper you can use the nearby mounted minigun to shoot it down.*

## REACH EXTRACTION

Retrace your steps back through the town, keeping your Optical Camo active to remain hidden from the patrolling chopper. The quickest path to the extraction site is through the building containing the weapon box, where you deployed your UAV from earlier. However, if you're eager to punish more mercs, take the path along the shore. Two riflemen advance along this wooden walkway. Mark them for your teammates or simply wait at the end of the walkway and mow them both down with your suppressed PDR.

## TACTICAL CHALLENGE: NO BLOOD NO FOUL

### CRITERIA: INFILTRATE THE OUTPOST, RETRIEVE THE DATA, AND EXTRACT WITHOUT RAISING THE ALARM

If you managed to secure Sykes's data without triggering an alarm, you complete this challenge when you board the chopper. As long as you utilize the UAV and carefully orchestrated sync-shots, it's relatively easy to cut through the mercs without being detected. However, you will need to replay the mission again if you were spotted at any time during the approach to the gas station or extraction point.

Before you can reach the extraction point, you must eliminate three more mercs. Find cover nearby and deploy your UAV. From the UAV view, mark the three riflemen patrolling the beach and order your team to take them out with a sync-shot. The path to the extraction point is now clear. Proceed to the waypoint on the beach and wait for your ride. Within seconds, a Blackhawk swoops into view and sets down on the beach, prompting the Ghosts to climb aboard for a swift departure. Now that you have Sykes's data, it will hopefully reveal more information about what you're up against.

### NOBLE TEMPEST: COMPLETION UNLOCKS

| Type | Category | Item |
| --- | --- | --- |
| Weapon | Sniper Rifle | MSR |
| Attachment | Optics | Custom Sniper Optic |
| Items | Grenade | Flashbang |
| Items | Drone | UAV + Crawler |
| Paint | Weapon paint | Brazilian Urban |

# TIGER DUST

## BRIEFING

LOCATION: PESHAWAR
OBJECTIVES: IDENTIFY, LOCATE, AND CAPTURE ARMS DEALER.
CURRENT CONTACT: SENIOR MASTER SERGEANT MARCUS KELSO

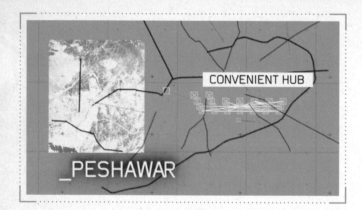

CONVENIENT HUB

_PESHAWAR

// IDENTIFY
// SECURE_
// EXTRACT

EXTRACTION

Officer Sykes is on his way to Ramstein Air Base. After they check him out, he'll be going home, thanks to you. In return, he gave us some critical intel. The pieces are coming together, gentlemen. All three supply chains lead us back to the same source: a gunrunner out of Pakistan with an international client list.

We're going into Peshawar, a convenient hub for illicit trade to and from Southeast Asia, the Middle East, and Africa. This isn't a small-time operation. Whoever he is, this guy is running serious hardware, mil-spec technology, maybe even radioactive material. We have to cut him off. We're cooperating with Pakistani forces on this one. Their operation will cover ours. They keep the local, we get his supplier, everybody wins. Your team will identify, secure, and extract the supplier. Get this guy and we're a major step closer to the big picture.

## MISSION CHALLENGES

### WEAPON CHALLENGE: BODY COUNT

| DIFFICULTY: | ★★★★★ |
|---|---|
| UNLOCK: | AK-200 |

- Kill eight enemies in under 30 seconds while using an assault rifle

### TACTICAL CHALLENGES

| DIFFICULTY: | ★★★★☆ |
|---|---|
| UNLOCK: | OPTIONAL 2 STOCK |

- Clean Kill: Assault the HQ and take out the hostiles without any misses
- Killer Pursuit: Destroy every enemy vehicle during the chopper gunride
- Bird in the Air: On Elite difficulty, take out the enemy RPG before your chopper gets shot

## GEAR SELECTION

| Equipment Slot | Default | Recommended |
|---|---|---|

### PRIMARY

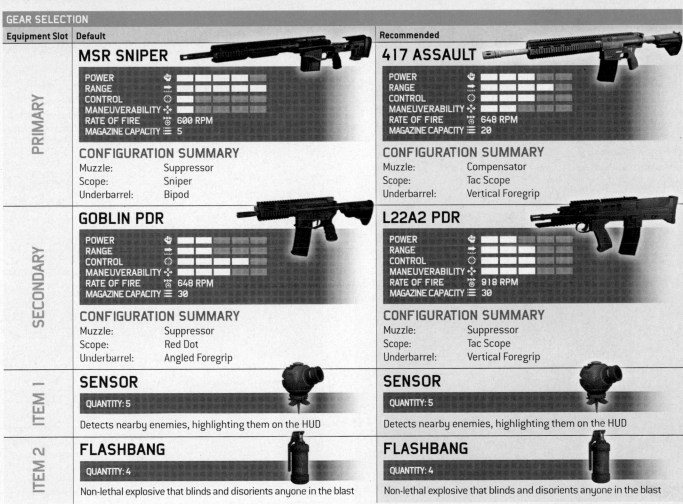

**MSR SNIPER**

| | |
|---|---|
| POWER | |
| RANGE | |
| CONTROL | |
| MANEUVERABILITY | |
| RATE OF FIRE | 600 RPM |
| MAGAZINE CAPACITY | 5 |

**CONFIGURATION SUMMARY**

| | |
|---|---|
| Muzzle: | Suppressor |
| Scope: | Sniper |
| Underbarrel: | Bipod |

**417 ASSAULT**

| | |
|---|---|
| POWER | |
| RANGE | |
| CONTROL | |
| MANEUVERABILITY | |
| RATE OF FIRE | 648 RPM |
| MAGAZINE CAPACITY | 20 |

**CONFIGURATION SUMMARY**

| | |
|---|---|
| Muzzle: | Compensator |
| Scope: | Tac Scope |
| Underbarrel: | Vertical Foregrip |

### SECONDARY

**GOBLIN PDR**

| | |
|---|---|
| POWER | |
| RANGE | |
| CONTROL | |
| MANEUVERABILITY | |
| RATE OF FIRE | 648 RPM |
| MAGAZINE CAPACITY | 30 |

**CONFIGURATION SUMMARY**

| | |
|---|---|
| Muzzle: | Suppressor |
| Scope: | Red Dot |
| Underbarrel: | Angled Foregrip |

**L22A2 PDR**

| | |
|---|---|
| POWER | |
| RANGE | |
| CONTROL | |
| MANEUVERABILITY | |
| RATE OF FIRE | 918 RPM |
| MAGAZINE CAPACITY | 30 |

**CONFIGURATION SUMMARY**

| | |
|---|---|
| Muzzle: | Suppressor |
| Scope: | Tac Scope |
| Underbarrel: | Vertical Foregrip |

### ITEM 1

**SENSOR**

QUANTITY: 5

Detects nearby enemies, highlighting them on the HUD

**SENSOR**

QUANTITY: 5

Detects nearby enemies, highlighting them on the HUD

### ITEM 2

**FLASHBANG**

QUANTITY: 4

Non-lethal explosive that blinds and disorients anyone in the blast

**FLASHBANG**

QUANTITY: 4

Non-lethal explosive that blinds and disorients anyone in the blast

# PESHAWAR

## LOCATE ARMS DEALER

Officer Sykes's intel has lead the Ghosts to Peshawar, Pakistan, where they're tracking a high-end arms dealer. The dealer is operating out of a nearby compound under heavy guard. The Ghosts are tasked with quietly infiltrating the compound and extracting the arms dealer. Intel also reports that the dealer is arranging a sale with a buyer. The buyer is off-limits during this operation—the Pakistanis want him alive.

Peshawar is a crowded city filled with civilians. Overlord advises to keep a low profile in an effort to avoid potentially dangerous engagements where innocents may be caught in the crossfire. It's also important to remain undetected to maintain the element of surprise. If the dealer has any clue of the Ghosts' presence, he'll bug out. The plan is to reach the target area by advancing across a series of rooftops. But the arms dealer is either paranoid or extremely prudent. The path to the arms dealer's compound is filled with hostiles occupying rooftops and towers.

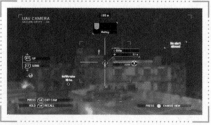

Start by climbing through the window where you begin the mission. Immediately after passing through the window, assume a crouched stance to activate your Optical Camo. There are five hostile gunmen nearby. The Optical Camo allows you to access the nearby rooftops without being spotted. Before moving too far, deploy your UAV to scout ahead. Veer to the left to spot a riflemen patrolling a rooftop near a minaret across the street—mark him. Two other riflemen are nearby on a lower rooftop, but ignore them for now—you need to take out the three hostiles on the high ground first. Instead, locate two other riflemen on a distant rooftop and mark them. Once your team has acquired the three marked targets, issue a sync-shot order to take them out. The remaining two hostiles on the lower rooftop can now be eliminated with a second sync-shot; mark them and give the shoot order. After eliminating these five hostiles, the immediate area is clear of threats. Recall the UAV and move out.

// TIP

If you choose to participate in any sync-shots during the advance to the arms
dealer's compound, make sure you have equipped a weapon with a suppressor.
The report of a non-suppressed weapon may alert nearby hostiles, resulting in
a mission failure.

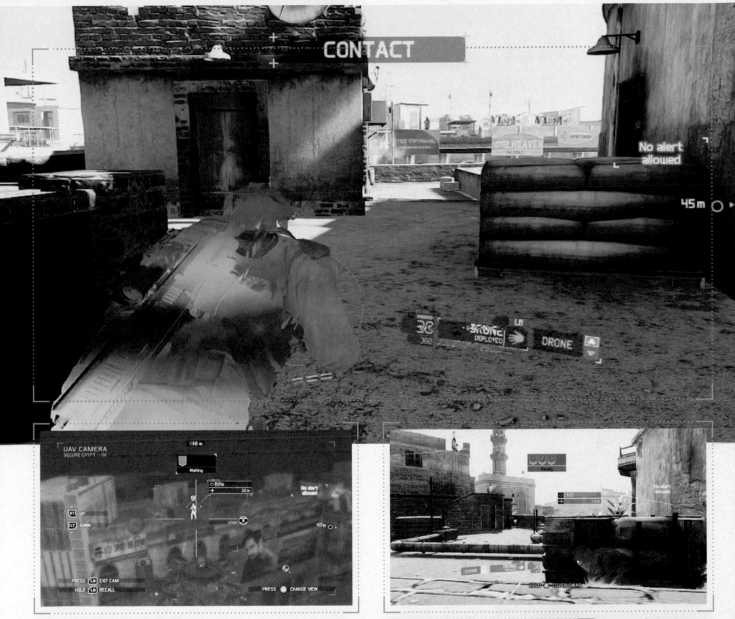

You can now stand up and advance along the rooftops for a few meters without being
spotted. Locate the waypoint marker in the distance and begin moving toward it. The
rooftops are uneven and you may need to climb over certain objects and low walls
along the way. Remember, you must take cover next to wall before you can climb over
it. Continue advancing toward the waypoint until the word "Contact" appears at the top
of the HUD—this indicates that a hostile is nearby. Immediately assumed a crouched
stance to activate your Optical Camo and find a piece of cover. A lone riflemen patrols a
rooftop across the street. Deploy the UAV to get a better view. You can either mark this
guy for your teammates or take him out yourself. There are no other hostiles within
view to see this guy die, so don't worry about triggering an alarm. If you do take the
shot yourself, use your weapon's scope view to score a headshot. If you miss or inflict
a less than lethal injury, the rifleman may trigger an alert. So if you're not confident in
your marksman skills, have a teammate take him out.

Keep your Optical Camo
active and creep toward
the waypoint marker. You're
not just outside the arms
dealer's compound. As
expected, the compound
is guarded by multiple
hostiles. There are a total
of eight guards in the area.
Before you can deal with
the four guards on the compound's rooftop, you need to take out the four guards
around the perimeter. These guys have elevated views of the compound from
neighboring rooftops and towers. Mark all four of these hostiles and perform a
sync-shot to take them all out simultaneously. When picking a target for yourself,
choose one of the nearby hostiles, especially if you don't have a sniper rifle.

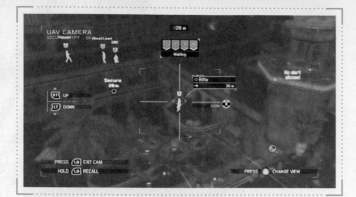

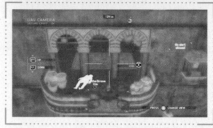

Next, mark the four guards on the compound's rooftop, including the guy on the balcony. Once all four targets are marked, move closer to the compound so that you have a clear view of the marked hostiles. From a covered position, take aim at the marked hostile on the balcony. This guy paces in and out of the compound. You need to wait until he steps out onto the balcony to get a clear shot. Once you have your shot lined up, squeeze the trigger to initiate the sync-shot. Within an instant, all the hostiles are down. You now have a clear path to the compound and can prepare to infiltrate.

Follow your teammates down onto the compound's rooftop and take a position along the skylight—move into the white ring to prepare for the breach. Before you can crash through the skylight and apprehend the arms dealer, you need to get a clear picture of exactly what you're jumping into. Chances are the dealer has surrounded himself with more guards. Once again, deploy the UAV and fly it toward the new waypoint marker on the balcony below, where you just eliminated the hostile. Descend onto the balcony and press the button shown on-screen to land the UAV. Once landed, the UAV is in Crawler mode. This transforms the UAV into a device that operates like a remote-controlled car.

## // CAUTION

*When securing the area around the compound, make sure the two patrolling riflemen at the compound are looking away from the enemies on the rooftop across the street. If they see one of these guys die, they'll go on alert, resulting in a mission failure.*

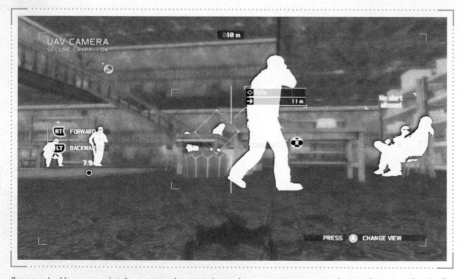

Drive the UAV into Crawler mode through a small vent in the wall opposite the balcony. This gives you access to the room where the deal is taking place. But there's one problem. You've located the buyer, but the arms dealer is nowhere to be found. After passing through the vent, turn right and drive the Crawler down the nearby staircase. The floor below is filled with riflemen. Judging by their relaxed postures, they don't expect anything. Although the arms dealer isn't present, Ghost Lead suggests following through with the assault. Drive the Crawler toward the center of the floor, marked by a waypoint. As you near the waypoint, make sure not to move too close to the guy pacing the floor while talking on a cell phone. Wait until his back is turned, then drive the Crawler to the waypoint marker. When you reach the waypoint, you're prompted to press the button shown on-screen to emit a sonic pulse.

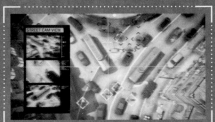

The sonic pulse serves as the perfect tactical aid, temporarily deafening the hostiles, giving your team the opportunity to crash through the skylight and attack. Although the room is filled with hostiles, during this sequence, you need to worry about only two. Upon entry, there are three targets within your view—you need to shoot the two guys on the left. Do not shoot the third guy on the right—he's the buyer! If you accidentally shoot the buyer, the mission ends in failure and you are forced to restart from the previous save checkpoint. Once you've gunned down the two hostiles, Kozak grabs the buyer and shoves him against the wall, frisking him for weapons before knocking him out. With the room secure, Ghost Lead checks in with Overlord for a mission update.

## TACTICAL CHALLENGE: CLEAN KILL

### CRITERIA: ASSAULT THE HQ AND TAKE OUT THE HOSTILES WITHOUT ANY MISSES

This challenge must be completed during the assault on the compound, during the sequence when you have to shoot the two hostiles after crashing through the skylight. To pull this off you need to kill both enemies without missing. So take your time to line up the shots before firing. When you do fire, simply tap the trigger to fire one round into each rifleman's head. Do not hold down the trigger and spray the room with automatic fire. All it takes is two bullets to complete this challenge, so steady your aim before you fire.

## OVERLORD INTEL UPDATE: ARMS DEALER LOCATED

Alright, we've got a read on the dealer. It's not looking good. They're boxed in on all sides. You're going to have to go to him. Stakes just went up. Pakistani forces are closing in on the area. Looks like they're going to try to grab both parties. Although it wasn't part of deal, it looks like they're making a new one. This just got real messy, gentlemen. You're going to have a lot of civilians in harm's way and multiple hostiles moving through traffic. Watch your targets, and watch what's behind 'em. We'll bring you in from the opposite direction of the Pakistani forces. That'll let the Pakistanis force the target your way, and avoid any accidental engagements.

HOLD Ⓐ COVER SWAP

# CAPTURE ARMS DEALER

The dealer has been spotted in a vehicle on the city streets of Peshawar's eastern district. When the Ghosts reach the nearby insertion point via Blackhawk, they're already under fire by hostiles. There's no need to sneak around anymore, so prepare for an all-out assault. Once you've found cover behind a car, immediately get the UAV up in the air to spot hostiles hiding among the congested city streets. The UAV makes it easy to spot hostiles hiding among the cars. In addition to spotting enemies, the UAV is also useful for issuing focus-fire orders. Start by marking enemies nearby, as they pose the biggest threat to your team. By having your team focus their fire on one enemy at a time, you can quickly prioritize and eliminate threats. Given the fast pace of this battle, Sensors are often more effective than the UAV, especially when it comes to identifying enemies nearby. The UAV can sustain damage if left hovering above the street, drawing fire from enemies. But don't worry-the UAV can repair itself. Consider using it to lure incoming fire away from your team.

## // CAUTION

Soon after arriving on the city street, there is a rifleman on the second floor of this building near the intersection. If you don't stay behind cover, you're likely to be picked off by this guy. While behind cover, use the UAV to locate this enemy and issue a focus-fire order on him. You need to take him out quickly or else he'll inflict heavy damage on your team.

## ENEMY PROFILE: SNIPER

The sniper is a long-range static threat, similar to RPG soldiers. Snipers don't move much and it can take them a while to acquire targets and reload. When encountering snipers, stay behind cover and never run out into the open. It is also wise to scan the snipers (with a Sensor or UAV) as it will show their laser sights in red. This is a good feedback to know when they are about to shoot. After that, it is a cat and mouse game in which you have to peek out of cover and shoot the sniper when he is reloading or acquiring a new target. Issuing focus-fire orders on snipers is also strongly advised.

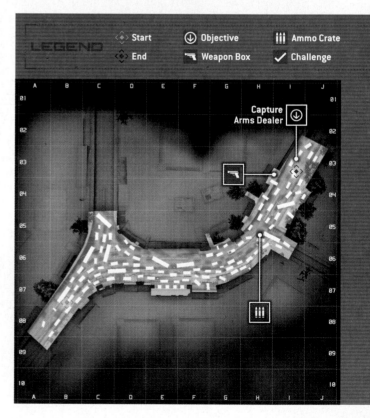

LEGEND

◈ Start  ⊙ Objective  ⦀ Ammo Crate
◈ End  🔫 Weapon Box  ✓ Challenge

Capture Arms Dealer ⊙

Even after you've dealt with the first group of hostiles, always assume you're under fire while moving through the streets. Fortunately, there is plenty of cover in the street. Instead of moving out of cover and advancing down the street, always utilize the cover swap method to move from one car to the next. This allows you to automatically sprint between covers, greatly minimizing your chances of getting hit by incoming fire. Even if you spot an incoming grenade, don't pull out of cover manually. Quickly find a nearby vehicle to take cover behind, and use the cover swap feature to move out of the path of the incoming grenade. Moving from one vehicle to the next, work your way toward the intersection at the end of the street. Watch your fire during this engagement. If you accidentally kill a civilian, the mission ends in failure.

Soon after reaching the intersection, your team comes under attack by more enemies, some of them armed with shotguns. Once again, deploy the UAV in an effort to identify the locations of the hostiles and mark them for your teammates. After using the UAV to pinpoint the locations of hostiles, exit the UAV view and help your team pick off enemies. The UAV continues updating enemy positions in real time if you leave it hovering above the street. There's no need to be quiet any longer, so don't bother using a suppressed weapon. You're better served by a weapon possessing significant stopping power (such as an assault rifle or LMG). Pay close attention to the enemies equipped with shotguns. These guys are very aggressive and will attack at close range, potentially downing you or your teammates with a single shot. Identify and neutralize these shotgun-toting bad guys before they get too close for comfort. If necessary, consider retreating to maintain a safe distance.

## // TIP

*If any of your teammates are brought down, you'll need to heal them. Approach the body and then press (and hold) the button shown on-screen to begin the healing process. Before rushing toward a downed teammate, make sure the*  *surrounding area is clear of threats. While healing a teammate you are exposed for a few seconds, making you vulnerable to incoming rounds. You won't do your downed teammate any good if you get shot while trying to heal him.*

RPGs aren't the only thing you need to watch for. You eventually encounter a couple of GAZ-2330 light vehicles, each armed with an automated machine gun turret. You need to destroy these vehicles before you can reach the target vehicles. Fortunately, GAZ-2330s can be destroyed with small arms fire or frag grenades. Mark these vehicles with a focus fire order to take them out quickly. But when these vehicle open fire, make sure you are behind cover and access the UAV to mark each GAZ-2330. By ordering your team to focus fire on each vehicle, you stand a good chance of taking them out without exposing yourself to incoming fire. Alternately, peek out of cover and fire a quick burst at each vehicle to assist your team. Stay behind cover until both vehicles are destroyed.

## ENEMY PROFILE: GAZ-2330 TIGER

*An all-terrain 4x4 vehicle, designed for maximum performance in even the roughest environments, from scorching sand dunes to the freezing cold of Siberia. The armor on the Tiger will withstand considerable fire so find cover and have an extra*  *magazine ready. The assault version comes equipped with a remote sentry gun.*

Further down the street you encounter a few hostiles armed with RPGs. These enemies are extremely deadly, capable of destroying the very vehicles your team is using for cover—you don't want to be near a vehicle that explodes! Either use the UAV to track down and mark these guys or simply follow the smoke trail of incoming rockets back to the shooter. Don't waste any time taking these guys out. As soon as you identify them, take aim through your weapon's scope and take them down with a headshot.

## // TIP

Don't forget to utilize your Sensors and Flashbangs during the advance through the street. Sensors are a great way to spot enemies hiding behind cover, highlighting them as red silhouettes on your HUD. In many instances, you can fire through the cars they're hiding behind, allowing you to engage enemies without exposing yourself. Flashbangs are perfect for engaging enemies hiding among civilians. When these nonlethal devices explode, they temporarily blind and deafen anyone in their blast radius. This causes enemies to stumble around for a few seconds before they regain their composure. While enemies are stunned by Flashbangs, target them before they recover. As you near the target vehicle, you can restock your supply of Sensors and Flashbangs by interacting with an ammo crate in the middle of the street. There's also a weapon box on the left side of the street that contains a PKP LMG.

Despite the urgency of the chatter, there are no time constraints during this advance. So there's no need to rush. Stay behind cover and methodically identify and engage enemies as you encounter them. When you're not shooting enemies yourself, use Sensors and the UAV to reveal the locations of hostiles for your teammates. Swap cover from one vehicle to the next while advancing toward the target vehicle, which is marked with a waypoint. When the word "Clear" appears on the HUD, all enemies have been eliminated.

Unfortunately, the arms dealer has gotten away. There's nothing in the target vehicle but a beeping cell phone Ɛ attached to an explosive device. The Ghosts recognize the booby trap, giving them just a few seconds to get away from the vehicle before the bomb goes off. As the Ghosts regain their composure and brush the dust off themselves, Overlord reports that the dealer has secured a new vehicle and is on the move. You'll have to track him from the air.

### OVERLORD INTEL UPDATE: ARMS DEALER IDENTIFIED

We've got positive ID on the dealer. She's Russian. Katya Prugova. We're working connections to see what we can find, but we've already got enough to be worried. Early reports have her linked to an international import-export corporation with known ties to criminal elements. These people are very good at making things disappear Ɛ weapons, money, people. If she goes to ground, we're going to have a hell of a time digging her back up again. DIA's involved, and our boys at NSA have a file, but nothing's as good as a face-to-face.

 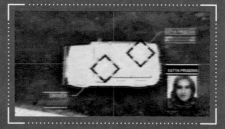

We need her alive, gentlemen. It's a hornet's nest down there. Looks like everyone with a gun is coming out to play. You'll have to deal with them before you stop her. And you will stop her. Our birds don't have the range to chase her into Afghanistan. If she makes the border, she's as good as gone.

# DESTROY ESCORT VEHICLES

The Ghosts split up into two Blackhawks, with Kozak and Pepper riding in one while Ghost Lead and 30K board a separate bird. The arms dealer, Katya Prugova, has been tracked racing toward the Pakistan/Afghanistan border. But she's not alone. She has surrounded herself with armed escorts in the form of GAZ-2330 light vehicles—just like the ones you encountered in Peshawar. This time, you have the firepower necessary to lay waste to these vehicles. While manning the Blackhawk's door-mounted minigun, open fire on these hostile vehicles. They're easy spot, thanks to an orange triangular icon that is superimposed over them on the HUD. Take aim and open fire on every hostile vehicle you encounter. However, watch your fire. The bad guys are sharing the road with civilians, so avoid collateral damage whenever possible. There are also enemy troops positioned along the road, some carrying RPGs—these enemies are marked with orange diamond icons on the HUD.

Now comes the tricky part. When you catch up with Prugova's SUV, you'll see it is escorted by two GAZ-2330 light vehicles. Start by opening fire on the GAZ-2330 trailing behind the Prugova's ride. With the rear vehicle destroyed, focus your fire on the GAZ-2330 in the lead. However, hold your fire as the GAZ-2330 slows and travels alongside the target vehicle—you can't risk destroying Prugova's SUV. Instead, wait for the light vehicle to fall behind the SUV before resuming your fire. Try to take out both escort vehicles before Prugova's SUV enters a tunnel.

Shortly after Prugova's SUV enters the tunnel, your Blackhawk comes under attack by an Mi-24 attack chopper. As soon as the enemy chopper comes into view, open fire on it with the minigun. Don't worry about collateral damage here. Simply hold down the trigger and continuously pepper the enemy chopper with automatic fire as it flies past from right to left. Following the first past, release the trigger and swing the gun to the left side to reacquire the target. Once again, open fire and score hits on the top of the enemy chopper as it passes beneath your Blackhawk. When the enemy chopper flies out of view, swing the gun to the left again and search for the Mi-24, which should now be trailing black smoke. Finish off the crippled chopper with another aggressive burst of automatic fire.

Once the enemy chopper is down, Ghost Lead's Blackhawk opens fire on Prugova's SUV, causing it to flip over at high speed and eventually come to rest near a small roadside settlement. Ghost Lead and 30K will provide fire support from their Blackhawk while Kozak and Pepper secure Prugova Ε assuming she survived the crash.

## TACTICAL CHALLENGE: KILLER PURSUIT

### CRITERIA: DESTROY EVERY ENEMY VEHICLE DURING THE CHOPPER GUNRIDE

To complete this challenge you must destroy every GAZ-2330 and the Mi-24 attack helicopter during the sequence when you're manning the Blackhawk's minigun. The challenge is completed immediately after shooting down the Mi-24. If the challenge is

not completed at this time, you must have missed one of the GAZ-2330s earlier in the sequence—immediately restart from the previous save checkpoint and repeat the gunride from the beginning.

# DISRUPT ENEMY COMMUNICATIONS

Getting information out of Katya Prugova hasn't been easy. She's more scared of her own people back home than she is of her captors—and for good reason. Prugova has been connected to a vast network of unsavory organizations, including everything from the private sector to organized crime syndicates. But Prugova has revealed one piece of actionable intel that leads the Ghosts to an abandoned weather station in Russia, not far from the Norwegian border on the Barents Sea. According to Prugova, this weather station is being used as a transfer point for weapons. The Ghosts are tasked with gathering intel and destroying the operation. But before they can move in on the weapons cache, the Ghosts must sever the enemy's communication system. As a secondary objective, the Ghosts are also responsible for field-testing the Warhound. This four-legged semi-autonomous weapon system won't play fetch, but it is capable of taking out hostile vehicles and personnel thanks to its mortar and guided missiles.

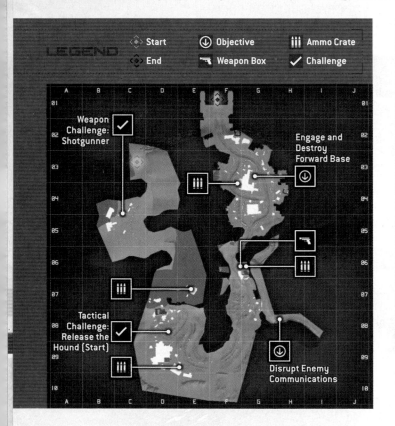

LEGEND

| | | |
|---|---|---|
| ◇ Start | ⊙ Objective | ⫼ Ammo Crate |
| ◈ End | 🔫 Weapon Box | ✓ Challenge |

Weapon Challenge: Shotgunner ✓

Engage and Destroy Forward Base ⊙

Tactical Challenge: Release the Hound (Start) ✓

Disrupt Enemy Communications ⊙

BARENTS SEA

At the insertion point, blizzard-like conditions have dropped the visibility to nearly zero. This could actually work in your team's favor, making it nearly impossible for hostiles to detect your approach. During this phase (and most of the mission), the Warhound leads the way, automatically advancing from one waypoint to the next. Rely on the Warhound to guide you through this snowstorm. To maintain visual contact with the Warhound and your team, activate Magnetic view. While Magnetic view doesn't have great range, it can still cut through the falling snow, allowing you to see distant objects (and enemies) before you trip over them.

Enemy contacts are detected in the distance, near a supply area. Your team must neutralize all enemies in this area before proceeding. While your team (and the Warhound) holds back, drop to a crouched stance to activate your Optical Camo. The combination of the blizzard and your Optical Camo makes you almost impossible to see. As you creep toward the supply area, you can spot one enemy rifleman pacing nearby. Although your Optical Camo decreases your visible profile, don't take any chances. Stay a safe distance from the hostile until he turns his back. Creep up behind the rifleman and take him out with a stealth kill. It doesn't matter where his body falls—the snow will make him hard to spot. Anyway, his comrades don't have long to live.

Shortly after eliminating the first hostile, a GAZ-66 truck pulls up nearby and two more hostiles get out. They gather near the front of the truck, standing near a third rifleman. A fourth rifleman can be spotted in the distance, patrolling the supply area on his own. This is the perfect opportunity for a sync-shot. Mark all four riflemen, pick out a target of your own, then initiate the sync-shot. If you don't have a suppressed weapon, don't worry. Nobody will live long enough to detect the report. Eliminating all four riflemen clears the supply area, allowing Warhound to proceed to the next waypoint.

## WEAPON CHALLENGE: SHOTGUNNER

**CRITERIA: WITH A SHOTGUN, TAKE OUT THREE ENEMIES USING EXACTLY THREE CARTRIDGES IN THREE SECONDS OR LESS**

Instead of using a sync-shot to take out the three riflemen near the truck, try to pull off this challenge by gunning all three hostiles down with a shotgun. The snowstorm and your Optical Camo allow you to get really close to these enemies without 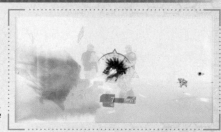 being detected. Wait until all three riflemen are standing together in a tight group, then attack. If you're close enough, you can kill each rifleman with one shotgun blast. But speed counts, too. You need to drop all three enemies in under three seconds to complete the challenge. If you miss this opportunity, consider restarting the mission and trying again. This is the very best spot in the mission to score these shotgun kills.

CONTACT

## ENEMY PROFILE: T-90

*A third-generation main battle tank, the T-90 means serious business. It comes equipped with 125mm/4.9 inch gun, anti-aircraft heavy machine gun as well as composite and explosive reactive armor. There is no way you can destroy one of these on your own, as most of your weapons won't even dent its heavy armor. If sneaking around it isn't an option, you will need to call in for support to stand a chance.*

Warhound leads the Ghosts to a low hill overlooking a motor pool. Take cover behind the steel vertical plate that is marked with a waypoint marker. From here, you have a clear view of the motor pool. Several enemy riflemen patrol the motor pool along with a T-90 tank. The priority target is the T-90. Follow the on-screen directions to gain access to the Warhound. The Warhound interface is overlaid on the HUD, allowing you to target and engage enemies using the Warhound's mortar. Place the Warhound's circular aiming reticle over the T-90 tank to aim the mortar. A white arc line appears on the HUD, similar to when you throw a grenade. This arc represents the trajectory the mortar round will take to reach the target. With the T-90 targeted, open fire with the Warhound's mortar.

It takes multiple mortar hits to destroy the tank, so keep lobbing mortar rounds to whittle away the tank's orange health meter, which is shown on the HUD. However, don't fire the mortar rapidly. Pay close attention to the Heat Level meter on the left side of the HUD. After each mortar round is fired, the Heat Level increases. If you fire multiple mortar rounds in quick succession, the mortar will overheat and go temporarily offline. To prevent overheating, fire mortar rounds slowly, at the rate of approximately one per second. This will allow you to keep hammering the tank without the risk of overheating.

After destroying the T-90, focus the Warhound's firepower on the enemy infantry scurrying for cover in the motor pool. The Warhound's mortar automatically snaps to targets, highlighting them with an orange diamond icon. Once a target is acquired, fire a mortar round. Mortar rounds are not guided and impact at the point where they're aimed. As a result, enemy infantry may escape incoming mortar rounds by running away. So if the first mortar round doesn't kill your target, follow up with more shots.

Eventually a GAZ-2330 light vehicle and GAZ-66 truck roll into view in the distance. Target the GAZ-66 truck first and destroy it with multiple mortar rounds before the infantry inside can unload. With the truck destroyed, bombard the GAZ-2330. A second set of vehicles arrive next. Prioritize the targets in the same fashion—take out the GAZ-66 first, then target the GAZ-2330. Once you've destroyed all the vehicles, hunt down any surviving infantry until the motor pool is clear. As you can see, the Warhound is an extremely powerful ally, capable of laying waste to a wide range of threats. Exit the Warhound view and follow your team through the smoldering wreckage at the motor pool. There is an ammo crate at the motor pool you can visit to replenish your stock of ammo and grenades.

Follow the Warhound out of the motor pool and advance along the adjoining road. The Warhound comes to a stop when the nearby commo array is detected in a nearby icy canyon. Access the Warhound and follow the on-screen instructions to launch a guided missile. When you fire the Warhound's guided missile, your view switches to a camera attached to the missile. From this view you can guide the missile toward the target, using the right control stick to steer. Start by steering the missile slightly to the left, then veer to the right so that you can line up with the narrow canyon, where the commo array is located. Once the commo array is within view, steer the missile straight ahead, through the canyon and directly into the array. If you miss, you can fire a second missile and try again. When you score a hit with the guided missile, the commo array collapses. The enemy is now cut off from the outside world. You can now assault the nearby forward base without setting off an international incident.

HEAT LEVEL

Mortar RT
Missile LT

Pepper

LB  EXIT WEAPON SYSTEM          HOLD  A  COVER SWAP

# ENGAGE AND DESTROY FORWARD BASE

Beyond the fallen commo array is a small supply depot. As the Warhound leads the way, your team comes under attack by several vehicles, including two GAZ-66 trucks full of infantry. Immediately take cover, then access the Warhound. Target the GAZ-66 trucks first before they can unload their troops. While the Warhound's mortar is sufficient for taking out these vehicles, guided missiles are very effective, too—it takes only one guided missile to destroy each vehicle. More infantry and vehicles attack from the distant pass and cliff side. Hammer the infantry with mortar rounds, then take out the vehicles with guided missiles. Hold behind cover until you're certain all hostiles are down at the supply depot.

## // TIP

There's an ammo crate and weapon box inside the garage-like shelter at the supply depot. The weapon box contains an M110 sniper rifle, a Skorpion SMG, a RPK LMG, 417 assault rifle, and a M590A1 shotgun. If you're not satisfied with your weapons, now's the perfect time to adjust your gear before attacking the forward base.

As the Warhound ascends the nearby slope leading to the forward base, a hostile GAZ-2330 pulls into view. Facing off against a hostile vehicle while traversing this open terrain is dangerous. So rush behind the Warhound for cover and engage the vehicle. You can take cover behind Warhound just like any other solid object. Now access Warhound and target the enemy vehicle with a guided missile. Follow up by firing some mortar rounds at any hostiles who may have exited the vehicle. The path to the forward base is now clear. But the enemy is ready for you. You'll need to assault with overwhelming force and aggression to overcome the loss of the element of surprise.

Sprint toward the forward base, and take cover behind the low sandbag wall on the perimeter. An Mi-24 Hind attack chopper can be seen in the distance, parked on a helipad—don't let it take off. Access the Warhound and immediately launch a guided missile toward the chopper—one hit prevents the Hind from taking off. After neutralizing the Mi-24 with a guided missile, focus the Warhound's attention on the enemy infantry scurrying about. Target the enemy troops with the Warhound's mortar. Don't let the intense action make you overheat the mortar. Fire the mortar at a steady and even pace, engaging one target at a time.

## // CAUTION

There are enemy troops in the guard towers posted around the forward base. From their elevated positions, these enemies can gain a line of sight on you and your team, even if you're behind cover. Deal with these threats as soon as possible. If you can't target these enemies directly, simply launch a single mortar round (or guided missile) at each guard tower to take them out.

The Warhound automatically moves into the forward base during the attack. While enemies are still visible, stay behind cover. But when you can't spot enemy activity, cautiously advance toward the Warhound's position. Even if you can't see enemies, always assume a threat is present. Use the swap cover feature to advance, sprinting from one piece of cover to the next. If you can't find suitable cover, remember that you can also take cover behind the Warhound. Eventually a BTR-90 rolls into view in the center of the forward base. This Armored Personnel Carrier (APC) is like a miniature tank, covered in thick armor. Start by hammering the enemy vehicle with two guided missiles fired from the Warhound. But these only damage the BTR-90. If necessary, scramble to new cover as the BTR-90 continues its advance. But it's best to keep up the pressure, hitting the BTR-90 with a constant barrage of mortar rounds until it explodes. Beyond the BTR-90 is another GAZ-2330 parked in the middle of the forward base. If you can't spot the GAZ-2330 from your current position, simply launch a guided missile. While steering the guided missile through the camp, locate the enemy vehicle and pilot the missile directly into it.

## ENEMY PROFILE: BTR-90

*More than just an 8x8 armored personnel carrier, the BTR-90 comes prepped for war with a high-speed auto cannon or other mounted weapons. On top of that, it's amphibious. The BTR-90 is a formidable threat since its heavy armor and powerful guns can pin you down while the troops it deploys can quickly flank you. Look around for heavier guns that you can use to your advantage.*

The Warhound automatically advances to a nearby dock, where a boat is waiting to take your team to a hardened submarine pen. Regroup with the Warhound to begin the boat ride to the target area—there isn't much left at the forward base, with the exception of an ammo crate. You can always stock up on supplies when you reach the sub pen.

Help your team mop up the remaining enemies at the forward camp, utilizing the Warhound's mortar to clear a path. As the Warhound moves ahead, you need to keep up to establish a line of sight with the new enemy contacts. Always use the cover swap feature when moving. There are several stacks of crates near the helipad that offer excellent cover during the final stages of the assault. By taking cover near the helipad you can get a clear view of the remaining hostiles and therefore engage them with the Warhound's mortar. When the word "Clear" appears at the top of the HUD, all enemies at the forward base have been neutralized.

// TIP

*Be careful where you take cover at the forward base. The red barrels are explosive. Of course, you can use this to your advantage. If you spot enemy troops taking cover nearby, simply target the barrels to trigger a potentially lethal explosion. Just make sure you're standing a safe distance away.*

# LOCATE WEAPONS CACHE

When the Ghosts arrive at the submarine pen, an alarm sounds. There's no need to be sneaky—the enemy already knows you're here. The alarm is accompanied by a countdown timer, which gives you exactly 10 minutes to reach the base's mainframe. If you're late, the base will go on lockdown, preventing you from accessing the critical data on the weapons cache. Follow closely behind the Warhound as it advances along the walkway. You can access two weapon boxes and an ammo crate along the way if you want to change your weapons or stock up on ammo. For the fight ahead, assault rifles and LMGs are recommended. When the word "Contact" appears at the top of the HUD, switch to Magnetic view to spot the hostiles waiting around the next corner. Find some cover and engage the hostiles with your own firearms—don't launch the Warhound's mortar at this close range.

When you reach the footbridge spanning the sub pen's central channel, take cover on the right side and access the Warhound. Multiple hostiles rush into view on the opposite side of the bridge, scurrying along the lower and upper walkways. Hold behind cover and pound these hostiles with mortar rounds. As the Warhound advances across the bridge, follow closely behind and seek cover. More enemies appear on the upper level walkway ahead. The walkway is lined with vertical steel plates, giving the hostiles plenty of cover. If you're having trouble spotting these enemies activate your Magnetic view, then target them with the Warhound's mortar.

While advancing along the central walkway, your team comes under fire by an automated machine gun turret on the right side of the sub pen—immediately take cover before you're hit. Once you've reached safety, use a guided missile fired from the Warhound to knock the turret out of commission. Compared to targets you've attacked with guided missiles thus far, the turret is quite small, making it a little difficult to score a direct hit. Fortunately, the guided missile's blast radius is quite large, so you don't need to hit the turret head-on. Instead, fly the missile as close to the turret as possible. Even slamming the missile into the wall behind the turret results in an explosion big enough to do the job. Just make sure the turret is down for good before moving out of your cover.

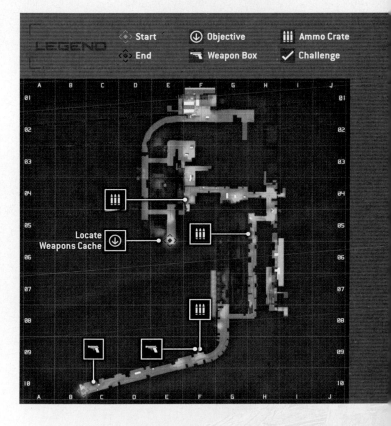

Keep an eye on the countdown timer as you advance through the sub pen. You need to carefully balance aggression and prudence to eliminate the hostiles while keeping yourself and teammates alive. Fortunately, the Warhound makes the advance much easier and faster. Stay closely behind the Warhound and always seek out cover. When you spot hostiles ahead, immediately target them with mortar rounds. Shortly after crossing another short bridge, your team comes under attack by two hostiles armed with RPGs—their positions are marked on the HUD. While holding behind cover, quickly target both of these hostiles with mortar rounds. The explosions trigger a large explosion, collapsing a few catwalks in the distance. Some enemies may be difficult to hit with mortar rounds, due to objects hanging from the sub pen's ceiling. So if you can't get a clear shot at enemies with the mortar, don't be afraid to target enemies with guided missiles.

The hostiles in the sub pen make their last stand on a loading dock. Sprint to cover near your teammates and the Warhound so you can get a clear view of the loading dock as well as the catwalk above it. While behind cover, target the enemies with the Warhound's mortar. If you're having trouble spotting enemies hiding behind cover, lob a few Sensors toward the loading dock. Likewise, watch out for incoming grenades tossed by the enemies. Also, pay close attention to the enemies on the catwalk. Two of these enemies are armed with an RPG and an LMG. Identify and neutralize these enemies as soon as possible.

## // TIP

*If your team needs a bit more firepower in the last fire fight in the sub pen, take control of mounted machine gun nearby. When used in combination with the Warhound, the machine gun can help cut through the resistance. But go easy on the trigger to prevent overheating. This is a good tactic when playing the mission with friends. AI-controlled teammates do not utilize mounted weapons.*

When the Warhound turns away from the loading dock, the sub pen is clear. Since you no longer have to worry about threats, don't linger behind the Warhound, especially if time is short. Instead, sprint along the walkways where a submarine is under construction. You must reach the next waypoint before the countdown timer expires. The door beyond the waypoint contains a terminal. Ghost Lead orders Kozak to upload the mainframe's data. Upon analysis of the data, Overlord reports the presence of what could be a cavern. Perhaps this is where the weapons cache is located? It's up to the Ghosts to check it out. With the Warhound in tow, the team boards an elevator and heads for the surface.

# DESTROY WEAPONS CACHE

BARRENTS SEA

**LEGEND**

◇ Start  ⊕ Objective  ⫿⫿⫿ Ammo Crate
◇ End  🔫 Weapon Box  ✓ Challenge

Tactical Challenge: Group Shot → ⊕ Destroy Weapons Cache

Tactical Challenge: Silent Talon

Upon exiting the elevator, you can access an ammo crate nearby. After stocking up on ammo and grenades, follow the Warhound out of the bunker-like facility. Your team emerges onto another base occupied by more hostiles. Immediately take cover behind one of the stacks of crates on the left to avoid getting hit by RPG rounds fired from the two guard towers connected by a catwalk. Once you've reached cover, access the Warhound and target the towers with mortar rounds—all it takes is one hit to bring the connected towers crashing down. Next, focus the Warhound's fire on the enemy infantry blocking the path ahead.

Just ahead, you can hear the sound of a mounted machine gun spitting rounds at your team. Using the swap cover method, dash to the right side of the path and take cover by the crates next to the forklift. Chances are the mounted machine gun will pin you shortly after you reach cover. Stay low behind your new cover and fire a guided missile from the Warhound. As the camera view switches, fly the missile toward the left side of the base. You'll spot the mounted machine gun (along with other hostiles) behind a row of sandbags. Fly the missile into the ground at the base of the mounted machine gun. This not only silences the machine gun, but the missile's large blast radius also takes out any hostiles nearby. With the machine gun out of the way, help your teammates clear out the remaining hostiles.

## TACTICAL CHALLENGE: RELEASE THE HOUND

**CRITERIA: USE THE WARHOUND TO KILL AT LEAST 75% OF THE ENEMIES DURING THE MISSION**

By this point in the mission you should have completed this tactical challenge, requiring you to eliminate at least 75 percent of the enemies with the Warhound. But if you haven't completed this challenge yet, there's still time to pull it off. Going forward, make an effort to target all remaining enemies with the Warhound's mortar or guided missiles. In most cases, you can eliminate the enemies before your teammates have a chance to "steal" kills from you.

Next, follow your team (and the Warhound) toward the nearby helipad. But don't let that ammo crate distract you just yet. Immediately take cover behind one of the concrete barriers on the helipad's perimeter and peer out toward the sea. Two Mi-24 Hind attack helicopters can be seen in the distance. Quickly access the Warhound and launch a guided missile at the first enemy chopper that comes into view. Hitting a moving target with the guided missile isn't easy. So lead the chopper slightly, flying the missile in the direction the chopper is traveling. It doesn't matter where you hit the chopper, but aim for the fuselage to guarantee a hit. It takes two guided missiles to neutralize each chopper-one crashes, but the other gets away. So act quickly to eliminate both threats before they lay waste to your team. There are also two mounted machine guns near the helipad. If you're playing this mission with friends, ask them to open fire on the choppers with the machine guns while you attack with the Warhound's guided missiles. These weapons are your best shot at bringing these choppers down quickly.

## TACTICAL CHALLENGE: SILENT TALON

### CRITERIA: ELIMINATE BOTH ENEMY CHOPPERS WITHOUT LOSING A SQUADMATE

To complete this challenge, it's imperative that your teammates stay behind cover when the two Mi-24 attack choppers attack. If the team stands out in the open, they run the risk of getting hit by incoming fire. But even if your teammates stay behind cover, they're  not entirely safe from the incoming explosive attacks. Therefore, you need to shoot down these choppers fast to limit your team's exposure. The Warhound's guided missiles are the quickest way to deal with these threats. If your aim is true, you can destroy both choppers with two guided missile hits each.

## // NOTE

*Shortly after shooting down both enemy helicopters, you can find a weapon box and ammo crate approximately 30 meters away from the helipad. The weapon box contains an M110 sniper rifle, a Skorpion SMG, an RPK LMG, a 417 assault rifle, and a M590A1 shotgun.*

Follow the Warhound up the nearby slope, leading to the mysterious facility believed to contain the weapons cache. As expected, the facility is heavily defended. Your team is greeted by the ripping sound of an automated turret opening fire. Sprint to cover behind the crates on the outskirts of the facility to avoid being cut down by the incoming fire. Once you've reached safety, bring the Warhound online and fire a guided missile at the turret. In addition to the turret, several enemy troops are also nearby. Stay behind cover and use the Warhound's mortar to engage all contacts. If you have trouble spotting enemies hiding behind cover, deploy Sensors or simply activate Magnetic view to uncover their positions.

 After clearing out the first layer of defenses, advance behind the Warhound as it marches fearlessly toward the facility. Swap cover, sprinting from one piece of cover to the next until you can make your way to the low sandbag wall overlooking the facility.

From this position, you can bombard the enemy troops below using the Warhound's mortar. Watch for enemy troops hiding behind cover as well as those positioned on the guard tower on the left and the rooftops on the right. During the fight, watch out for a GAZ-2330 light vehicle that approaches from the left—if you're not careful, you'll get flanked. When this vehicle arrives, immediately target it with a guided missile. Also, keep an eye open for incoming RPG rounds-one hit can be fatal. Hold on the small hill hill overlooking the facility until you're certain you've eliminated every threat. If necessary, lob Sensors toward the facility to reveal any enemies hiding.

## TACTICAL CHALLENGE: GROUP SHOT

### CRITERIA: KILL FIVE OR MORE ENEMIES WITH A SINGLE WARHOUND MORTAR ROUND

If you haven't completed this challenge yet, the assault on the weapons cache facility presents you with multiple opportunities to score five or more kills using the Warhound's mortar. During the firefight, reinforcements appear outside the facility, moving  through narrow doorways—keep an eye on the right side of the facility. These doorways serve as natural choke points, funneling large groups of enemies into tight clusters. This makes them extremely vulnerable to explosive attacks. But instead of lobbing a barrage of mortar rounds in their direction, simply fire one mortar round at a time. The challenge requires you to kill at least five enemies with a single mortar round, so go easy on the trigger.

## // TIP

*The enemies on the second floor of the large concrete building cannot be easily targeted with the Warhound's mortar. The narrow slit that serves as a window is best targeted with guided missiles. This is the best way to take out enemies manning the mounted machine gun here. Even after you kill the gunner with a missile, watch out for reinforcements arriving on this floor and manning the machine gun.*

When you're certain the area outside the facility is clear, rush down the nearby slope and take cover. Keep an eye on the large concrete structure on the right—a large door slides open and more enemy infantry rush out. Another group of enemies also occupy the second floor of the facility, firing at your team through the window slit. Take out the enemies on the ground first, targeting them with the Warhound's mortar. Next, take aim at the hostiles on the structure's second floor by launching a guided missile at the mounted machine gun. Stay behind cover and keep up the attack until the word "Clear" appears at the top of the HUD.

Regroup with your team and enter the now open doorway in the large concrete structure. Before moving toward the waypoint marker, interact with the ammo crate just inside the door—you won't have much time to resupply later. Just beyond the ammo crate is a large blast door. Wait nearby while Overlord cracks the door, finally giving your team access to the weapons cache. What the Ghosts find inside is far more disturbing than they ever imagined. The bunker-like facility contains stockpiles of heavy weapons largely consisting of long- and intermediate-range missiles. What are these people up to? Overlord orders the Ghosts to take it out. Turn to the right side of the catwalk and located the white ring icon next to large missile. Move into the ring and press the button shown on-screen to place a C4 charge on the missile. The C4 charge is more than enough to trigger a chain reaction of explosions within the facility, wiping out the weapons cache. But do the Ghosts have enough time to get away before this place blows sky high?

## REACH EXTRACTION

You have exactly three minutes to escape the facility before the C4 charge explodes—a countdown timer appears on the right side of the HUD. To make matters worse, the Mi-24 attack chopper that escaped earlier, has returned outside, blocking your path to the extraction point by deploying troops. The chopper hovers overhead and drops off a new group of hostiles. Rush through the door and immediately take cover outside. Once you're behind cover, access the Warhound and target the Mi-24 with guided missiles. All it takes is one hit to cause the chopper to spin out of control and crash into a nearby cliff. With the chopper out of the way, focus on the infantry by targeting them with the Warhound's mortar. The infantry are eventually joined by a GAZ-2330 light vehicle—hit it with a guided missile before it can unload more troops.

While engaging the hostiles outside the facility, keep an eye on the countdown timer on the right side of the HUD. If there's only a minute remaining, you need to move out whether the area is secure or not. Swap cover while working your way toward the waypoint marker. Don't worry if the Warhound lags behind—it will survive the weapons cache explosion, but you won't. Shortly after you reach the extraction point, the weapons cache goes up in a spectacular explosion. It'd be nice to think this was the last of the weapons, but Ghost Lead has a feeling that this is just the beginning.

### // EOD

*achievement trophy*

This achievement/trophy is unlocked upon the completion of the Silent Talon mission.

| SILENT TALON: COMPLETION UNLOCKS | | |
|---|---|---|
| Type | Category | Item |
| Weapon | Sniper Rifle | SRR |
| Weapon | SMG | P90 |
| Attachment | Side Rail | OTR Scanner |
| Items | Grenades | Incendiary |
| Items | Goggles | Night Vision |
| Paint | Weapon paint | Russian Digital |

# INFILTRATE AIRPORT

Katya Prugova's involvement with Raven's Rock only ups the ante. The CIA has determined that Raven's Rock is in the process of transporting a cutting-edge missile guidance system to some unsavory characters. This intel has brought the Ghosts to a heavily guarded airfield within Russia, where they must covertly infiltrate the facility and prevent the weapons shipment from leaving. Overlord reports that the airfield is guarded by military personnel. If the Ghosts are detected, the response will be swift and deadly. Therefore it's vital to the mission's success to reach the cargo and destroy it without being heard or seen—suppressed weapons are a must.

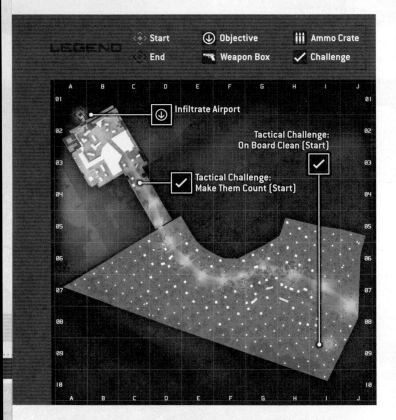

LEGEND

◇ Start    ◷ Objective    ⫿⫿⫿ Ammo Crate
◈ End    ▨ Weapon Box    ✓ Challenge

ↂ Infiltrate Airport

Tactical Challenge:
On Board Clean (Start) ✓

Tactical Challenge: ✓
Make Them Count (Start)

The Ghost team inserts within a small forest, approximately 200 meters from the airfield's checkpoint entrance. While moving through the woods, Ghost Lead detects movement nearby. Remain crouched to keep your Optical Camo activated. Next, switch on your Night Vision Goggles (NVGs) to get a better view of your surroundings. Just ahead you can spot the heat signatures of two riflemen moving in your direction. Stay low and creep away from them. Once you're a safe distance from the patrol, mark both riflemen and take them out with sync-shot. This clears the forest, but there are plenty of hostiles nearby, advancing along a road outside the airfield. Stay in the woods to avoid being spotted and resume your advance to the airfield's checkpoint, which is marked with a waypoint.

## // TIP

*You do not need to engage the large group hostiles patrolling the road—there's no need to risk triggering a firefight this early in the mission.*

When the checkpoint comes into view, deploy the UAV to scout ahead. The UAV detects four riflemen guarding the checkpoint—two of the riflemen patrol while the other two stand still. Make sure you can spot all four enemies and mark them all. Exit the UAV view and prepare to perform a sync-shot. Find your target and aim through your weapon's scope to guarantee a hit. When your team is ready, squeeze the trigger to initiate the sync-shot, dropping all four hostiles simultaneously. Your team can now infiltrate the airfield. The lighting conditions within the facility differ, but for the most part, you won't need your NVGs.

Next, mark all four riflemen in the middle layer. This group consists of two stationary riflemen (on the left and right) as well as a pair of patrolling riflemen that are walking along a catwalk in the distance. Once all four enemies are marked, exit the UAV view and take aim at one of the hostiles. Once again, use your weapon's scope to line up your shot before initiating the sync-shot. The final two riflemen, on the lower level, can now be eliminated with a simple sync-shot. Return to the UAV view to mark both targets, then order your team to drop them with a sync-shot. The area is now clear. Regroup with your team at the sliding door by the waypoint marker and prepare to breach.

## TACTICAL CHALLENGE: MAKE THEM COUNT

### CRITERIA: FINISH THE MISSION USING LESS THAN 50 ROUNDS OF AMMO

Follow your team past the checkpoint, but don't let your guard down. Keep your Optical Camo active by remaining crouched. When the word "Contact" appears atop the HUD, seek cover on the left side of the road and deploy the UAV. This next area is guarded by an eight-man squad, mostly consisting of riflemen. But there's also two snipers watching from elevated positions. You need to attack this area in three layers, working from the top down. Start by identifying both snipers on the top layer—mark them, then order your team to take them out with a sync-shot.

If you're interested in completing this difficult challenge, it's best to start working toward this goal early. This challenge requires you to complete the mission by firing fewer than 50 rounds. While infiltrating the airfield, it's easy to keep your shot count down by

utilizing the UAV and setting up sync-shots for your team. Doing this, you can reach the target area by firing less than 10 rounds. The tricky part comes toward the end of the mission, when you must escape. Resist the urge to swap your primary weapon for something with a higher rate of fire. Using any automatic weapon will make completing this challenge nearly impossible. So keep your slow-firing sniper rifle throughout the entire mission and rely on your teammates to do the bulk of the heavy lifting when a firefight breaks out. By deploying Sensors and issuing focus-fire orders, you can help direct your team during engagements. When you do take shots, make sure they hit. Fortunately, most sniper rifles are lethal with a single hit, which helps you keep your shot count low. You can monitor the challenge's progress by accessing the Tactical Map. Here you can see exactly how many rounds you've fired in the mission thus far.

## AIRSHAFT

**LEGEND**

◈ Start    ⊕ Objective    ⦂⦂⦂ Ammo Crate

◈ End    ⟋ Weapon Box    ✓ Challenge

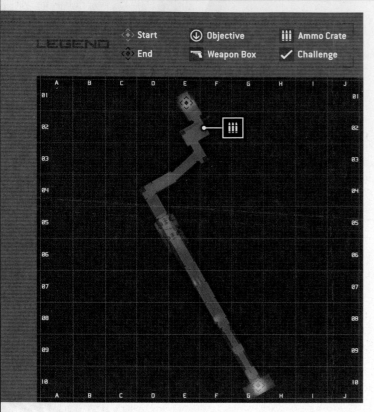

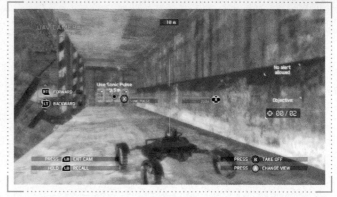

Beyond the sliding door is a dark maintenance tunnel—consider activating your NVGs. The tunnel eventually turns into a large airshaft. These shafts run beneath the airfield. The Russians pipe hot air through them to keep ice off the runways. Your team's path through the shaft is blocked by a pair of large fans. You need to find a way to deactivate these fans. Deploy the UAV and fly it to the right side of the shaft, where there's a small ledge. Land the UAV on the ledge to transform into Crawler mode. Drive the Crawler through the adjoining tunnel on the right. At the end of the tunnel is a control panel. Drive the Crawler next to the control panel and emit a sonic pulse—this deactivates the first fan. Recall the Crawler to return the UAV to your hand.

Next, deploy the UAV a second time. Fly past the deactivated fan, then veer to the left side of the shaft where there's another ledge. Land the UAV on the ledge to enter Crawler mode, then drive the Crawler through the nearby tunnel. Just like with the first fan, emit a sonic pulse near the control panel at the end of the tunnel to deactivate the second fan. Recall the UAV and follow your team past the two disabled fans. While you are moving through the adjoining corridor, Overlord reports that you're approaching a stretch of runway with a heavy enemy presence. There's another airshaft on the opposite side that will get you closer to the target. At the end of the corridor is an ammo crate and a ladder. Stock up on ammo before moving toward the ladder.

# REGROUP AT THE VENTILATION SHAFT

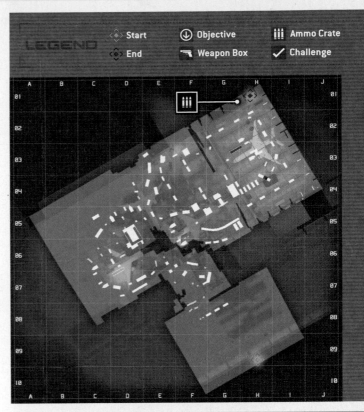

LEGEND
◇ Start    ⊘ Objective    ⦀ Ammo Crate
◇ End      🔫 Weapon Box   ✓ Challenge

The ladder leads up to a small hatch that opens next to a large runway. Activate your NVGs and follow your team across the runway. Contacts are detected just ahead. Take cover behind one of the exhaust barriers to avoid being spotted—even with the Optical Camo active, you're not completely invisible. To get a better view of the hostiles, deploy the UAV. There are a total of seven riflemen here. You'll need to take out these guys in groups, beginning with the lone rifleman on the rooftop to the left—mark him and order one of your teammates to take him out. Next, wait for the two enemies on the far right to isolate themselves; they move behind some trailers. Mark both enemies on the right, and order your team to take them out with a sync-shot—three down, four to go. The final group of riflemen, in the center of the tarmac, can be taken out with one sync-shot. Mark all four targets, then exit the UAV view to take aim at one of the hostiles. When all your teammates are ready, initiate the sync-shot by squeezing your trigger.

## // TIP

*Suppressed weapons aren't completely silent. If you fire a suppressed weapon within close proximity of an unalerted enemy, it may get their attention.*

Follow your team toward another group of hostiles. Stay low and take cover near one of the crates on the tarmac. Get the UAV into the air to identify seven more riflemen. Once again, it's important to take out these guys in isolated groups. Start by marking the lone rifleman standing on the scaffold in the distance—but don't shoot him yet. Wait for two of the patrolling riflemen to move toward the scaffold. When these two riflemen are a safe distance from the other four, mark them and order your team to take out the three marked targets with a sync-shot. Quickly mark the remaining four hostiles, including the group of three that is chatting between the two large planes. Exit the UAV view, take aim at one of the hostiles, and drop all four enemies with a sync-shot.

While still crouched, creep between the two planes on the tarmac while moving toward the next waypoint marker. There are multiple hostiles in this next area. They are guarding access to the massive hangar that your team must infiltrate to reach the next ventilation shaft. Don't get overwhelmed by the large enemy presence. If you're careful, you can isolate these enemies and pick them off in small groups. As you pass between the planes, glance to the right to spot your first victim standing on a scaffold. This guy is stationary and has a clear view of the tarmac in front of the hangar. Even at this close range, don't take any chances. Take aim with your weapon's scope, and center the target's head in the crosshairs—this will prevent you from hitting the railing around the perimeter of the scaffold.

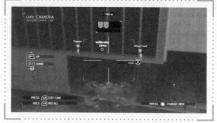

With the first enemy down, creep forward and take cover behind a crate on the tarmac. Keep your Optical Camo active and stay behind cover to avoid being spotted by the two riflemen patrolling nearby—but these guys aren't your next targets. Deploy the UAV and fly it directly toward the large hangar. Just above the hangar door is a catwalk occupied by two snipers. Mark both snipers and order your team to take them out with a sync-shot. With the snipers down, clearing the remaining hostiles on the tarmac is far less dangerous.

Fly the UAV back toward your position and mark the two hostiles patrolling nearby. Order your teammates to take them out with a sync-shot. Next, fly the UAV to the right side of the tarmac to locate two more riflemen near the port-side wing of the large aircraft. Mark these guys and have your teammates drop them with another sync-shot.

Cautiously advance toward the hangar and take cover behind one of the exhaust barriers near the entrance. From here, you have a clear view of all five enemies inside the hangar. For good measure, deploy the UAV to scout ahead. Your first target is the patroling rifleman on the right side of the hangar. Mark this guy and order one of your teammates to take him out. Immediately mark the remaining four riflemen on the left side of the hangar—there are three hostiles chatting near the hangar door and a fourth rifleman on the scaffold by the plane. Once all four targets are marked, exit the UAV view and take aim at one of the marked targets. Initiate the sync-shot once all teammates are ready and on target. When all four targets are down, recall the UAV and prepare to move out.

Four more riflemen are on the tarmac, and all are located on the right side of the hangar's entrance. Mark all four enemies with the UAV, then move to a position closer to the hangar. The scissor lift near the aircraft's port engine is a good cover spot for engaging this next group. Assume a position along the scissor lift and target one of the stationary riflemen on the far right. Once again, peer through your weapon's scope and line up the rifleman's head in the crosshairs to guarantee a clean kill. When all teammates are in position and ready, squeeze the trigger to initiate the sync-shot. This clears the tarmac, but there are still a few more enemies you need to deal with in the hangar.

## VENTILATION SHAFT

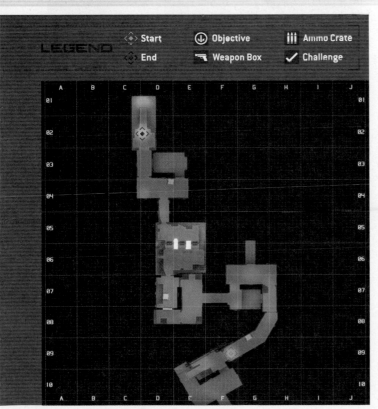

LEGEND
Start — Objective — Ammo Crate
End — Weapon Box — Challenge

The hangar is now clear. Rush inside and move toward the stairs on the left side; they are marked with a waypoint. Just beyond the stairs is a blast door, leading into a maintenance corridor. Regroup with your team at the blast door and enter the corridor together. The corridor leads you to the next ventilation shaft, which is blocked by three parallel fans. Deploy the UAV and fly it through one of the small openings above the fans. Land the UAV behind the fans on the waypoint marker to enter Crawler mode—a large transformer box is next to the waypoint marker. While in Crawler mode, emit a sonic pulse to knock out power to the fans. Recall the UAV, then drop prone to crawl beneath one of the three disabled fans. As you regroup with your team at a blast door, Overlord reports that the missile guidance system has been loaded onto a cargo plane.

Pass b
hangar
equippe
can't pa
better w
issue fo
teamm
trio. Thi
damage
more in
The har
multiple
the unn
site. Be
grenade
promise
hangar.

ENE

# EXTRACTION POINT

As the Ghosts move through the double doors, the extraction point can be seen only a few meters away. But you'll need to secure the area before you can hitch a ride out of here. In the distance, a GAZ-66 truck is moving into view and unloading troops. Immediately rush to cover near the weapon box and ammo crate. From this position, toss Sensors in the direction of the enemies. This makes it possible to spot the enemies hiding behind cover, allowing you to issue focus fire orders on them. Most the cover used by the enemies is solid and cannot be penetrated by bullets. So wait for the enemies to peek out of cover before firing. You can help flush them out of cover by tossing incendiary grenades in their direction.

the prote
so look f
shield ca
cause th
they may
and ince
grenades

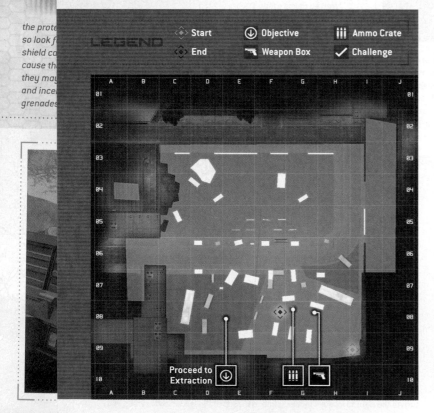

| LEGEND | ⬥ Start | ⬇ Objective | ⦀ Ammo Crate |
|---|---|---|---|
| | ⬥ End | 🔫 Weapon Box | ✓ Challenge |

Proceed to Extraction ⬇   ⦀  🔫

While engaging the first group of enemies, watch for reinforcements arriving on the right side from the nearby hill. At this point you must shift to a new covered position to avoid being flanked—watch where your teammates move and follow them. Once again, lob a few Sensors in the direction of the reinforcements on the hill. If you're running low on Sensors, carefully make your way to the ammo crate and resupply. Watch out for LMG fire coming from the hill. Identify the LMG-toting enemies and place a focus-fire order on them. During this engagement, keep an eye on your right flank. Placing a Sensor here will allow you to spot flanking attempts by enemy troops. Mow them down as they try to encircle your team. Their advance can be slowed by tossing incendiary grenades along their path.

## // TIP

During the attack, watch out for incoming GAZ-66 trucks filled with more reinforcements. When a truck stops, open fire on the back end to mow down enemy troops exiting the vehicle.

## TACTICAL CHALLENGE: GHOST ESCAPE

### CRITERIA: ONCE THE OBJECTIVE'S COMPLETE, MOVE TO THE EXTRACTION ZONE WITHOUT BEING SHOT DOWN

The challenge begins back at the cargo plane crash site, following the ride in the LAV. From that moment, you must reach the extraction point without suffering any serious injuries. If you fall the to ground and must be healed by a teammate, the

challenge is failed and you must start the mission over. As long as you utilize cover and avoid taking any unnecessary risks, you can pull off this challenge. The most difficult part of the challenge is surviving the enemy attack near the extraction point at the end of the mission. When calling in the air strike, make sure you're a safe distance away from the tank. Otherwise you may be killed by your own missile.

The action is briefly interrupted by a cinematic showing the arrival of a T-90 tank. You don't have enough firepower to take out this tank, so stay behind cover to avoid getting killed. Eventually that air strike Overlord promised becomes available. Press the button shown on-screen to initiate the strike. This switches the view to a missile camera, allowing you to guide the weapon toward the tank—you don't need to hit the tank directly to destroy it. The enemy attack ends with the destruction of the T-90. As a Blackhawk hovers overhead, the Ghosts attach themselves to a line suspended from the chopper before being yanked out of the extraction point. While the missile guidance system has been destroyed, it's unclear what the fallout of this mission will be.

### FIREFLY RAIN: COMPLETION UNLOCKS

| Type | Category | Item |
| --- | --- | --- |
| Weapon | Assault Rifle | ACR |
| Weapon | Shotgun | M1014 |
| Attachment | Optic | Magnified HWS |
| Paint | Weapon paint | Air Force ABU |

# EMBER HUNT

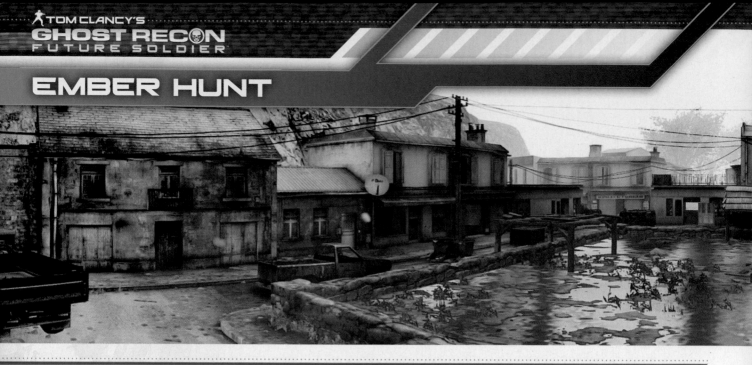

## BRIEFING

LOCATION: DAGESTAN
OBJECTIVES: LOCATE AND EXTRACT GEORGIAN SPECIAL FORCES. RECOVER INTEL ON NUCLEAR LAUNCH.
CURRENT CONTACT: SENIOR MASTER SERGEANT MARCUS KELSO

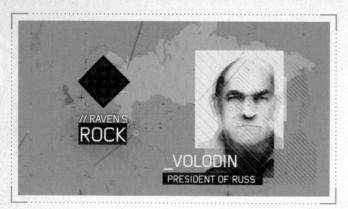

// RAVEN'S
**ROCK**

_VOLODIN
PRESIDENT OF RUSS

EXTRACTION
INSERTION
// RECOVER TEAM_
// ANSW

We're on the brink here, gentlemen. That missile might have not been launched by the Russian government, but it came out of Russia. Whether Raven's Rock is responsible for the launch or not, we believe they're behind the internal pressure calling for President Volodin's replacement. Momentum is building and it's not looking good. We're not in position to do much about Russian politics. We'll have to go where we can do some good instead.

Trajectory analysis puts the launch site in Dagestan, just east of the Georgian border. A Georgian spec-ops unit was deployed to investigate, but they dropped contact and disappeared near the target zone. We've agreed to help the Georgians recover their team. With luck, we'll find some answers, too.

## MISSION CHALLENGES

### WEAPON CHALLENGE: TIGHT BURST

DIFFICULTY: ★☆☆☆☆
UNLOCK: TYPE 95

- Take down five enemies with an LMG while firing nonstop

### TACTICAL CHALLENGES

DIFFICULTY: ★★★★☆
UNLOCK: DRAGON'S BREATH

- **No Safe Distance:** Stealthy kill all Russian riflemen assaulting the house
- **Neck Breaker:** Kill 40 enemies by snapping their necks
- **Countersniper:** Kill all Bodark snipers during your escape

## GEAR SELECTION

| Equipment Slot | Default | Recommended |
|---|---|---|

### PRIMARY

**ACR ASSAULT**

| | |
|---|---|
| POWER | |
| RANGE | |
| CONTROL | |
| MANEUVERABILITY | |
| RATE OF FIRE | 915 RPM |
| MAGAZINE CAPACITY | 30 |

**CONFIGURATION SUMMARY**

Muzzle: Standard
Scope: Holomag
Underbarrel: Vertical Foregrip

**MK48 LMG**

| | |
|---|---|
| POWER | |
| RANGE | |
| CONTROL | |
| MANEUVERABILITY | |
| RATE OF FIRE | 702 RPM |
| MAGAZINE CAPACITY | 150 |

**CONFIGURATION SUMMARY**

Muzzle: Compensator
Scope: Tac Scope
Underbarrel: Bipod

### SECONDARY

**M1014 SHOTGUN**

| | |
|---|---|
| POWER | |
| RANGE | |
| CONTROL | |
| MANEUVERABILITY | |
| RATE OF FIRE | 600 RPM |
| MAGAZINE CAPACITY | 8 |

**CONFIGURATION SUMMARY**

Muzzle: Standard
Scope: Iron Sights
Underbarrel: Nonc

**PDR-C PDR**

| | |
|---|---|
| POWER | |
| RANGE | |
| CONTROL | |
| MANEUVERABILITY | |
| RATE OF FIRE | 702 RPM |
| MAGAZINE CAPACITY | 20 |

**CONFIGURATION SUMMARY**

Muzzle: Suppressor
Scope: Tac Scope
Underbarrel: Vertical Foregrip

### ITEM 1

**FRAG**

QUANTITY: 3

High-explosive grenade intended to kill or wound

**SENSOR**

QUANTITY: 5

Detects nearby enemies, highlighting them on the HUD

### ITEM 2

**INCENDIARY**

QUANTITY: 3

Sets fire to an area, injuring any who attempt to pass through

**FRAG**

QUANTITY: 3

High-explosive grenade intended to kill or wound

# REACH GEORGIAN UNIT

An attempted nuclear missile attack on London has the international community on edge. Public panic has been avoided by declaring the incident a "satellite collision." The missile defense shield was capable of rendering the nuclear warhead inert, but the falling debris resulted in multiple civilian casualties on the ground. If an incident like this happens again, it will be difficult to keep things under wraps. The missile launch site has been traced back to Dagestan. Initially, Georgian Special Forces were tasked with investigating. But the Georgian spec-ops team has been out of contact. Overlord confirms that some members of the Georgian team are still alive, but they've been unable to establish contact. Russian troops, possibly affiliated with Raven's Rock, have been spotted searching nearby.

LEGEND  ◇ Start   ⊙ Objective   ⫼ Ammo Crate
        ◇ End     ▭ Weapon Box   ✓ Challenge

Tactical Challenge:
Neck Breacker (Start)

From the insertion point, remain crouched to keep your Optical Camo active while creeping toward the distant waypoint marker. Along the way, the word "Contact" appears across the top of the HUD, indicating enemies have been detected. Keep moving toward the waypoint and take cover behind the wooden fence. From this elevated position, you can observe a large number of Russian troops gathered around the ruins of a small bombed-out settlement. Deploy the UAV to get a better view of the area. Most of the enemies are riflemen. But there's an RPG soldier on the rooftop to the left and a mounted machine gun on the rooftop to the right—you'll want to take these guys out before a full-blown firefight breaks out. But before devising a frontal assault, consider pushing forward on your own in an attempt to silently eliminate a few hostiles.

# TACTICAL CHALLENGE: NECK BREAKER

## CRITERIA: KILL 40 ENEMIES BY SNAPPING THEIR NECKS

If you want to complete this challenge, you need to start early. The first group of enemies you encounter, near the town ruins, is the best place to start. Start by sneaking along the left side where a lone rifleman patrols. Stay low to keep your Optical Camo active, but don't forget to utilize cover as well. Even Optical Camo doesn't make you completely invisible. If you run the risk of being spotted, immediately drop prone to significantly reduce your profile. When the rifleman turns his back, sneak up behind him and take him out with a stealth kill—one down, 39 to go. Stealth kills result in various melee animations, including neck breaking. But any melee-based kill counts toward the total required to complete this challenge.

After taking out the patrolling rifleman on the left, avoid the road and creep toward the building where the RPG soldier is positioned. There is another rifleman pacing on the front side of this structure. Get as close as you can to this guy without being spotted. Given his tight patrol pattern, it may be necessary to drop prone and crawl toward him. But when he turns his back, sneak up behind him and perform a stealth kill.

Now enter the building and head upstairs. The RPG soldier is pacing on the rooftop. While on the second floor, glance up at the ceiling to spot the RPG soldier's position. If the UAV is still deployed overhead, you can see him through the ceiling, appearing as a yellow silhouette. If the UAV isn't deployed, you can spot this soldier through the ceiling by activating Magnetic view. When the RPG soldier moves away from the staircase leading to the rooftop, creep up the stairs and take him out with a stealth kill. The rooftop is home to an ammo crate, as well as a great view of the mounted machine gun on the neighboring rooftop. Using a suppressed weapon, take out the machine gunner or order one of your teammates to do it. You cannot kill the machine gunner with a stealth kill, as there is no way to climb up to his perch. This rooftop is a good spot from which to stage an assault on the remaining enemies. But, you don't need to attack yet—there are more stealth kills you can score.

Head downstairs and advance toward the building where the mounted machine gun is positioned. As you exit, notice the one stationary guard standing near the road. Carefully sneak up behind him and take him out with a stealth kill. You can now cross the road and enter the neighboring building where the now-vacant mounted machine gun is positioned. On the first floor, two riflemen are staring out a window, both with their backs turned. Since they're standing so close to one another, it may be tough to take out one hostile without being spotted by the other. So mark both riflemen and take out one with a stealth kill. The second you perform the stealth kill, one of your teammates shoots the other marked rifleman—you don't even have to issue the sync-shot order.

At this point, there are six more enemies in the area—two on the road, and four standing among the ruins. You can easily eliminate the remaining hostiles with a pair of sync-shots. If an alert is raised, you don't have to worry about reinforcements showing up. So consider sneaking around and trying to eliminate a few more hostiles with stealth kills— if you want to complete the Neck Breaker Tactical challenge, never pass up the opportunity to score stealth kills. Keep nearby targets marked as you stalk

your prey. If you run the risk of being detected, immediately issue a sync-shot order to give your team the attack order. Depending on where the bodies fall, an alert may be raised. But no reinforcements arrive—you must simply contend with the remaining hostiles. If the word "Engage" appears on the HUD, forget about being quiet. Find cover and aggressively attack with grenades and unsuppressed weapons while issuing focus-fire orders for your team. Once the area is "Clear," resupply at one of the nearby ammo crates located in the buildings by the road. Afterward, regroup with your team at the waypoint marker down the road.

## RAVINE

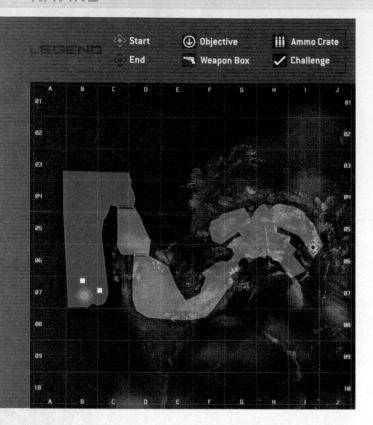

From the road, drop down into the ravine on the left and move to the next waypoint marker. The Ghosts take a short break as Overlord connects the team with the Georgian spec-ops. Sergeant Osadze from the Georgian Special Forces reports in. Osadze is the last living member of his team and he's surrounded by Russian troops—you need to reach him soon. After speaking with Osadze, advance through the ravine. Along the way, the team encounters a few glitches in their Cross-coms, causing details on the HUD to flicker on and off. Overlord has no solutions but suggests that the terrain may be causing interference.

## RESCUE OSADZE

Reach Georgian Unit ⊕
⦀⦀⦀

Tactical Challenge: No Safe Distance ✓

As the Ghosts continue the advance through the ravine, enemy contacts are detected just ahead. At approximately the same time, Sergeant Osadze reports that he's been discovered by Russian troops—you need to get to him before the enemy does. With your Optical Camo active, creep toward the waypoint marker. Just ahead you can see multiple enemy troops scurrying about. Two of the enemies assume a fixed position on a hill overlooking a courtyard—the enemy on the left is a rifleman and the guy on the right is a sniper. Mark both targets and keep your eye on the rifleman as he peers through binoculars. This enemy occasionally shifts positions. When the rifleman has his back turned to you and raises his binoculars, sneak up behind the sniper and perform a stealth kill—a teammate shoots the rifleman at the same time.

Now swing back to the left side of the courtyard and mark the four enemies in the street—ignore the three soldiers standing next to the house for now. Once your team has acquired their target, exit the UAV view and line up your own shot. If using a suppressed PDR or SMG, aim at the enemy closest to your position. For greater accuracy, you can even creep down into the courtyard to reduce the range to your target. Once you have your target sighted, squeeze the trigger to initiate a sync-shot, dropping all four enemies at once. Now all that remains are the three enemies outside the house where Osadze is holed up. Mark all three hostiles and order your team to take them out with a sync-shot.

## TACTICAL CHALLENGE: NO SAFE DISTANCE

### CRITERIA: STEALTHY KILL ALL RUSSIAN RIFLEMEN ASSAULTING THE HOUSE

To complete this challenge you must eliminate all the Russian troops gathered outside the house where Osadze is hiding out—and you must do it without triggering an alert. Sync-shots are the safest and most effective method of completing this challenge. Follow the text provided in the walkthrough to complete this challenge, eliminating the enemies with a series of sync-shots. You can orchestrate most of these sync-shots entirely from the air with the UAV.

Once the courtyard is clear, cautiously approach the Osadze's position, which is marked with a waypoint. As you advance through the courtyard, a GAZ-66 truck pulls up near the house and multiple enemy troops pour out. They're joined by more hostiles appearing on the rooftop of the house and within the second-story windows of the adjoining building—some of these guys have LMGs. When the truck pulls into view, immediately take cover behind the low stone wall running parallel with the street. Toss a Sensor toward the truck to get a better read on each enemy, then open fire. Toss grenades toward the truck and other vehicles in an effort to deprive the enemy of cover. If you have an LMG, you can explode vehicles with prolonged automatic bursts. Watch out for enemies attempting to flank. While your team holds one side of the courtyard, cross to the other side and confront these threats head-on.

Shortly after wiping out the enemy reinforcements, the sound of squealing tires is heard in the distance, as a vehicle speeds away. When you reach the house where Osadze was hiding, it becomes apparent what just happened—the Russians have taken Osadze captive and driven away with him. Before moving on, interact with the ammo crate inside the house to resupply. Once you're well stocked with ammo and grenades, follow your teammates by hopping through the window at the back of the house.

---

There's a weapon box near the sniper. It contains a PSL-54C sniper rifle, a MP7 SMG, a L22A2 PDR, a Mk48 LMG, and a PDR-C PDR. The PSL-54C is equipped with a Thermal Optic scope, ideal for spotting enemies in the fog. This weapon comes in handy when the Cross-coms malfunction.

Sergeant Osadze has barricaded himself in a house on the far side of the courtyard. Take cover along the low wall where the sniper was positioned to get a better view of the situation. Osadze is holding off a group of 13 Russian troops. Deploy the UAV to get a better view of the courtyard. Despite the urgency in Osadze's voice, you don't need to rush this rescue effort. All of the hostiles currently have their backs turned to your team, making it possible to eliminate all of the enemies with a series of carefully orchestrated sync-shots. Start by marking the three enemies closest to your position. There's one rifleman on the left side of the courtyard, and two enemies on the right. Order your team to take the sync-shot to eliminate these enemies.

## // CAUTION

It's possible to eliminate multiple enemies in the courtyard with stealth kills, and thus work toward achieving the Neck Breaker Tactical challenge. But if you're spotted, it's impossible to complete the No Safe Distance Tactical challenge, requiring you to silently eliminate the Russian soldiers attacking the house.

Next, target the three remaining hostiles on the right side of the courtyard—two are standing in the street, and one is pressed up against a building not far from the Osadze's position. You can kill these three enemies with a sync-shot without alerting the other troops on the left side of the courtyard.

# LOCATE AND SECURE OSADZE

LEGEND    ⬥ Start    ⊙ Objective    ⅲ Ammo Crate

⬥ End    🔫 Weapon Box    ✓ Challenge

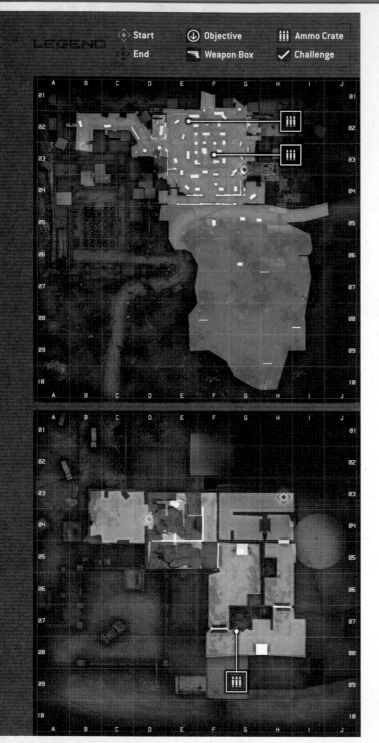

Back outside, regroup with your team and follow them through the city street toward the next waypoint. Interference continues to plague the Ghosts' Cross-coms, as false enemy readings appear on the HUD. But don't let these false readings tempt you to let your guard down. When you reach a large plaza, a few Russian troops ambush your team. Immediately take cover and toss a Sensor toward the center of the plaza. There's no need to be quiet, so don't worry about going loud. Frag grenades are particularly effective at taking out enemies hiding behind cover in the middle of the plaza. Once the plaza is clear, resupply from one of the two ammo crates, then regroup with your teammates at the double doors in the nearby building.

Upon passing through the double doors, your team's Cross-coms continue showing signs of interference. Follow your team through the cramped building. Along the way you encounter the bodies of two Georgian spec-ops team members. Apparently the Russians aren't taking prisoners. If Osadze is still alive, he probably doesn't have much time. Continue advancing through the damaged structure, hopping over obstacles and crawling through low openings. Despite what your Cross-coms show on the HUD, there are no enemies nearby. So don't let those red and yellow silhouettes make you panic. Near the building's exit, Overlord reports that they're still trying to clear up the interference your team is experiencing. In the meantime, Overlord suggests checking out a nearby church the hostiles are using as an outpost. It's believed Osadze is being interrogated in this church.

# RESCUE OSADZE

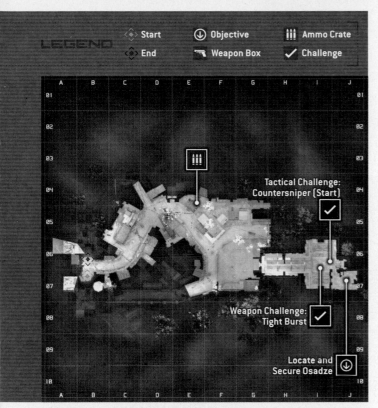

LEGEND

◇ Start    ⊘ Objective    ⫼ Ammo Crate
◇ End    ⬛ Weapon Box    ✓ Challenge

Tactical Challenge:
Countersniper (Start) ✓

Weapon Challenge:
Tight Burst ✓

Locate and
Secure Osadze ⊘

Return to the street and take cover behind a crate on the left side. Just ahead you can spot the two other patrolling riflemen moving toward a GAZ-66 truck. There's also a shotgunner standing on the left side of the street just ahead—mark all three enemies. Return to the alley and take cover in the small shop, not far from the shotgunner's position. While behind cover, take aim at the driver inside the truck. You can't mark the driver inside the truck, but you can shoot him through the driver-side window. Take aim at the driver and issue the sync-shot order to your team. As soon as your team takes their shots, put a few bullets through the driver's left ear. If you're detected, a couple of enemy troops may hop out of the back of the truck, so be ready to deal with this possibility. Being detected here will not alert the enemy troops posted near the church.

## // TIP

*If you encounter enemies at close range, it's often easier (and faster) to take them out with a melee attack than it is to shoot them. Simply rush toward them and press the stealth kill button. However, never attack a shotgunner in this fashion unless you're certain you can take the enemy by surprise.*

Shortly after Overlord's transmission, a timer appears on the HUD, giving you four minutes and thirty seconds to reach the church where Osadze is being held. Assume a crouched stance to activate your Optical Camo, then creep outside into a city street. This time when the word "Contact" appears on the HUD, your Cross-com isn't lying. Stay low and creep up the street until you spot four enemies patrolling up ahead—toss a Sensor in their direction to guarantee detection. Hold back and wait for two of the riflemen to enter an alley on the left. This allows you to creep up behind them and take both out with stealth kills, one at a time.

The clock is ticking, so don't waste any time making your way toward the church. Continue the advance along the street until new enemies are detected. Move through an alley on the left side of the street and resupply from an ammo crate. Just beyond the ammo crate is a narrow staircase leading up to a balcony overlooking the church's courtyard. Take cover along the balcony's low wall and saturate the area outside the church with Sensors. Two riflemen patrol a covered walkway on the right side of the courtyard—mark these guys first and order your team to take them out with a sync-shot. Next, mark the two riflemen patrolling the street below the balcony.

## // NOTE

*As interference continues to plague the Cross-coms, false enemy detection icons, represented by yellow diamonds, appear on the HUD. Don't trust these icons until you can visually confirm the presence of an enemy. Sensors also can highlight the positions of real enemies.*

Chances are, there isn't much time left. At this point there are five more enemy soldiers outside the church. Mark four of them and issue a sync-shot to take them out. Quickly located and gun down the last soldier to clear the courtyard. If a firefight breaks out, deploy your LMG's bipod on the balcony's low wall and rake the courtyard with automatic bursts. With the support of your team, it doesn't take long to eliminate this last group of enemies. Don't worry about using unsuppressed weapons at this point. The sound of gunfire (and grenades) won't alert the enemies inside the church.

With the courtyard clear, sprint to the church. There are no enemies inside the chapel, so don't waste any time getting to the waypoint marker. Along the way, Overlord reports that they need to bring the whole Cross-coms system down. At this point, all details on the HUD disappear, along with the interference. The timer stops once you step into the white ring icon next to a wooden door. Ghost Lead stacks up on the same door while Pepper and 30K set up on a door around the corner. Magnetic view reveals four hostiles inside along with Sergeant Osadze sitting in a chair in the middle of the room—it looks like he's being tortured with some sort of electrical device. Give the breach order, then target the enemy opposite the door, panning your aim slightly to the right.

One of the enemy soldiers ducks behind a cabinet in the left corner of the room. Don't try to shoot him upon entry, as you might hit Osadze in the process. Kozak automatically throws Osadze to the floor and covers him with his own body while drawing a pistol. Take aim at the soldier behind the cabinet and fire multiple pistol rounds at him until the room is clear. If you miss or fail to take out the enemy soldier in time, he will kill you, forcing you to restart the entry. Once Sergeant Osadze is safe, Ghost Lead hands him a weapon pulled off one of the dead soldiers. Osadze will now move and fight with your team. Overlord reports that the Georgians are sending a chopper to extract Osadze and your team.

# EXTRACT WITH OSADZE

While moving back through the chapel, Kozak notices a red laser sight centered on his chest—Ambush! Kozak moves out of the way, taking cover behind a pillar on the left just before the bullets start flying. These enemies aren't standard Russian soldiers. These are elite Raven's Rock spec-ops units known as Bodarks. They're equipped with a variety of weapons, including sniper rifles. Multiple snipers are in the chapel along high perches on the walls and ceiling. Locate and mark these enemies with focus-fire orders. Avoid taking on these snipers by yourself, because one sniper round can knock you flat on your back, requiring you to be healed by a teammate. It's important to eliminate every sniper during your escape if you wish to complete the Countersniper Tactical challenge.

## ENEMY PROFILE: BODARK

Bodarks are elite enemy units equipped with state-of-the-art weaponry, including assault rifles, shotguns, sniper rifles, and LMGs. They utilize the same tactical behavior as other enemies, but they're equipped with more items, such as EMP grenades and Flashbangs. Bodarks are also equipped with Optical Camo, making them difficult to spot and invisible to Sensors. Their Optical Camo can be disabled with EMP grenades. If EMP grenades are not available, rely on Magnetic view to locate these dangerous threats.

Bodark snipers aren't the only threat in the church. Keep an eye on the floor to spot Bodark infantry closing in on your position. These guys are equipped with Optical Camo, which makes them difficult to spot, especially if they're not moving. Since the Cross-coms are down, you must rely on your own eyesight and Magnetic view to locate these threats. Sensors won't work without the Cross-coms. Bodark troops are relentless, attacking aggressively along the church floor while attempting to flank your team. Advance to the altar using the cover swap method, then help your team clear the floor. Keep scanning the left and right sides of the church to watch for flanking maneuvers attempted by Bodarks armed with shotguns—don't let these guys get behind you. From the altar, you can also spot more snipers. Issue focus-fire orders on them, and let your team take them out.

## WEAPON CHALLENGE: TIGHT BURST

### CRITERIA: TAKE DOWN FIVE ENEMIES WITH AN LMG WHILE FIRING NONSTOP

The ambush in the church is the perfect opportunity to complete this challenge. Once your team has eliminated the snipers overlooking the altar, take aim at the Bodark infantry on the floor. Instead of firing from behind the altar, cover swap to one of the pillars beyond. While peeking around a pillar, you're much more difficult to hit. Load a fresh magazine in your LMG and take this opportunity to rake the central aisle with automatic fire—don't let go of the trigger. Your bullets can easily splinter the wooden pews, killing any Bodarks hiding behind them. Keep firing until you've killed at least five enemies with a single burst.

Wait for your teammates to advance before following suit. Always use the cover swap method to move from one piece of cover to the next. For best results, zigzag across the central aisle, rushing between the pillars on the left and right. As you near the exit, watch for more snipers posted on ledges above. While behind cover, issue focus-fire orders on these dangerous threats. Avoid engaging these guys on your own, as you're likely to lose. Hold behind cover and help your teammates clear out the church before moving toward the exit.

Upon exiting the church, the fountain in the center of the courtyard is slammed with an incoming RPG round. Sprint toward the fountain and take cover next to it. Just ahead there's a sniper and RPG soldier on a distant rooftop. Immediately mark both enemies for your teammates and open fire—take out the RPG soldier before he can fire another rocket in your direction. Next, turn to the right to locate two more snipers on another rooftop. Once again, issue a focus-fire order on both enemies and help your teammates take them out.

Once all four rooftop threats are eliminated, cross the courtyard and drop down onto the street. Take cover behind the nearby concrete barrier and look for another RPG soldier on the rooftop ahead. Issue a focus-fire order on him, then open fire before he can send a rocket in your direction. While your team focuses their attention on enemies advancing along the street, cut through the alley on the right. Be prepared to gun down a Bodark moving through this alley, not far from the ammo crate. While in the alley, activate your Magnetic view. This allows you to spot snipers and RPG soldiers posted on the nearby buildings without exposing yourself to them. Issue focus fire orders on these enemies, and wait for your team to take them out before stepping back out onto the street.

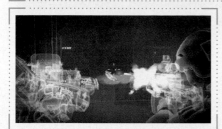

## TACTICAL CHALLENGE: COUNTER SNIPER

You can usually complete this challenge without too much effort. Starting back at the church, you need to eliminate every Bodark sniper you encounter. In each instance, snipers make their presence known, so it's nearly impossible to advance through the church and city streets without encountering every sniper along the path. When you do encounter a sniper, take cover and issue a focus-fire order on them. Snipers are always positioned in high elevations, usually on rooftops. So keep looking up during the advance to the extraction point.

Rejoin your team in the street and continue the advance toward the extraction site. Just ahead, a couple of GAZ-2330 light vehicles appear in the road and unload some Bodarks. Take cover behind the large concrete block on the right side of the street and open fire on the new arrivals. With the Cross-coms down, it makes it difficult to spot these enemies, especially as they hide behind the vehicles and other pieces of cover. So activate your Magnetic view to reveal enemy locations. With sustained automatic fire, you can even destroy the vehicles they're hiding behind.

Next, swap cover to the concrete barrier in the middle of the street, not far from the two GAZ-2330s. Here you can attack more Bodark troops further down the street. But the most significant threat are a few RPG soldiers in the distance. Activate the Magnetic view to get a better read on the smoke trails left behind from each incoming rocket. Trace the smoke trails of the rockets back to each shooter's location and issue a focus-fire order. While being attacked by rockets, stay clear of the vehicles parked along the sides of the street. All it takes is one RPG hit to cause these vehicles to explode.

Continue advancing through the street, swapping cover along the way while engaging the remaining Bodarks. When Sergeant Osadze races ahead, the path is clear. Regroup with your team at a set of double doors on the right side of the street—you must advance through this damaged building to reach the extraction point. Follow your team through the building, hopping over low walls and crawling through small gaps. Along the way, look for a weapon box on the left. This box contains an L22A2 PDR, an Mk40GL Explosive grenade launcher, an Ultimax Mk.5 LMG, an Mk48 LMG, and a PDR-C PDR. Consider swapping out your secondary weapon for the Mk40GL grenade launcher. The extra firepower afforded by this grenade launcher will come in handy later. Suppressors are no longer necessary.

## // CAUTION

If you see an orange hexagonal icon marked with a rocket icon on the HUD, it means you're being targeted by one of the RPG soldiers. Instead of trying to beat the enemy to the draw, immediately swap cover to a new location. If you ignore this warning, you'll be killed by an incoming rocket, with no chance of revival. Instead, you must restart from the previous save checkpoint, way back at the church courtyard.

LEGEND ◈ Start ⊙ Objective ⫼ Ammo Crate
◇ End 🔫 Weapon Box ✓ Challenge

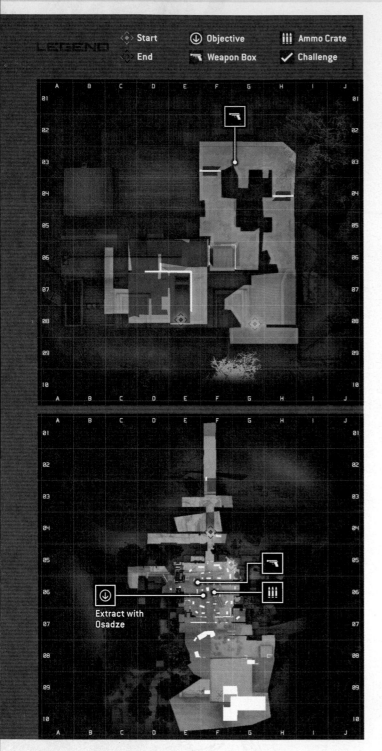

Exit the building and head toward the extraction point in the middle of the plaza. Overlord reports that a Georgian helicopter is on its way. The Ghosts deploy a flare in an effort to guide the helicopter through the mist. But instead, the flare attracts an incoming RPG. Overlord reports that multiple hostiles are closing in on the extraction point. Immediately take cover and open fire on the incoming Russian troops. The Cross-coms are still offline, so you need to rely on your eyesight and Magnetic view to keep tabs on these enemies. Watch out for flanking maneuvers as the enemies fan out across the plaza. If necessary, retreat within the small shelter in the center of the plaza to avoid being flanked. The Mk40GL grenade launcher is perfect for taking out large groups of enemies. It can also explode vehicles, like the incoming GAZ-2330s, with one hit. When you're not blasting enemies with the grenade launcher, open up with your LMG. If you haven't completed the Tight Burst Weapon challenge yet, this is a good spot to score five kills with one burst. For best results, target large groups of enemy riflemen as they advance through the street. If you run low on ammo or grenades, you can get more from the ammo crates in the center of the plaza.

Shortly after eliminating the Russian attackers, the Georgian helicopter pilot advises that he's near the extraction point. But due to enemy activity, he can't loiter long. After the helicopter flies into view, it hovers near the edge of the plaza. Suddenly an RPG round streaks toward the chopper, causing it to explode. It looks like the Ghosts and Osadze will need to find another way out.

HOLD Ⓐ COVER SWAP

# WAIT FOR INSTRUCTIONS

The destruction of the Georgian helicopter triggers the arrival of another wave of Bodark attackers. These enemies attack from the direction of the downed helicopter. But if you're not careful, they can encircle your team, attacking from the plaza's perimeter. In an effort to spot the Optical Camo-enabled attackers, activate your Magnetic view. Also, retreat within the shelter at the center of the plaza and take cover behind one of the large stone pillars. These pillars will help protect you against incoming tank rounds when a T-90 rolls into view near the helicopter's wreckage. Always keep a solid piece of cover between yourself and the tank. There's nothing you can do to take out the T-90, so just stay out of its line of sight. If you must move, do so with the cover swap method.

 Soon after the T-90 attacks, your team seeks shelter on the opposite side of the plaza, putting as much distance as they can between themselves and the tank. At this point, Osadze is struck by enemy fire—he'll survive, but he needs help. Osadze is down in the street, next to a concrete barrier. Swap cover until you can get close to his position. Once you're within view, swap cover to the concrete barrier he's lying next to—this move completes the mission. In the concluding cinematic, the Ghosts retreat from the plaza, only to come face-to-face with another T-90. With no other options, the Ghosts and Osadze leap off the side of a stone bridge, escaping with only seconds to spare.

## // Blood Brother

This achievement/trophy is unlocked after reaching the injured Sergeant Osadze.

### EMBER HUNT: COMPLETION UNLOCKS

| Type | Category | Item |
|------|----------|------|
| Weapon | Sniper Rifle | KSVK |
| Weapon | LMG | LSAT |
| Attachment | Magazine | Incendiary Ammo |
| Attachment | Optic | Backscatter Optic |
| Paint | Weapon paint | Chinese Type 07 Oceanic |
| Paint | Weapon paint | Canadian Cadpat |

# DEEP FIRE

## BRIEFING

LOCATION: NORWEGIAN SEA
OBJECTIVES: SECURE DRILLING SHIPS FOR RUSSIAN RESISTANCE FORCES.
CURRENT CONTACT: SENIOR MASTER SERGEANT MARCUS KELSO

_\\TWO MAJOR PLAYERS

**BUKHAROV**

GENERAL BUKHAROV

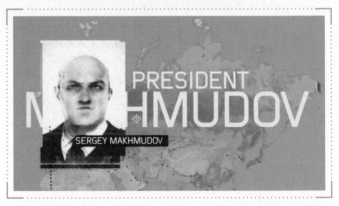

**PRESIDENT MAKHMUDOV**

SERGEY MAKHMUDOV

I know things went sideways in Dagestan. Believe me, I wouldn't be sending your team out again so soon if we could avoid it. Raven's Rock just came out of the shadows, full force. The group must've been preparing for this moment for years. Now they've taken the Kremlin, and with it, the country. We've ID'd two major players. The first is General Bukharov. He's running the military arm of the coup. The other is the new "president," Sergei Makhmudov.

Raven's Rock has established remarkable security in a short time. Resistance forces are fighting back, but they're critically short of fuel supplies. We're going to give 'em a little lift. Forces loyal to General Bukharov have seized drilling ships in the North Sea, and may have sabotaged them. We need your team to secure the facilities.

## MISSION CHALLENGES

### WEAPON CHALLENGE: RIFLE MASTER

| DIFFICULTY: | ★★☆☆☆ |
| --- | --- |
| UNLOCK: | AN-94 |

- Kill eight enemies in under 30 seconds using an assault rifle

### TACTICAL CHALLENGES

| DIFFICULTY: | ★★★★★ |
| --- | --- |
| UNLOCK: | ARMOR PIERCING AMMO |

- Undetected: Reach the drilling ship entrance without killing any guards
- Roger Dodger: Once the timer has started, make it to the control room in under 2 minutes
- Wrecker: Destroy all enemy vehicles during the gunride

NORWEGIAN SEA

## GEAR SELECTION

| Equipment Slot | Default | Recommended |
|---|---|---|
| PRIMARY | **LSAT LMG**<br>POWER<br>RANGE<br>CONTROL<br>MANEUVERABILITY<br>RATE OF FIRE — 660 RPM<br>MAGAZINE CAPACITY — 150<br><br>**CONFIGURATION SUMMARY**<br>Muzzle: Compensator<br>Scope: Backscatter<br>Underbarrel: Vertical Foregrip | **ACR ASSAULT**<br>POWER<br>RANGE<br>CONTROL<br>MANEUVERABILITY<br>RATE OF FIRE — 823 RPM<br>MAGAZINE CAPACITY — 75<br><br>**CONFIGURATION SUMMARY**<br>Muzzle: Suppressor<br>Scope: Backscatter<br>Underbarrel: Angled Foregrip |
| SECONDARY | **PDR-C PDR**<br>POWER<br>RANGE<br>CONTROL<br>MANEUVERABILITY<br>RATE OF FIRE — 702 RPM<br>MAGAZINE CAPACITY — 20<br><br>**CONFIGURATION SUMMARY**<br>Muzzle: Suppressor<br>Scope: Tac Scope<br>Underbarrel: Vertical Foregrip | **M1014 SHOTGUN**<br>POWER<br>RANGE<br>CONTROL<br>MANEUVERABILITY<br>RATE OF FIRE — 600 RPM<br>MAGAZINE CAPACITY — 8<br><br>**CONFIGURATION SUMMARY**<br>Muzzle: Compensator<br>Scope: Red Dot<br>Underbarrel: Vertical Foregrip |
| ITEM 1 | **SENSOR**<br>QUANTITY: 5<br>Detects nearby enemies, highlighting them on the HUD | **SENSOR**<br>QUANTITY: 5<br>Detects nearby enemies, highlighting them on the HUD |
| ITEM 2 | **FLASHBANG**<br>QUANTITY: 4<br>Nonlethal explosive that blinds and disorients anyone in the blast | **FLASHBANG**<br>QUANTITY: 4<br>Nonlethal explosive that blinds and disorients anyone in the blast |

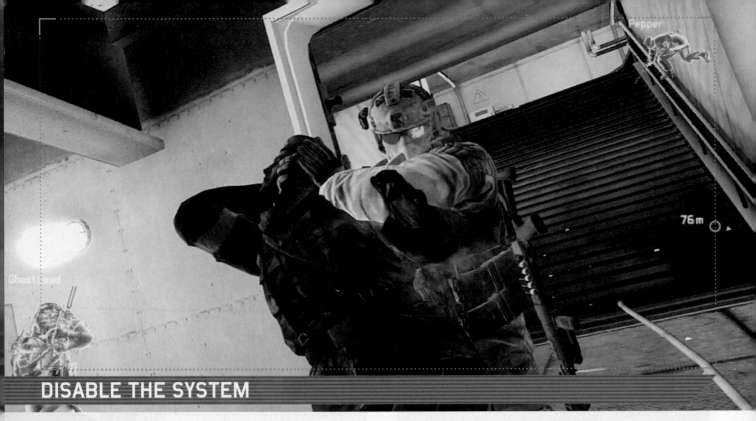

# DISABLE THE SYSTEM

After passing through the doorway, creep down the corridor while crouched and descend the short flight of stairs to the right that lead to the generator room. A rifleman can be seen through the doorway at the bottom of the stairs with his back turned to you. Sneak up behind him and take him out with a stealth kill. A second rifleman patrols the floor below. While still crouched, creep up behind the patrolling rifleman and perform another stealth kill.

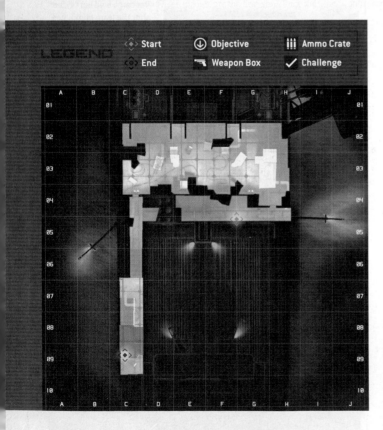

Next, toss a couple of Sensors along the perimeter of the generator room. The Sensors detect five more riflemen—two patrol a catwalk above the room, and three more are on the generator room's floor. Mark the two rifleman on the catwalk as well as two of the three riflemen on the floor. Next, move to the far right side of the generator room and climb a set of steps to reach a perimeter catwalk—this catwalk is below the one patrolled by the other hostiles, so utilize cover and keep your Optical Camo active to prevent being detected. While your teammates set up their shots on their targets, take aim at one of the marked enemies on the floor. Since there are five enemies and only four marked targets, you'll need to take down your marked target as well as the unmarked enemy on the floor. Wait until your two targets are close together then perform the sync-shot. During the sync-shot, time slows for a couple of seconds. This gives you just enough time to take aim at the unmarked rifleman and shoot him before he realizes what's happening. If things go well, all five hostiles will be dead within a couple of seconds. The generator room is now clear. Regroup with your team in the adjoining corridor, which is marked with a waypoint marker. Just inside the corridor, turn right to resupply from an ammo crate.

# HACK THE SYSTEM

As you enter the corridor beyond the generator room, Overlord warns that the hostiles have initiated a lockdown sequence. You must reach the control room before the lockdown is complete. Otherwise you'll be locked out of the control room, which results in a mission failure. As you advance through the corridor toward the drill room, a timer appears on the HUD, giving you three minutes and 30 seconds before the control room is sealed. There isn't time for a quiet approach any longer. Toss a Sensor through the doorway on the left, then rush into the drill room and begin opening fire on all enemy troops. Multiple enemies are near the drill room's entrance, including a couple on the catwalk to the left. You can drop most of them before they have a chance to scramble for cover. As you move in and open fire, issue focus-fire orders on enemies that are outside your line of sight.

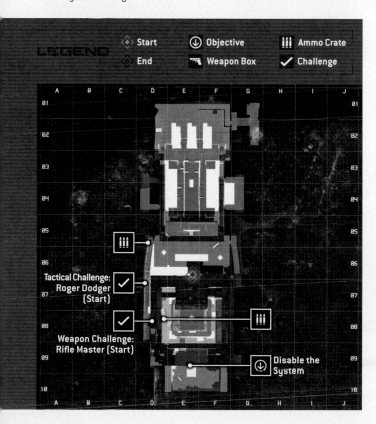

## // NOTE

The assault on the drill and control rooms is the perfect opportunity to complete a couple of challenges, as long as you attack aggressively. The Rifle Master Weapon challenge requires you to kill eight enemies in under 30 seconds with an assault rifle. To complete the Roger Dodger Tactical challenge you must reach the control room in under two minutes. Keep both of these challenges in mind as you race toward the control room. If you feel you can't complete either challenge, restart from the previous save checkpoint to reset the timer and begin the attack again.

After eliminating the first group of enemies, race up a series of staircases to reach an elevated perimeter walkway. While moving up the stairs, sprint. Every second counts and there's no enemies in this area to worry about. If you fail to sprint when not engaging enemies, you cannot complete the Roger Dodger Tactical challenge When you reach the next walkway, take aim at a lone rifleman in the distance and drop him with a quick burst from your assault rifle.

You're soon attacked by three rifleman on the catwalk above. Toss a Flashbang in their direction to stun them, then race up the nearby steps to flank them, mowing them down while they're still stunned. A shotgun works well when engaging stunned enemies at close range—all it takes is one shot. Flashbangs stun enemies for several seconds, making it easy to close the distance and attack at point-blank range. This is particularly useful if enemies are hiding behind cover. Stun them with a Flashbang, then flank them at close range before they can return fire.

Race up the next set of stairs to reach another catwalk. Here, you encounter three more riflemen, along with more on the distant stairway landing. As you race up the stairs, toss a Sensor and a Flashbang to detect and stun these enemies. Some enemies may not be stunned by the Flashbang, depending on their proximity to the device when it detonates—stunned enemies usually drop to their knees and rub their eyes. So don't assume every enemy is stunned. In such cases, prioritize the enemies who are not stunned, as they pose the biggest threat. Once you've dealt with the active threats, neutralize the stunned enemies before moving on.

Once again, deploy a Sensor and Flashbang toward the next walkway as you rush up the stairs. There are only two riflemen on the this platform, but four more are firing at you from the catwalk ahead. Mow down the two riflemen on the platform while moving toward the ammo crate by the next stairway—chances are you're running low on Sensors and Flashbangs. Once you have resupplied, toss a Flashbang toward the four riflemen on the next catwalk, then flank them while they're still stunned—this is a great way to score four assault rifle kills within a few seconds, putting you closer to completing the Rifle Master Weapon challenge.

You're not far from the control room now, and only two more riflemen stand in your way. Before rushing up the next set of stairs, lob a Sensor and Flashbang up toward the next platform. The Flashbang should stun at least one of the riflemen, but one may escape the blast by running down the stairs in your direction—be ready to gun him down at point-blank range. Alternately, press the stealth kill button to perform a quick melee attack. Clear out the second rifleman on the platform, then race to the nearby control room.

Before entering the control room, lob a Sensor and Flashbang through the doorway—there are four rifleman waiting inside, gathered around the central console. The Flashbang may not affect all of the enemies, so stay on your toes. As you enter, side step to the left and circle-strafe around the console, picking off riflemen as you move laterally. Once you've mowed down all four riflemen in the control room, approach the waypoint marker next to the console and interact with the terminal. Kozak hacks the ship's terminal, uplinking data to Overlord—the techs back home will crunch the data and see what they can find. Meanwhile, Overlord advises the Ghosts to reach a helipad on the upper deck. It's time to secure the second ship.

## TACTICAL CHALLENGE: ROGER DODGER

**CRITERIA: ONCE THE TIMER HAS STARTED, MAKE IT TO THE CONTROL ROOM IN UNDER TWO MINUTES**

This is by far the most difficult challenge to complete in this mission. It requires you to blaze through the drill room in under two minutes. Since the timer starts with three minutes and thirty seconds, it means you need to race into the control room before

the timer reads one minute and 30 seconds. The timer stops as soon as you enter the control room. So if you're running low on time, simply sprint all the way into the control room, even if it means racing past stunned enemies. While speed and aggression are important during this advance, don't get careless. Getting gunned down at any point during the advance almost guarantees failure, as you have to wait for a teammate to heal you. You can help minimize the danger by stunning enemies with Flashbangs along the way. If reaching the control room in time looks hopeless, restart from the last save checkpoint and try again. Once you've played this sequence a few times, it's easier to remember the placement and appearance of enemies, allowing you to shave a few precious seconds off your time.

## WEAPON CHALLENGE: RIFLE MASTER

**CRITERIA: KILL EIGHT ENEMIES IN UNDER 30 SECONDS USING AN ASSAULT RIFLE**

The large concentration of enemies near and inside the control room make this the best spot to complete this challenge. Four riflemen are on the catwalk leading to the control room, and two riflemen guard the control room's entrance. Add the four riflemen

inside the control room, and you have a total of ten possible targets. The trick is killing at least eight of these enemies in 30 seconds or less. Stunning enemies with Flashbangs is the key to plowing through these enemies quickly. You can also benefit from a larger magazine for your assault rifle. If you completed the Tactical challenges in Noble Tempest, you have access to the Drum Magazine. This increases your weapon's magazine capacity to 75 rounds, making for fewer reloads. Regroup with your team at the door marked with a waypoint and enter the adjoining corridor.

NORWEGIAN SEA

## REACH THE HELIPAD

LEGEND

◇ Start    ⊙ Objective    ⦙⦙⦙ Ammo Crate
◇ End    🔫 Weapon Box    ✓ Challenge

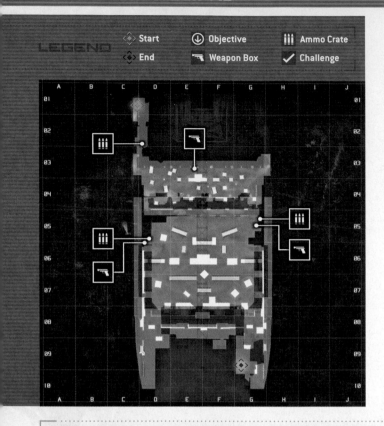

Apparently your work on the ship hasn't gone unnoticed by Raven's Rock. As the Ghosts enter the corridor beyond the control room, Overlord warns that multiple hostiles are closing in on your location—the Russians have deployed a Quick Reaction Force (QRF) in an effort to stop your team. You need to fight your way through the reinforcements to reach the helipad at the aft of the ship. Friendly choppers are inbound and will provide fire support upon arrival. In the meantime, you need to hold out as long as you can. Advance toward the waypoint marker, but drop to a crouch when the word "Contact" appear across the top of the HUD. Just ahead, there's a staircase guarded by three riflemen. Take cover along the wall on the left, and peek around the corner to the right to spot all three enemies—deploy a Sensor if you still have one. There's no need to for an elaborate takedown here. Simply peek around the corner and mow down all three riflemen before they have a chance to seek cover. Even if you're spotted, it won't trigger a wide-scale alert. Once the riflemen are down, approach the metal door and wait for your teammates to breach.

You're now on the deck of the ship. In preparation for the fight ahead, access the ammo crate to the left to stock up on Sensors and Flashbangs. As your team advances, more enemies are detected patrolling nearby. Take cover behind one of the crates and toss a Sensor toward the patrolling riflemen. There are a total of seven enemies here—make sure all seven are detected by your Sensor. Mark the four enemies farthest from your position and setup a sync-shot. When all your teammates are ready, select a target and squeeze the trigger to initiate the sync-shot. Killing four of the riflemen leaves three more standing. You need to take these guys out fast before they can realize what happened. If the remaining riflemen are nearby, you can quickly mow them down before they spot the bodies of their dead comrades and trigger an alert.

Even if you eliminate all seven riflemen on the deck without triggering an alert, it doesn't prevent your team from coming under attack by four snipers posted on the ship's conning tower. Immediately put a solid piece of cover between yourself and the snipers.

At this distance, it's tough to see the snipers, and they're way beyond the range of your hand-thrown Sensors or Backscatter scope. So activate your NVGs and watch for incoming tracers. While behind cover, issue focus-fire orders on each sniper and let your team take them out.

## // TIP

After dealing with the snipers, consider accessing the nearby weapon box. It contains a KSVK sniper rifle, an M12 shotgun, an SA58 OSW PDR, an ACR assault rifle, and an M1014 shotgun. If you don't have an assault rifle yet, choose the ACR now. You'll want a weapon with range and a high rate of fire for the next phase of the mission. One of the shotguns isn't a bad option as a secondary weapon. A weapon box containing the same weapons is available on the lower portion of the deck, next to an ammo crate.

With the four snipers down for the count, follow your team down a short ramp leading to a walkway. When you reach the bottom of the ramp, your team comes under attack by more enemies, including two more snipers. Immediately take cover along one of the crates or steel plates on the edge of the walkway. The snipers are posted on the walkways just beneath the conning tower—there's one on the left and one on the right. Stay behind cover and issue focus-fire orders on both snipers. Once your team has dispatched both snipers, deal with the riflemen on the lower part of the deck. Toss a Sensor toward them to make them easier to spot, then help your team pick them off one by one. Although your team has the height advantage in this fight, the riflemen below outnumber you and can unleash a lot of lead in your direction. So don't get overconfident. Issue focus-fire orders, then peek over the railing and engage one target at a time.

Once all enemies are eliminated, follow your team down to the lower deck of the ship. When you drop off the walkway, immediately move to the left side of the ship to access an ammo crate—the nearby weapon box contains the same weapons you encountered in the previous box. When you're resupplied, join your team near the center of the deck. Suddenly several spotlights on the ship's conning tower bathe the deck in blinding light while a Russian voice can be heard saying something over a loudspeaker—it looks like you just walked straight into an ambush!

Take cover behind the cluster of pipes in the center of the deck. The adjoining stacks of barrels on each side create a handy U-shaped defensive position, which helps to provide cover from three directions. The first group of enemies attack from the right side, moving along the catwalk. Toss a Sensor in their direction and begin opening fire. Most of the enemies take cover behind the metal plates beneath the catwalk's railing. Fortunately your assault rifle can punch through these metal plates. If your Sensor hasn't revealed these hiding enemies, your Backscatter scope will.

## // TIP

*During the ambush on the ship's deck, your teammates are likely to be downed by enemy fire. Instead of leaving cover to heal them, aim at them and issue a heal order. This allows you to stay behind cover while one of your teammates handles the medic duties.*

Listen to the chatter of your teammates during this attack. They often provide helpful cues as to where the enemy is attacking from. When they announce the enemy is flanking from the left, move to the left side of your defensive position, taking cover behind the stack of barrels. Toss a Sensor toward the catwalk on the left side of the ship to reveal the next wave of attackers. Once again, identify the enemies hiding behind the metal plates beneath the catwalk's railing and engage them through cover.

After you've dealt with the enemies on your flanks, focus on the hostiles firing from the catwalk straight ahead, beneath the conning tower. Some of these enemies are armed with LMGs that make them particularly deadly. Stay behind the cluster of pipes at the center of the deck and issue focus-fire orders on these enemies. As the enemy attack intensifies, your team is saved by two Blackhawks flying overhead that rip into the enemies with their miniguns. There's no need to risk injury during the Blackhawk attack. Stay behind cover and let them mop up the rest of the enemies. When the word "Clear" appears across the top of the HUD, it's safe to move out of cover. The path to the helipad is now clear. Follow your teammates up a ladder and regroup at a door leading into the ship's conning tower.

## HELIPAD

LEGEND

◇ Start
◇ End

⊙ Objective
🔫 Weapon Box

▥ Ammo Crate
✓ Challenge

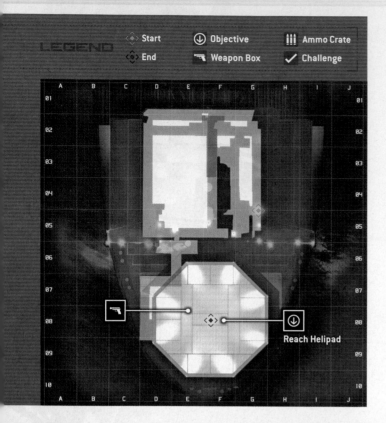

🔫 ─────
◇ ⊙ ─── Reach Helipad

Pass through the corridors behind the door and proceed to the helipad, which is marked on the HUD with a waypoint. A weapon box on the helipad contains a Stoner 96 LMG, but you won't be needing it. Instead, move to the white ring icon on the helipad and prepare to climb aboard one of the Blackhawks. Kozak and 30K board one chopper while Ghost Lead and Pepper are hoisted onto the other Blackhawk. Once onboard, Overlord reports that US decryption analysts have managed to lock down the control system of the second ship remotely, preventing any tampering by the enemy. However, realizing they've lost control of one ship, Raven's Rock is moving large numbers of reinforcements to secure the second ship.

## SECURE SECOND SHIP

During this sequence, you man the Blackhawk's door-mounted minigun. Focus your fire on the enemy convoy consisting of GAZ-2330s and GAZ-66 trucks. However, don't neglect the enemy troops on the ground, as many of them are armed with RPGs capable of shooting down your chopper. So prioritize infantry and the GAZ-2330s first, as they pose the biggest threats. The GAZ-66 trucks are defenseless and explode after absorbing a short burst from the minigun. When an enemy Mi-24 appears on the horizon, Ghost Lead advises Kozak and 30K to stay focused on the convoy. Pepper and Ghost Lead will attack the enemy chopper from the other Blackhawk.

You eventually come to an enemy field HQ that is filled with a variety of targets. While inbound, focus your fire on the infantry first; they appear as small orange diamond icons on the HUD. But don't neglect the BTR-90 APC here, as its powerful weapons can knock your bird out of the sky. Hit the BTR-90 with a prolonged burst from the minigun until it explodes. Once the BTR-90 is destroyed, open fire on the parked GAZ-66 trucks at the HQ. Even though these trucks aren't part of the convoy, you need to destroy them if you want to complete the Wrecker Tactical challenge, which requires you to destroy every vehicle you see during this sequence. Beyond the HQ, hunt down any surviving vehicles that may have escaped and take them out before they can get away.

Your NVGs are automatically activated as you approach the second ship. The ship is covered in orange diamond icons indicating the presence of enemy troops—some of which are armed with RPGs. There's no time to distinguish between enemies carrying rifles or RPGs, so mow them all down. As the Blackhawk flies along the port side of the ship, take aim at the enemies lined up along the perimeter walkways. Establish your aim vertically, then simply open fire. The Blackhawk's forward movement allows you to strafe the whole port side of the ship with only minor aiming adjustments.

After making a strafing run alongside the ship, another Mi-24 attack chopper is detected. This time, Ghost Lead tells Kozak and 30K to take care of the Hind while he and Pepper continue engaging enemy troops on the ship. Turn your attention to the enemy chopper and continue hammering it with the minigun. As you pass the ship's massive drill tower, lay off the trigger and let the minigun cool down for a few seconds. The Mi-24 is on the other side of the tower and is hard to hit. When you have a clear line of sight on the enemy chopper, open fire and finish it off. The damaged chopper spins out of control, slamming into the ship's drill tower, causing it to topple. Once the Hind is down, the ship is secure and the mission concludes.

## TACTICAL CHALLENGE: WRECKER

### CRITERIA: DESTROY ALL ENEMY VEHICLES DURING THE GUNRIDE

If you destroyed every vehicle you encountered during the gunride sequence, this challenge is completed after you shoot down the Mi-24 Hind attack chopper guarding the second ship. If this challenge isn't completed at this point, you probably

missed an enemy vehicle along the way—probably one of the GAZ-66 trucks parked back at the field HQ. You must destroy every vehicle, not just those that are part of the convoy.

 **// Fuel for the Fire**

This achievement/trophy is unlocked after successfully competing the Deep Fire mission.

| DEEP FIRE: COMPLETION UNLOCKS | | |
| --- | --- | --- |
| Type | Category | Item |
| Weapon | Sniper Rifle | M110 |
| Attachment | Magazine | EXACTO Ammo |
| Items | Grenades | Smoke |
| Paint | Weapon paint | ATACS |
| Paint | Weapon paint | Australian DPCU Urban |

# VALIANT HAMMER

## RUSSIA

## BRIEFING

**LOCATION:** RUSSIA CAUCASUS
**OBJECTIVES:** AMBUSH RAVEN'S ROCK FORCES TO EASE PRESSURE ON RESISTANCE GENERAL ALEXEI DOUKA.
**CURRENT CONTACT:** SENIOR MASTER SERGEANT MARCUS KELSO

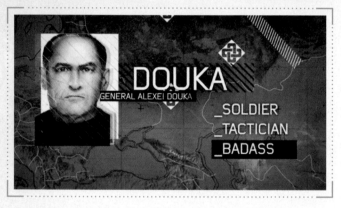

DOUKA
GENERAL ALEXEI DOUKA
_SOLDIER
_TACTICIAN
_BADASS

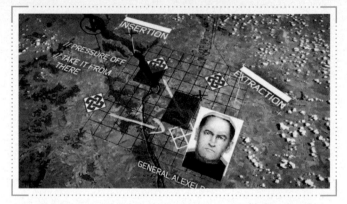

The Russian resistance is putting up a hell of a fight, and the resources you sent will go a long way. Unfortunately, the movement is still scattered and disorganized. DIA's identified a leader who could bring them together: General Alexei Douka. He's a career soldier, an impressive tactician, and a badass, and he might be the hero the Loyalists need. Raven's Rock forces must know it, because they've pinned him in. We don't know the exact situation on the ground, but we know he needs a hand. Get in there and take the pressure off. If he can take it from there, I'd say he's the man for the job.

## MISSION CHALLENGES

### WEAPON CHALLENGE: SHOTGUN MASTER

| DIFFICULTY: | ★★☆☆☆ |
| --- | --- |
| UNLOCK: | MTS-255 |

- With a shotgun, take out three enemies using exactly three cartridges in three seconds max

### TACTICAL CHALLENGES

| DIFFICULTY: | ★★★☆☆ |
| --- | --- |
| UNLOCK: | HIGH POWER SCOPE |

- **Ghostly Recon:** On Veteran difficulty, reach the observation point without alerting any enemies
- **Engraved:** Rack up kills on all enemy snipers in the cemetery without being shot
- **Innovative Diversity:** Your squad must kill enemies with at least 15 different weapons

## GEAR SELECTION

| Equipment Slot | Default | Recommended |
|---|---|---|
| PRIMARY | **M110 SNIPER**<br><br>POWER<br>RANGE<br>CONTROL<br>MANEUVERABILITY<br>RATE OF FIRE — 600 RPM<br>MAGAZINE CAPACITY — 20<br><br>**CONFIGURATION SUMMARY**<br>Muzzle: Suppressor<br>Scope: Sniper<br>Underbarrel: Angled | **M110 SNIPER**<br><br>POWER<br>RANGE<br>CONTROL<br>MANEUVERABILITY<br>RATE OF FIRE — 600 RPM<br>MAGAZINE CAPACITY — 20<br><br>**CONFIGURATION SUMMARY**<br>Muzzle: Suppressor<br>Scope: Sniper<br>Underbarrel: Angled Foregrip |
| SECONDARY | **GOBLIN PDR**<br><br>POWER<br>RANGE<br>CONTROL<br>MANEUVERABILITY<br>RATE OF FIRE — 648 RPM<br>MAGAZINE CAPACITY — 30<br><br>**CONFIGURATION SUMMARY**<br>Muzzle: Standard<br>Scope: Tac Scope<br>Underbarrel: Vertical Foregrip | **M590A1 SHOTGUN**<br><br>POWER<br>RANGE<br>CONTROL<br>MANEUVERABILITY<br>RATE OF FIRE — 180 RPM<br>MAGAZINE CAPACITY — 8<br><br>**CONFIGURATION SUMMARY**<br>Muzzle: Compensator<br>Scope: Red Dot<br>Underbarrel: Vertical Foregrip |
| ITEM 1 | **SMOKE GRENADE**<br>QUANTITY: 4<br>Creates a smokescreen, providing concealment | **SMOKE GRENADE**<br>QUANTITY: 5<br>Creates a smokescreen, providing concealment |
| ITEM 2 | **FRAG**<br>QUANTITY: 3<br>High-explosive grenade intended to kill or wound | **SENSOR**<br>QUANTITY: 5<br>Detects nearby enemies, highlighting them on the HUD |

# REACH OBSERVATION POINT

Now that the Russian resistance has access to fuel, they need a leader to rally around. Without a strong leader, Raven's Rock will continue making gains in their attempt to establish total control, both politically and militarily. Communication lines with the Loyalists do not extend to General Douka. But it looks like Douka is the best chance the resistance has—Raven's Rock appears to feel the same way, judging by the way they're mobilizing to crush him. Douka's won impossible fights before, which makes him a good candidate for myth-making. But despite his impressive reputation, he's in a tough spot and needs assistance, whether he'll admit it or not. The General is currently pinned by Raven's Rock forces in the Caucasus—that's where the Ghosts come in. The Ghosts are tasked with thinning out the Raven's Rock forces surrounding the General's position. But before they assist General Douka, they must reach an observation point to scout Raven's Rock assets in the area of operations.

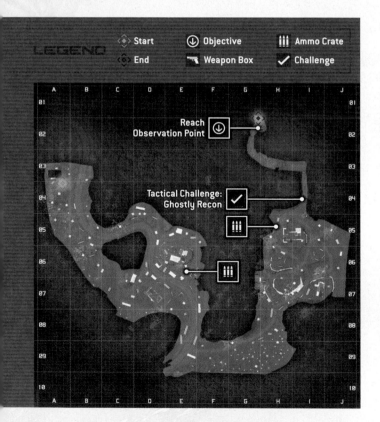

The area is crawling with Raven's Rock troops, so be ready to activate your Optical Camo as soon as the word "Contact" appears across the top of the HUD. Just ahead is a lumber camp guarded by several riflemen. Take cover behind one of the stacks of logs and deploy the UAV to get a closer look. There are a total of ten enemies here, most patrolling around the camp. Fortunately, most of these riflemen are isolated in small groups, which makes them easy to eliminate with a series of sync-shots. Orchestrate the takedowns from the air, with the UAV, picking off two or three enemies with each sync-shot. Start by eliminating the enemies near the large shed on the left, then work your way to the right, across the camp. Before issuing the sync-shot order, always makes sure the marked targets are a safe distance away from their unmarked comrades—you don't want to risk setting off an alert this early in the mission, especially if you want to complete the Ghostly Recon Tactical challenge, which requires you to reach the observation point without being detected.

After clearing out the lumber camp, Overlord reports that they may have picked up a communication signal from General Douka. From the sounds of it, the General is scrambling to keep his unit alive. If you expended any ammo or items during the assault on the lumber camp, you can resupply from an ammo crate near road. Recall your UAV before proceeding to the next waypoint.

Regroup with your teammates and advance along the road until you spot more enemy troops in the distance. Nine enemies have established a makeshift checkpoint near an abandoned cabin. These enemies block the path leading to the observation point, and there's no way around—too bad for them. Once again, deploy the UAV and start clearing the area by utilizing sync-shots. Start by taking out the two nearby riflemen along with the two enemies in the cabin that are equipped with LMGs. Follow up by taking out the three riflemen to the right of the cabin—two are stationary and one patrols. Finally, clear the checkpoint by eliminating the two guards standing behind the cabin. When the area is clear, recall your UAV and regroup with your team at the waypoint marker. Along the way, you can resupply from the ammo crate on the left side of the cabin.

## TACTICAL CHALLENGE: GHOSTLY RECON

### CRITERIA: ON VETERAN DIFFICULTY, REACH THE OBSERVATION POINT WITHOUT ALERTING ANY ENEMIES

To complete this challenge, you must play the mission on Veteran or Elite difficulty and reach the observation point without triggering an alert. That means you must silently clear the lumber camp as well as the cabin checkpoint. All together there are 19 enemies you must eliminate in these two areas. Mark targets with the UAV and utilize sync-shots to whittle down their numbers, eliminating isolated groups of two or three enemies at a time. It's also possible to sneak up behind some of these enemies and perform stealth kills. But if you're spotted, you run the risk of failing this challenge. It's safest to keep your distance and orchestrate the assault from the air.

Regroup with your team at the cliff behind the cabin and proceed down the adjoining path to the observation point, which is marked by a white ring on the HUD. The hilltop observation point offers a sweeping view of a nearby lumber mill that Raven's Rock troops are using as a field headquarters. Lacking intel on Raven's Rock and General Douka's positions, Ghost Lead feels the enemy field HQ is a good place to start gathering information. If the Ghosts can locate and eliminate Raven's Rock artillery positions, General Douka will have an easier time maneuvering. Ghost Lead confirms the game plan with Overlord. But Overlord warns that if things get ugly, there's nothing they can do to help—the area is simply too hot. In other words, the Ghosts are on their own.

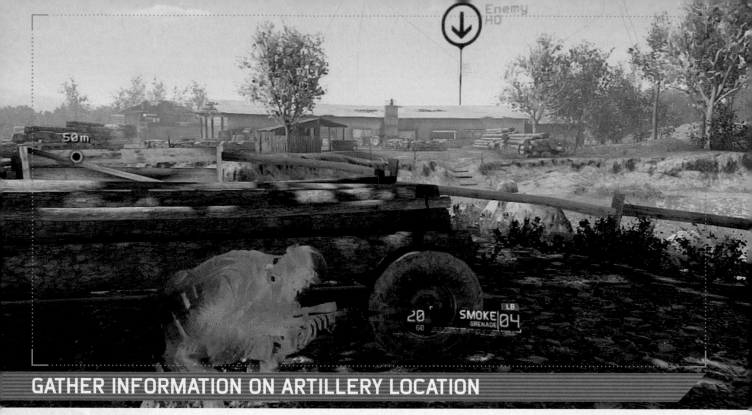

# GATHER INFORMATION ON ARTILLERY LOCATION

Follow the road down from the observation point toward the lumber mill. As you near the bridge leading into the lumber mill, assume a crouched stance to activate your Optical Camo—enemy troops are posted on the other side of the bridge, including one behind a mounted machine gun. Take cover behind one of the lumber piles near the bridge. Before you deal with the enemy troops near the bridge, locate a rifleman standing atop a cylindrical tower attached to one of the lumber mill's main structures. Peek over your cover and take aim at this hostile through your sniper rifle's scope. As long as your weapon is suppressed, you can take this rifleman out without alerting the enemy troops near the bridge.

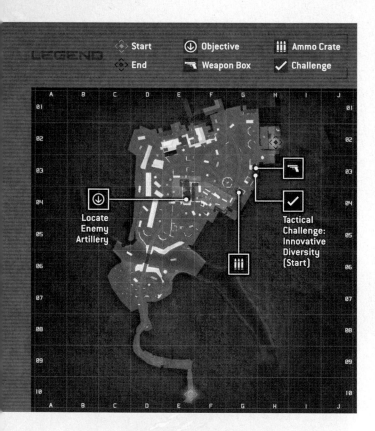

## LEGEND

◇ Start   ⊙ Objective   ≡ Ammo Crate
◇ End     ⬚ Weapon Box  ✓ Challenge

⊙ Locate Enemy Artillery

✓ Tactical Challenge: Innovative Diversity (Start)

## // NOTE

If you equipped your sniper rifle with EXACTO ammo, you'll notice a slight addition to the scope view when you're targeting enemies. While aiming at an enemy, an intel box appears in the scope; it marks the distance to the target provides

an "Acquiring" reading, ranging from 0 to 100 percent—a yellow ring icon also appears over your target's head. EXACTO rounds are guided to help ensure pinpoint accuracy. But you must lock on to a target before firing if you want to guarantee a hit. The acquisition process takes only about two seconds, then the words "Target Acquired" appear and the ring icon over your target's head turns from yellow to red. Once a target is acquired, you can fire and score a headshot, regardless of where the scope's crosshairs are aimed. EXACTO rounds are great for engaging targets at long range, but they're not magic. The bullets still fly in a straight line and cannot negotiate around cover, even if a lock is established. So only fire when there are no solid objects between yourself and the target's head to guarantee a hit. EXACTO rounds can also be fired without achieving a lock; in this case they perform like a standard bullet.

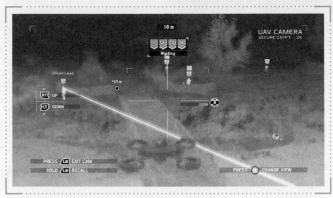

With the rifleman on the tower down for good, you can now clear out the enemies guarding the bridge. Deploy the UAV and start marking targets. In addition to the three riflemen positioned near the bridge, there's also a fourth rifleman patrolling not far from the tower where you claimed your first victim—mark all four enemies and prepare a sync-shot. Exit the UAV view and take aim at any of the four targets while waiting for your team to line up their shots. When everyone is ready, squeeze your trigger to perform the sync-shot. You can now gain access to the makeshift enemy field HQ. But don't let your guard down—the place is still swarming with hostiles. Cross the bridge and recall your UAV.

On the opposite side of the bridge, veer to the left and creep forward while using the large stacks of logs for cover. Just beyond a parked BTR-90 and UAV-66 is a house-like structure. A rifleman is posted on the roof of this building, standing behind a low sandbag wall. There are other hostiles in the area, too, but don't worry about them just yet—as long as you keep your Optical Camo active and stay behind cover, you won't be detected. Take aim at the rifleman on the rooftop and drive a suppressed bullet through the center of his forehead—alternatively, you can have one of your teammates take the shot.

Take cover behind one of the sandbag walls on the perimeter of the large courtyard and monitor the enemy movements in the courtyard. There is no way to secure the field HQ without triggering a firefight. But before attacking, take a few moments to scout the area. Start by tossing two or three Sensors into the courtyard to land at varied distances so their detection radii overlap—take note of the two mounted machine guns, not far from the weapon box and ammo crate. Follow up by deploying the UAV and leave it hovering just above the courtyard so it can monitor the patrolling riflemen during the fight. In addition to the riflemen patrolling the courtyard, there are also multiple hostiles in the large shed and wooden structure to the right—don't overlook these enemies.

## // CAUTION

Remember, the UAV cannot see through rooftops. Therefore you must rely on Sensors and Magnetic view to locate enemies positioned inside structures.

Once you have a clear view of the opposition, creep up to the elevated walkway of the building on the right. Stay clear of the doorway because there's a rifleman inside—you'll deal with him soon enough. But for now, focus your attention on the riflemen in the courtyard.

You can't mark them all, but pick out targets closest to the mounted machine guns, as they pose the biggest threat to your team. When you have four riflemen marked, take aim at one of the marked targets and prepare to initiate chaos—as soon as you initiate the sync-shot, all hell will break loose. You must act quickly and aggressively to eliminate the surviving troops. When you're ready to begin the assault, squeeze your rigger to initiate the sync-shot.

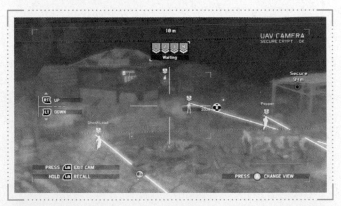

Now it's time to deal with the four other riflemen posted nearby. Deploy the UAV and begin marking targets. There are three riflemen patrolling near the house-like structure, and a fourth rifleman stands on the house's elevated balcony. Mark all four targets, then exit the UAV view. Take aim at the rifleman on the balcony while your teammates take aim at the three patrolling soldiers. When everybody is ready, squeeze your trigger to perform a sync-shot, instantly neutralizing all four threats. Recall the UAV, then creep toward the next waypoint marker. Be careful to avoid being spotted by the numerous enemy troops patrolling the large courtyard.

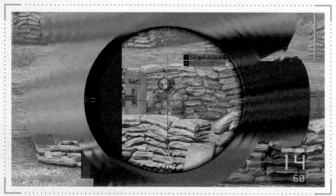

As four riflemen drop dead simultaneously, an alert is triggered and the remaining enemies in the courtyard to scramble for cover. Let your team deal with the enemies in the courtyard. Immediately following the sync-shot, equip your shotgun (or any other secondary weapon) and rush through the doorway on the right, gunning down the startled rifleman before he has a chance to react. As he falls to the ground, pass through the next doorway to the left and blast another rifleman posted on a balcony overlooking the large equipment shed—at this close range, a melee kill may be easier. Take cover on the edge of the balcony and begin engaging enemy troops in the shed. If necessary, deploy more Sensors to get a better view of their hiding spots. Issue focus-fire orders on the enemies in the shed, or take them out yourself using your sniper rifle or shotgun.

## // TIP

*Immediately following the firefight in the field HQ, resupply at the ammo crate beyond the mounted machine guns. You won't have much time to resupply once the enemy counterattack commences.*

From the balcony within the equipment shed, you can also view the two mounted machine guns in the courtyard. Throughout the battle, riflemen will attempt to rush to these weapons and open fire on your teammates—don't let that happen. Monitor the mounted machine guns and pick off anyone that tries to reach them. When you're not targeting enemies behind the mounted machine guns, issue focus-fire orders on hostiles in the courtyard and within the equipment shed. Hold your position on the balcony overlooking the equipment shed and continue supporting your teammates until the field HQ is clear. You can now search the facility for intel on the enemy artillery locations.

Regroup with your team in the structure where you began your shotgun assault. Approach the desk next to the large map and gather intel on the enemy artillery positions. Kozak discovers that General Douka is surrounded by enemy artillery. Douka needs some breathing room, and knocking out those artillery guns may give him the chance to break out. But before moving out, Ghost Lead wants to inspect another building.

As you follow your team outside, deploy more Sensors in the courtyard and rush to the mounted machine guns—enemy reinforcements have arrived! Take control of the mounted machine gun on the right and aim it at the incoming BTR-90. The slow-moving APC is joined by a small group of infantry. Immediately open fire on the enemy attackers, focusing mostly on the BTR-90. This machine gun is equipped with a steel plate that protects you from incoming fire. However, watch out for enemy troops attempting to flank from the right. If you don't, that steel plate won't do anything for you. Go easy on the trigger, firing the machine gun in short bursts. If the machine gun overheats, it will become inoperable for several seconds while it cools down, leaving you defenseless. Keep an eye on the weapon's heat meter, which is shown on the HUD. If the heat meter turns orange, release the trigger to prevent overheating. As the BTR-90 moves to the right side of the courtyard, continue tracking its movements and mow down the troops that exit the vehicle. Keep up the attack until the BTR-90s is destroyed and all enemy troops are down for the count. You can finally inspect that other building.

## TACTICAL CHALLENGE: INNOVATIVE DIVERSITY

### CRITERIA: YOUR SQUAD MUST KILL ENEMIES WITH AT LEAST 15 DIFFERENT WEAPONS

If you want to complete this challenge, you need to make use of the various weapon boxes scattered throughout this mission as well as weapons dropped by enemies. You might as well start early. The first weapon box you encounter is located in the courtyard

at the field HQ and contains an MSR sniper rifle, an Mk48 LMG, an AK-47 assault rifle, an M110 sniper rifle, and an M1014 shotgun—the remaining weapon boxes contain the same weapons. At this point in the mission, your squad has probably performed kills with at least six weapons. To reach the 15 weapons required, you'll need to swap weapons often. Kills with mounted machine guns don't count toward the total, but frag and incendiary grenade kills do. Ideally this challenge is easiest to complete when playing the mission with a friend or group of friends. This allows you to diversify your gear from the beginning. But it's possible to complete while playing the mission solo, as long as you swap weapons frequently—you only need to get one kill with each weapon. Just make sure you maintain possession of a suppressed weapon at all times. You may also want to keep a shotgun handy as a secondary weapon until you've complete the Shotgun Master weapon challenge.

Regroup with your team at the wooden structure on the right side of the courtyard. There are no enemies inside, but there is a radio. Kozak translates the Russian chatter, reporting that Raven's Rock reinforcements are approaching from the west, attempting to trap General Douka's men. In an attempt to warn the General, Overlord patches Kozak in to Douka's communication frequency. Careful not to identify himself or the Ghosts, Kozak speaks directly with General Douka in Russian, warning him of the enemy's plan to encircle his position. Douka seems reluctant to accept information from strangers. Taking out Raven's Rock artillery will certainly help earn the trust of the besieged general.

## DESTROY ARTILLERY UNITS

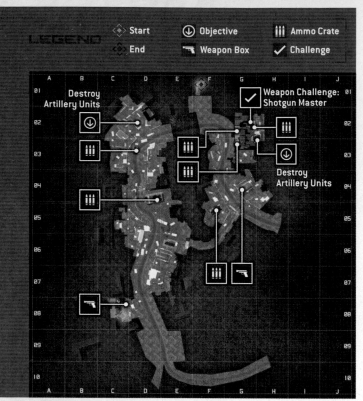

LEGEND

◆ Start
◉ Objective
▥ Ammo Crate
◆ End
▥ Weapon Box
✓ Challenge

Destroy Artillery Units

Weapon Challenge: Shotgun Master

Destroy Artillery Units

With your Optical Camo active, follow your team toward the next waypoint marker—artillery guns can be heard in the distance. Take cover behind one of the stacks of wood on the left side of the road to avoid being detected by nearby hostiles. The abandoned town ahead has been occupied by Raven's Rock forces. You'll need to clear out several enemy troops before you can reach the first artillery unit. Deploy the UAV and conduct a quick flyby to detect a mix of stationary and patrolling enemies—there are 12 in this area. Start by marking the three hostiles in the distance standing on elevated platforms. The guy on the far left is equipped with an LMG and standing on the roof of a bus. Another soldier equipped with an LMG paces along a balcony on the far right. Then there's a rifleman on a balcony in the middle. You need to take out these three hostiles before you can begin picking off the enemies on the ground. Mark these targets and have your teammates perform a sync-shot.

Next, turn to the enclosed courtyard on the left side of the road. This area is isolated from the rest of the town, making it the perfect kill zone to ambush unsuspecting enemy patrols. Wait until at least three patrolling riflemen enter this courtyard, then mark them for a sync-shot. But once you've killed enemies in this courtyard, you don't want anyone else to enter, or they'll discover the bodies of their comrades. So continue monitoring movement around this courtyard and quickly eliminate any enemies that get too close for comfort.

Following the brief conversation with General Douka, step outside and immediately take cover behind the trailer, next to a weapon box. A T-90 tank pull into view on the road ahead and stops only a few meters away. As long as you stay behind the cover of the trailer, the T-90 crew won't spot you. Hold behind cover while a convoy of tanks and trucks roll along the nearby road. Don't try to access the nearby weapon box until all enemy vehicles have passed by and are safely out of sight. Like the previous weapon box at the enemy field HQ, this one contains an MSR sniper rifle, an Mk48 LMG, an AK-47 assault rifle, an M110 sniper rifle, and an M1014 shotgun.

There are six more riflemen, mostly patrolling around the bus by the gas station. The bus is equipped with a mounted machine gun, but there's currently nobody behind it. However, that will change if your team is detected. Watch the movements of the remaining hostiles and pick them off in groups of three. Usually three enemies gather near the front of the bus, and another three loiter around the back of the bus and gas station. These areas are close together so you need to rush these sync-shots to avoid triggering an alert. If you've lost count of how many enemies you've taken out, perform a thorough search with the UAV before moving out. You can also deploy Sensors or activate your Magnetic view to locate enemies you may have missed.

Once you've cleared out the enemy troops guarding the town's entrance, creep toward the next waypoint, marking the position of the first artillery gun. As expected, more hostiles are gathered around the gun—you'll need to take them all out before you can destroy the gun. While moving along the road, and past the gas station, veer toward the left side. There's a bus parked along the road. You can access the roof of the bus by climbing the nearby slope. The bus' rooftop is lined with sandbags, making it the perfect spot to hide while scouting for enemies. Deploy the UAV and search the area for enemies. There are 11 enemy soldiers here as well as three more manning the artillery gun. A rifleman stands next to a mounted machine gun in the center of the road. But ignore this threat for now. Instead, slide to the right side of the road and locate two more riflemen standing on a slight hill—one is stationary and one patrols. Mark both enemies and drop them with a sync-shot.

To eliminate the remaining enemies, you need to carefully monitor the patrols and wait for enemies to isolate themselves from their allies. You can pick off individual riflemen in the courtyard on the left side of the road and within the house beyond the courtyard. There is one stationary enemy standing guard in the courtyard that you cannot eliminate with a sync-shot due to limited sight lines. You can sneak up behind him and take him out with a stealth kill instead. The two riflemen guarding the road near the mounted machine gun must be eliminated carefully. Mark both enemies then watch the patrolling rifleman near the artillery gun. Wait until he turns his back and walks away behind the artillery gun before giving the sync-shot order.

Once you've cleared out most of the enemies in the area, focus on the artillery gun. There are three riflemen standing directly behind the gun. They are responsible for loading and firing artillery shells. There's also a lone rifleman patrolling around the platform on which the artillery gun is placed. Mark all four enemies and prepare to initiate a sync-shot. Exit the UAV view and take aim at any of the marked enemies—squeeze the trigger to initiate the sync-shot, causing the gun to fall silent. You can now approach the artillery gun and destroy it.

## // CAUTION

After eliminating the artillery gun's crew, carefully scour the surrounding area for any riflemen you may have missed from the air with the UAV. Magnetic view and Sensors are helpful for locating enemies that may have been obscured by rooftops or other overhead obstructions. Eliminate all the enemies in this area before setting a charge on the artillery gun. This is a good opportunity to score some stealth kills. You'll know the area is secure when the word "Clear" appears across the top of the HUD.

RUSSIA

To reach the artillery gun you must climb a ladder on the left side of the platform. From there, you can plant a C4 charge on the gun—step into the white ring icon next to the artillery gun and press the button shown on-screen. Once the charge is placed, you have five seconds to get away before it detonates. Instead of climbing down the ladder, simply drop off the side of the platform and seek cover nearby. The C4 charge's detonation knocks out the artillery gun. But another gun can be heard firing in the distance. You'll need to silence it, too.

Follow your team back toward the gas station. Be sure to resupply along the way. There are ammo crates next to the mounted machine gun in the road as well as within the nearby building. When you near the bus by the gas station, your team comes under attack by enemy reinforcements that arrive in GAZ-2330s and GAZ-66 trucks. Immediately toss a couple of smoke grenades on the driver's side of the bus to create a smoke screen. Next, enter the bus and take control of the mounted machine gun. To see through the smoke screen, activate Magnetic view. This helps you see the enemies, but they can't see you as long as the smoke screen is up. Sensors can also help you identify targets through the smoke. Destroy the enemy vehicles, then focus your fire on the infantry. The machine gun in the bus does not have a protective steel plate. So once your smoke grenades have been depleted, take cover within the bus and help your teammates fend off the attackers. The attack is over when the word "Clear" appears across the top of the HUD. Following the attack, resupply from the nearby ammo crate in the building, then follow your team through the bus on the left side of the gas station—you'll need to hop through the window of the bus to access the next area.

## // TIP

*During the firefight at the gas station, target the fuel pumps to trigger large, fiery explosions. This is a good way to take out a few enemies at the start of the fight. Just make sure no teammates are standing nearby when they blow up.*

After passing through the bus, you come to another section of the town where the second artillery gun is positioned. But before you assault the gun, you must clear out the enemy troops. Keep your Optical Camo active and creep along the road, then move toward the damaged barnlike structure on the left side of the road. Climb the ladder on the left side of the structure to access the barn's loft. The loft offers an ammo crate as well as a great view of the area. Lob Sensors all around the barn to get a good picture of the enemy presence. Send the UAV up to get an even better view. Five riflemen are patrolling the nearby road and a sixth is standing on a balcony across the road. Two of the patrolling riflemen can be picked off with a sync-shot as they patrol the area beneath your position in the loft. That leaves four more by the road that you can eliminate with a sync-shot.

## // TIP

*After eliminating all six hostiles near the road, you can find a weapon box in the building where the lone rifleman stood on a balcony. This weapon box contains the same weapons as the previous boxes. But it provides a good opportunity to switch weapons if you're still chasing the Innovative Diversity Tactical challenge.*

Before approaching the cabin structure marked with a waypoint, search for one more rifleman patrolling nearby—use the UAV or Magnetic view to locate him. You don't want this guy flanking your team as you assault the next artillery gun, so track him down and take him out.

The second artillery gun is located in a fenced-off courtyard behind a cabin structure. The only way to reach the gun, is through the cabin. There's no quiet way to do this so prepare for an aggressive assault. Start by tossing Sensors over the cabin's roof to identify enemy soldiers around the artillery gun and within the cabin. Fly the UAV over the artillery gun to provide your team with an updated feed of enemy movements during the attack. When you're ready to begin the assault, stack up on the cabin's door and activate your Magnetic view. This reveals a rifleman inside the cabin staring right at the doorway you're about to enter. You'll need to take this guy out fast before he can raise his weapon.

Give the breach order and drop the rifleman inside the cabin, preferably with a quick shotgun blast. Next, move to the left side of the cabin's interior and approach the back door leading out to the courtyard. Toss a smoke grenade into the courtyard, then open fire on the large group of enemy troops scrambling for cover. Use Magnetic view to engage the hostiles through the smoke screen. But watch out for enemies attempting to rush inside the cabin. Be ready to take them down with a point-blank shot or a melee attack. From the cabin's back door, continue lobbing smoke grenades into the courtyard during the attack. This hinders the enemy's visibility, making it difficult for them to target your teammates. You can always grab more smoke grenades from one of the two ammo crates in the cabin. There is a mounted machine gun on a hill overlooking the courtyard behind the cabin. Use Magnetic view to spot this gunner through the cabin's walls and issue a focus-fire order on him. Continue blasting enemies from the cabin's back door until the word "Clear" appears across the top of the HUD.

## WEAPON CHALLENGE: SHOTGUN MASTER

### CRITERIA: WITH A SHOTGUN, TAKE OUT THREE ENEMIES USING EXACTLY THREE CARTRIDGES IN THREE SECONDS MAX

The assault on the second artillery gun is a great spot to complete this challenge. Saturate the courtyard behind the cabin with smoke grenades, then activate your Magnetic view to go on a killing spree. The courtyard is filled with a number of enemy riflemen, often hiding behind low sandbag walls in tight groups. But before opening fire, first locate your three victims and plan your attack. It's easiest to sweep your weapon across all three targets in one smooth motion, downing each with a shotgun blast.

Now it's time to take out the second artillery gun. Approach the gun and plant a C4 charge on it. Once again, you have only five seconds to move away before the charge detonates. Seek a piece of cover in the courtyard and wait for the boom. Ghost Lead reports the success to Overlord. Overlord feels General Douka should be able to handle things on his own now that the artillery guns have been silenced. It's time to find a way out of this war zone. Ghost Lead relays the team's plan to head east, toward the river. In the meantime, Overlord will arrange ground transport for the Ghosts' extraction. Follow your team through a doorway leading into a garage. Once inside, Kozak contacts General Douka, reporting the destruction of the enemy artillery. Douka is grateful for the assistance but warns Kozak of enemy troops still in the area along the town's perimeter. It sounds like it won't be a relaxing walk to the extraction point.

### // Breathing Room

This achievement/trophy is unlocked after destroying the second artillery gun.

RUSSIA

HOLD Ⓐ COVER SWAP

# REACH EXTRACTION

As you step outside the garage, immediately rush behind the stone wall ahead and take cover—the adjoining cemetery is filled with enemy snipers. Don't even think about accessing the nearby ammo crate or weapon box unless you want to be perforated by a sniper's bullet. Instead, swap cover to one of the nearby tombstones or crypts. When you've reached cover, deploy the UAV to scout ahead. From the UAV view, you can spot enemy snipers atop the crypts and mausoleums in the cemetery—issue focus-fire orders on each sniper you detect.

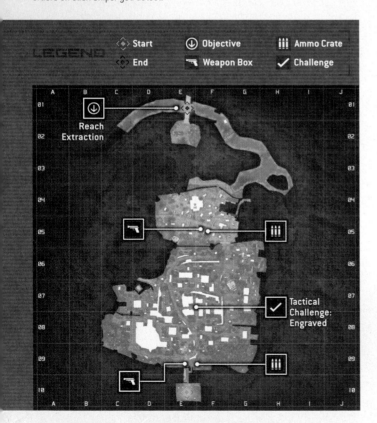

There are only a few snipers in the cemetery, but more lurk beyond. Two snipers are in the church and a couple of snipers are in the dacha on the right. Instead of trying to identify these targets on your own, use the UAV to mark them for your teammates. At this range, Sensors don't offer much help, as the snipers are far beyond their detection radius. Smoke grenades and Magnetic view don't offer much help either. So utilize the tombstones and low walls to advance through the cemetery. Swap from one piece of cover to the next to reduce your chances of getting hit.

## TACTICAL CHALLENGE: ENGRAVED

### CRITERIA: RACK UP KILLS ON ALL ENEMY SNIPERS IN THE CEMETERY WITHOUT BEING SHOT

*During firefights, the UAV can sustain damage from enemy fire. If the UAV takes heavy damage, it is disabled for several seconds while it conducts self-repairs. Recall the UAV any time it begins taking fire to prevent it from being disabled.*

There are two parts to this challenge. First, you need to avoid getting shot by snipers while advancing through the cemetery. The easiest way to do this is by staying behind cover. When you need to move, always use the cover swap method, sprinting from one tombstone to the next. The UAV is the safest way to locate enemy snipers. While in the UAV view, you can spot white glints in the distances, as the sun reflects off each sniper's scope. Use these glints to zero-in on each sniper then peek out of cover to take a shot. While peeking out of cover, you run the risk of getting shot, resulting in failure of this challenge. So quickly duck back behind cover if you see a red aiming laser pointed in your direction. Using the sniper rifle's EXACTO ammo allows you to lock onto each sniper you encounter, guaranteeing a hit. But if you get shot at any time during this sequence, restart from the previous checkpoint (by the garage) and try again. You need to take out these snipers on your own. If your teammates kill all the snipers in the cemetery, the challenge will not be completed.

After clearing out the snipers, approach the exit to the cemetery and prepare to engage more hostiles. There's no need to sneak around—these guys are waiting for you. Target the enemy troops positioned on the dacha's balcony, but watch for more reinforcements approaching from the church on the left—don't let them flank you. Deploy Sensors to keep tabs on the nearby enemies, then issue focus-fire orders for your team. A few enemies may attack beyond the range of your hand-thrown Sensors. So use the UAV to track down these distant enemies and mark them for your team.

Once the area around the church and dacha is secure, follow your team through the nearby shallow river and regroup beneath a bridge. While pausing beneath the bridge, the Ghosts detect enemy reinforcements moving toward General Douka's position. If these troop transports manage to flank the General, the whole mission will be in jeopardy. It looks like the mission isn't over quite yet. It's time to take out those reinforcements in an effort to secure General Douka's flank.

RUSSIA

# ELIMINATE HOSTILE REINFORCEMENTS

Instead of proceeding to the arranged extraction point, the Ghosts decide to stick around a bit longer. Creep out of the river and approach the next waypoint. As you detect enemy troops nearby, take cover behind one of the hay bales and deploy the UAV. There are several enemy troops here, all within eyesight of one another. This makes a stealthy attack nearly impossible. However, you can whittle down the enemy's numbers before launching a full-on assault. Start by marking the hostile armed with an LMG on the upper-floor balcony of the building on the opposite side of the road. You can pick this guy off without anyone noticing.

Next, set up a four-way sync-shot, targeting a selection of the eight remaining enemy soldiers. While it makes little difference which enemies you target initially, be sure to take out the hostile carrying the LMG patrolling the field on the opposite side of the road to the right. Once you have four targets marked, take aim and initiate the sync-shot. As expected, the remaining enemy soldiers go on alert when they see their buddies drop dead. But your team has eliminated half of the hostiles, making it easy to wipe out the remaining troops—especially if you attack quickly before they can reach cover. If you haven't completed the Shotgun Master weapon challenge yet, this is a good spot to rack up three quick kills. Immediately following the sync-shot, equip your shotgun and blast three of the riflemen patrolling the road before they can run to cover. By starting the assault with a sync-shot and following through with an aggressive attack, you can clear out this group of enemies within a matter of seconds. But don't pat yourself on the back just yet. Prepare to engage reinforcements approaching from the town. From the UAV view, locate and mark these incoming enemies.

## // TIP

*There's a weapon box on the left side of the road. After eliminating the first batch of enemies, consider swapping your weapons once again to continue making progress toward the Innovative Diversity Tactical challenge. If you haven't used it already, now is the perfect time to grab the Mk48 LMG.*

Cautiously advance along the left side of the road while engaging enemy troops. The enemy has deployed an automated turret in the center of the road and it begins firing as your team approaches. The turret can be easily destroyed with EMP or Frag Grenades. But if those weapons aren't available, it can also be destroyed with small arms fire. Issue a focus-fire order on the turret and let your team handle the dirty work. Or if the turret isn't firing at you, peek out and fire a quick burst to take it out—these things aren't very durable. A second automated turret is positioned farther down the road. Stay behind cover while approaching this threat and issue a focus-fire order on it as soon as possible. With the turrets out of the way, mop up the remaining hostiles. If you're having trouble spotting them, use Sensors and the UAV to locate them. Keep up the fight until the word "Clear" appears at the top of the HUD. Before regrouping with your team, resupply from one of the various ammo crates in the area—there's one right next to each automated turret.

There's an ammo crate and weapon box beyond the crawl space, but for now, turn your focus to the remaining hostiles. After exiting the crawl space, turn left and take cover behind a low wooden fence. This fence won't last long so toss a smoke grenade in front of your position to limit the amount of incoming fire. With the smoke screen in place, activate your Magnetic view and begin engaging hostiles through the smoke. Reinforcements continue streaming into the area, so stay focused and deploy Sensors to keep tabs on enemy movement.

Eventually a T-90 tank arrives on the nearby road—you need to find better cover fast! Ghost Lead suggest moving into the ruins of an old church on the right. Sprint into the church and seek cover among the interior walls. There's not much left of this church except for a few crumbling brick walls. But it will provide your team with life-saving protection until Overlord can come through with an air strike. You'll need to hold out at this location for a while. Start by deploying smoke around the church. This will

help reduce the amount of incoming fire, allowing you to engage hostiles around the perimeter by using Magnetic view. Deploy Sensors around the perimeter of the church, too. This helps you spot enemies attacking at close range. Throughout the attack, hold near the center of the church, as you're less likely to be injured by tank shells slamming against the exterior walls. When Overlord reports the air strike is ready, initiate it by pressing the button shown on screen. The camera then switches to the view of an incoming missile. Guide the missile toward the tank to save your team and complete the mission. The air strike destroys the tank and kills all remaining hostiles. The Ghosts walk away from another close call.

Regroup with your team at a gate (marked with a waypoint), and prepare to breach. Just inside the gate is a damaged cabin structure blocking your path. But there's plenty of trouble waiting behind this building. Toss a couple of Sensors over the cabin's roof to detect a few hostiles on the other side. Deploy the UAV and fly it over the roof to get a better view. Due to limited sight lines, you can mark only two of these enemies—the one patrolling near the cabin and the one on a distant balcony to the left. Before issuing the sync-shot order, exit the UAV view and drop down into the crawl space beneath the cabin. Once you're in position, give the sync-shot order to initiate the attack.

| VALIANT HAMMER: COMPLETION UNLOCKS | | |
| --- | --- | --- |
| Type | Category | Item |
| Weapon | SMG | Vector |
| Weapon | LMG | Ultimax Mk.5 |
| Attachment | Optic | Thermal Optic |
| Paint | Weapon paint | Danish T90 |
| Paint | Weapon paint | Iraqi Urban |

# GALLANT THIEF

SIBERIA

## BRIEFING

LOCATION:     RUSSIA, SIBERIA
OBJECTIVES:   INFILTRATE BLACK PRISON AND EXTRACT RUSSIAN PRESIDENT VOLODIN
CURRENT CONTACT:   SENIOR MASTER SERGEANT MARCUS KELSO

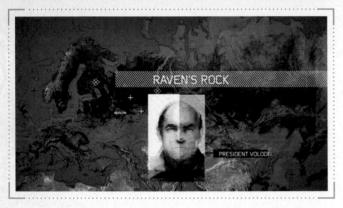

RAVEN'S ROCK

PRESIDENT VOLODIN

You guys risked a lot for General Douka. But you made it work and it's paying off. The resistance is making a strong push, rallying around Douka. But Raven's Rock still has an ace in the hole. President Volodin is locked up in a black prison, near borders even we don't even dare cross. If the Loyalists are going to restore their government, they need proper authority to do it with. General Douka has a force standing by to transport Volodin back to Moscow. We just need to go get him. Kozak, you're taking point. You'll infiltrate the prison, locate President Volodin, and bring him out.

## MISSION CHALLENGES

### WEAPON CHALLENGE: UP THE ANTE

| | |
|---|---|
| DIFFICULTY: | ★★☆☆☆ |
| UNLOCK: | PP2000 |

- Take down 12 enemies with an SMG without reloading

### TACTICAL CHALLENGES

| | |
|---|---|
| DIFFICULTY: | ★★★★★ |
| UNLOCK: | GRIPOD |

- Quigley: Kill two enemies with a single bullet
- Hands On: Reach the canteen without firing a weapon
- Secret Service: On Elite difficulty, find President Volodin inside the prison in under two minutes

## GEAR SELECTION

| Equipment Slot | Default | Recommended |
|---|---|---|

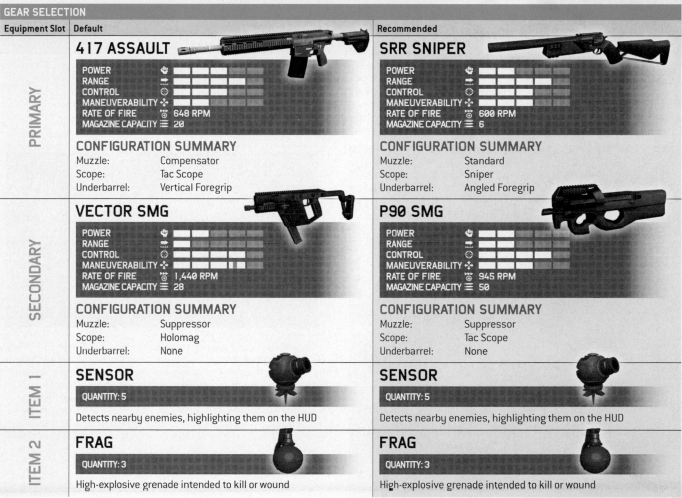

**PRIMARY**

### 417 ASSAULT

| | |
|---|---|
| POWER | |
| RANGE | |
| CONTROL | |
| MANEUVERABILITY | |
| RATE OF FIRE | 648 RPM |
| MAGAZINE CAPACITY | 20 |

#### CONFIGURATION SUMMARY

Muzzle: Compensator
Scope: Tac Scope
Underbarrel: Vertical Foregrip

### SRR SNIPER

| | |
|---|---|
| POWER | |
| RANGE | |
| CONTROL | |
| MANEUVERABILITY | |
| RATE OF FIRE | 600 RPM |
| MAGAZINE CAPACITY | 6 |

#### CONFIGURATION SUMMARY

Muzzle: Standard
Scope: Sniper
Underbarrel: Angled Foregrip

**SECONDARY**

### VECTOR SMG

| | |
|---|---|
| POWER | |
| RANGE | |
| CONTROL | |
| MANEUVERABILITY | |
| RATE OF FIRE | 1,440 RPM |
| MAGAZINE CAPACITY | 28 |

#### CONFIGURATION SUMMARY

Muzzle: Suppressor
Scope: Holomag
Underbarrel: None

### P90 SMG

| | |
|---|---|
| POWER | |
| RANGE | |
| CONTROL | |
| MANEUVERABILITY | |
| RATE OF FIRE | 945 RPM |
| MAGAZINE CAPACITY | 50 |

#### CONFIGURATION SUMMARY

Muzzle: Suppressor
Scope: Tac Scope
Underbarrel: None

**ITEM 1**

### SENSOR

QUANTITY: 5

Detects nearby enemies, highlighting them on the HUD

### SENSOR

QUANTITY: 5

Detects nearby enemies, highlighting them on the HUD

**ITEM 2**

### FRAG

QUANTITY: 3

High-explosive grenade intended to kill or wound

### FRAG

QUANTITY: 3

High-explosive grenade intended to kill or wound

# INFILTRATE THE PRISON

About a third of the legitimate Russian government has been liquidated or "shot trying to escape." Raven's Rock is keeping the rest on ice in prisons around the country. They're keeping President Volodin alive until they can trot him out to legitimize the new government. But the Resistance needs Volodin, too. Once General Douka takes back Moscow, the Loyalists need Volodin to help restore the government. Kozak is on his own for this mission; he is tasked with breaking President Volodin out of prison. Performing a High Altitude-Low Opening (HALO) jump, Kozak covertly inserts by air, reaching the outskirts of the Siberian prison where President Volodin is being held. Overlord advises that alerts must be avoided until the prison's security system is isolated.

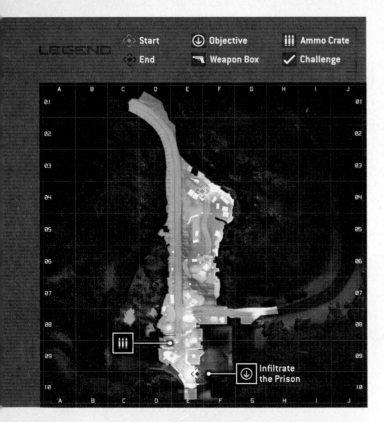

A lone rifleman patrols the area near the insertion point. Sneak up behind him and perform a stealth kill. Melee kills like this are essential if you want to complete the Hands On Tactical challenge, which requires you to infiltrate the prison without firing a shot. However, not every enemy needs to die. Whenever possible, avoid contact. The discovery of dead bodies by patrols can result in a alert, instantly making the mission a failure. So before you kill an enemy, think twice. It's often much easier to slip by undetected with the aid of your Optical Camo. If you do kill an enemy, you'll need to take out all nearby enemies to prevent anyone from finding a dead body.

Creep up the nearby hill, moving toward the prison. Take cover near one of the shipping containers and deploy the UAV to locate two riflemen and a sniper patrolling nearby. Exit the UAV view and leave the drone hovering over the hill, so it can monitor the enemy movements. These enemy troops are spread out, so they are easy to take out with stealth kills. Or, you can simply slip past them and proceed to the prison's entrance. But if you do kill one of these enemies, take out all three to prevent a body from being discovered. Since this is a night mission, Kozak is equipped with Night Vision Goggles (NVGs). In addition to the UAV hovering overhead, the NVGs come in handy for highlighting enemy heat signatures in the darkness. Using the NVGs in combination with the UAV and Sensors is the best way to identify threats around you.

Descend the hill and approach the left side of the prison's gate. As expected, there are multiple riflemen nearby, including some posted in guard towers. Fly your UAV toward the entrance so it can monitor the enemies while you sneak into the prison. Exit the UAV view and begin moving toward the gate. Stay on the far left side of the entrance to avoid being detected by the rifleman standing near the checkpoint booth—he's looking right at you! But as long as you keep your Optical Camo active and move slowly, he won't detect you. Just beyond the checkpoint are two more riflemen patrolling near the road. Stay on the left side of the road and wait for the riflemen to move away before slipping past them. Once you have moved beyond the two patrolling riflemen, recall your UAV and proceed to the waypoint marker leading into one of the prison's administrative buildings. You can deactivate your NVGs once you're inside.

## // TIP

*If you're about to be spotted by enemy troops, move behind cover. If no cover is available, drop prone and remain still.*

# ADMINISTRATIVE OFFICES

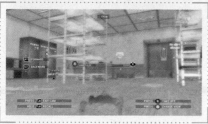

Overlord reports that you can now hack into the prison's security system. Enter the automatic door on the left side and advance through a series of corridors until you come to a room with an open floor-level vent. Time to deploy the UAV. Land the UAV near the vent and enter Crawler mode. Drive the Crawler through the lengthy ductwork until it comes to a room with a pair of consoles that is marked with a waypoint. Move the drone to the base of these two consoles and emit a sonic pulse. This fries the electronics in the consoles, causing the nearby door to open. Follow a series of waypoints through the corridors of the administrative building until you exit, emerging outside on the prison grounds.

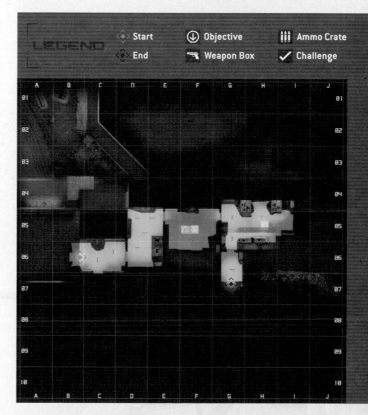

LEGEND

◇ Start  ⬇ Objective  ⫿⫿⫿ Ammo Crate
◇ End  🔫 Weapon Box  ✓ Challenge

# ENTER SECURITY AREA

Upon exiting the administrative building, turn right to spot a sniper in the distance; his back is turned. Sneak up behind the sniper and take him out with a stealth kill—don't worry, nobody will find his body. Beyond the sniper is a door marked with a waypoint. But Overlord reports that this door can only be opened through the security room—a new waypoint marker appears on your HUD. Before moving out, deploy the UAV in the direction of the new waypoint to identify several riflemen patrolling the nearby road. Activate your NVGs and creep toward the waypoint, being careful to keep your distance from the enemy troops. Stay along the left side of the road and pass through a small concrete structure containing an ammo crate. This allows you to bypass the troops near the parked GAZ-2330 parked in the center of the road.

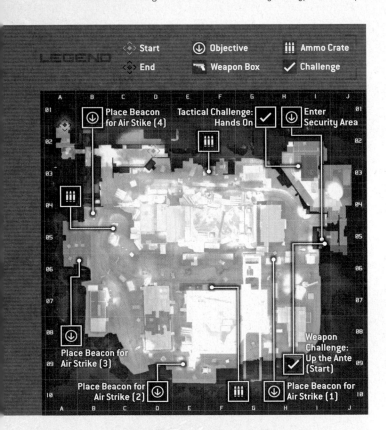

When you reach the door by the waypoint marker, you see it's guarded by a rifleman. There is no way to sneak around this guy. While you can easily take him out with a suppressed weapon, doing so will make you fail the Hands On Tactical challenge. Get as close to the rifleman as possible without being detected. Moving to cover just outside the entryway is a good place to prepare your attack. While still crouched with Optical Camo active, move directly toward the rifleman and take him out with a stealth kill as quickly as possible. The rifleman will see you during the approach, but if you act quickly, you can kill him before he can raise an alert. It's a somewhat risky move, but it's the best way to get through this area without firing a weapon.

After eliminating the rifleman by the doorway, Kozak discovers that the next door is protected by a retinal scanner—it looks like you'll need to borrow someone's eyes. Follow a new waypoint toward the canteen. Move to the white ring icon outside the canteen's window to trigger a cinematic. Kozak sneaks through the window and grabs a soldier from behind before guiding him back to the retinal scanner. Once the soldier has opened the locked door by using the retinal scanner, Kozak guides him into the next corridor and knocks him out with a choke hold.

## TACTICAL CHALLENGE: HANDS ON

### CRITERIA: REACH THE CANTEEN WITHOUT FIRING A WEAPON

This challenge is completed when you reach the canteen's window. Of course, completing this challenge hinges on your success with infiltrating the prison without firing a shot. By simply utilizing your Optical Camo, you can make your way into the

prison without being spotted, so there's little need to open fire on anyone. Any hostiles that stand in your path can all be eliminated with melee stealth kills.

Advance down the corridor and enter the first doorway on the right to enter the security room. Here, you find two riflemen standing in front of a few computer terminals—both enemies have their backs turned. Given their close proximity to one another, it isn't

possible to stealthily kill both riflemen without triggering an alert. Your best option is your suppressed SMG. Take aim at one of the riflemen, centering the aiming reticle on the back of his head. Shoot the first enemy, then immediately swing your aiming reticle over the next rifleman and drop him before he can respond. With both enemies out of the way, approach the white ring icon in front of the center terminal. Kozak transmits the prison's security data to Overlord. Overlord reports that they've received the data, but it will take some time to decrypt. In the meantime, Overlord advises Kozak to begin placing air strike targeting beacons around the prison in preparation for the escape.

## WEAPON CHALLENGE: UP THE ANTE

### CRITERIA: TAKE DOWN 12 ENEMIES WITH AN SMG WITHOUT RELOADING

Gunning down the two riflemen in the security room is a good place to start this challenge. Just make sure you have your SMG equipped before opening fire—and don't reload. The P90's 50-round magazine capacity gives your plenty of ammo to

spare, but always go for headshots at relatively close range to ensure a kill while expending as few rounds as possible. SMGs have incredibly high rates of fire when fired automatically, so consider fitting your SMG with a semi-auto trigger group. This will guarantee you fire only one round with each pull of the trigger. This makes it much easier to manage your ammo while completing this challenge. From the security room, you have many opportunities to kill unalerted enemies at close range with your SMG while sneaking around the prison grounds. But remember, every body you leave behind could potentially lead to an alert. So choose your victims carefully.

# PLACE FOUR TARGETING BEACONS FOR AIR STRIKE

Exit the security room and follow the waypoint marker to return outside. The prison's alarm system has been isolated, so it's no longer necessary to remain silent. However, it's still in your best interest to avoid detection. Before you can enter the cell block where President Volodin is being held, you must first deploy four targeting beacons around the prison grounds at predetermined locations marked on your HUD as waypoints. The first location is only a few meters away from the security room's exit. Before moving out, drop to a crouch to activate your Optical Camo. There are plenty of enemy troops patrolling the prison grounds, but your Optical Camo will help you avoid being detected—just keep your distance from enemies. There are no enemies near the first beacon location. Move toward the waypoint marker until you see a white ring icon at the base of a large white fuel cell—step into the white ring to place the first beacon. One down, three to go.

Before moving toward the second beacon location, deploy the UAV to scout ahead. This will help you keep tabs on enemy patrols during the advance. Exit the UAV view and begin moving toward the next waypoint. Instead of taking the most direct route, circle around

the large garage-like building so you can avoid moving directly toward the guard tower near the beacon location. This allows you to approach the location from the side, where you're less likely to be spotted by the rifleman in the guard tower or any patrols nearby. The second beacon must be placed between two large white fuel cells.

On the way to the third beacon location, you pass a building on the left occupied by two riflemen. One of these enemies patrols while the other remains stationary, staring out a window. Before planting the third beacon, take out the rifleman who patrols nearby. But you must kill him outside the line of sight of his stationary comrade. Wait for him to exit the building and begin walking toward the third beacon location. When he turns back to the building, sneak up behind him and take him out with a stealth kill once he's inside. For good measure, sneak up behind his buddy, staring out the window, and take him out quietly, too. Both of these enemies can be shot with your SMG to help you complete the Up the Ante weapon challenge.

## TACTICAL CHALLENGE: QUIGLEY

### CRITERIA: KILL TWO ENEMIES WITH A SINGLE BULLET

The two riflemen standing in front of the GAZ-66 truck by the checkpoint offer the perfect opportunity to complete this challenge. After eliminating all the remaining enemies around the checkpoint, move toward the checkpoint booth until you can get a clear view of both riflemen. Move laterally until the riflemen are perfectly aligned, with one standing directly in front of the other. Next, equip a suppressed semi-auto rifle (like the SRR sniper rifle), take aim, and fire. If your targets are properly aligned, the bullet will pass through the first enemy and kill his buddy standing a few feet away. A semi-automatic weapon is important to complete this challenge. If you fire more than one bullet, the challenge will not be completed.

Now move back toward the third beacon location, not far from an enemy check-point. Before planting the beacon, consider eliminating the nearby enemies. Toss one Sensor toward the checkpoint booth on the right side of the road and another Sensor toward the vehicle shelter on the left side. Get your drone into the air, too, to provide a view from above. There are a total of six enemy troops loitering around the checkpoint. Without the support of teammates, you'll need to take these enemies out on your own. Start by picking off the rifleman on the rooftop not far from the checkpoint booth. Before firing, make sure you're a safe distance away from any of the patrolling troops. Even when using a suppressed weapon, the report may draw the attention of enemies. This is a good opportunity to use a suppressed sniper rifle or assault rifle—your SMG simply doesn't have the range.

With the rooftop rifleman down, approach the check-point and begin stalking more enemies. Start by taking out the rifleman inside the checkpoint booth—the Sensor you deployed earlier should highlight his position. But before killing the enemy in the checkpoint booth, monitor the patrol of the nearby sniper. When the sniper is far away, sneak into the checkpoint booth and neutralize the rifleman. You can now stalk the patrolling sniper—just be sure to take him out a safe distance away from the checkpoint, where his body won't be noticed by the two riflemen standing in front of the truck in the middle of the road. Finally, go after the rifleman patrolling the vehicle shelter on the opposite side of the road. Wait until he's within the vehicle shelter, then take him down so that his body falls behind one of the parked GAZ-2330s. The two remaining riflemen standing in front of the truck can be eliminated with one bullet, to complete the Quigley Tactical challenge.

With the checkpoint clear of hostiles, get on with placing the third and fourth beacons on large white fuel cells near the vehicle shelter. After you place the fourth beacon, Overlord reports that they've decrypted the prison data and can now open the door leading to the subterranean maximum security area. Before leaving the area, resupply from the ammo crate next to the checkpoint booth and recall your UAV. Upon reaching the next waypoint, wait for Overlord to hack the door, then step inside the adjoining corridor. Proceed to the next waypoint to board a lift that provides access to the underground cell block where President Volodin is being held. During the ride down, Overlord reports that they have no visibility on the facility's lower levels. You'll have to infiltrate the cell block and find the President on your own.

# FREE VOLODIN

Following the ride on the lift, you find yourself in a narrow corridor. Activate your Optical Camo (by crouching) and creep forward. A few paces down the corridor, you spot a row of bars on the left side. Standing just beyond the bars is a rifleman. While you can easily sneak past this guy, he's an easy target if you're still pursuing the Up the Ante weapon challenge. Take aim at the rifleman with your suppressed SMG, and take him down with a headshot—his body won't be discovered.

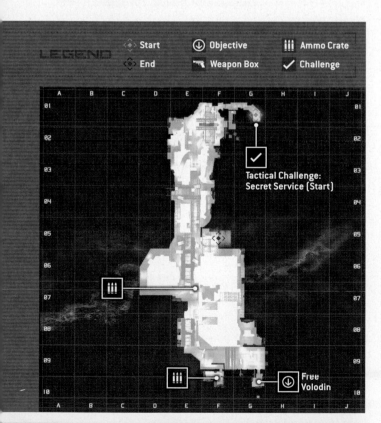

**LEGEND**

◇ Start    ⊙ Objective    ⦀ Ammo Crate

◇ End    🗃 Weapon Box    ✓ Challenge

✓ Tactical Challenge: Secret Service (Start)

⊙ Free Volodin

The corridor leads to a large storage room that is occupied by a few riflemen, including one patrolling a catwalk above the room. Take cover behind one of the pallets and deploy a Sensor to get a reading on all the enemies in this area. Don't think about eliminating enemies here—there are too many. Instead, sneak toward the doorway on the opposite side of the room, utilizing cover and Optical Camo during the advance. But before moving, make sure the rifleman on the catwalk is looking away. Immediately after you pass through the doorway, turn to the left and perform a stealth kill on the soldier peering through the window—his body won't be discovered.

The small office near the supply room is connect to a perimeter passage. But watch out for a rifleman patrolling this passage. Deploy another Sensor if necessary to spot the nearby patrols. If you're not careful, this rifleman can sneak up behind you. So hold at the intersection in the passage and wait for him to pass by. At that point, you can take him down in the passage without anyone seeing. But the path ahead isn't clear. Take cover behind one of the crates at the end of the passage and monitor the nearby riflemen. When you have an opening, proceed to the steps just ahead.

## // CAUTION

*If you're playing this mission on Elite difficulty, the Secret Service tactical challenge begins immediately after exiting the lift. This challenge requires you to reach President Volodin's cell within two minutes. Every second counts, so don't waste any time.*

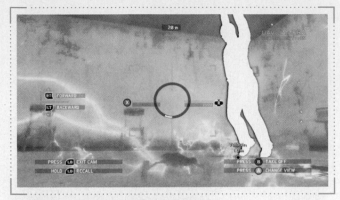

When you reach this next area at the top of the steps, you're prompted to use the UAV, in Crawler mode, to inspect the nearby cells. But while controlling the Crawler, you run the risk of being spotted by one of the enemy riflemen patrolling nearby. So before deploying the Crawler, thin out the number of guards in this area. First, deploy at least a couple of Sensors here so you have a good reading on your surroundings before going on the attack. The enemy riflemen here are often isolated, making them easy to eliminate one at a time. This is a good opportunity to use your SMG to rack up some easy kills for the Up the Ante weapon challenge. Still, be mindful of where bodies fall. Try to eliminate enemies along the perimeter so that their bodies aren't easy to spot. Six riflemen are patrolling or posted in this area—quietly stalk and kill them all before deploying the Crawler.

Each cell door has an open floor vent next to it, marked by an "Explore" waypoint. Once you're certain all nearby enemies have been eliminated, deploy the UAV, and land it next to one of the open vents to initiate Crawler mode. While the first two cells contain captives, unfortunately neither of them is President Volodin.

## // TIP

There's no need to waste your time investigating the first three cells. Volodin is located in the final cell, at the end of the cell block corridor. If you search each cell with the Crawler, you'll never complete the Secret Service tactical challenge in time. Make a beeline for the final cell, which is marked on the map.

Continue through the corridor and ignore the rifleman that is visible through a window as you make a left turn toward the final two cells. As long as you keep your Optical Camo active and keep your distance, the rifleman in the window won't notice you. However, there are two more riflemen near the cells at the end of the corridor and you'll want to eliminate them before freeing the president. One of the riflemen patrols the area in front of the cell doors. Wait for him to walk away from the cell doors, then sneak up behind him and perform a stealth kill. The second rifleman is in the boiler room, staring through a window, looking directly at President Volodin's cell. Step inside the boiler room and fire a bullet through the side of his head using your suppressed SMG.

You can now deploy the Crawler to locate President Volodin in the final cell—he's dangling from the ceiling by shackles attached to his wrists. Once you've found the president, emit the Crawler's sonic pulse to disable the electronic lock on the cell door. Enter the cell and approach Volodin to free him from his shackles. Kozak tries to put Volodin at ease and hands him a Vector SMG. Unlike some VIPs, Volodin can handle himself. Plus, it will be good to have backup during the escape. Now it's time to get out of here without drawing too much attention.

## TACTICAL CHALLENGE: SECRET SERVICE

### CRITERIA: ON ELITE DIFFICULTY, FIND PRESIDENT VOLODIN INSIDE THE PRISON IN UNDER TWO MINUTES

To complete this challenge you must be playing the mission on Elite difficulty. This challenge begins as soon as you exit the lift, at the start of the maximum security area. To reach Volodin's cell in less than two minutes, you need to move quickly without being detected. If an alert is sounded, you'll have a difficult time fighting your way to President Volodin in under two minutes. Only kill enemies that are in your way and that can't be detected by patrols. Also, don't bother searching the first three cells with the Crawler. Take the side passage that cuts through the boiler room, bypassing the first two cells. This shortcut will shave several seconds off your time, helping you to reach Volodin's cell before time runs out.

### // Special Election
achievement/trophy

This achievement/trophy is unlocked after freeing President Volodin.

# ESCORT VOLODIN TO EXTRACTION

Instead of retracing your steps back through the cell block, pass through the boiler room directly across the hall from Volodin's cell. This is connected to a narrow passage that leads directly to a lift. However, when you reach the end of the corridor, pause before ascending the steep flight of stairs on the left. There's a rifleman patrolling here. If you can't spot him, toss a Sensor toward the top of the stairs. Wait for the rifleman to begin descending the stairs, then shoot him with your suppressed SMG. Carefully scout the area at the top of the stairs, then turn right to enter a lift leading to the surface. Soon after Kozak and Volodin enter the lift, Overlord reports that the air strike is about to begin. Seconds later, a series of loud explosions rock the prison facility, causing the elevator shaft to shudder under the concussive blasts.

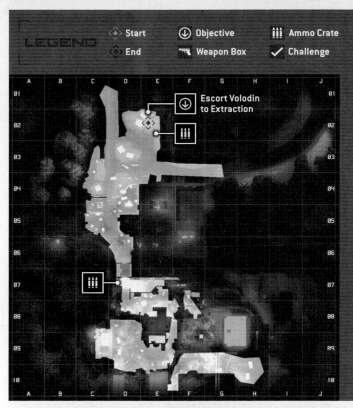

| | | |
|---|---|---|
| ◇ Start | ⊙ Objective | ⫶⫶⫶ Ammo Crate |
| ◇ End | ▀ Weapon Box | ✓ Challenge |

⊙ Escort Volodin to Extraction

When the lift reaches the surface, you find that the prison facility has been transformed in a hellish landscape, bathed in fire and rocked by secondary explosions. The air strike worked; it is serving as the perfect distraction while you escape with President Volodin. Let Volodin lead the way. With the exception of some soldiers performing CPR on their fallen comrades, you encounter no living enemies while advancing through the prison. You don't need to shoot the soldiers doing CPR—they're eventually take out by a secondary explosion. There's no need to be quiet any longer, so consider looting weapons off the dead bodies you pass along the way—you can usually find an SA58 OSW PDR among the dead. Proceed to the extraction point on the hill overlooking the prison facility.

On the way to the extraction site, President Volodin is struck by an incoming bullet fired by pursuing enemy troops. You'll need to hold off these attackers while waiting for extraction. Immediately move behind the low wall for cover, next to an ammo crate. Propped up against the wall are an Ultimax Mk.5 LMG and a SA58 OSW PDR. Swap your sniper rifle for the LMG and begin firing on the attackers. The enemy troops approach from the prison, some charging up the hill toward you. Toss a few Sensors in the direction of the prison to highlight the attackers. This makes it easier to spot and engage enemy troops (armed with shotguns) charging up the hill. Don't let these shotgun-toting enemies flank your position. Be ready to gun them down at close range as they sprint toward President Volodin. A Blackhawk eventually arrives to pick you up. The Blackhawk performs a couple of strafing runs before hovering over your position. At this point, a white ring icon appears next to President Volodin. Step into this ring to begin the extraction process. Kozak attaches a cable to himself and the president and within seconds they're lifted to safety as the prison burns in the background.

| GALLANT THIEF: COMPLETION UNLOCKS | | |
|---|---|---|
| Type | Category | Item |
| Weapon | Assault Rifle | TAR-21 |
| Attachment | Underbarrel | 40mm HEDP Launcher |
| Paint | Weapon paint | Army ACU |
| Paint | Weapon paint | Estonian |

# INVISIBLE BEAR

## BRIEFING

| | |
|---|---|
| LOCATION: | RUSSIA, MOSCOW |
| OBJECTIVES: | SUPPORT RESISTANCE FORCES IN THEIR PUSH INTO MOSCOW |
| CURRENT CONTACT: | SENIOR MASTER SERGEANT MARCUS KELSO |

President Volodin will never publicly acknowledge your role in his rescue. Hopefully his return to power will be thanks enough. In the meantime, Douka's people are pushing into Moscow. We're sending you in to support them. The crowds should draw most of the attention. I want your team to shadow the procession, and make sure their way is clear.

Once they're clear, we're going after Raven's Rock military head. General Bukharov is on site, coordinating final efforts. This will be a victory for the people of Russia. We're not here to save the country for them, but we'll sure as hell do what we can to make sure they win.

## MISSION CHALLENGES

### WEAPON CHALLENGE: MASTER SNIPER

| | |
|---|---|
| DIFFICULTY: | ★★☆☆☆ |
| UNLOCK: | VSS |

- Using a sniper rifle, kill 15 consecutive enemies without any misses

### TACTICAL CHALLENGES

| | |
|---|---|
| DIFFICULTY: | ★★★☆☆ |
| UNLOCK: | RAUFOSS AMMO |

- Dodge the Dot: Avoid being taken out by a sniper during the mission
- Clean Sweep: Clear General Bukharov's room in under 20 seconds
- Disruptor: Kill at least 10 Bodark while they are still under the effects of an EMP

## GEAR SELECTION

| Equipment Slot | Default | | Recommended | |
|---|---|---|---|---|

### PRIMARY

**TAR-21 ASSAULT**

| POWER | ✊ | |
|---|---|---|
| RANGE | ➡ | |
| CONTROL | ⊙ | |
| MANEUVERABILITY | ✛ | |
| RATE OF FIRE | ⏱ | 720 RPM |
| MAGAZINE CAPACITY | ≡ | 30 |

**CONFIGURATION SUMMARY**

| Muzzle: | Standard |
|---|---|
| Scope: | Red Dot |
| Underbarrel: | HEDP GL |

**M110 SNIPER**

| POWER | ✊ | |
|---|---|---|
| RANGE | ➡ | |
| CONTROL | ⊙ | |
| MANEUVERABILITY | ✛ | |
| RATE OF FIRE | ⏱ | 600 RPM |
| MAGAZINE CAPACITY | ≡ | 20 |

**CONFIGURATION SUMMARY**

| Muzzle: | Flash Hider |
|---|---|
| Scope: | Sniper |
| Underbarrel: | Angled Foregrip |

### SECONDARY

**VECTOR SMG**

| POWER | ✊ | |
|---|---|---|
| RANGE | ➡ | |
| CONTROL | ⊙ | |
| MANEUVERABILITY | ✛ | |
| RATE OF FIRE | ⏱ | 1,440 RPM |
| MAGAZINE CAPACITY | ≡ | 28 |

**CONFIGURATION SUMMARY**

| Muzzle: | Suppressor |
|---|---|
| Scope: | Holomag |
| Underbarrel: | None |

**L22A2 PDR**

| POWER | ✊ | |
|---|---|---|
| RANGE | ➡ | |
| CONTROL | ⊙ | |
| MANEUVERABILITY | ✛ | |
| RATE OF FIRE | ⏱ | 918 RPM |
| MAGAZINE CAPACITY | ≡ | 30 |

**CONFIGURATION SUMMARY**

| Muzzle: | Suppressor |
|---|---|
| Scope: | Tac Scope |
| Underbarrel: | Vertical Foregrip |

### ITEM 1

**SENSOR**

QUANTITY: 5

Detects nearby enemies, highlighting them on the HUD

**SENSOR**

QUANTITY: 5

Detects nearby enemies, highlighting them on the HUD

### ITEM 2

**EMP GRENADE**

QUANTITY: 3

Disables equipment and disrupts HUD of any caught in blast

**EMP GRENADE**

QUANTITY: 3

Disables equipment and disrupts HUD of any caught in blast

# PROTECT THE CROWD

General Douka's men have broken through Raven's Rock's defensive line and are currently securing the streets of Moscow. Crowds have swarmed the streets, greeting Douka's men as heroes. But there are still a few Raven's Rock hardliners in town hoping to spoil the victory parade. The Ghosts are here to make sure Douka's advance and President Volodin's return go off without a hitch. In addition to supporting Douka's advance, the Ghosts are tasked with tracking down and eliminating General Bukharov. Intel reports place Bukharov in the city, organizing Raven's Rock defenses from the old FSB headquarters. But for now, the Ghosts must protect the crowds rallying support for the Resistance. The more chaos the crowd creates, the better your shot at taking out Bukharov.

LEGEND

- ◈ Start
- ◈ End
- ⊕ Objective
- ▤ Weapon Box
- ⫼ Ammo Crate
- ✓ Challenge

The Ghosts begin on the street, ready to move to high ground in an effort protect demonstrators. Not far from the insertion point, a T-90 tank rolls through the intersection ahead. Keep your Optical Camo active and follow the tank through the intersection, toward a large plaza filled with Russian troops loyal to Raven's Rock. You can't risk an alert, so forget about an assault. Plus, you don't have the firepower to take out that tank. Instead, look for a way to slip past these hostile units. Deploy the UAV over the plaza to get a better view.

Ascend the stairs on the far right side of the plaza to reach an elevated walkway ringing the perimeter. Follow this path to reach the entrance of the nearby apartment building. However, you'll need to clear out a couple of riflemen first. Pause at the top of the steps and wait for two riflemen to approach from the left. Keep your distance and stay behind cover to avoid being spotted. The

pair climb a second set of steps parallel to the path and begin to move along the walkway away from you. Stay behind cover and take aim at their backs with your suppressed weapon—shoot them both in the back of the head with short, controlled bursts. If you act quickly (and aim accurately) you can eliminate both riflemen without raising an alert.

With the two patrolling riflemen down, the path to the apartment building is now clear. However, you still need to keep a low profile to avoid being detected. As the path turns left, toss a Sensor toward the waypoint to highlight two riflemen standing on the edge of the walkway staring out toward the plaza. Each rifleman is standing next to a mounted machine gun. But you don't need to kill these guys. Their backs are turned, so simply walk past them and proceed toward the apartment building's entrance. Unfortunately this building isn't equipped with an elevator. So follow your team up several flights of stairs until a cinematic is triggered, showing thousands of protestors filling the streets below.

## OVERWATCH

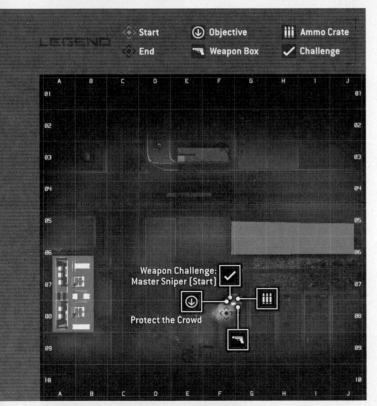

LEGEND

◇ Start    ◎ Objective    ⫼ Ammo Crate
◈ End    🔫 Weapon Box    ✓ Challenge

Weapon Challenge: Master Sniper (Start) ✓

Protect the Crowd

Shortly after eliminating the two snipers, Overlord reports that President Volodin has joined the procession in the streets. There are reports of enemy infantry occupying buildings along Volodin's route. You need to clear out any nearby threats before the President arrives. At this point, a timer appears on the HUD, giving your team seven minutes until President Volodin arrives. Take cover below the window and deploy the UAV. Fly the UAV toward the "Secure" waypoint marker to spot a lone sniper standing on the corner of a distant rooftop. Mark the sniper, then have one of your teammates take him out—or take the shot yourself.

Eliminating the sniper causes a flurry of activity on the rooftop, as two more snipers rush into view; they are attempting to target your team. Spot the new snipers through your rifle's scope, or with the UAV and mark them for your team. While peeking out of cover, you're vulnerable to incoming sniper rounds. If you wish to complete the Dodge the Dot tactical challenge, you need to avoid getting hit by a sniper for the entire mission. So consider staying behind cover and issuing focus fire orders for your team through the UAV view. If you do engage the enemy snipers, watch for red aiming lasers pointed in your direction. If you see an aiming laser, immediately duck behind cover before you're acquired by one of the snipers and shot.

Following the cinematic, the Ghosts stack up next to a room occupied by two Raven's Rock snipers. Stay behind cover on the left side of the doorway and mark both snipers. Next, peek through the doorway and take aim at one of the snipers while a teammate aims at the other one—squeeze your trigger to initiate the sync-shot. Eliminating the two snipers clears the floor. Step inside the room and resupply from the ammo crate. If you didn't bring along a sniper rifle, grab the KSVK from the nearby weapon box.

After eliminating the two snipers on the rooftop, shift to the right side of the room and scan the large skyscraper across the street. Three snipers are hiding in this building, barely visible through the windows. Stay behind cover and fly the drone over toward the building to locate and mark the snipers. From the UAV view you can see the glint of sunlight reflecting off each sniper's scope. Use this reflection to zero-in on each sniper and issue a focus-fire order so your teammates can take them out.

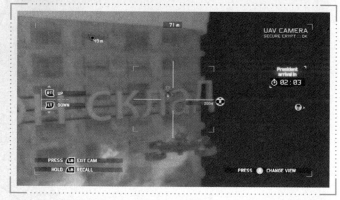

Now shift back to the left side of the room and refocus on the distant rooftop, which has been occupied by one more enemy sniper. Locate the sniper with the UAV, and mark him for your teammates. While scanning for the sniper, listen for the sound of an approaching chopper. Make sure you're behind cover when an Mi-24 appears and begins strafing the floor with its chin-mounted turret. There's no way to counter the chopper's attack, so just stay behind cover and wait for the strafing run to end. Following the chopper attack, more snipers appear at both buildings. Mark the sniper on the rooftop first, then shift to the skyscraper across the street, where two more snipers are positioned in windows. Once again, use the UAV to locate and mark these snipers.

Once all the snipers have been eliminated, the area is clear, allowing President Volodin to join the demonstrators without incident. The Ghosts can now hunt down General Bukharov. Resupply from the ammo crate before regrouping with your team in the adjoining hallway. A cinematic shows news coverage of President Volodin arriving in the street and whipping the crowd into a frenzy.

## WEAPON CHALLENGE: MASTER SNIPER

### CRITERIA: USING A SNIPER RIFLE, KILL 15 CONSECUTIVE ENEMIES WITHOUT ANY MISSES

The counter-sniping sequence in the apartment building is a good place to start this challenge. However, if you get shot in the process, you risk not completing the Dodge the Dot tactical challenge. So take this into account before peeking out of cover to engage the enemy snipers. This challenge is made much simpler with EXACTO ammo. While it takes some time for each bullet to acquire a target, once locked on, a hit is virtually guaranteed. Although EXACTO ammo can punch through light cover, you should avoid engaging enemies through cover because one miss resets the kill count, which means you must restart the challenge. So don't rush your shots and make sure each bullet fired has a clear, unobstructed path to the target.

# PROCEED TO GENERAL BUKHAROV'S HQ

Following the cinematic, stack up on a door with your team and prepare to enter a large floor of the apartment building still under construction. Just ahead, a Mi-24 hovers in the distance and unloads several enemy troops—prepare for an attack. Take cover behind the low crates straight ahead and lob a couple of Sensors out, throwing one to the right and another to the left. The overlapping detection radii of the Sensors allow you to spot incoming troops. Deploy the UAV as well, leaving it hovering just ahead of your position. Once you've spotted enemies, issue focus-fire orders for your teammates while helping them engage. Using your sniper rifle, engage the hostiles on the scaffolding in the center.

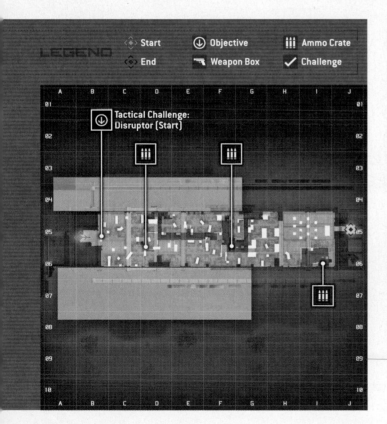

| Start | Objective | Ammo Crate |
|---|---|---|
| End | Weapon Box | Challenge |

**LEGEND**

Tactical Challenge: Disruptor [Start]

## // CAUTION

Watch out for the Bodark units during the firefight in the construction site. Their Optical Camo makes them tough to spot. If you don't engage these enemies, they'll advance aggressively in an attempt to flank your team. During close encounters, rely on melee attacks to take these guys out.

## TACTICAL CHALLENGE: DISRUPTOR

**CRITERIA: KILL AT LEAST TEN BODARKS WHILE THEY ARE STILL UNDER THE EFFECTS OF AN EMP**

To complete this challenge, you must have EMP grenades in your inventory, which are chosen at the start of the mission. You encounter the first Bodark units at the construction site. Toss EMP grenades in their direction to disable their Optical Camo. The EMP

affects the Bodark troops for only a few seconds, so you need to kill them before they recover. You must kill a total of ten Bodark units in this fashion to complete this challenge.

Hold behind cover and continue deploying fresh Sensors to detect incoming enemies. The hostiles throw a variety of objects in your direction, too, including Flashbangs and EMP grenades. If an EMP grenade goes off nearby, your Cross-com system is temporarily disabled along with your Optical Camo. When this happens, all your HUD elements disappear, essentially leaving you blind. Stay behind cover and wait a few seconds for the Cross-com system to come back online.

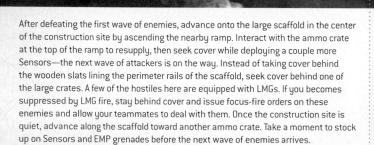

After defeating the first wave of enemies, advance onto the large scaffold in the center of the construction site by ascending the nearby ramp. Interact with the ammo crate at the top of the ramp to resupply, then seek cover while deploying a couple more Sensors—the next wave of attackers is on the way. Instead of taking cover behind the wooden slats lining the perimeter rails of the scaffold, seek cover behind one of the large crates. A few of the hostiles here are equipped with LMGs. If you becomes suppressed by LMG fire, stay behind cover and issue focus-fire orders on these enemies and allow your teammates to deal with them. Once the construction site is quiet, advance along the scaffold toward another ammo crate. Take a moment to stock up on Sensors and EMP grenades before the next wave of enemies arrives.

After resupplying at the ammo crate, move to the far left side of the scaffold system and take cover behind a cluster of metal barrels. As your team announces the arrival of more hostiles, toss Sensors ahead, including at least one toward the large two-floor wooden structure on the right. Multiple hostiles are holed up in this small building, firing at your team through windows. Fortunately, you don't have to wait for them to peek their heads out. Using your sniper rifle, engage these enemies directly through the wooden exterior walls. But don't let the enemy troops in the wooden structure distract you from the Bodark units scurrying along the floor. Lob EMP grenades in their direction in an attempt to halt their aggressive advance, then pick them off one by one as they scramble for cover. Hold your position on the scaffold and help your team engage the hostiles until the word "Clear" appears across the top of the HUD. Before exiting the construction site, resupply at one of the ammo crates, then regroup with your teammates at the waypoint marker. If it's still deployed, don't forget to recall your UAV.

# MOSCOW STREETS

**LEGEND**

◇ Start　　⊙ Objective　　▥ Ammo Crate
◇ End　　🔫 Weapon Box　　✓ Challenge

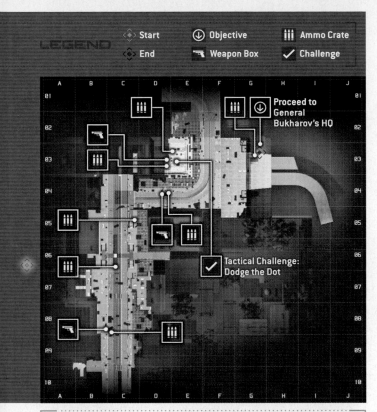

Proceed to General Bukharov's HQ

Tactical Challenge: Dodge the Dot

Once you've initiated the attack, reinforcements appear in the distance. Immediately deploy Sensors, tossing one to the right side of the street and another to the left side. This helps you keep tabs on incoming enemies, making it easier to issue focus-fire orders, even if the hostiles are hiding behind cover. When the street falls silent, cautiously swap cover, advancing toward the parked GAZ-2330 on the left side of the road. There's an ammo crate here as well as a weapon box. The weapon box contains an LSAT LMG, an M110 sniper rifle, an AK47 assault rifle, and an L22A2 PDR. If you don't have a sniper rifle, consider grabbing the M110 in an effort to complete the Master Sniper tactical challenge. Otherwise, the LSAT LMG is a good option for the fight ahead.

## // TIP

*The UAV will sustain heavy damage if it is left hovering above the street. You're better off relying on Sensors and Magnetic view to spot enemies once the firefight begins. If you do deploy the UAV, use it briefly to mark targets for your teammates, then recall it.*

Now move back to the center of the street and take cover behind the large crates just beyond the GAZ-2330. Here, you come under attack by another wave of enemy troops. Once behind cover, deploy a couple of Sensors ahead to detect the incoming enemies. In addition to the enemy troops in the street, there are two snipers posted on the apartment balconies to the left. Given the amount of incoming fire, it's a bit risky to peek out of cover and try to take out these snipers on your own—especially if you're trying to earn the Dodge the Dot tactical challenge. So issue focus-fire orders on these enemies. If you have trouble spotting them, use the UAV to scout their positions and mark them. But while focusing on the snipers to the left, don't neglect the sidewalk on the right. Make sure you have adequate Sensor coverage here to spot enemies attempting to flank you.

Following a brief cinematic showing an irate President Sergei Makhmudov breathlessly criticizing the demonstrations, the Ghosts finally emerge from the apartment building. Activate your Optical Camo and creep outside—be careful to avoid the numerous enemy troops loitering in the street. Take cover behind the concrete barrier in the center of the street and deploy the UAV. There are a total of nine enemy soldiers here. You can't take them out silently, but you can whittle down their numbers significantly with a sync-shot. Before marking targets, identify the two soldiers carrying LMGs in the distance—mark them first. Next mark other distant enemies, including the lone rifleman standing on the right side of the street. Exit the UAV view and shoot any of the marked targets to initiate the sync-shot. Immediately after hitting your target, while time is still slowed, open fire on as many other nearby enemies standing in the middle of the street as possible. If you're quick, you can score three more kills.

Hold behind cover until no more threats can be spotted—conduct a quick patrol with the UAV to ensure that the street is clear. Continue advancing down the center of the street toward a row of sandbags next to another ammo crate. Just ahead, a GAZ-2330 pulls into view and begins firing with its machine gun turret. Issue a focus-fire order on the vehicle then help your team destroy it. Peek out of cover when the turret isn't firing and shoot the vehicle with automatic fire. But don't get greedy. Be ready to duck back down behind cover before the turret resumes firing. If you have a grenade launcher, you can take out this vehicle quickly.

After taking out the GAZ-2330, a GAZ-66 arrives in the distance and unloads more enemy troops. Toss more Sensors in the direction of the truck and issue focus-fire orders on the new arrivals. Some of these troops are equipped with ballistic shields— make these enemies your priority. Even your sniper rifle won't penetrate these shields, so don't even bother trying. If you don't have Frag grenades (or a grenade launcher), a frontal attack does no good. Instead, issue focus-fire orders on these guys and try to flank them before they get too close for comfort.

## // CAUTION

*Shortly after the arrival of the GAZ-66 truck, a sniper appears on the balcony of a distant apartment building on the left side of the street. If you don't deal with this threat quickly, he'll pick your team apart. It's safest to locate and mark this guy with the UAV. If you take the shot yourself, wait until just after the sniper has taken a shot before peeking out of cover. This will give you just enough time to pick him off before he can fire again.*

Your team emerges from the underground stairway near the adjoining intersection, across the street from an Admiral Burgers fast food restaurant, and only meters from the former FSB building where General Bukharov was last spotted. But as you emerge from the stairway, make sure your Optical Camo is active—otherwise you'll be spotted by a BTR-90 parked in the street just ahead. Unless you have a grenade launcher, you don't have adequate firepower to take out this vehicle. Fortunately, you can find a grenade launcher in the weapon box behind the truck on the left side of the street. The grenade launcher is attached to an AK47 assault rifle. With the AK47 in hand, take cover behind one of the concrete barriers in the street and begin launching grenades at the BTR-90. After your first shot, the BTR-90 retaliates, firing its cannon in repetitive bursts. Wait to return fire until the BTR-90 stops firing, then peek out of cover and fire another grenade. Repeat in this fashion until the BTR-90 explodes. Overlord reports that General Bukharov has dispatched a convoy to deal with the demonstrators. Keep the AK47 with the grenade launcher attachment—it will come in handy. But make sure to stock up on ammo before regrouping with your team.

The tram in the center of the street blocks your line of sight, so move toward the sidewalk on the left side of the street to resume the advance. Stay behind cover at all times, using the cover swap method to advance from one piece of cover to the next. There are a few more enemy troops hiding among the vehicles in the street. Deploy Sensors to locate them, then issue focus-fire orders. There's also one more sniper at the far end of the street on a balcony to the right. Once you've located him, issue a focus-fire order and let your teammates score the kill. The sniper is usually the last enemy standing in the street. But wait for the word "Clear" to a appear on the HUD before leaving cover. There's an ammo crate on the right side of the street where you can resupply. Afterward, regroup with your team in the underground stairway nearby.

Follow your team into the Admiral Burgers restaurant and seek cover as enemy units emerge from Bukharov's HQ across the street. The attack is lead by a GAZ-2330, which sprays the restaurant with automatic fire. Issue a focus-fire order on the vehicle, then attack with your grenade launcher. When you're taking cover, deploy Sensors in the street to keep tabs on the enemy troops outside. If you're not careful, enemy troops will enter the restaurant and attempt to flank your team at close range. Stop these flanking advances before enemy troops can gain a foothold in the restaurant. If enemies do gain entry, hunt them down quickly. During the attack, a second GAZ-2330 opens fire. Stay behind cover and fend off the infantry attacks first, then eliminate the GAZ-2330 with your grenade launcher.

Two ammo crates and a weapon box are inside the Admiral Burgers restaurant. The weapon box contains an AK47 with a grenade launcher, just in case you happened to ditch the one you used earlier. Remember, Sensors are only active for a limited time, so you'll need to deploy fresh Sensors throughout the fight. Stay near one of the ammo crates so that you have an endless supply of Sensors and grenade launcher ammo.

Another BTR-90 appears outside the restaurant and begins bombarding the interior with its cannon. As long as you stay behind solid cover (such as one of the pillars), the BTR-90 can't hurt you. In the meantime, turn your attention toward the infantry swarming around you. A few are equipped with ballistic shields. Target the shield soldiers directly with your grenade launcher. When the bulk of the infantry are down, focus your fire on the BTR-90, pounding it with your grenade launcher until it explodes. When the word "Clear" appears across the top of the HUD, the enemy attack is over. Resupply, then join your team at the waypoint across the street. It's time to pay General Bukharov a visit.

// TIP

In addition to a grenade launcher, there's also a mounted machine gun outside the restaurant that you can use to destroy the BTR-90. However, make sure all the enemy troops have been eliminated before leaving the relative safety of the restaurant.

Watch out for a GAZ-66 truck to come crashing through the front of the restaurant. Immediately fire a grenade at the truck to destroy it before enemy troops can get out. But there are plenty more enemy troops in the street. Deploy more Sensors to get a reading on the latest group of attackers. Once again, keep an eye on the left and right flanks to prevent enemy troops from infiltrating the restaurant. If enemies manage to breach the restaurant, engage them through their cover—your bullets will pass right through the flimsy tables and booths.

## TACTICAL CHALLENGE: DODGE THE DOT

### CRITERIA: DODGE THE DOT: AVOID BEING TAKEN OUT BY A SNIPER DURING THE MISSION

This challenge is completed immediately following the enemy attack on the Admiral Burgers restaurant, assuming you managed to reach this point without being dropped by an enemy sniper. The easiest way to avoid incoming sniper rounds is by staying behind cover. When snipers are present, use the UAV to locate and mark them. Any time you peek out of cover, you're vulnerable.

## ELIMINATE BUKHAROV

After entering the HQ, a brief cinematic shows the demonstrators continuing their march through the streets of Moscow. The Ghosts have certainly done their fair share of keeping the heat off the procession, but it's not over yet. General Bukharov has barricaded himself in this office building, surrounding himself with Raven's Rock fanatics. As soon as your team enters the office, you come under fire by a mounted machine gun. Sprint to cover and issue a focus-fire order on the gunner. Due to the steel plate in front of the gun, it's tough to get a clear shot. But even the steel plate won't protect the gunner from a direct hit with a grenade launcher. Simply launch a grenade at the steel plate to kill the gunner behind it. In addition to the mounted machine gun, there are Bodark units lurking about. Lob EMP grenades at them, then take them out before they can recover.

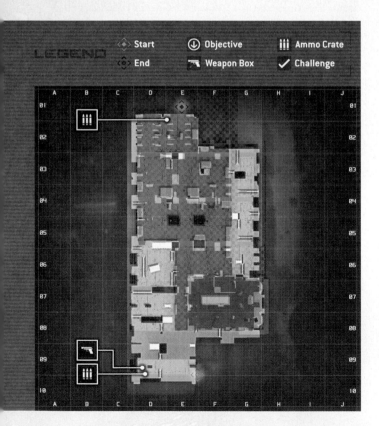

A second mounted machine gun opens fire as your team pushes deeper into the office. Once again, stay behind cover and wait for a pause in the firing, then peek out and launch a grenade at the steel plate on the front of the machine gun. Beyond the second machine gun are a few hostiles equipped with ballistic shields. Don't waste time flanking these guys. Just knock them out with a blast from your grenade launcher. Deploy Sensors to locate any other enemies hiding among the cubicles. However, Sensors won't detect Bodark units. So advance cautiously. When Bodark units are encountered, toss EMP grenades at them and gun them down. When the office is "Clear," according to your HUD, regroup with your team at the elevator, which is marked with a waypoint. The elevator is out of service, so the Ghosts must climb a ladder in the elevator shaft to reach Bukharov's office. As they move into position, a cinematic shows President Makhmudov being evacuated from a news conference.

# BUKAHROV'S OFFICE

Upon reaching the exterior of Bukharov's office, Ghost Lead conducts a Magnetic view reading that reveals multiple hostiles inside. Instead of barging through the front door, Ghost Lead suggests making a new entrance. Move to the wall next to Pepper and step inside the white ring icon on the HUD. You're prompted to plant a C4 charge to initiate the breach. Before planting the charge, use Magnetic view to get a quick glimpse of the enemies waiting inside. This can help you plan which targets to attack upon entry. When you're ready to attack, plant the charge on the wall and prepare to enter.

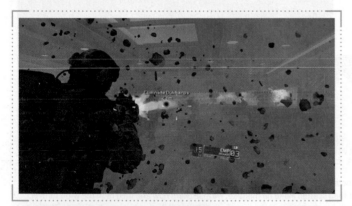

Time slows as your team assaults the office, so you have time to take down multiple enemies. Sweep your aim from the right to the left, blasting all enemy troops within sight. You automatically take cover behind a conference table following the breach.

Toss a Sensor ahead to locate any remaining enemies and engage them through cover. Bukharov hides behind a desk at the far side of the room. But you don't need to wait for him to peek out. Simply fire through the desk to strike him. Once Bukharov is dead, the mission is over. Ghost Lead reports the success to Overlord. The mission ends with a newscast cinematic detailing the capture of President Makhmudov and the death of Bukharov—the media reports the general was killed by his own security forces.

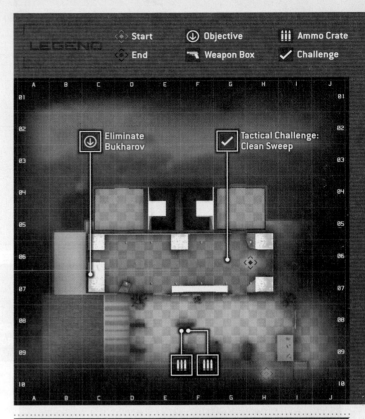

| LEGEND | | |
|---|---|---|
| ◇ Start | ⊕ Objective | ⫲ Ammo Crate |
| ◇ End | ▭ Weapon Box | ✓ Challenge |

## TACTICAL CHALLENGE: CLEAN SWEEP

**CRITERIA: CLEAR GENERAL BUKHAROV'S ROOM IN UNDER 20 SECONDS**

From the moment the C4 charge detonates, you have exactly 20 seconds to wipe out every enemy in the office, including General Bukharov. If you're quick, you can eliminate all the riflemen in the office during the breach sequence. When the breach sequence is over, immediately identify any remaining hostiles in the office with a Sensor and engage them by firing through their cover. Don't waste time flanking or waiting for enemies to pop out of cover. Simply blast through the overturned tables and desks to take them out.

### // Relieved of Command

This achievement/trophy is unlocked after eliminating General Bukharov.

| INVISIBLE BEAR: COMPLETION UNLOCKS | | |
|---|---|---|
| **Type** | **Category** | **Item** |
| Weapon | Shotgun | M12 |
| Weapon | Assault Rifle | A-91 |
| Paint | Weapon paint | Marine Marpat |

# 3

# MULTIPLAYER

*Ghost Recon Future Soldier's* multiplayer modes allow you to experience the future of warfare like never before. Select from three classes (Rifleman, Engineer, and Scout) and unlock new gear to battle on ten maps. During your online career you gain experience and levels, all leading to decisions that you make to customize and develop your character. But it's not all about you. You won't be successful without teamwork. The multiplayer modes offer many opportunities to work together and help your team gain the upper hand in each battle. Gather intel on your opponents' positions and share it with your teammates. Or use the suppression system to pin your enemies down while your teammates flank them. Hours of intense online action await. Study the maps and tactics in

# INTRODUCTION

## ADVERSARIAL

The ultimate measure of your skills not just as a lone Ghost, but as a squad, were put to the test throughout the Campaign. Now it's time to put that tested mettle to use against actual living, breathing combatants. *Ghost Recon Future Solider*'s Adversarial modes pit you against the rest of the world in ten wildly different maps across four distinct game types, each with its own nuances, quirks, and strengths. Mastering not just the basics of the modes, but the ins and outs of each of the maps is key to securing objectives before hostiles on the other team can do the same. Make no mistake; this is just as team-oriented as the Campaign ever was. To come out on top, you'll have to work together with other members of your squad and team to ensure victory. Those that seek singular glory will find themselves at the bottom of the leaderboard at best, and kicked out of the squad as a likely consequence. Communicate, collaborate, and concentrate. Adversarial modes are where good Ghosts go to become great.

## MODUS OPERANDI

### CONFLICT

A decidedly objective-based approach is required for all Conflict maps, meaning it's not enough to just shoot the other guys, you have to beat them to the punch in gaining control of objectives and then *hold* those objectives until the timer runs out. Objectives are randomized, and can offer a variety of side effects, including intel on hostile players, the ability to shut down their HUDs with an EMP blast, being able to restock ammo and deployables and more. Kill counts aren't the goal here; only by taking and holding more valuable sites on the map will your team come out on top. Most objectives are two-sided, meaning if an attacking team is trying to destroy or capture an objective, it is marked as a defensive objective for the opposing team.

### EMP BLASTS

Repelling demolition attempts on the EMP generator until it can unload affords defenders a huge advantage for about 30 seconds, effectively turning the normally high-tech operations of the attacking team's HUD dark. That means no radar, no advanced optics (even when aiming through scopes), no Optical Camo, no objectives markers, no UAVs, no deployables. ... You get the idea. Needless to say, if you're on the attacking team, planting a demo charge on the EMP is of the utmost importance.

### INTEL SENSOR

Having knowledge of the enemy's position and direction is the single most important deciding factor in getting the drop on the other team. Intel Sensors can reveal location data on key members of the opposing team, but they have to be powered up and defended. It's not a one-way objective, however; if the enemy can clear out defenders and recapture a Sensor, the data is flipped, revealing information on *your* team's whereabouts and movement.

### INTEL SWEEPS

The data you view on enemies is always being collected for distribution to the rest of your squad, but it needs to be uploaded from time to time. Though it is a team-wide objective, only one carrier has the information necessary and must bring it to a laptop to transmit the information. The carrier is marked as a High Value Target. Protect the HVT on the way to the upload location. The enemy needs only to kill the carrier to fulfill their objective, while your team must reach the objective and then defend it as the data is uploaded. Doing so successfully sends out a level-wide pulse that reveals information about the other team.

### RESUPPLY POINTS

With no way outside of a Rifleman's Ammo Box to restock on ammo short of looting weapons off fallen enemies, and no way to grab more deployables like grenades, Sensors, cameras, and UAVs without respawning, Resupply Points are an invaluable means of allowing the whole team to replenish their stores after protracted firefights. Just capturing the Resupply Point isn't enough, however. Denying the other team the spoils is a key way to leave them ill-equipped for the race to the next objective, so be ready for attempts by the opposing team to capture it for themselves. If you *do* manage to take an enemy's Resupply Point, stock up quickly before they can retaliate. Whatever team is in control should be making the most of their bottomless supplies by lobbing every deterrent possible while the Resupply Point is active.

### ASSASSINATION

High Value Targets aren't limited to Intel Sweep carriers. Occasionally, members of a team will be singled out as targets for assassination. HVTs must be protected (or killed) at all costs.

# ACCESS YOUR BONUS EGUIDE NOW!

The print book was reviewed and approved by Ubisoft, however we're aware that future game updates may result in some inaccuracies. To keep you up to date with these changes we're giving you FREE access to the Prima Official eGuide. The eGuide includes interactive maps for the Adversarial modes as well as Campaign Challenge videos and will update when there's a major change to the game, keeping you prepared for battle.

## 1.

Go to www.primagames.com. Register or Log in.

## 2.

After you are logged in, click your username located at the top right-hand corner of the home page.

## 3.

Click on the "INFO" tab.

## 4.

Scroll down the page until you see the "UNLOCK GUIDE WITH VOUCHER CODE" box. Enter the voucher code in the text field and click the "unlock guide" button. You will be redirected to your content now.

### PRIMAGAMES.COM

- Ask strategy questions and get real answers in the *Any Answers* section and in the Prima forums

- Get free tips, hints and FAQs on *Tom Clancy's Ghost Recon Future Soldier*

- Receive the latest news, screenshots and videos on your favorite games

www.primagames.com

Your eGuide offer expires May 22, 2013.

Follow us on Twitter

Like us on Facebook

## VOUCHER CODE

## 5a68ae33-5ef4-4bb7-97f0-fdf4b6ff2171

## DECOY

For this, teams are tasked with attacking or defending a trio of objectives. Decoy puts a new spin on the familiar bomb-planting modes seen in other competitive online games by randomizing a "true" objective. If successfully hacked, the "true" objective will reveal a final bomb plant location for the attacking team. Neither team knows which of the three main objectives holds the key information, making strategy a key part of picking targets.

### ATTACKERS

The team seeking to capture the objectives has an interesting dilemma: Since neither team knows which of the objectives will reveal the final bomb site, is it better to divide and conquer, seeking to spread the defense's resources as thinly as possible, or is a unified rush from one target to the next more warranted? It only takes finding the right objective, but that could be the first or the last. Deception here can be as important as outright firepower; popping a smoke grenade at one objective while chasing another, using guerrilla-style hit-and-runs to divert attention as well as full-on rushes are all equally viable strategies. The key is understanding how the other team will react to each.

### // CAUTION

#### THE CONSEQUENCE OF CHOICE

*While the attacking team in Decoy has the advantage of being able to capture objectives in any order, there is a price to choosing the wrong objective: a Sensor pulse will wash through the level, revealing the position of the entire team. Although this effect dissipates fairly quickly, it's valuable intel for the defending team, showing them where their foes are moving—that is, to which of the remaining objectives. Savvy attackers might be able to use this against them, however, with a fake toward one objective until the "DETECTED" message fades, then a redirected move toward another.*

### DEFENDERS

Defenders have the most to lose during their rounds, as they must hold all three positions as long as possible to drain the clock. Careful use of triggered explosives, cameras, Sensors, and more can help provide valuable intel that can then be shared with the entire team. Be wary of decoys and hit-and-run tactics. Often it can be wise to employ a few "floater" squad members to run to the nearest objective under siege. Communication is absolutely crucial to holding back the enemy for the full round.

## SABOTEUR

If Decoy represents a new take on the familiar, Saboteur is the old standby. Two teams race to pick up a bomb and plant it in the enemy's designated space. Expect plenty of seesaw battles here. And woe be unto any foolish player thinking they can just grab the bomb and run it in. Team tactics are incredibly important, since neither side has an advantage and the bomb placement areas are usually equidistant from the central bomb location. Working as a tactical unit is paramount, but so, too, is putting effects like suppression from LMGs for covering fire and real-time observational feedback from cameras and Scope Detectors to good use. The shared intel between squads will make or break any attempts to move the bomb, so learn the level layouts well before attempting to strike.

That intel is doubly important once the bomb has been picked up, as it disappears from view for the opposing team. Only by collecting intel on the bomb carrier (or forcing him to drop his package) can your team keep track of the bomb's location. If discovered as a carrier, beware: you have just become an objective on the enemy team's HUD.

## SIEGE

One of the best time-tested modes available, Siege challenges defenders to protect a key capture point, while attackers must break through the enemy defenses and capture the objective. This has one important difference from any other modes: You get one spawn, and one spawn only. If you go down, your team is left without you. Defenders are given a slight advantage; they spawn a few seconds earlier near the objective to set up for the incoming attack wave, which makes high-ground, pre-planted devices and coordination core tenets. Attackers, on the other hand, have the challenge of not only infiltrating the capture point from a random location, but also staying alive long enough to capture the objective itself.

# BATTLEFIELD EFFECTS

## CONFIDENCE

Just as the name implies, confidence is a measure of your team's ability to complete an objective. By sticking close together, capturing that objective becomes progressively quicker, the more teammates that are nearby. For every additional teammate in range, a pip will be added to the objective meter, helping to fill it more quickly. Moving as a group and making concerted pushes toward objectives isn't just sound defensive strategy, it's literally beneficial to the overall objective.

## DATA HACKING

Not every takedown has to be a lethal kill. Using less-than-lethal attacks like the Stun Pistol or Stun Mines make for incapacitation rather than outright death, and that means you can jack into the enemy network by "capturing" an incapacitated enemy and mine data on where other players are. Be forewarned, however, that the process isn't instantaneous, and you're open to getting killed while hacking. Still, the benefits of being able to see the other team through walls without the need for Sensors, UAVs or cameras can be momentum-shifting.

## COORDINATION

Even vets get a little turned around now and again, but both they and rookies have the same tool at their disposal: the Coordination System. Pulling up the Coordination Dial or Tac Map and selecting an objective, teammate, ammo supply, or inteled enemy from the list of available options draws a line in the level itself, showing the most direct route to that location. Make extensive use of Coordination when exploring a map for the first time to learn the shortest route to that objective, then exploit that intel by placing explosives or cameras along the most traveled routes in tighter areas for maximum effect. Generally speaking, if an object is marked by one player, others on the team can use the Coordination System to navigate to that object, so even silent players can communicate with their team.

## SHARED VISION

Thanks to advanced information networks, what one of your squad sees, you all see, marking enemies on your HUD and broadcasting their position in the world whenever they're targeted. Although this information can be turned against you with data hacking, it's far too valuable to waste. Planting cameras, lobbing Sensors, and using UAVs not only allows you mark targets or track incoming threats, but also shares the intel with your team. Use this to your advantage in modes like Saboteur by serving as lookout without engaging the enemy so that your entire team can see the bomb carrier and prepare an intercept.

## DETECTION

Thanks to the laws of cause and effect, the same systems that allow someone to peek through walls also emit a signature that often lets the person being seen *know* it's happening. If the enemy has intel on you, your screen will flash with the word "Detected" indicating that your position has been compromised. In addition the equipment name and type (heat or X-Ray) will appear above your minimap, giving valuable information to counter the enemies' intelligence.

# THE COMBATANTS

Divided into three distinct classes, the combatants on either the Ghost or Bodark teams are not necessarily carbon copies of each other. On the contrary, they have their own weapons, unlock progression, XP levels, and abilities, allowing for full customization of not just a particular style of play per class, but also per round. Learning when you'll be attacking or defending is key to choosing how you upgrade your characters, and while we won't tell you *how* to upgrade, we'll certainly tell you what *types* are available for every class on every side. At certain points along the upgrade path, you'll be forced to make a choice between two equally tempting options. Don't make those choices lightly; the only way to undo an upgrade choice is to use a Respec Token, which everyone gets at Level 1 and again at Level 50, and can only be used once. Reaching Level 50 with that team's class will also unlock an additional class-specific character customization slot, allowing you to level up again and choose another set of options.

## BE LIKE WATER

One of the most interesting things about *Ghost Recon Future Soldier*'s Adversarial multiplayer is just how variable each and every match is. Every mode requires a different strategy and squad makeup, and one game will almost never go the same as the next. As a result, being able to quickly adjust to the situation is just as important as the upgrade progression. In the pages to come, you'll find each of the maps dissected and laid out, as well as tips straight from the testers who have spent hundreds of hours in direct competition. Take their advice to heart and use this information well, for no asset is more valuable when going head-to-head with other living players than intelligence.

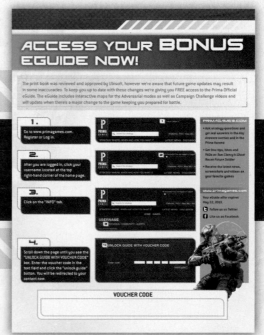

# EQUIPMENT

## UNIVERSAL – ALL CLASSES

### EMP GRENADE

The EMP is an invaluable tool for dealing with emplacements like Turrets, Sensors, and UAVs. Any hostiles that are hit by an EMP will lose the use of any of their electronically-aided equipment, meaning their heads-up display, mini-map, intel, threat indicators and targeting reticule.

### CAMERA SENSOR

Cameras are one of the most valuable items in any soldier's arsenal, allowing for 360 degree views of the nearby area, tracking threats and exposing them for the entire team. Cameras do have one problem, however: their all-seeing eye is limited to heat-based detection, meaning optical camouflage can mask an approach. Unlike other deployables, cameras are not one-time-use items; they can be retrieved and re-deployed as needed unless destroyed.

### MEDICAL KIT

Though any soldier can heal a squadmate that is bleeding out, they can do so much faster with a Med Kit. In addition, the Med Kit will raise your downed squadmate with greater health. Better still, those carrying a Medical Kit can revive themselves if they're caught bleeding out, turning a potentially fatal injury into nothing more than a scratch and a chance to seek revenge.

### ARMOR PIERCING AMMO

The Rifleman's Interceptor Armor gives him a noticeable advantage when going up against non-armored classes. Equipping Armor Piercing rounds helps even those odds, adding more effectiveness to every shot thrown toward a Rifleman.

## SCOUT–SPECIFIC EQUIPMENT

### OPTICAL CAMO (PASSIVE)

So long as a Scout has stopped moving for a few seconds, his Optical Camouflage will kick in, making him far less visible not just to the naked eye, but to all thermal detection equipment (UAV, Camera Sensor, Sentry Turret, OTR Scanner, and NVT Scope). This makes Scouts perfect eyes-on infiltrators, allowing them to hide in plain sight. Just remember, the second you move as a Scout, the effect is broken, and it takes a few more seconds of inactivity to restore the cloak.

### CLAYMORE

Point a Claymore in the direction of an approaching enemy and get ready for some serious fireworks. Just as effective as a kind of early warning system as they are an explosive deterrent, Claymores are often noticed at the last second—far too late for a hostile to react in time to escape the blast.

### STUN MINE

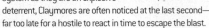

Like the Claymore, a Stun Mine can only trigger in one direction, but the disabling effect can also hit multiple targets. This is one of the only ways short of using a Stun Gun to take out enemies that can then be Data Hacked to reveal the opposing team's position, and the element of surprise means placing a Stun Mine around corners can be a great way to scoop up intel without risking a firefight.

### NVT SCOPE

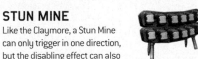

The single greatest advantage of the NVT Scope is its ability to highlight enemies in a thermal view when peering through the optics, though it also adds a modicum of magnification for taking down long-range targets as well.

### EXACTO ROUNDS

You aren't a Future Solider without gaining access to some seriously cutting-edge tech. Case in point: EXACTO Rounds, which have the ability to lock onto enemies and actually adjust their trajectory mid-flight. You won't be firing around blind corners or anything, but an enemy on the run is no longer a target that will escape just because you were only able to shoot near them. Also if your team has intel on the enemy, you can pre-lock onto them through obstacles. When the targeted enemy enters a clear line of sight, you're immediately ready to fire.

### RAUFOSS ROUNDS

Being a sniper already has its advantages, but adding RAUFOSS Rounds ups a sniper's lethality even more by making each and every shot explosive in addition to packing the normal long-range punch.

### AUGMENTED CAMO

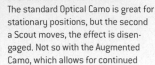

The standard Optical Camo is great for stationary positions, but the second a Scout moves, the effect is disengaged. Not so with the Augmented Camo, which allows for continued cloaking even while moving at a controlled speed. This is a great way to slip by all thermal detection equipment (UAV, Camera Sensor, Sentry Turret, OTR Scanner and NVT Scope). Note that firing, running and rushing will still break the effect.

### OTR SCANNER

If Intel is the most valuable asset on the battlefield, the OTR Scanner allows for collection and relay of that intel just by observing enemies caught while looking through this side-rail attachment. Note that one must be in a scoped view to actually collect the data, but the limited field of view is more than made up for by the ability to relay any enemy positions to the rest of your squad.

### FLASHBANG GRENADE

Anyone caught in the blast radius of a Flashbang is rendered completely blind for many seconds. This makes the Scout-only deployable a great means for breaching into a new area or confusing an attacking squad, opening them up to fire from your squadmates before they ever have a chance to return fire or find cover.

### DECOY GRENADE

A soldier's HUD delivers tons of tactical data in real time, but it can be fooled. That's precisely what a Decoy Grenade does, spamming an enemy's display with false data, indicating incoming fire from multiple angles and creating the illusion of an intense firefight on their mini-map. Even an enemy's ears are fooled, as the Decoy also confuses with the sounds of scattered gunfire wherever it's been thrown.

# ENGINEER-SPECIFIC EQUIPMENT

## SCOPE DETECTOR (PASSIVE)
Engineers' ability to gather intel isn't just delivered by way of equipment that must be used, they have the ability to detect when an enemy has scoped in and from what direction. It's not a laser-precise indicator, but no other class has the split-second advantage of knowing incoming fire is about to happen before it actually happens.

## INTEL SENSOR
The Engineer is the only class that gains access to Sensors which create a complete bubble of X-Ray-based observation, allowing detection of enemies as they approach. Sensors are absolutely invaluable to providing data on objectives and areas that may be hotly contested, and should be used whenever entering a hot zone for the first time.

## SMOKE GRENADE
You can't hit what you can't see, and the single best means of obscuring basic vision on the battlefield is with smoke. Thick plumes render anyone or anything inside the field near invisible, with only certain scopes that allow for alternate vision modes to peer through the haze. Smoke grenades work equally well on offense or defense, helping to create cover for advancing attackers or hiding the location of defenders.

## SLUGS
This magnum shotgun round fires a single projectile which increases range over standard buckshot but decreases control.

## UAV
These unmanned aerial vehicles are a great means of peering down onto the battlefield to gather intel without actually needing to be constantly controlled. Park a UAV near an objective with a clear line of sight and any moving, non-cloaked enemies will instantly be painted for your squad to see. An Engineer that knows a level's layout has the ability to detect incoming threats from almost any angle.

## SENTRY TURRET
By dropping a Turret, Engineers can single-handedly control and lightly defend an area until reinforcements arrive. Turrets placed in a room's corner, or around a blind turn have an even greater chance of unloading on enemies before they can be disabled with an EMP. They also serve as a warning system, indicating when enemies are drawing near from a direction the Turret is facing and will engage UAVs as well as human targets.

## JAMMER
Engineers aren't just gifted at gathering intel, they're equally capable of masking it. When a Jammer is deployed, any allies inside the protective bubble are completely shielded from intel gathering equipment. Useful for not only infiltration, but defense, the Jammer effectively reduces a hostile's ability to acquire a target. In addition, the Jammer will interrupt an enemy's HUD when they're within the bubble.

## FIELD COMPUTER
While the Confidence System is the best way to cut down on the time it takes to capture an objective or data hack, the Field Computer can effectively take the place of a teammate by adding an extra pip to a filling objective meter. It's no exaggeration to say that a Field Computer has the potential to completely change momentum in just a few seconds.

## DRAGON'S BREATH
If stunning isn't your thing, there's always the intense heat of Dragon's Breath rounds, which burp fire in a wide cone of effect. Any shots that happen to tag a hostile will continue to damage them, burning for a few seconds after the initial impact. As with all incendiary effects, if you find yourself on fire, go prone and roll by moving left or right to put out the flames.

## UCAV
Quite possibly the most potent deployable in an Engineer's arsenal, the UCAV is a UAV packing the ability to fire fairly weak explosives at targets. This makes them a fantastic harassment tool, and should an enemy be slow to react, the UCAV is more than capable of taking them out with a few shots. The potential to sneak in crippling and disorienting shots makes this far more than a simple UAV; it can both gather intel and annoy in equal measure.

# RIFLEMAN-SPECIFIC EQUIPMENT

## INTERCEPTOR ARMOR (PASSIVE)
The always available additional armor that Riflemen carry means they can take more hits and dish it right back out with high rate-of-fire weapons like Assault Rifles and LMGs. Their Interceptor Armor is standard no matter the level, making Riflemen great at leading a charge into an objective and deadly for other classes trying to win in a one-on-one shootout.

## FRAG GRENADE
The only ones capable of lobbing high explosive firepower, a Rifleman's frags are, hands-down, one of the most effective deterrents available when trying to quickly stop a hostile from capturing an objective. A relatively short fuse means there's often little to no time to avoid an incoming frag, and when coupled with the blindness of a Smoke or EMP grenade, they're even more effective.

## UB STUN GUN
By attaching the Stun Gun not as a secondary weapon, but an underbarrel option for Rifles, a Rifleman gains the ability to administer less-than-lethal attacks without sacrificing the secondary firearm. A stunned enemy is vulnerable to being Data Hacked, turning their team's own shared intel into a liability.

## AMMO BOX
Short of a Resupply Drop objective or looting an enemy's weapon off their dead body, there's no way to stock up without respawning. No way, that is, except for an Ammo Box, which lets teammates load up on both ammo and grenades, and giving the Rifleman experience for their assistance to boot.

## INCENDIARY AMMO
In much the same way Incendiary Grenades can create an area of deterrence, Incendiary Ammo is capable of creating small zones of denial, but they also continue to burn hostiles that have been struck with a round. Even if an enemy happens to make it around a corner, if they've been hit with enough shots and don't have time to go prone and roll, the damage of the ammo burning can finish them off.

## INCENDIARY GRENADE
The thermite payload of incendiary deployables creates an area of effect that is deadly to any hostiles attempting to pass through. Best used in choke points to deny access to areas beyond, these grenades will set anyone foolish enough to get close ablaze, allowing for damage over time. The enemy might make it past a burning Incendiary Grenade, but they won't make it far before succumbing to the intense heat unless they can drop, drop, and roll quickly.

## 40MM SMOKE/ EMP/HEDP GRENADE LAUNCHER
By attaching a grenade specific underbarrel to the Rifleman's assault rifles, he's capable of launching covering smoke or debilitating disruptions much farther than a hand-thrown grenade. Not only that, but grenades shot from a launcher have an area effect, allowing EMPs to take down uavs without actually having to hit them directly.

## BACKSCATTER OPTIC
Though the Rifleman is often seen as a heavy weapons/defender class, he's the only one that gains access to the Backscatter scope, allowing for X-ray vision modes revealing both players and equipment through walls. A Scout that would normally be invisible to UAVs and thermal scopes is now lit up as if they were never cloaked to begin with.

TOM CLANCY'S
# GHOST RECON
FUTURE SOLDIER

## THE SCOUT  WEAPONS: SNIPER RIFLES, SUBMACHINE GUNS

Scouts represent a squad's eyes and ears. They are able to see long distances thanks to their sniper rifles and slip through defenses with Optical Camo. As the only class that can cloak, Scouts excel at seeing without *being* seen, and their cameras can be deployed and picked up again to create a disc of constant observation. The Optical Camo also hides all Heat signatures, making UAVs, night vision scopes, and Sensors blind to their presence.

## GHOST

### GHOST SCOUT—STARTING GEAR

| Appearance | Watch Cap V1 | | |
|---|---|---|---|
| Primary Weapons | M110 | MP7 | |
| Secondary Weapons | 45T | STUN GUN | |
| Grenades | FLASHBANG | EMP | |
| Equipment | CAMERA | | |

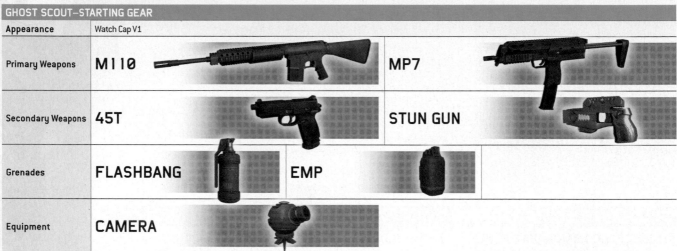

## // TACTICAL ANALYSIS

The Ghost Scout's Level 4 choice could largely influence the choices later on. Would you rather be a hang back and be a long-range shooter, using the distraction and cover of the early Decoy Grenades and Optical Camo to snipe from afar, or do you opt for a close-range fighter who can get an early peek through smoke? Use those early levels to feel out both options by changing your loadout every few rounds. If you like the long-range game, there are plenty of options to make you even more effective, and if you like playing closer to the action, the same is true. While you certainly *can* toe the line between both ranges, the end result will be a Scout that is arguably spread too thin. Instead, decide on one, sniper or scrapper, then commit to that decision, with the respective branching upgrades down the line.

Level 16 offers rounds that can auto-adjust mid-flight at the cost of actual damage (sniper) or an OTR Scanner that can relay spotted enemies to the rest of your squad, while Level 20 gives you yet another sniper rifle (this one has a built-in silencer) or SMG. By the time you've made it to Level 28, you should absolutely be locked in (save a Respec Token for level 25—if you still don't feel comfortable in that role, then switch choices), because the Augmented Camo option is best used at a distance. You can move while staying crouched, but that movement will almost certainly give you away to natural eyes (but not auto-turrets or UAVs, making it great for sneaking around to sniping spots), while Stun Mines are a fantastic way to take down enemies (even ones chasing if you're fast enough) and then hack them to give your team intel on the entire enemy team.

Level 32's MSR (sniper) or Vector (scrapper) weapon choices should be obvious; the former is a one-hit kill in most instances, while the latter has a blistering 1440 rounds per minute firing rate. Coupled with the Raufoss Ammo found in level 40, very few unarmored opponents could survive unless they get the jump on you, and even then it would be close. Then again, Claymores (also an option at 40) and ladders are one of the most potent combinations of triggers out there, making staking out a sniping spot that much safer. It's your choice, but make it early to yield the best results.

### PROGRESSION

| Level | Reward |
|---|---|
| 4 | NVT Scope OR Decoy Grenade |
| 6 | Watch Cap V2 |
| 8 | Med Kit |
| 12 | BLD-3 Flash Bulb |
| 14 | CW Mask V1 |
| 16 | EXACTO Rounds OR OTR Scanner |
| 20 | SRR OR P90 |
| 22 | CW Mask V2 |
| 24 | KARD |
| 28 | Stun Mine OR Augmented Camo |
| 30 | CBRN V1 |
| 32 | MSR OR Vector |
| 36 | Armor Piercing Ammo |
| 38 | CBRN V2 |
| 40 | Claymore OR RAUFOSS Rounds |
| 44 | Hood V1 |
| 50 | Hood V2 |

## BODARK

### BODARK SCOUT—STARTING GEAR

| Appearance | CWH-1 V1 | | |
|---|---|---|---|
| Primary Weapons | PSL-54C | PP2200 | |
| Secondary Weapons | GSH-18 | STUN GUN | |
| Grenades | FLASHBANG | EMP | |
| Equipment | CAMERA | | |

### PROGRESSION

| Level | Reward |
|---|---|
| 4 | NVT Scope OR Decoy Grenade |
| 6 | CWH-1 V2 |
| 8 | Med Kit |
| 12 | BLD-3 Flash Bulb |
| 14 | CWM-1 V1 |
| 16 | EXACTO Rounds OR OTR Scanner |
| 20 | VSS OR PP19 |
| 22 | CWM-1 V2 |
| 24 | OTS-33 |
| 28 | Stun Mine OR Augmented Camo |
| 30 | MTM-1 V1 |
| 32 | KSVK OR Skorpion |
| 36 | Armor Piercing Ammo |
| 38 | MTM-1 V2 |
| 40 | Claymore OR RAUFOSS Rounds |
| 44 | CWH-2 V1 |
| 50 | CWH-2 V2 |

### // TACTICAL ANALYSIS

Bodark Scouts should loosely follow the same general mantra as Ghosts, specifically "pick one discipline and stick to it," but without the same need for stringency, as there is one key difference: at Level 20, you're given the option to stick with an SMG with a slower rate of fire, but more rounds per clip (14 of them to be precise), or go with a higher powered SRR that can actually spray bullets. While neither the Ghost or Bodark option is explicitly a sniper rifle in the conventional sense, they both offer significant power over traditional SMGs—the only other option for a Scout—yet the Bodark option is fully automatic, meaning the stopping power is both more effective, *and* the magazine is larger to compensate. Simply put, in a Ghost vs. Bodark showdown of the exact same choices, the Bodark option has the range and the number of rounds to end things faster at distance.

This is the single largest distinction, but it's one that could pay dividends during the middle XP levels. In contrast, the Ghost SMG option at Level 20 gifts a higher rate of fire with the exact same stats as the Bodark SMG, but with a smaller clip. As a result, Bodark Scouts opting for the sniper route have an easy quick-fire option on both ends of the development spectrum that offer more shots per mag (though a slower fire rate in the SMG department) than Ghosts, meaning regardless of progression path, mid-progression Bodarks can leverage their equipment while staying CQC-ready in a way Ghosts can't—at least not in terms of sheer mag size.

Where this turns into a liability is at Level 32, where the Bodark SMG option is both plainly slower—just 900 rounds a minute vs. Ghosts' vastly superior 1440 with the same stats, *and* the Ghosts' clip holds eight more rounds. So Bodark tactics should shift toward using that Optical Camo (especially the Advanced version if you're a scrapper) to get the drop on Ghosts.

### // Ghosts vs. Bodark

It's clear that while most of the progression between the two teams is similar, the late-level unlocks give Ghosts a bit of an advantage. Use of disruptive tactics like Stun Mines can be the turning point, allowing Bodark squads access to Ghost networks to tip the balance, especially because Ghosts end up defending more often than not.

# THE ENGINEER | WEAPONS: SHOTGUNS, PERSONAL DEFENSE RIFLES

Neither as stealthy as Scouts, nor as heavily armed as Rifleman, Engineers are the information brokers of the battlefield. They can both hack and observe in equal measure, and have the unique ability to see when enemies have them scoped in, allowing them a split-second opportunity to avoid being gunned down during firefights. Yet they can bring intense firepower into close-range fights. Engineers are the all-seeing eye of the battlefield, able to capture enemy positions from on high with UAVs and Sensors, and hack objectives faster than any other class (with the proper item equipped). Their handiness with electronics means they can just as easily disrupt enemies. When leading a charge into an area, an Engineer is simultaneously the most diverse and specialized part of a squad.

## GHOST

### GHOST ENGINEER – STARTING GEAR

| Appearance | Tac Cap Opt A V1 | | | |
|---|---|---|---|---|
| Primary Weapons | GOBLIN | | M590A1 | |
| Secondary Weapons | 45T | | STUN GUN | |
| Grenades | SENSOR | | EMP | |
| Equipment | CAMERA | | | |

## // TACTICAL ANALYSIS

Unlike the Scout, the Engineer has a bit more leeway in how he want to progress through their unlocks. Level 4 gifts two different but equally useful options: a Field Computer, which allows for not only faster captures of objectives than any other class, effectively making the Engineer point man on any captures, but also lets him data hack faster than others, too. The UAV, on the other hand, is an invaluable tool for gaining intel passively. It relays enemy position data from on high without drawing too much attention. Better still, UAVs are incredibly mobile and can be left "in reserve" while fighting enemies. Park them and peer through them at any time. Both options have serious advantages, making the Engineer's decisions difficult—and they don't get easier as the levels go up.

Level 16 is a perfect example because if offers a means of creating cover in the form of Smoke Grenades, something not available to other classes (unless a Rifleman equips an underslung Smoke Grenade Launcher, which still must be unlocked). It's an extremely effective way to feint an approach from one angle while ambushing from another, or just a great way to create the illusion of activity where there is none. The Dragon's Breath ammo creates lasting damage over time with each hit, but it sacrifices both range and overall power, so it's best used with a weapon that can dispense multiple rounds quickly. Fittingly, Level 20 offers a choice between the Engineer's two weapon disciplines: the M1014 shotgun with fantastic stopping power, or the PDR-C that fires its 20 round mag at 780 rounds per minute. PDRs give you range flexibility, but shotguns, when properly aimed in close quarters, will nearly always win a head-to-head shoot-out. They're simply more powerful. If you opted to observe from afar with a UAV, PDRs are probably more your style. If you wanted to hack more quickly, however, shotguns are the ultimate repellent against would-be attackers and a great way to overwhelm hostiles trying to capture an objective.

Level 28's Jammer and Slugs further split the Engineer's play styles. The latter offers better range for shotgun blasts (at the cost of accuracy), while the former masks approaching allies from all surveillance equipment. Having more shotgun range is nice, but being able to deploy a bubble of electronic (though not visual) invisibility can be a huge asset. Remember that it's a deployable item, however, so you'll lose the use of a UAV or other equipment if you elect to use it. Level 32's shotgun and PDR options are formidable, gifting a shotty with full auto fire for applying a huge amount of damage, though the kick obviously means it's not exactly precise. The bullpup PDR means quick aiming and a great rate of fire for a 30 round magazine, so if you opted for longer range, definitely give this new toy a try.

When you finally reach Level 40, a unique opportunity presents itself: Do you opt for a Sentry turret that can automatically destroy UAVs (and non-cloaked enemies), or do you go with a UAV that can actually *attack*? The UCAV is startlingly good at destroying lone hostiles trying to capture an objective, and its nagging ability is fantastic. Opting for the UCAV effectively means you can spot targets *and* begin engaging them immediately. The vehicle's agility means shots can be rained down from above and cover is whatever building is nearby. The Sentry turret can be easily taken out with EMPs, which makes the UCAV an even more tempting option.

### PROGRESSION

| Level | Reward |
|---|---|
| 4 | UAV OR Field Computer |
| 6 | Tac Cap Opt A V2 |
| 8 | Med Kit |
| 12 | BLD-3 Flash Bulb |
| 14 | Tac Cap Opt B V1 |
| 16 | Smoke OR Dragon's Breath |
| 20 | M1014 OR PDR-C |
| 22 | Tac Cap Opt B V2 |
| 24 | KARD |
| 28 | Slugs OR Jammer |
| 30 | Tac Cap Opt C V1 |
| 32 | M12 OR L22A2 |
| 36 | Armor Piercing Ammo |
| 38 | Tac Cap Opt C V2 |
| 40 | Sentry Turret OR UCAV |
| 44 | Watch Cap V1 |
| 50 | Watch Cap V2 |

## BODARK

### BODARK ENGINEER—STARTING GEAR

| Appearance | GFC-1 V1 | | |
|---|---|---|---|
| Primary Weapons | AKS-74U | RMB-93 | |
| Secondary Weapons | GSH-18 | STUN GUN | |
| Grenades | SENSOR | EMP | |
| Equipment | CAMERA | | |

### PROGRESSION

| Level | Reward |
|---|---|
| 4 | UAV OR Field Computer |
| 6 | GFC-1 V2 |
| 8 | Med Kit |
| 12 | BLD-3 Flash Bulb |
| 14 | CWC-1 V1 |
| 16 | Smoke Grenade OR Dragon's Breath |
| 20 | MTs-255 OR SR-3M |
| 22 | CWC-1 V2 |
| 24 | OTS-33 |
| 28 | Slugs OR Jammer |
| 30 | GWC-1 V1 |
| 32 | Saiga 12 OR SA58 OSW |
| 36 | Armor Piercing Ammo |
| 38 | GWC-1 V2 |
| 40 | Sentry Turret OR UCAV |
| 44 | GFC-2 V1 |
| 50 | GFC-2 V2 |

### // TACTICAL ANALYSIS

While the Bodark Engineer doesn't diverge from his Ghost counterpart until Level 20, the split is interesting. The shotgun is equal to the Ghost version in all stats save for one: It has a three round deficit in capacity, leaving just five shots before a full reload is necessary. By contrast, the PDR sports the same stats as its Ghost doppelganger *and* has a higher rate of fire. The MTs-225 shotgun has amazing stopping power, but that's an awfully low number of shots before having to stop to reload. Fortunately, the OTS-33 sidearm offered to Bodark teams is a beast, spitting out 900 rounds a minute—that's right, it's a fully automatic *pistol*. The magazine is three rounds larger to compensate, too, making the Bodark sidearm choice a clear advantage—but only once you get to Level 24.

The Saiga 12 shotgun available at Level 32 helps tip the advantage back toward Team Bodark. It is a little more clunky, but fires 25 percent faster and with a tighter spray. The SA58 OSW PDR, on the other hand, is a quirky thing that offers a two-round burst shot instead of the 1,000+ round per minute stream of the Ghosts' counterpart. Like the shotgun, the Bodark version of the PDR is a little slower, but it's also got more punch with those double-tap bursts than the Ghosts' version. The burst fire will require changing up engagements a little (more aiming at a target first rather than unloading with a hail of gunfire), but it can be a surprisingly effective long-range option the shotguns could never be.

### // Ghosts vs. Bodark

In terms of raw power, the Bodark Engineer can outpace the Ghosts' version, but most of the weapons have a slight maneuverability deficit. This means overall movements are a bit more sluggish, but if they're able to get the drop on a lone Ghost, the battle will be over before a firefight has a chance to break out. The automatic sidearm in particular is a great tool for CQC, and shouldn't be forgotten when creating late-level loadouts.

# THE RIFLEMAN — WEAPONS: LMGS AND ASSAULT RIFLES

Because he's the source of a squad's heavy firepower, the impact of a Rifleman cannot be ignored. The only unit capable of wielding an LMG and its devastating suppression effect, Riflemen are tasked with providing covering fire, keeping enemies pinned to allow flanking by other squad members, or using underbarrel attachments on their ARs to lob grenades or reveal enemies (even through thin walls) that would be otherwise invisible to Heat-detecting equipment. Riflemen don't just dish out the heat, they can take more of it, too, thanks to their increased armor over other classes.

## GHOST

### GHOST RIFLEMAN—STARTING GEAR

| Appearance | MICH 2015 V1 | | |
|---|---|---|---|
| Primary Weapons | ACR | MK48 | |
| Secondary Weapons | 45T | STUN GUN | |
| Grenades | FRAG | EMP | |
| Equipment | CAMERA | | |

## // TACTICAL ANALYSIS

A difficult choice should be made early on with the Ghost Rifleman: LMGs or assault rifles? LMGs are essential to suppressing enemies, and their effectiveness is increased even more when a Bipod attachment is added to stabilize while prone or using low cover, but the Assault Rifle's ability to use underbarrel attachments like grenade launchers or the incredibly useful stun gun makes it formidable as well. The ability to propel grenades (including Frags, which only the Rifleman gets) long distances with an AR means both explosives (or debilitating effects like EMPs) and normal firepower is always at the Rifleman's fingertips. Conversely, opting for an AR over an LMG means no suppression effect, which is a key component in securing and holding objectives.

Unlocked at Level 4, the underbarrel Stun Gun can be an incredibly effective intel-gathering option. The alternative, a Smoke Grenade Launcher, does have its own advantages in that it can lob smoke over huge distances for both distraction and obstruction of views. Both are AR upgrades, however, so keep that in mind if you've chosen the LMG route. At level 16, things get more interesting. Another Grenade Launcher (this time an EMP version) is great for taking out equipment (it will auto-detonate near UAVs, for instance), but the Ammo Box can provide valuable resupplies of not just ammo, but also grenades anywhere in the field for the whole squad. If you've chosen the LMG route, the Ammo Box is doubly important because it allows full refills of the large-magazine suppression weapon.

AR users will fall in love with the 417 unlocked at Level 20. Although it's only a single-fire rifle, the stopping power works wonders even at range. The Stoner 96 is also a beast of an LMG, spraying at 960 rounds a minute with a big, 150 round clip. Accuracy or overwhelming firepower—your choice. Level 28 further cements the underbarrel options for AR users, as it offers a High-Explosive Dual Purpose Grenade Launcher or the lasting effect of an Incendiary Grenade. Again, the Rifleman is the only class that can use these types of grenades.

If you stuck with the LMG, the LSAT that is unlocked at Level 32 offers a tighter cone of fire, which should make up nicely for its lower rate of fire than the Stoner. On the AR side, the TAR-21 adds a three-round burst and ten more rounds per mag than the previous weapon. This comes in handy when it's coupled with the Incendiary Ammo that is unlocked at Level 40. But the Backscatter Optic (which can attach to both an LMG and AR) offers X-ray detection—something even Scouts can't hide from. Once again, the Rifleman is the only class that gains access to this scope, so make good use of it in situations where Heat detection isn't working.

### PROGRESSION

| Level | Reward |
|---|---|
| 4 | 40mm Smoke Launcher OR UB Stun Gun |
| 6 | MICH 2015 V2 |
| 8 | Med Kit |
| 12 | BLD-3 Flash Bulb |
| 14 | FAST-B Opt A V1 |
| 16 | Ammo Box OR 40mm EMP Launcher |
| 20 | 417 OR Stoner 96 |
| 22 | FAST-B Opt A V2 |
| 24 | KARD |
| 28 | Incendiary Grenade OR 40mm HEDP Launcher |
| 30 | FAST-B Opt B V1 |
| 32 | TAR-21 OR LSAT |
| 36 | Armor Piercing Ammo |
| 38 | FAST-B Opt B V2 |
| 40 | Incendiary Ammo OR Backscatter Optic |
| 44 | IWH-2014 V1 |
| 50 | IWH-2014 V2 |

## BODARK

### BODARK RIFLEMAN—STARTING GEAR

| Appearance | GPH-3A V1 | | | |
|---|---|---|---|---|
| Primary Weapons | **AK-200** | | **PKP** | |
| Secondary Weapons | **GSH-18** | | **STUN GUN** | |
| Grenades | **FRAG** | | **EMP** | |
| Equipment | **CAMERA** | | | |

### PROGRESSION

| Level | Reward |
|---|---|
| 4 | 40mm Smoke Launcher OR UB Stun Gun |
| 6 | GPH-3A V2 |
| 8 | Med Kit |
| 12 | BLD-3 Flash Bulb |
| 14 | GPH-1A V1 |
| 16 | Ammo Box OR 40mm EMP Launcher |
| 20 | AN-94 OR Type 95 |
| 22 | GPH-1A V2 |
| 24 | OTS-33 |
| 28 | Incendiary Grenade OR 40mm HEDP Launcher |
| 30 | GPH-2A V1 |
| 32 | A-91 OR Ultimax Mk.5 |
| 36 | Armor Piercing Ammo |
| 38 | GPH-2A V2 |
| 40 | Incendiary Ammo OR Backscatter Optic |
| 44 | GPH-3B V1 |
| 50 | GPH-3B V2 |

## // TACTICAL ANALYSIS

The Bodark Rifleman's weaponry differences offer an interesting twist on more than just base stats. In contrast to the Ghosts' AR option, the AN-94 unlocked at Level 20 offers a two-round burst and ten more rounds per mag, while the LMG is seriously limited. With almost half the firing rate and only 80 rounds per magazine, the Bodark Type 95 LMG is no match in raw output for what the Ghosts have, but its bullpup design means it's quite a bit more maneuverable to offset the lack of spraying power. Not surprisingly, then, the Level 32 differences even things out a little more. Though the Ultimax Mk.5 LMG still doesn't have the firing rate to match the Ghosts' option, like the other Bodark weapon options, it's more maneuverable and is more in line with the Ghost LMG for this level, with a bigger mag (150 rounds) and a solid 540 RPM firing rate to the Ghosts' 660. The A-91 Assault Rifle is even more formidable, ratcheting up to 858 rounds a minute (the Ghosts' AR is a three-round burst) and offering more power without losing that maneuverability.

## // Ghosts vs. Bodark

You've seen it mentioned more than once, but what the Bodark team lacks in sheer firing speed or capacity, they make up for across all their weapons in maneuverability. Of course, maneuverability can be key when acquiring targets and shooting from the hip. Still, when properly set up, Ghosts have a distinct advantage with their weapons' base stats. As a result, LMG players may have an easier time on Ghosts, while the augmented abilities and better chance for intel hacking while using an Assault Rifle can help Bodark players be more agile.

# PIPELINE

## SITUATION REPORT

Precious natural resources are precious for a reason: they're limited. Eventually, all oil fields run dry, and when they do, the only option left is to move on to more plentiful fields. The locals here did just that, leaving behind a sand-blasted hovel nestled along a pipeline that slices right through the middle of what used to be a town. Far from abandoned, the mix of crumbling masonry and slapdash tin walls ruin any long lines of sight in this hot spot. That makes this an almost exclusively close-quarters engagement, with rare moments of medium-range fire. Gear up accordingly.

# SPAWN POINTS (CONFLICT, DECOY, AND SABOTEUR)

**SHARE AND SHARE ALIKE**

*Though their actual gameplay is fairly different, most of the competitive multiplayer modes in Ghost Recon: Future Soldier share common ground, most notably spawn locations for each team. Use the experience in one mode to help guide how you exit from the spawn areas in subsequent modes, paying attention to the various locations of objectives or hazards. Forget the basics and you're going to be seeing a lot of those spawn points.*

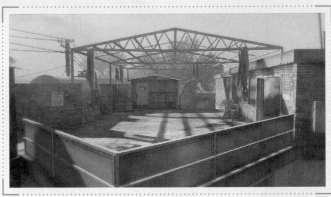

Ghosts spawn outside what's left of the town's Hotel, with a ramp downward and out into the main combat zone, which is littered with low cover, or a long tunnel that leads to either a set of stairs down through a door or a limited vantage from which to snipe. In Conflict, Decoy, and Saboteur modes, this area is completely protected, but in Siege, it's left open to either team. Keep this in mind when moving back toward the spawn point, and use the other side of the wall to flank enemies that might snipe from the relative comfort of the hallway. Once flanked, anyone still foolish enough to be caught in the hall will likely get gunned down with ease; there's no cover inside the long, narrow stretch, and only one way out if one end is covered.

The Bodark team begins in and around the Maintenance area for the nearby bridge, which offers small bits of low cover, plus a much more protected side route that parallels the bridge and exits out into plenty of cover to the left. Be wary of the Maintenance building's multiple levels; during Siege matches, they offer multiple routes of entry *and* elevations to cover. Unlike the hallway on the Ghosts' side, there's bits of cover along the approach from the bridge, which also offers a vantage point to fire down on enemies trying to sneak along the side path.

# POINTS OF INTEREST

## ELEVATED POSITIONS

Pipeline's raised platforms aren't exactly plentiful, but they can be deadly. A trio of them face inward toward the center pipeline area that forms the basis of both the bomb location in Saboteur and the central capture point being defended in Siege. Control of the center forces opposing teams to skirt the edges of the map, so expect plenty of tug-of-war fights over these key spots.

Of the three elevated platforms, only this Garage overlooking the center of the camp offers multiple routes of entry that are entirely ramp-based. While it's a solid spot for brief sniping, the fact that there are no less than three separate entrances means the position should only be held by an entire squad, which allows teammates to cover all the ramps leading up to the rooftop, where a sniper can take out enemies trying to sweep through the middle of the map.

This upper area offers limited angles to fire down into the center of the action, and has at least one ladder that can slow down approaching attackers. The other end, however, is a long, sloping ramp with decent amounts of cover on the approach so multiple attackers can approach at once. Use this to your advantage while attacking and keep it in mind if you're defending the position.

Like the elevated position tucked into the corner of the map, the Admin building will be a source of more than a few firefights thanks to its prominence as a very common hot spot for objectives in Conflict mode. The long, narrow walkway is bookended on one end by a ramp that can allow sneak attacks and, at the other end closer to the objective, a ladder with very little cover. Use this to your advantage when assaulting: Use the ramp area's limited cover to take out enemies at the far end, or placing claymores near the ladders to catch those trying to sneak up from ground level. Like the other elevated positions, most of the cover-based sight lines are focused on the center of the map.

**THE PATH MOST TRAVELED**

*Use claymores where there's less chance of them being detected and skirted. Since claymores only trigger in one direction, it's important to face them toward the most logical routes enemies will take. This means that ladders in particular are a great place to catch an enemy by surprise.*

## CONFLICT

1 HOTSPOT

☰ DEPLOY

🛡 DEFEND

⚙ CONTROL/INTEL

💥 DEMOLITION

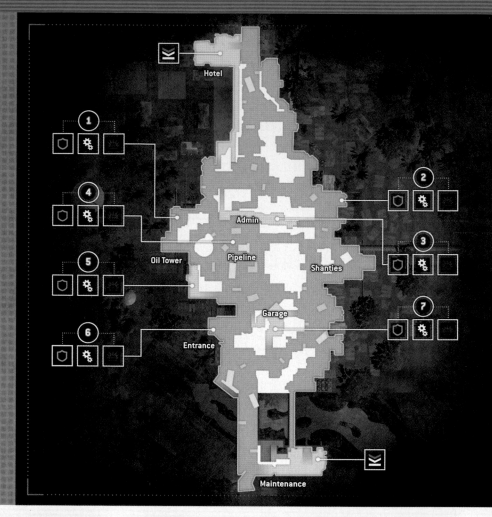

Hotel

Admin

Oil Tower

Pipeline

Shanties

Garage

Entrance

Maintenance

1 One of the most dangerous hot spots on the map, this objective looks out into the large central Pipeline area and can be easily covered by way of the nearby L-shaped set of walls opposite a large gas tank. Running directly toward the objective through the open areas of the map is foolhardy, as there's simply too many sight lines into the courtyard area. When capturing, be sure to cover the rear; enemies in the long elevated walkway can make their way down the ramp and sweep around the corner to take out a would-be capturing enemy.

2 Although it looks relatively unprotected, the sight lines on those trying to capture or destroy an objective here mean attacks will likely come from the cover of the nearby sandbags. The small stitch of corrugated metal can provide some low cover for defenders, but this is not an objective that should be attempted alone by either team.

(3) For the very same reasons that make this spot such a dangerous sniping spot, it also can mean death for those rushing to capture the objective. The corridor-like nature of the platform offers only one means of escape if opposing forces attempt a pincer attack by coming up the ramp and climbing the latter at the other end: a sprint toward the ladder in the middle. Remember, though, that jumping down can immobilize you for a few seconds—often the difference between a clean getaway and adding to the enemy's kill count.

(6) Like the objective on the opposite side of the map, this one is largely unprotected and has clear lines of sight from the elevated walkway opposite and the more open central part of the map. Attempt a capture only as a unit or suffer the consequences.

(4) With all elevated positions looking in at this spot, making a run without a coordinated offense amounts to suicide unless opposing squads are being distracted. Avoid approaching from the open area near the truck if possible and slip in from the sides or after scouting the nearby elevated areas. Defenders need only line up their shots or throw a well-timed grenade.

(7) Although there is limited cover to mount a counteroffensive, the sheer number of routes up to this platform can make surprise attacks inevitable. If you are stuck under heavy fire with no way out, running off the edge facing toward the central part of the map is an option, but probably the only way this objective will be taken or held is by coordinating with teammates.

## // CAUTION

The print book was reviewed and approved by Ubisoft, however we're aware that future game updates may result in some inaccuracies. To keep you up to date with these changes please refer to the insert card giving you FREE access to the Prima Official eGuide. The eGuide includes interactive maps for the Adversarial modes as well as Campaign Challenge videos and will update when there's a major change to the game, keeping you prepared for battle.

(5) This upper area has two key advantages for those already occupying it: the ladder can slow down approaches and the cover looking out over the ramp leading in from the other side makes assaults difficult.

# DECOY

 **OBJECTIVE**

**DEMOLITION**

**A** Objective A has only two routes of entry, which can make a pincer attack by invading forces a hugely effective technique. Likewise, when defending or capturing the area, be sure to position support with eyes on both routes of entry. There's precious little time to react to enemies that swoop in.

**B** Once again, the upper walkway where Objective B rests is fraught with multiple entry routes and nothing in the way of cover if you are trying to capture. Those repelling a capture should approach from the ramp to avoid surprise claymores at the top of the stairs and eagle-eyed sharpshooters firing from ground level near the large tower connected to the oil pipeline. Get in and out as fast as possible, as there's little room to escape if things go south.

**C** Objective C is closest to the attackers' spawn point in Maintenance, so it's likely to be a first strike for beginning players. Use this to your advantage: Take cover on the opposite side while waiting for the enemy to try to capture the objective. Scoot around the truck bed to take them out quickly, then head back to the relative safety until your cover is blown. Likewise, attacking players should be wary of those laying in wait, though the short distance to the objective may allow them to get there first.

When the "proper" objective has been secured, the task quickly turns to bombing one of three locales. The first, the familiar, scarcely protected corner of the map with only a low bit of metallic cover is left wide open for attacks from the direction of the nearby sandbags. Those seeking to defend the position should approach from there to maximize sight lines.

Just past the sandbags is the other possible planting location, which is a bit more generous on cover. Although the two most obvious angles of attack are from the direction of the stairs leading down from the elevated platform and nearby alleyway or the sandbags near the other demo location, remember that the defenders' spawn point allows them to drop right in from the relative protection of the long hallway.

Past the slightly more protected second plant location is a third, far more deceptive area that faces back toward the Admin area and its narrow choke point. While it's easy to assume that most defenders attempting to stop bomb placement will come from this area or the second bomb plant location's direction, there's a far more dangerous route of entry: the staircase leading directly to the long hallway connected to the defenders' spawn point. The entire route to this third bomb plant location is completely protected, and Team Bodark can't move toward the staircase as it's the enemy spawn location. Be wary of shots raining down from above; this will likely be the toughest of the locations if it's not seized as quickly as possible.

# SABOTEUR

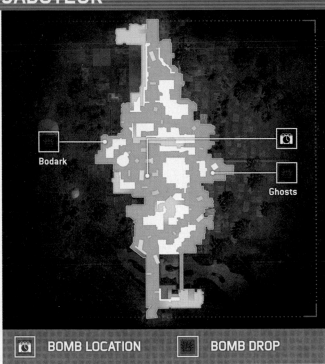

☐ Bodark

📷 (Bomb Location icon)

Ghosts

| 📷 BOMB LOCATION | 🎇 BOMB DROP |
|---|---|

# SIEGE

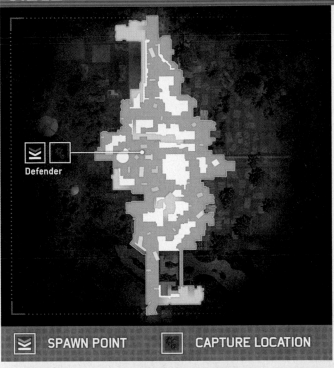

≽ ☐ Defender

| ≽ SPAWN POINT | 🎇 CAPTURE LOCATION |
|---|---|

The central location of the bomb near a dusty truck means it's sitting smack-dab in the middle of plenty of crossfire. Both elevated areas at either end of the map have clear sight lines and should be cleared out first, if possible. Even if you manage to make it to the bomb unscathed, there's little guarantee that a Rambo-style dash to plant it will go as smoothly.

It's tempting to make a beeline for the enemy demolition location, but there's a bottleneck when squeezing through that opens into two wide-open flanks. If you *must* head straight for the plant location, have a teammate pop smoke to cover your approach. (Remember, while carrying the bomb, you're limited to your secondary weapon.) Alternatively, you can have them do it from another location to lure the enemy away. Keep in mind that smoke works both ways; you won't be able to see out and they can't see in with normal weapons, but a enemy with the right scope can see right through the fog and mow you and your buddies down before you know where the gunfire is coming from.

Unlike the Ghosts' bomb planting location, both the approach and planting area for Team Bodark is fairly well protected from crossfire. Tuck into the corner of the bomb planting area to avoid sticking out too much, and remember to cover both routes in. Keep an eye out for grenades, too, as there's very little room to maneuver in here.

## // CAUTION

### HARDEST OF THE HARDCORE

*Unlike the other modes, Siege requires a very specific mindset going in. With only one life for the entire round, every firefight needs to be considered, and Pipeline's map design in particular makes the attackers' approaches toward the objective extremely harrowing. It's best to get to know the map well in other modes where there are respawns before jumping into the more tactical play found in Siege mode.*

Those defending the central capture point have just a scant few seconds to set up their defense before the attacking team approaches. Use the combination of nearby elevated positions and high cover to deal with those that would rush toward the objective blindly, but beware of sneak attacks from the many alternate routes up to those elevated positions. Remember, you get only one life in Siege mode, so be sure to make it count; stay in constant communication with other defenders to prevent being overwhelmed and, where possible, use the buddy system to cover flanking positions.

Avoid heading directly for the objective on ground level unless you have an overwhelming amount of force. More patient players will realize that they have the whole map to play with, and keeping in mind that there are no respawns can shift the momentum toward the attacking team if defenders can be dealt with one at a time. Scout out the elevated positions, and use guerilla hit-and-run moves; the defenders can't leave the objective unprotected for long, so avoid running through the middle of the map and stick to the sides, pulling back if needed to regroup around the one-time Bodark spawn near the bridge.

# MARKET

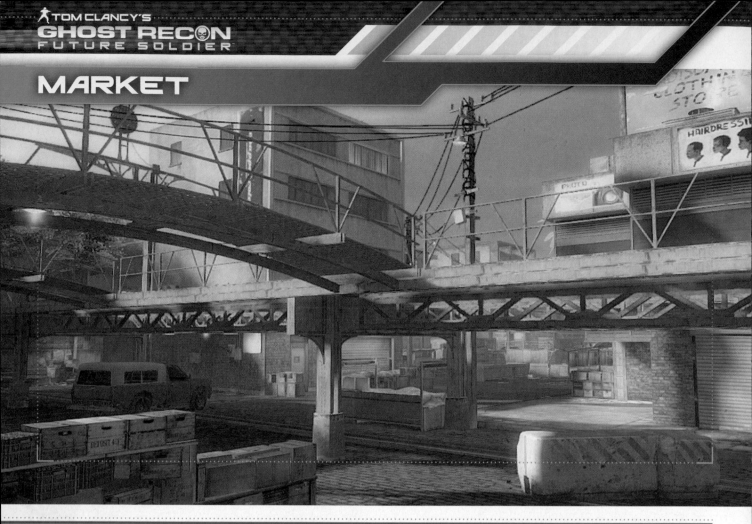

## SITUATION REPORT

Not long ago, this Market was filled with the din of shopkeepers hawking their wares, customers haggling for a deal, and lively conversation. Now, the only sounds one is likely to hear are sporadic bursts of gunfire, as the once-bustling Market is nothing more than a ghost town in a constant tug-of-war between opposing factions. Littered with alleyways and side routes, the main Market is a clear funnel for activity, but shoot-outs can happen just as easily while navigating the tight spaces surrounding it. The Market itself doesn't sport terribly long sight lines, thanks to plenty of cover, but the bus station is wide open for snipers, so stick to cover or avoid it altogether.

# SPAWN POINTS (CONFLICT, DECOY, AND SABOTEUR)

An elevated back alley dubbed Overlook serves as the Ghosts' area of deployment. Just a quick sprint to the elevated railway system stop, the Ghosts' spawn point is filled with clean right angles that are perfect for grabbing cover—a good thing considering one of the key Conflict objectives and a bomb planting location in Decoy are both situated in and around that station stop. A trio of entrances down into the main Market offer quick routes into the alleyway system on either side, which make covert approaches into the level simple and with cover along the way.

A covered garage serves as the Bodark source of deployment. They'll have to sprint out and past a vehicle-strewn parking lot before they can get to the Market itself, but they've also got better, direct access to some of the back alleyways that skirt the Market, as well as a more protected route up to the second-floor Apartments overlooking the Market.

# POINTS OF INTEREST

## MAIN MARKET

The central Market area is, well, a death trap. There's simply no other way of putting it. There there is plenty of cover and multiple opportunities for snipers, such as from the upper walkway Apartments overlooking the Market itself and the rooftop camping spots that are accessed by climbing a ladder near the Courtyard and simply jumping down off the upper walkway. Not surprisingly, then, most modes feature some form of an objective here, making it a hotbed of crossfire. The one upside to having so much cover is that lobbed explosives like grenades aren't quite as effective—as long as there's enough warning. Don't even think about attempting to take an objective here alone. Too many sight lines mean you're just asking for death if you try.

## SHOPS AND ALLEYWAYS

Running through the center of the map is foolhardy, which makes it fortunate that the level is skirted by a series of back alleys and shop fronts with rear exits. Both the Butcher Shop near the Bodark spawn and Medicine Shop closer to the Ghosts' home feed into a series of channels cutting through the buildings flanking the Market. Use these side routes to work your way through the map and ambush hostiles trying to secure objectives tucked into the corners of these side areas.

## APARTMENTS

One of the biggest areas of conflict will be the Apartments, both because of their proximity to the main Market area itself, and the strategic upper area that allows for longer sight lines out over the rest of the level. A Conflict objective at the top of the stairs means plenty of fighting in and around the upper walkway, but the stairwell itself shouldn't be discounted as a place to ambush and be ambushed. The tighter confines of the stairs make for a great place to toss explosives or plant mines in preparation for an assault.

# CONFLICT

- (1) **HOTSPOT**
- ⟱ **DEPLOY**
- 🛡 **DEFEND**
- ⚙ **CONTROL/INTEL**
- 💥 **DEMOLITION**

Bus Station · Parking Garage · Market Entrance · Back Alley · Butcher Shop · Courtyard · Market · Medicine Shop · Apartments · Train Station · Residential District · Overlook

(1) The clean right angles and tight confines of this alleyway make bouncing grenades off the walls a common practice, but the alley also has ample opportunity for easy corner cover and can be held relatively easily with a couple of supporting squadmates. Smoke and flashbangs can be incredibly helpful here to obscure or blind, so if you're capturing, make the most of the Confidence system to boost capture speed, and if you're defending, be on constant watch for incoming equipment. UAVs and Cameras can help alert those trying to capture an objective here to incoming enemies, too. So don't be afraid to make a sweep of the area and throw down some early warning systems before attempting the capture.

## TESTER TIP: CONTROL DENIED

Frag grenades are one of the quickest and most effective ways to disrupt a capture of an objective. Get in the habit of practicing a lob from multiple spots on a map (where a particular map will afford the chance, of course). A properly lobbed grenade can force someone capturing an objective to break it off and go for cover. Even if the Frag doesn't get them, they'll have to start the whole capture process over again, no matter how many of their buddies were there trying to help them capture it faster.

(2) With a direct route from the Bodark spawn point to the left and a stairway entrance on the right, this lofty perch can be a prime sniping spot until it actually activates as an objective. A Camera placed near the objective itself does a great job of warning of incoming threats from the Bodark spawn, but be cautious of taking cover with your back to the open Market. A scoped enemy can take you out before you'll ever get the chance to ambush an incoming threat.

(3) This little nook just outside the Medicine Shop's rear exit tends to be a heavily accessed area, not just because of the objectives spawning here, but because it's one of the main routes into the Market. Make sure to cover the alleyway exits, the shop itself and the wider area leading in from the Market. The ladder leading up to a raised platform can be a decent place to provide overwatch for a cloaked Scout, but anyone else will be a fairly easy target from the raised Apartments area, so don't stay up there too long.

(6) Tucked into the corner of an alleyway, the dumpster near this objective almost makes it seem somewhat protected, but there's ample room to get sandwiched by an EMP or Flashbang. Thankfully, this is one of the few objectives where attacks can really only come from two cardinal directions, so hit it quickly and with some backup to secure the location.

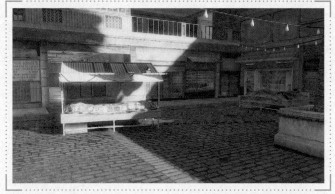

(4) Expect this area to seesaw more or less constantly when trying to capture or defend an objective here. As said before, the number of approaches, elevations, and routes of entry make covering every angle extremely difficult even for a full team. Grab cover where you can. (The fruit stand looking out toward the lower Apartment entrance works and the objective itself is a solid place to hide, but the flanks need to be watched.) Overwhelming firepower or defense is the key to taking and keeping this objective.

(7) Tucked in next to the stairs leading down from the train platform, this little magazine rack is rather horribly exposed from the direction of the Market. Scouts can try setting up overwatch from the smallish outcropping at the top of a nearby ladder, but the sight lines are ruined by the elevated train tracks. The key here is to try to tuck into the alcove and apply as much fire toward the Market and nearby alleyway as possible. Remember that if you're on team Bodark, this is the closest objective to the Ghost spawn location, so keep an eye out for hostiles dropping down from the Train Station.

// CAUTION

The print book was reviewed and approved by Ubisoft, however we're aware that future game updates may result in some inaccuracies. To keep you up to date with these changes please refer to the insert card giving you FREE access to the Prima Official eGuide. The eGuide includes interactive maps for the Adversarial modes as well as Campaign Challenge videos and will update when there's a major change to the game, keeping you prepared for battle.

(5) The Apartments are difficult mostly because they have a completely unprotected flank in the direction of the stairwell, but the fact that opposing forces can approach from either of the walkway directions certainly doesn't help either. Early warning intel-gathering items like UAVs and Cameras are vital to understanding where the enemy is coming from, so keep an eye out. If approaching, a bait-and-switch tactic of teasing an approach near the stairs while attacking from the upper walkway seems to work like a charm.

# DECOY

**A** OBJECTIVE

**✹** DEMOLITION

**A** The familiar locale of the Apartments makes for the first of three possible "real" objectives in Decoy. As always, the key is having awareness of which direction the enemy is approaching from. Sensors dropped below can warn of an approach from the stairs, while support trained on either side of the corner cover, looking out toward either route of entry from the walkway, can warn of incoming hostiles.

**B** Because it is flanked on either side by the elevated platforms accessible from the Apartments and Courtyard, there's plenty of danger in trying to capture this location. In fact, a well-placed sniper or even a prone Rifleman with an LMG can make it extremely annoying trying to capture this objective from the Courtyard raised platform. Move cautiously here, and begin capturing only once the area has been swept clear of hostiles

**C** While not subject to the same number of sight lines, the third possible objective is nonetheless a source of considerable danger. The doorway leading out from the Medicine Shop is a bit of a bottleneck, so expect enemies to try to peek out and take potshots while the objective is being taken. Tucking in near the benches to force them further out of the doorway can mean you get the drop on them before they can do the same to you. Keep an eye on the alleyway entrances, too, as they're a more likely route for enemies than directly from the Market itself.

**✹** Once the real objective has been captured, a trio of options for bomb planting are possible. The first is in the center of the Market, right near one of the hardest Conflict objectives. Planting here should begin only after most of the area has been swept clear to avoid your teammates being taken out by snipers or onlookers from the Apartments above.

Another familiar locale, tucked in next to a dumpster, serves as the second possible bomb plant location. Just as before, cover the two main routes of entry, and watch for things like EMP or flashbangs while planting.

The third locale is also the hardest by far to capture, thanks to its being smack-dab in the middle of the Train Station, which is connected directly to the defenders' spawn point. Those defenders can approach from either of the station's flanks near stairs, or they can slip down those stairs, climb up the ladder leading to the platform just below the plant location, and attack from the covered position there while trying to plant the bomb.. Expect a fairly steady flow of defenders pouring from their spawn point, as it's not a long trip back to the Train Station.

## SABOTEUR

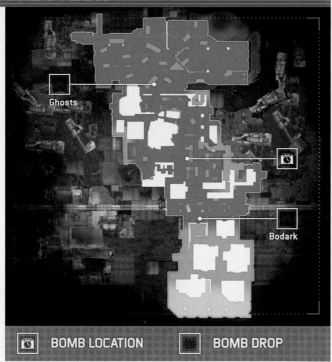

|  BOMB LOCATION |  BOMB DROP |

Placed smack-dab in the middle of the Market, the bomb here is vulnerable to a snatch and grab from quite a few angles, although the most likely angle is a dash out from the Courtyard area and back into the more claustrophobic confines of the alleyways. The single largest job of the support team is to protect the identity of the bomb carrier, so keep them out of sight unless making a move toward the plant location. Opting for a secondary weapon like the Stun Pistol can turn a potential ambush while running the bomb in into a chance to data hack the opposing team and see where they're waiting for you.

The abandoned parking lot that makes up the bomb plant location for the Ghosts is a sniper's paradise. Bodark team members can grab cover next to plenty of vehicles. A common ambush point is the long hallway that leads down from the raised walkway overlooking the Market. There's a smaller entrance to the left of the main one, but it's a bottleneck and isn't nearly as protected on the left as the bus near the plant location.

The Bodark bomb plant area is almost as bad, with the whole Market to their backs and three separate staircases leading down to where the bomb must be placed. There's also the ever-present Train Station, which can make approaches difficult. An approach from the direction of the alleyway leading to the Apartments might allow for proper cover, but no matter what, it's a long run through plenty of open ground to get to the bomb plant location.

## SIEGE

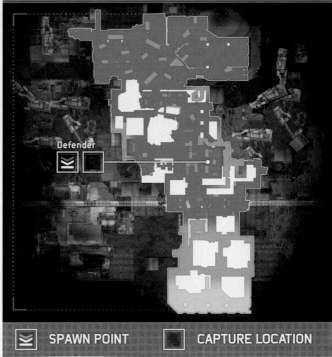

|  SPAWN POINT | CAPTURE LOCATION |

Well *of course* the Market would serve as the central capture and defend point. Given the ridiculous number of possible approaches, expect Siege matches to be incredibly tense. Defenders should grab high ground where possible and remember that attacks can come from any direction. Smart attackers will approach from odd angles in the hope of picking off defenders that are waiting for threats to approach from the usual forward positions. Try to head them off by covering the alleyways that would allow attackers to sneak around the Market itself. That means locking down the Apartments area as much as possible to deny access to the upper walkway and watching the side alley near the Medicine Shop.

### TESTER TIP: OBFUSCATION

One of the greatest combinations available to any Adversarial player is a thermal scope coupled with the use of smoke. Capable of peering through smoke to see threats inside, the scope works just as well as an *offensive* item as it does a defensive one. Popping smoke and then using it as a kind of blanket to avoid detection is the logical use, but throwing it into a crowd of hostiles being scoped with thermal and then taking them down while they can't see precisely where the hits are coming from can add confusion and chaos to a routine objective capture. Pop smoke often to make the most of your ability to see where others can't.

For the same reason defenders are trying to hard to keep the side areas locked down, attackers should try to distract and slip through into those areas. Use guerrilla tactics to bait defenders into focusing fire on an alleyway before making a smaller push up through the Apartments (or, if you prefer, swap the "true" objective). Defenders have nothing but time, so chances are unless they're rookies, they aren't going to feel the need to pursue if they've locked down all the routes of entry from the Train Station. Be patient here, since that one life is all you get in this round.

# OVERPASS

## SITUATION REPORT

Mother Nature has a way of turning something seemingly solid into rubble in seconds. Such was the case with this busy town along a major road, complete with overpass allowing for plenty of through traffic. Unfortunately, an earthquake brought that overpass down with impunity, cutting off travel and leaving the town without major access. Residents and commuters alike abandoned their cars where they stood, leaving strategic places of cover ready-made for pushing up into the various buildings skirting the road. Intel is especially valuable in Overpass because the area is small and filled with tight channels of activity, which allows the tracking of enemies through walls and across the small map. Snipers for either team have high points that look out over the entire expanse of the street.

## SPAWN POINTS (CONFLICT, DECOY, AND SABOTEUR)

Ghosts funnel into the area from a dry creek bed that offers plenty of protection from prying eyes. Shortly after leaving the creek bed, players find a pair of staircases leading up to a well-protected Pedestrian Bridge that serves as a sniping vantage point pointed toward the Bodark spawn point. Make note of the three main areas off the road: the Gas Station, Arcade and residential area, as all three are littered with capture locations that will be used in the battles to come.

What's left of the freeway Overpass marks the starting location for the Bodark forces. Because it offers a clearer line of sight out toward the road, the Bodarks can engage hostiles a bit more quickly than Ghosts right out of the gate, and their snipers have the freeway from which to take potshots at enemies trying to use the road to move up. The Arcade is a hotbed of activity, as is the route toward the Flea Market and the area that the Red House overlooks. Use the cars for cover if moving up, but be wary of enemy forces using the residential area to make sneak attacks.

## POINTS OF INTEREST

### CAMPERS' DELIGHT

High, cover-rich areas that bookend the street mean snipers will have plenty of room to practice without too much risk of retaliation (at least from anything other than counter-sniping). Their positions of overwatch can help light up enemies trying to make a move through the streets. And although the various cars and trucks that litter the roadway make for more than enough cover from sniper fire, only careful movement between bits of cover will save them from crack shots.

### TESTER TIP: THE COVER SWAP SHUFFLE

While performing a cover to cover swap, turning the camera while your player is rushing can save you time by aiming toward another cover point and immediately performing another cover to cover swap. Try to plan your routes so that you're spending as little time between cover points as possible when trying to make a push toward the end point. Sprinting around in the open is tantamount to begging for a free bullet to the noggin, especially on smaller maps like this one.

### RED HOUSE

The Red House has such an innocuous name, but it's home to three different areas rife with capture points. The two-tiered nature of the building and the fact that its windows overlook the street and parts of the alleyways mean it is a great place to dig in, and the right angles of the interior provide great corner cover spots from which to return fire. Learn quickly which of the two interior objectives is above and below so that you know which route to take to reach it. The upper objective will be on the right side of the building, while the lower one is in the middle. Many a rookie will head upstairs in an attempt to cut off an objective capture that's actually taking place down below and lose valuable seconds in the process.

### FLEA MARKET

The labyrinthine back alleyways that lead off the main road provide ample cover from which to repel advancing enemies. Whenever proceeding through this area, particularly when there's a nearby objective, keep an eye out for enemies that would try to ambush you. Use cover to cover movements to minimize exposure, and don't even think of charging right up the middle of the main road leading to and from the Bodark spawn point. It's far too open and enemies have plenty of time to set up their shots on you.

# CONFLICT

- ① HOTSPOT
- ⩔ DEPLOY
- 🛡 DEFEND
- ⚙ CONTROL/INTEL
- ▦ DEMOLITION

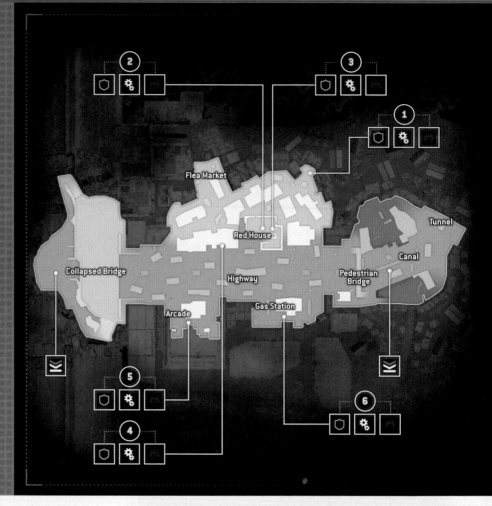

① Many an Intel Sensor or Sweep will be fought over here, so spread out your team when defending around the low bits of cover. There are no less than four routes to attack from when trying to take the position, so coordinate with your squad members to either attack en masse or break up the assault along multiple channels. Likewise, spreading your defense here can help identify threats, but moving to quickly repel them is just as important.

## TESTER TIP: COORDINATED ASSAULT

The Coordination System allows for easy waypoint markers and the ability to call out a simple objective seen on the TacMap while playing, but just pointing your crosshairs toward an alleyway or bit of cover and tapping the mark button as if you were highlighting an enemy can also indicate a point on the TacMap and in the level itself. Use this system often to help relay information to your teammates and coordinate movement from one objective to the next. It's also a great way to warn of potential flanking positions, but only one highlight can be shown at a time.

② The Red House's lower floor can be incredibly dangerous, thanks to wide openings at either end of its hallway. Capturing here should be done with teammates watching both sides, as either one has an equal chance of being the source of some kind of offensive effort. Grab corner cover to avoid standing in the open, and keep a watchful eye out for grenades from either side.

**3** Although most players that are starting out will use the entrances near the staircase or the adjacent room to infiltrate the upper floor of the Red House, experienced players will know that the window looking out into the alleyway can actually be jumped through once a player takes cover underneath it. Use this to surprise enemies covering the doorways on either side, but only if they aren't looking in the direction of the window, as the climbing animation takes a while to finish, which leaves you vulnerable.

**5** It's never easy to capture an objective near an enemy's spawn point, but the Arcade is especially perilous to Ghost teams trying to sneak in just seconds from the Bodark spawn. Expect grenades to be not just commonplace, but nearly constant. Trying to engage enemies from the right entrance is probably your best bet, but there's no denying that this objective is going to be hard-fought. Use Confidence to reduce capture time as much as possible, but scramble as soon as the grenades come bouncing in. If one ally can survive an attack wave, spawning on him can help turn the tide, but it must be properly timed with as many squadmates as possible.

**4** This little alcove near the closed shops just off the street is dangerous indeed, mostly because of all the easy cover the cars and trucks nearby provide for your enemies. Only attempt to capture this objective with squadmates, using the Confidence system to cut down on the amount of time it will take to grab it, then use the easy cover as a means of repelling any enemies that might try to retake the objective.

**6** Nestled behind the Gas Station proper, the final objective for this map offers little in the way of cover from the direction of the gas pumps, and only a tiny bit more from the direction of the Ghost spawn area. UAVs above the Gas Station can catch enemies trying to sneak in, so deploy them whenever possible to give your team eyes in the sky. Remember that a UAV needn't be manned to detect enemies, so park the aerial overwatch and switch back to your normal view to engage hostiles as they appear.

## // CAUTION

*The print book was reviewed and approved by Ubisoft, however we're aware that future game updates may result in some inaccuracies. To keep you up to date with these changes please refer to the insert card giving you FREE access to the Prima Official eGuide. The eGuide includes interactive maps for the Adversarial modes as well as Campaign Challenge videos and will update when there's a major change to the game, keeping you prepared for battle.*

# DECOY

 **OBJECTIVE**

**DEMOLITION**

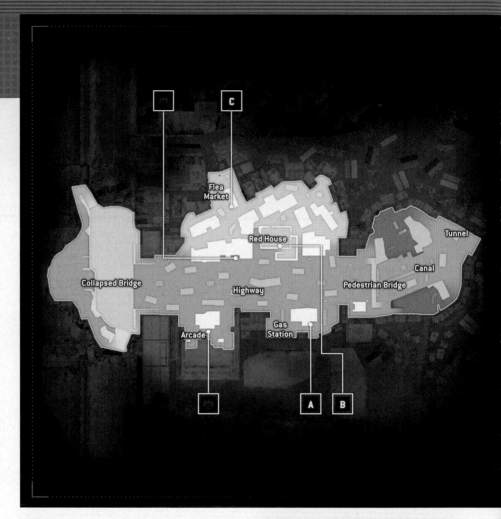

**A** The Gas Station once again serves as a central capture point, and will likely be well-defended. For attackers, using an Engineer with an equipped Field Computer can help to cut into the time it takes to capture the objective. Remember that attackers only need to capture the objective to remove it from the list of possibilities; there's no recapturing the point, so if you are defending, mark enemies as they appear to allow your whole squad to know where the threats lie so they can engage them quickly.

**B** The upper area of the Red House serves as home to the second possible capture point. The window entrance can offer a quick peek into things, but a well-placed Camera near the entrance does a great job on both offense and defense by revealing enemy forces. Cover all entrances for the best chance of taking or holding the position.

**C** The Flea Market has quite a few areas where cover is plentiful, making it a great place for defenders to dig in and watch the main road leading toward the Market as well as the two alleyways that are potential points of entry. The elevation of the capture point means advancing enemies coming from the direction of the Bodark spawn point will have to move up before they can see anyone, so keep this in mind when defending or attacking.

Upon revealing the true bomb plant location, things get considerably dicier. One location, not surprisingly, is the Arcade, making grenade battles common.

The second potential bomb plant location happens to be the same largely unprotected storefronts right off the main road, which means plenty of resistance from the nearby cars. Lobbing Sensors to get a peek through those bits of cover or using a UAV to peer down can help defenders spot incoming threats or attackers weed out the defense.

# SABOTEUR

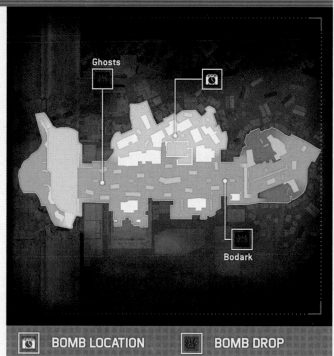

|  BOMB LOCATION |  BOMB DROP |

The bomb this time is actually located up and out of the way of the main street, near the Red House. Securing the bomb isn't terribly difficult, but the multiple routes to it mean that *holding onto* the bomb is quite a bit worse. UAVs can simply be parked near rooftops out of easy sight lines to spy on the bomb carrier, and having that kind of intel is crucial to stopping bombing attempts. Move in quickly, secure the bomb as a group, and then move toward the objective with speed.

The Ghosts must bring the bomb to the hotly contested Arcade area, so expect plenty of grenade-flavored opposition. Because of the long sight lines, snipers can be extremely dangerous. Use UAVs and Sensors to paint a picture of the surrounding area before moving into it.

While Ghosts have a fairly well-protected bomb drop, Bodarks must bring the bomb to the gas station, an area that's vulnerable to long-range fire from the Red House and flanking fire from the other side of the gas station. The same advice holds true here, including getting as much intel-collection equipment out into the area beforehand as possible. But remember that sniper Scouts can cloak to shield themselves from Heat detection. Watch the Pedestrian Walkway carefully.

# SIEGE

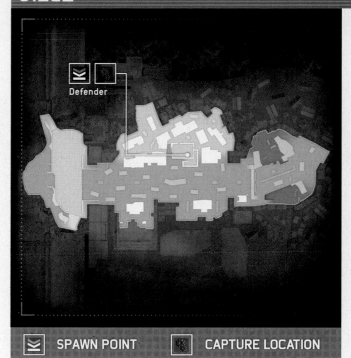

|  SPAWN POINT |  CAPTURE LOCATION |

Sensors and UAVs are a must here in the cramped quarters of the Red House. Luckily, the routes of entry aren't all that numerous, though the approach routes *into* the house area definitely are. Intel is key here, and defenders should expect plenty of smoke, EMPs, and grenades chucked in from the outside. Keep a few teammates around as floaters to manage incursions. They should move between entrances as needed to repel the invasion but stick to cover. These are valuable lives at risk.

Attackers have the disadvantage of being pretty easy to spot with intel-gathering devices. A concentrated rush, however, or a pincer attack that crashes multiple entry points at the same time could overwhelm unprepared defenders quickly, allowing time to set up and begin capturing. Again, just as in the case of Decoy, using a Field Computer can help speed up the process, but the key here is clearing out the defenders before ever moving in to attempt to capture.

# HARBOR

## SITUATION REPORT

Clearly there was some very clever infrastructure planning that went into making this harbor a major source of industry. Massive boats pull in, then cranes off-load the shipping containers and load them directly onto rail lines that speed the contents off to parts unknown. All that metal, both from machinery and containers means lots of safe cover free from the usual ballistics worries of lighter cover like wood or thin masonry. The deep channel cut into the middle of the level by the train tracks offers long sight lines for those foolish enough to try to enter from the bridge above. Instead, stick to the side routes unless the coast is clear. And it's never clear.

# SPAWN POINTS (CONFLICT, DECOY, AND SABOTEUR)

The docks serve as the Ghosts' place of refuge and respawning, allowing for a few entrances into the greater Boat House area. At the far end of the cranes is a Container Spill rich with bits of long cover. There's also a small side route down and into the Trainyard on the right end of the docks that offers a sneaky way to move around the map. The dual-level nature of Harbor means shoot-outs can come from nearly any angle down in the Trainyard, so keep your head on a swivel.

A huge Warehouse allows Bodarks to deploy out into the area of a giant Gantry Crane that also overlooks the central Trainyard. Like the Ghosts, they have an entrance down into the yard itself so they have the same sneaky routes throughout the map. Although the long shipping containers loaded onto and around the trains mean plenty of cover, the upper area can offer a few areas from which to fire down on enemies. Keep an eye out for conflicts breaking out around the Crane area, as there's a fairly wide-open section that should only be traversed when the coast is clear.

# POINTS OF INTEREST

## THE LONGEST YARD

With its series of lengthy corridors framed by the various train cars and shipping containers, the Trainyard offers plenty of sniping possibilities if hostiles are dumb enough to try to move around this area without taking cover. Sharpshooters would do well to take up positions at either end and watch for approaching enemies. UAVs will have great success peering out over the level. Just remember not to let them hang out for too long up above, as they can be easily targeted and taken down with longer-range weapons.

### TESTER TIP: RAUFOSS AND TUMBLE

Scouts gain access to Raufoss Ammo at Level 40, and although it can be tempting to go with the Claymore option that's also presented, know that the Raufoss's explosive secondary effect can take out enemies even if the rounds hit near their feet. It's splash damage, sniping-style.

## CRANES

Both sides of Harbor are littered with massive cranes that serve as the source of multiple objectives. Their wide bases and lengthy metallic feet are great for sneak attacks and flanking maneuvers, but bear in mind that the length has its own disadvantages: Should an enemy slip around the feet to your position, there's very little in the way of immediate cover to avoid getting gunned down.

## BRIDGE

Harbor's central bridge isn't a terribly lengthy stretch, and it's dotted with bits of cover in the middle and at the edges that make possible quick shots down into the Trainyard, but be wary of trying to use the boxcar parked below to make an incursion into the Yard proper. A properly positioned sniper at the far end can easily target and level would-be attackers before they ever reach the ground.

# CONFLICT

- (1) HOTSPOT
- ≽ DEPLOY
- 🛡 DEFEND
- ⚙ CONTROL/INTEL
- ▦ DEMOLITION

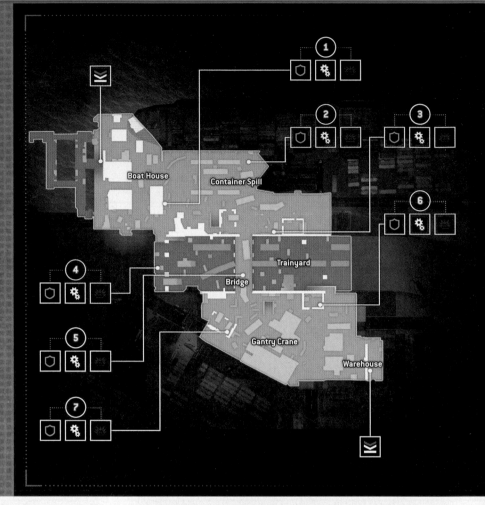

Boat House
Container Spill
Bridge
Trainyard
Gantry Crane
Warehouse

(1) Protected by low concrete walls but vulnerable to assaults coming up from the Trainyard and in the direction of the nearby cranes, this objective offers a great place to dig in to repel invasions. However, while capturing, players must try to avoid the wide-open flanks from being compromised. UAVs operating around the rooftops of the Boat House can do a great job of highlighting enemies on approach.

## TESTER TIP: SEEING STARS
The proximity to the Ghosts' spawn point means this objective is prone to some choice stun attacks. Should a teammate go down, don't immediately move to revive them, but instead hang back and let the enemy attempt a Data Hacking move. While they're occupied, you can gun them down and pocket a few extra points before moving in to help out your buddy.

(2) A tumbling mess of containers marks the second objective area, and it's one primed for corner cover. Keep an eye out for encroaching enemies while taking or defending the objective from the direction of the Bridge and Boat House, keeping in mind that the blind corners are great for ambushes. Cover to cover movement while assaulting the objective can help avoid those ambushes, as can a well-placed Sensor throw.

(3) This little alcove of activity near a building is fairly open to long-range attacks, so take up a position with allies to avoid getting ambushed. Confidence helps here, as always, but a well-placed UAV to look out over the more open area can do a great job of protecting your back from would-be intruders.

(6) Tucked inside a corner of a strategically placed storage building, this hot spot is great for grabbing cover along the walls, but is just a grenade throw away from being disastrous. Beware of approaches from the nearby staircase leading up from the Trainyard, as well as the Bodark Warehouse spawn.

(4) The twin columns on either side of this objective make great places for cover while a squadmate is attempting to capture the objective, but be wary of a small crack near the Ghosts' entrance down into the area. Barrels keep shots from sneaking through, but a well-thrown grenade will make short work of anyone not paying attention. Popping smoke here helps obscure the actions down below, forcing a ground-level assault even with enemies that can see through the smoke.

(7) This garage offers multiple routes of entry that make it rather difficult to pin down, but that can also be used to bait hostiles into trying to retake the objective. Fire can be applied from multiple doorways at once. If you're using the low concrete cover facing out toward the Warehouse, be careful of flanking fire from the direction of the bridge.

## // CAUTION

The print book was reviewed and approved by Ubisoft, however we're aware that future game updates may result in some inaccuracies. To keep you up to date with these changes please refer to the insert card giving you FREE access to the Prima Official eGuide. The eGuide includes interactive maps for the Adversarial modes as well as Campaign Challenge videos and will update when there's a major change to the game, keeping you prepared for battle.

(5) With multiple routes of entry, the bridge capture location is difficult to hold to say the least, but the bridge's supports can offer limited cover from incoming attacks. Keep an eye out for long-range snipers to avoid getting attacked as you secure the location.

# DECOY

 **A** OBJECTIVE

**DEMOLITION**

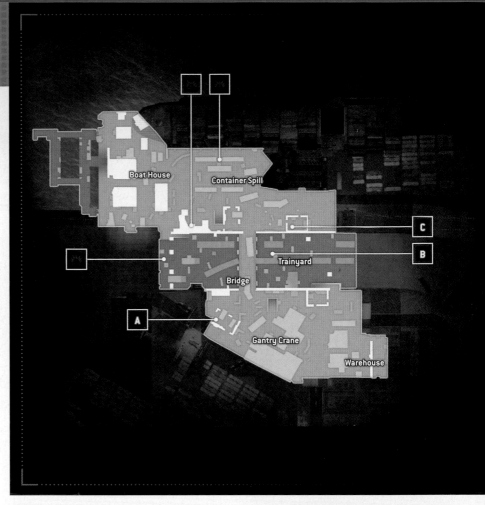

**Boat House** | **Container Spill** | **C** | **B** | **Trainyard** | **Bridge** | **A** | **Gantry Crane** | **Warehouse**

**A** That same garage area seen in Conflict makes for an equally precarious potential capture location in Decoy. The same rules apply, though: Watch for approaches from the bridge and the rear of the building, and protect the squad member that tries to hack into the objective. If defending, try luring enemies into the area with a pre-planted Sensor nearby, then open fire from multiple doorways to confuse and disorient.

**B** Tucked in between two rail cars, the second objective is more than a little dangerous. Sniping is possible from multiple spots along the Trainyard itself, but that also means support can be trained on either side of the expanse to limit the surprises that come in while capturing. Defenders can stealthily grab cover under the bridge or the low bits of concrete to mount a surprise attack.

**C** The small wooden building that serves as the third possible capture location affords three routes of entry, but be forewarned if you're trying to grab cover near the doorjamb of the rightmost doorway (which, incidentally, doesn't show up on the map): The length of wood on the right side of the outside part of the opening restricts the amount of cover-based aiming you can have. It only allows firing toward the doorway on the other side of the building and the objective itself.

The rubble surrounding the Container Spill makes for plenty of detritus to skirt while planting the bomb between the legs of one of the giant cranes. Position defenders along the legs, but stack up near the edges where it's possible to slip around the legs to attack the bomb planter.

Potential spot number two is actually fairly well protected on three sides, but that just funnels firepower down in the direction of the one open site facing out toward a mess of containers. Move quickly, using intel-gathering equipment to scout the area and protect it from incoming attackers while the bomb is planted.

The final location is actually down in the Trainyard itself, tucked behind the end of the tracks. Once again, grabbing cover along the nearby pillars is helpful, but be wary of grenades slipped through the crack up above.

# SABOTEUR

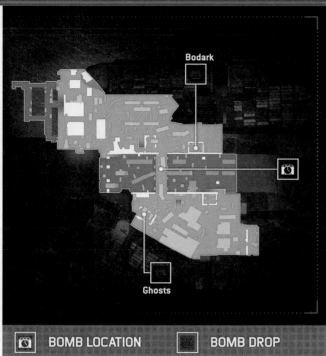

Bodark

Ghosts

📷 BOMB LOCATION        ▦ BOMB DROP

The explosive prize for this round is neatly sandwiched between two concrete bits of cover. These are directly in front of two tunnels leading down and right under a bridge that offer quick jumps down to ground level. There's an awful lot of ways to grab this bomb, and even more ways to attempt to take down the bomb carrier. The columns of the bridge can help to protect against light fire, but the safest route out is back up into the tunnels leading up to the bomb planting locations.

A Ghost bomb carrier has a tough battle to get near the empty garage that serves as the plant location. Heading up through the tunnels is a direct route, but the stairs make for a blind exit, so send a UAV up to scout out the area before hand if possible, and keep an eye out for hostiles taking cover behind the lip that looks out over the staircase itself.

Bodark carriers face the exact same dilemma: Head through the tunnels or brave the Trainyard in an attempt to take one of the side routes up. The latter is a long slog with high visibility, and the narrow passages up and out of the Yard are a natural bottleneck. Intel-gathering attempts are a must, but so, too, is quick movement to get out of sight. Remember, as soon as an enemy spots the bomb carrier, they're marked as an objective for the team, turning the carrier into a walking bull's-eye.

# SIEGE

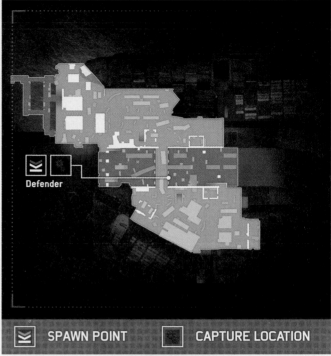

Defender

≪ SPAWN POINT        ▦ CAPTURE LOCATION

The Bridge once again plays host to a valuable objective. Defenders should make the most of the time they have and set up to cover the different routes of entry into the lower part of the level. Cover the tunnel leading down, keep an eye on the top of the bridge, and cover the narrow walkways in. Stay in cover and try to bait enemies into taking the "undefended" objective, then unload on them and quickly pop back into cover. Sensors near entrances do a great job of tipping off your team to enemy locations, but eyes-on will always be the most important.

## TESTER TIP: SILENT BUT DEADLY

When you have only a single life per round, stealth is the ultimate weapon. Suppressed weapons aren't just quiet, they're undetectable on the minimap, full TacMap, and a target's HUD, which means the enemy won't know where the shots are coming from. Using this from a covered position on a group of enemies while their backs are turned will cause absolute chaos as they scramble to find the direction of fire so they can grab cover to stop it. A few well-placed headshots will ensure that they never do.

Fake outs here are a great way to confuse and distract your foes, leading them into shifting their forces toward an entrance that is mostly unoccupied. Decoy Grenades are a great way to spook hiding defenders into thinking there's either a fight happening elsewhere, or that they should move, which opens them up to getting popped while changing cover. UAVs and Sensors, as usual, are also great for getting a good picture of the defenders' positions.

# CARGO

## SITUATION REPORT

A hijacked cargo ship lies nearly silent on the open waters. Only the intermittent sound of gunfire interrupts the briny pall. With sight lines broken regularly by tall shipping containers, Cargo means plenty of close-quarters combat both inside the bowels of the ship and around the various parts of the deck. Stick with weapons made for quick firing. And learn the layout of the ship as completely as possible in modes like Conflict before attempting to brave the blind corners and cramped corridors in Siege, or get used to watching the action unfold from the sidelines.

# SPAWN POINTS (CONFLICT, DECOY, AND SABOTEUR)

Ghosts deploy from the Stern of the ship, leaping down from shipping containers at the rear of the boat to join the fray as it erupts toward the middle. Despite the size of the ship, making one's way along the sides is a relatively speedy affair. Just remember to stick to cover along the way and transition from one cover position to the next. There are multiple routes down into the ship's hold, and it behooves the entire team to learn them quickly.

The Bow is Bodark territory, and like the Ghosts' spawn, there is ample opportunity to move both across the deck and down below. Cover—much of it quite high—is everywhere, so there's no reason to go charging through an area without sticking to something. Watch your flanks and move as a group, leapfrogging as needed between bits of cover to avoid detection on the way to the objectives.

# POINTS OF INTEREST

## PORT AND STARBOARD DECKS

The left and right sides of the ship are flecked with bits of heavy cover, which is good because the Stern of the ship has plenty of height and well-covered spots for snipers to take shots at anyone foolish enough to be waltzing along outside of cover. With all those chunks of metal, there's no reason not to be pushed up against them at all times.

## TESTER TIP: SPAWN POINTERS

Just because you can spawn on your squadmates, it doesn't mean it's always the best option. Select the squadmate when spawning, then wait and see what the situation surrounding them is. Are they under fire? Capturing an objective? Doing something stupid? It's probably a bad idea to spawn on that person lest you pop in right in the line of fire or next to a grenade. Careful planning of spawning on a teammate, however, can mean huge surges around a forward position, something that can get you and your squad back into the fray without having to navigate your whole way back to the fight. Just don't be too eager to jump in or you'll be treated to yet another spawn countdown screen.

## BELOW DECK

Not many maps in *Ghost Recon Future Solider* are as symmetrical as Cargo, but the simple layout below deck can help make learning it all much easier. Memorize where long sections without cover are, and what exits lead to sections of the hold that will allow quickest access back into firefights. With so many ladders, staircases, and corridors, it can be a bit overwhelming, but the combatant that knows the map layouts best is often the one that will arrive at an objective first, or know the best way to ambush an enemy if they aren't.

## WALKWAYS

Six walkways connect the two sides of the ship above deck, with one walkway each on the Bow and Stern protected by a respective team's safe zones (save for in Siege Mode where there are no safe zones). Learning which of these is the closest to your current position can speed movement between Port and Starboard locations, or facilitate a hasty retreat when coming under fire.

# CONFLICT

① HOTSPOT

⩔ DEPLOY

🛡 DEFEND

⚙ CONTROL/INTEL

▦ DEMOLITION

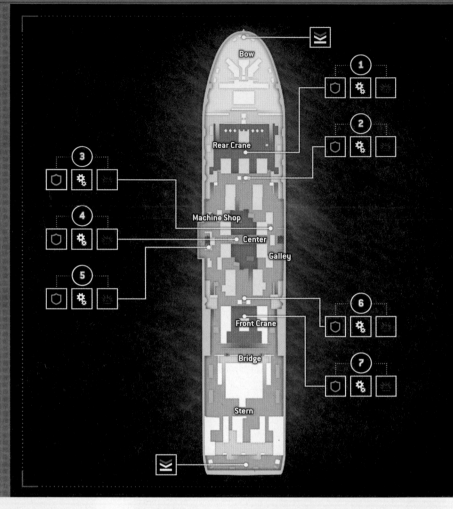

① Swaddled in nearby containers, this objective hot spot has multiple routes of entry, which can make defending a bit of a chore. Keep an eye on the stairs leading down into the hold area, as well as the exits from below the nearby bridge. The latter has plenty of cover to fire from, making it a favorite direction of attack and recapture.

② The two routes of approach on either side of the smokestacks containing the second objective are common routes of attack, but don't ignore the ramp leading up from the other section of the cargo hold ahead. All three present quick means of getting in or out, but keep one eye trained on either of the elevated sections flanking the area. A placed, cloaked sniper is easy to spot, but they have no cover from return fire, so spotting them quickly is key to removing the threat.

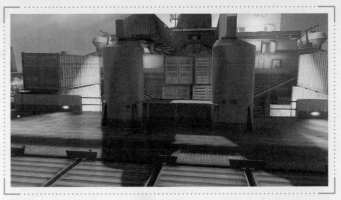

**3** The corner cover surrounding this objective makes it fairly easy to defend it from ground troops, but snipers from the back of the ship can sneak in potshots, so keep necks craned for incoming shots and the odd grenade being tossed from afar.

**6** A mirror of the second objective, the dangers here are more or less identical: entry routes from the left and right, elevated platforms where shooters can get the drop on those trying to capture, and a ramp up from the hold area—this time in the form of a covered shipping container.

**4** Digging in with all the bits of cover available underneath the bridge means holding this area isn't especially tough, but trying to take it certainly is. The cramped quarters make grenade tosses especially dangerous for anyone trying to capture the objective, though setting up the right angle for a grenade throw isn't exactly easy either. Once it's captured, be ready for attacks from both sides of the hold area and try to stay low to avoid enemies shooting through the holes in the cover.

**7** Much like the first objective, this hold area hot spot lets enemies fire down from above, enter by way of a pair of staircases and slip in from the innards of the ship. Use Sensors to track movement from below decks, UAVs to watch from the skies, and Confidence captures to speed things up.

**5** Tucked into a little alcove just above a set of ladders, this objective requires close-quarters combat to clear out any hostiles. Grenades can flush out potential enemy players trying to capture, and attacking from down below toward the top of the ladders can work well—so long as defenders aren't looking down at you.

# DECOY

 **A**   OBJECTIVE

   **DEMOLITION**

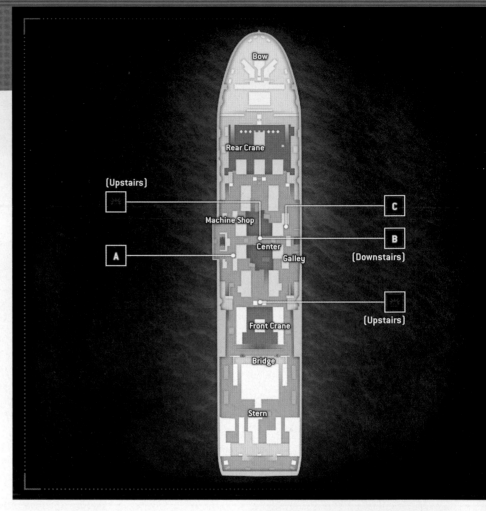

**A** For once, the capture and defend locations are purely symmetrical, offering the same kind of loose cover for the first of the possible true objectives next to a bunch of shipping containers. Watch for snipers from the Bow, and move quickly to capture the point or repel attackers if you're defending.

**B** Much as it was during Conflict objectives, the multiple covering walls that surround the below-bridge capture location make it a great place for grenade kills and a hardy place to stick in when repelling attackers.

**C** The mirror image of the first objective, this potential objective requires eyes trained toward the Stern to avoid sniping shots and solid corner cover while you're defending.

The first of three bomb planting locations sits in the dead center of the ship. Unprotected and vulnerable to plenty of crossfire, the bridge is a formidable challenge. Scout with intel-gathering equipment first before leaving the safety of the container cover on either side.

The second option will be familiar to Conflict vets: the twin smokestacks in all their hair-raising glory. Three routes of entry and those infernal sniping spots on either side without cover mean all escorts should be looking left and right as much as possible, while another squadmate keeps an eye on that shipping container route up from the hold below.

# SABOTEUR

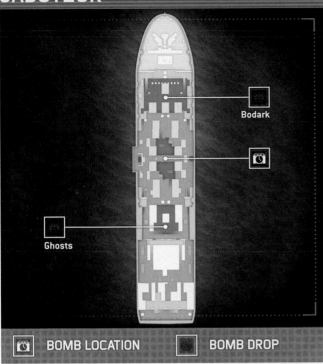

**Bodark**

**Ghosts**

🎦 **BOMB LOCATION**　■ **BOMB DROP**

Tucked down below the main walkway cutting across the middle of the ship, the bomb must be carried to hold area farthest from each team's spawn—a harrowing journey that starts by first securing the area and then moving the carrier as quickly as possible toward some more solid cover.

The Ghosts need to bring the bomb to the hold area closest to the Bow, which can mean a trip through the hallways of the ship below or a scramble to get there by way of the deck. Whatever the route, make sure to send scouts ahead to watch for enemy forces as they stack up in and around the hold. Only after deploying UAVs or Sensors should the group with the bomb carrier make their way toward the objective. And whatever you do, keep an eye out for snipers looking to take out carriers above deck.

Bodark's have largely the same trip back toward the Stern, though there's more in the way of cover leading through the corridors below. The crane at the Stern end of the ship can make sniping difficult, but not impossible, so use UAVs where possible to spot and mark potential threats before heading out of the ship's underbelly.

# SIEGE

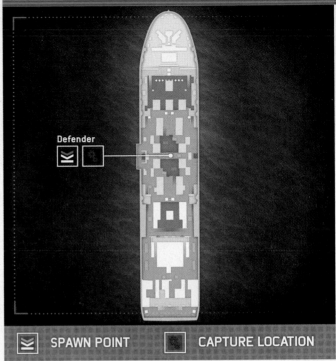

**Defender**

⋙ **SPAWN POINT**　■ **CAPTURE LOCATION**

Once again, semi-encased in a metallic cage, the objective and spawn point for the defenders offers multiple routes of entry, but a fairly difficult inner sanctum to crack. Keep an eye out for intrusions from the corridors below, as well as attacks from the hold areas fore and aft. Snipers can and will take shots at those that choose to stand with their faces showing through the holes in the cover surrounding the bomb location itself, so stay low whenever possible.

Imagine the chaos that would happen if a Flashbang were thrown into the area surrounding the bomb. Now imagine if it were followed up with a frag or EMP grenade. Attackers actually have a pretty solid means of dealing with the defenders, but the single life offered for the entire round means gung-ho antics aren't advised. Work slowly around the perimeter of the ship, taking shots where possible at the defenders and luring them out into the adjoining corridors or out into the hold where they can be taken out. In a pinch, remember that the walkway on top of the bomb *does* allow those above to jump down, but doing so with defenders present and aware is suicide.

## SITUATION REPORT

A drilling platform in the middle of the ocean, drinking everything it can from the sea floor below, Rig is by design the most square of all the maps available in Adversarial Mode. It's not nearly as symmetrical as Cargo was, save for the central areas making up the drill itself, the command center, and some of the rear areas. The outlying areas are filled with multiple elevations and a confusing set of rooms and open-air passageways that offer plenty of cover and ambush points. Data hacks are incredibly valuable here due to the lack of clear sight lines, so make the most of that stunning equipment.

# SPAWN POINTS (CONFLICT, DECOY, AND SABOTEUR)

Interestingly, the Ghost and Bodark deploy locations are quite close, but they're separated by a huge bulkhead that forces deployment out and around the main spawn. Ghosts move out from a Cargo Lift area into a set of Pump units. Stairs lead to multiple floors both above and below the starting location. To keep from losing your squad, make sure everyone is using the Command System to follow a similar path toward an objective, and be ever-vigilant about checking flanks as you move through the many open areas.

On the other side of the bulkhead, Bodarks mass their forces out from the Storage Room into a wide-open area, including a Locker Room just beyond the spawn area. Like the Ghosts' area, there are plenty of places to change elevations, and though some of the walkways can be shot through for sneaky kills, the multi-tiered nature of the level means most firefights will happen on the same plane. Command System waypoints are a key way to learn the lay of the land here, as the pathways can become quite convoluted if one isn't paying attention.

# POINTS OF INTEREST

## THE DRILL

At the Rig's core, on the bottom floor, lies the now-dormant drill, decoupled from the boring shaft. This area is a hotbed of potential sniping and multitiered fighting, as multiple floors have some form of a vantage point. Move quickly through this area to avoid being spotted, using it for more stealthy access into the main control room.

### TESTER TIP: BACKUP GENERATORS

With so many floors, it's not unusual to find oneself low on ammo or at the end of a magazine. Keep this in mind before reloading that main weapon in the heat of a firefight, though: Both a melee strike and switching to your secondary weapon are faster than the time it will take to reload even the quickest primary weapon, and that goes double for bigger weapons like the LMG. Of all the classes, the Scout has the most devastating melee strike—a quick jab to the throat of someone they attack head-on. Taking an enemy out and grabbing cover quickly could mean the difference between taking an objective or sitting there waiting for the respawn counter to hit zero.

## THE HELIPAD

The topmost level of the Rig might seem like a sniper's dream come true, but there's literally zero cover (aside from the floor, of course), and sneak attacks from the rear are common. Still, a suppressed sniper rifle from on high has the ability to strike foes running around on almost any level without them realizing where the attacks are coming from. A UAV launched from up here also has a great view of the action down below, making the Helipad a great place to build intel.

## HIGHWAYS AND BYWAYS

Trying to list the myriad levels and connecting crossways that litter the different levels of the Rig would make your head spin, but suffice it to say there's often more than one way to traverse a particular section of the Rig. When in need of some fast travel, try taking the side routes that skirt the lip of the rig's main floor, or use the causeway just below the helipad to slip into the Drilling Tower to take shots at enemies. Learning where walkways end up spitting a player out can mean heading off some forces before they can reach their destination—or skirting around them completely to gather more intel.

# CONFLICT

- ① HOTSPOT
- ⌄ DEPLOY
- 🛡 DEFEND
- ⚙ CONTROL/INTEL
- ✹ DEMOLITION

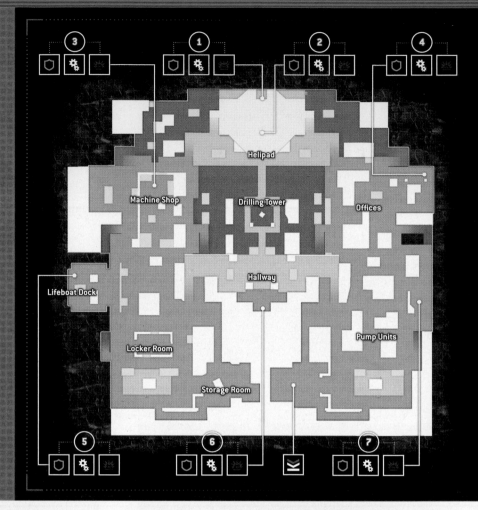

Helipad

Machine Shop

Drilling Tower

Offices

Lifeboat Dock

Hallway

Locker Room

Pump Units

Storage Room

① The first objective hot spot can be a little difficult to locate at first. It appears directly under the ladder leading down from the Helipad, but it's actually a full two floors below that level, behind a pulley holding a crate. This area has wide-open flanks that make captures difficult. Those on support duty should grab low cover near the barriers surrounding the suspended crate.

② Just above the first objective, in a command center that has seen better days, lies the second objective. This area is tight, flanked on either side by doorways that can create pincer attacks with quite a bit of effectiveness. Because there's so little room to move, grenades tossed in here have a great way of flushing enemies out.

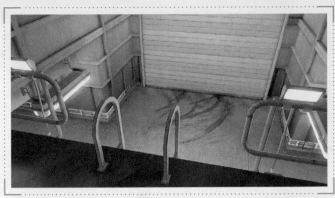

③ The Rig's Machine Shop serves as base for the third objective hot spot. There are entrances into the area from three of the four directions, and a window looks in from the forth, which make it hard to hold the position without incurring a few losses. Stacking up outside the three entrances and window and then unloading from all angles has a huge benefit, but be warned that a Sensor dropped in the middle of the room will allow those inside to see what's happening outside all four potential firing positions.

⑥ Tucked into a tiny back room on the middle floor of the Rig, the sixth objective hot spot seems fairly easily defendable—until one realizes there a ladder up to a floor that looks right down on the objective. Train your view toward this platform whenever defending or risk having your squadmate take a bullet to the face. There's no reviving a guy with ammo lodged in his dome.

④ The offices play host to the fourth location, with an objective that is woefully unprotected from fire coming from the direction of the Helipad. This can be an extremely hard position to infiltrate, with good snipers finding plenty of fodder while sitting prone on the Helipad. If you have an LMG in your squad, make sure they're suppressing as often as possible to allow the person capturing the objective to survive unscathed.

⑦ Situated fairly close to the Ghosts' spawn point, the final objective waits in a room just off the Pump units that is vulnerable to attacks from the north and south. Large doorways make it difficult to contain fire, and since enemies can grab cover behind a pump to the north and pop up from a stairwell to the south, it's important to use as many intel-gathering pieces of equipment as possible.

## // CAUTION

*The print book was reviewed and approved by Ubisoft, however we're aware that future game updates may result in some inaccuracies. To keep you up to date with these changes please refer to the insert card giving you FREE access to the Prima Official eGuide. The eGuide includes interactive maps for the Adversarial modes as well as Campaign Challenge videos and will update when there's a major change to the game, keeping you prepared for battle.*

⑤ The open-air Lifeboat Dock contains yet another objective, and while this one is still painfully exposed from some angles, it's not as prone to easy sniper fire as the last objective hot spot. Grab cover where possible to quickly eliminate those that would seek to put down your squadmate trying to capture the area, but stick close so the Confidence bonus can be applied.

# DECOY

**A** OBJECTIVE

**[demolition icon]** DEMOLITION

**A** The Machine shop holds the first of the three possible locations for capture and defense. As mentioned before, a Sensor in the center of the room can reveal immediate threats, but the number of attack angles means retaliation could come from anywhere. An LMG suppressing from the window can keep enemies pinned behind cover that's accessible from the sides, so either pop smoke before entering, or deal with the defenders on all sides before attempting to capture.

**B** The control room holds the second objective, with clear views from the outside of anyone trying to hack the location. While it's possible to mask this to a degree with smoke (if the enemy doesn't have thermal scopes), the near-straight firing lines mean just spraying into the general area can negate the usefulness of the smoke. Try to position defenders on either side of the two routes toward the objective to hold off advances, but don't neglect the ladders. One leading down from the helipad and two coming up from the floor below could catch defenders by surprise if they aren't paying attention.

**C** Unlike the Conflict objective in this area, the final of the three potential key locations is protected by some light cover. There's even a decent amount of room to move around should a grenade drop in, and those attacking the location have to sweep around two primary directions to get a firing angle. Taking cover from here and unloading can repel those invasions quite handily—at least until the grenades start flying.

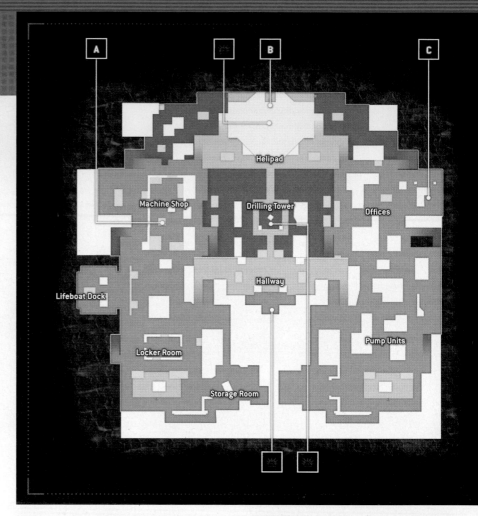

**[demolition icon]** The great big H of the Helipad may as well be a B, for it's exactly where one of the bomb locations appears. Holding this area is extremely difficult due to the lack of cover, but Stun Mines, Claymores and other deployables can help to a degree. In most cases, the side with a more coordinated effort is going to win—which usually means a pincer attack from both sides at once to spread out the defense.

The drill itself serves as the waiting recipient of another bomb plant location. Due to the sheer number of angles from which defenders can fire in on those trying to plant the bomb, intel here is essential. Having a UAV flitting around to mark targets before actually charging in could make all the difference.

Just through the Drilling Tower and down a ladder is the final bomb placement location. Just as in the case of this Conflict hot spot, the ladder is both a means of getting to the location and a great way to defend it or kill would-be bomb planters. Keep eyes up and to the sides to avoid getting overrun while the bomb planter does his thing.

## SABOTEUR

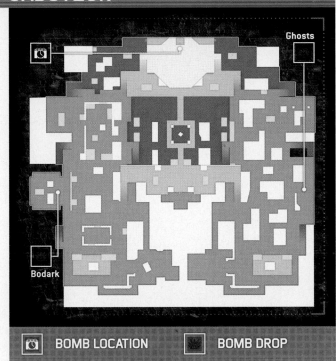

Ghosts

Bodark

BOMB LOCATION          BOMB DROP

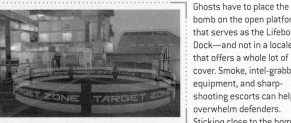

The bomb sits waiting for its captor inside the command center. Those seeking to capture it would do well to make sure the return route is clear before grabbing the bomb, as there's quite a bit of open space that needs to be crossed on the way to either bomb plant location.

Ghosts have to place the bomb on the open platform that serves as the Lifeboat Dock—and not in a locale that offers a whole lot of cover. Smoke, intel-grabbing equipment, and sharp-shooting escorts can help overwhelm defenders. Sticking close to the bomb carrier or using a Field Computer can speed up the process of actually setting the bomb.

Sneaking the bomb into the Pump Units is the task set forth for any Bodark bomb carriers. Consider taking the lower level side catwalk to avoid too many enemies, but remember that there are plenty of angles for flanking fire around the Pumps, so speed is the key to beating defenders to the punch. As always, a UAV sent out into the area beforehand can help to spot all but cloaked Scouts, and it can be parked somewhere to watch flanks while the carrier moves into position.

## SIEGE

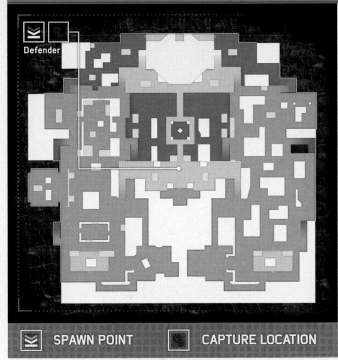

Defender

SPAWN POINT          CAPTURE LOCATION

The dangerous domain of the drill holds the location of the capture point and the spawn area for defenders. Quickly grab elevated positions to cover the flanks, but keep a few defenders down on the ground floor to sweep the area of threats. Note that an attacker trying to capture the location is protected by the nearby logs and must be taken out from the widely exposed flanks. The defenders have the advantage here, but there are quite a few routes of entry. Be ready for intel-gathering devices, EMPs, and smoke attempting to mask entries.

If protecting the attacker, make sure to keep eyes trained toward those nearby bits of cover at the flanks and up toward areas where a well-placed headshot could end everything. Popping smoke in a location *other* than the actual attack vector is a wise move, given how many multitiered routes of attack there are. Above all else, take things slowly and try to pick off the defenders one at a time.

# SAND STORM

## SITUATION REPORT

There's no telling when blinding gusts of wind will blow in and obscure almost everything in this desert encampment. Those caught without thermal or backscatter scopes are going to be left trusting their instruments, which is precisely why this map is such an EMP-lover's paradise. Intel is more important here than on any other map when the winds kick up, so stay on your toes at all times. When things are clear, a few elevated bunkers can make sniping shots rather favorable, but as soon as the storm blows in, visibility is severely hampered.

# SPAWN POINTS (CONFLICT, DECOY, AND SABOTEUR)

Even for a map in the desert, the Ghosts' spawn area is pretty bleak, necessitating a push into the camp proper. Longer-range shooters can take up cover on a slightly elevated platform to try to catch enemies flanking the bunker position in the middle of the map, but sight lines here are regularly disrupted by tents. Be sure to make the most of cover-to-cover movement whenever changing to a new area to avoid ambushes, especially during storms. There's plenty of low cover here, so weapons with Bipods are a smart choice.

Bodark squads have a bit more in the way of interesting clutter near their spawn point, but the actual usable cover here isn't really worth a whole lot. Therefore, like the Ghosts, they'll have to push into the middle of the map to start engaging. Remember to snap to cover as much as possible and keep out of sight when conditions are clear. When the storms move in, Scouts with Advanced Camouflage that lets them skulk around without breaking their Optical Camo are going to have a field day, so make sure a few are on your team.

# POINTS OF INTEREST

## HIGH GROUND

Two locations provide limited views over a decent portion of the camp: a bunker up on a ridge that overlooks all the low cover in the center of the map, and an radio building with a wide enough roof to allow for some cloaked sniping. Neither is particularly secure, but under the cover of the storm and with a properly scoped weapon, snipers can make a literal killing by just staying patient and watching their backs. Eventually, some poor rookie is going to go trotting through the middle of the camp and that will be the time to strike.

### TESTER TIP: THE BOY SCOUTS HAD IT RIGHT

Having an inventory that's right for the occasion isn't just good advice, it can be a lifesaver. In close-quarters environments, shorter-range SMGs and shotguns are going to win nearly every head-to-head firefight. Likewise, maps with long sight lines are going to favor assault and sniper rifles. For smaller maps like this, it's important to balance the two. Long enough sight lines mean an accurate PDR or AR can wreck the other team's chances, but there's more to building your loadout than just picking a particular weapon and calling it a day. Pay attention to the way different equipment affects all stats; low Maneuverability means moving around will be difficult, while low Control means bullets will have a harder time consistently finding their target. By constantly playing with your loadouts, you can find the right weapon for the situation—a situation that could change as much based on the people you're playing against as the actual map being played at the time.

## THE HANGAR

The plane prepping to take off is the source of more than a few objectives across the various modes, but controlling the hangar nearby can mean the difference between slipping onto the plane unseen and having a massive shoot-out every time you take a step toward the plane's rear. Lock down the hangar whenever possible. It has an objective hot spot of its own, but it's also one of the few covered areas on the map and a great place to regroup where squadmates can respawn on you (or you on them).

## THE LARGE TREE

Simply named, sure, and littered with the doleful reminders of what can happen to children in war-torn areas like this, the Large Tree also stands in as a landmark that can be used for regrouping during the storm. Its backside is one of the few true bottlenecks in this level, with a forward cover point in the middle and a rear that faces the Ghost spawn point (so if you're a Bodark trooper, be sure to keep your weapons trained back toward that camp). The fact that it is marked on the TacMap means it's an easy point for everyone to use the Communication System and head back toward even at the height of a sandstorm.

# CONFLICT

- (1) **HOTSPOT**
- **DEPLOY**
- **DEFEND**
- **CONTROL/INTEL**
- **DEMOLITION**

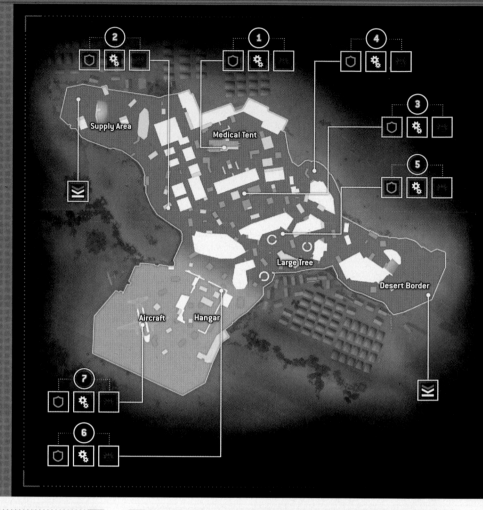

(1) Expect to head back to this radio building often to capture objectives, and get used to not feeling terribly safe while up there, too. Without a ton of cover and with two ladders leading up, it can be a daunting task to keep this location out of enemy hands. Use what cover there is to mount a forward assault, with your squadmates staying on the ground to repel attacks from flanks and behind the top-mounted cover.

(2) The massive generator truck makes for a pretty lousy place to grab cover. The rear is exposed and all it takes is an enemy slipping around the vehicle to make a mess of any capture attempts. Have your squadmates grab cover long the nearby structures to hold off assaults from the direction of the Bodark spawn and the area leading in from the airplane and hangar. Using Confidence and a Field Computer can ensure that the objective is taken quickly to allow you to set up to push back against incoming enemies.

**3** This large tent offers one of the better pieces of cover you're going to find in this dusty camp. Make sure to capture the objective from the direction of the long back wall to ensure as much protection on the flanks as possible, while the rest of your squad grabs cover along each of the three crates to hold off enemies and maximize Confidence. Attackers will likely find that a well-thrown grenade can break up the party rather well, so if you're defending, be ready to quickly move to adjacent cover to avoid the blast.

**6** The hangar's objective is shoved right into the corner of the building, making infiltration from one of the four doorways fairly easy. Unfortunately, that also means it's difficult to guard once it's taken, so stack up near the doors and use intel-gathering equipment like a UAV pointed out toward the main camp to help catch would-be enemies trying to sneak into the hangar. As a prime area for capturing and holding strategically, this is bound to experience heavy fighting.

**4** The forward-facing part of this bunker is a fantastic place for LMGs to set up a cone of suppression, but the unprotected back area has absolutely no cover, making it difficult to contain when the objective hot spot moves here. Be agile, shifting fire to the rear as needed, but don't be afraid to unload the LMG to pin down forces that would attempt to move toward the bunker from the front and left flank.

**7** Gassed up and waiting to taxi down the runway, the transport plane's belly holds an objective hot spot. Well protected from the outside, the plane's cramped quarters mean it's a favorite of Frag and Incendiary Grenades, both as a deterrent and an interruption for those already capturing the objective. It's best not to hang out in the plane if possible, but nearby, since the other way toward the plane is on either side of the hangar (or moving through it).

**// CAUTION**

*The print book was reviewed and approved by Ubisoft, however we're aware that future game updates may result in some inaccuracies. To keep you up to date with these changes please refer to the insert card giving you FREE access to the Prima Official eGuide. The eGuide includes interactive maps for the Adversarial modes as well as Campaign Challenge videos and will update when there's a major change to the game, keeping you prepared for battle.*

**5** This little cluster of village huts offers very little in the way of defensible cover, but it can at least put something between you and an attacker in a pinch. Unfortunately, the objective sits in a rather open area, so try to form a perimeter to guard against incoming threats from the east, west, and south. A Stun Mine or Claymore facing north can turn the capturing squad member into a bit of bait if you're looking to data hack an enemy (and with the sandstorm getting as bad as it does, it *always* pays to have that kind of intel).

## DECOY

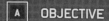

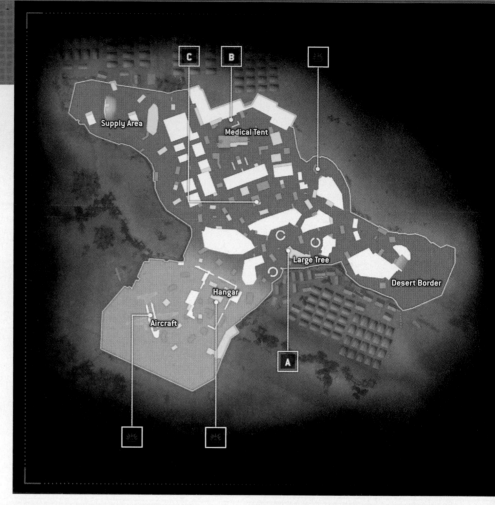

**A** The Large Tree overlooks the first objective, which is exposed from three sides by easy cover that will make taking the objective a pain. Smoke will help here, as can the cover of the sand storm, but a UAV high enough can help establish some semblance of overwatch while trying to infiltrate. The crates nearby make for an easy way to skirt around incoming attacks, so if you're defending, don't be afraid to pop out of cover and slip around to catch a quick breather.

**B** The cover scattered around this big tent, again, makes it a great place to dig in and repel incoming waves (though a well-thrown grenade works great to disrupt those that are using the crates for cover). Because the objective is sitting on one of those crates, capturing it can be difficult, as the flanks are exposed to fire coming from the bits of cover outside the tent.

**C** The final objective waits behind the radio building, which of course means that elevated position is great for overwatch while on defense. Thanks to support walls, the tent that holds the objective can be occupied to hold off invaders, but grenades can be snuck in rather easily, too. Keeping attackers on the other side of the radio building is important, as there are wide areas from which to slip in and flank.

The bunker ready-made for LMG suppression serves its purpose well, keeping attackers from planting the bomb if they attempt a frontal assault. That likely means the best route in will come by way of slipping up the back, so have plenty of defenders ready to hold the attackers back. Attackers can make use of Sensors and UAVs to scope out the situation before charging in, but it'll be a hard-fought position to take no matter what.

The hanger once again proves its usefulness by being the site of the second bomb placement spot. Defenders can prep by dropping Claymores and Stun Mines if there are enough high-level squadmates to command those tools, while attackers should attempt a breach from multiple angles to spread out the defense as much as possible.

The final location is, of course, the plane, meaning even if the hangar isn't the actual bomb spot this round, it's still a position worth holding decisively. Sitting inside the plane on defense isn't necessary, but making sure both entrances into the belly of the beast are covered most definitely is. Drop a sensor inside for an easy way to alert your squad to enemy attempts to sneak aboard.

# SABOTEUR

🕘 **BOMB LOCATION**   ▨ **BOMB DROP**

It's time to return to the plane to grab the bomb, taking care not to alert the other team to your presence once you've done so. The hangar can provide cover while moving to secure the bomb drop locations (which are startlingly close to each other in the village).

Ghosts must make their way back over toward the radar building, skirting the left side of the hangar. It's a longer trip than the Bodark drop, but it's also packed with more cover, making a stealthy approach all the more important. Send scouting teams out to scour the tents; all that cover makes for good hiding spots for hostiles too.

Bodark attackers will have to carry the bomb a bit farther into the village and drop it right in the middle. The round huts should be cleared on all sides (and insides) before attempting any sort of movement into the village. Crafty players can try popping smoke along one of the side routes into the village to pull defenders away, but the key here is taking out hostiles before they can mount a counterattack, then quickly moving in to secure the location.

# SIEGE

▼ **SPAWN POINT**   ▨ **CAPTURE LOCATION**

Defenders spawn around a tent that is well-protected against threats from the sides. At least one squad member should take up a position on top of the radio building for maximum sight lines, and deploying UAVs and Sensors to watch the left and right flanks is a great way to keep tabs on anyone trying to sneak through. There's quite a bit of cover throughout this part of the camp, so watch for attackers trying to take a wide route and slip in from behind the radio building.

Attackers have plenty of options when choosing to move in, but should split forces to help confuse and spread thin the defenders. Work toward the end goal by using guerrilla attacks, whittling down the defense one at a time to slowly thin their numbers until a combined assault from both sides helps punish any defenders still lucky enough to have avoided your drawn-out offensive. Slowly moving up the left side and getting around to take out any defenders on top of the radio building is a great way to limit their ability to attack from the building's sides.

# UNDERGROUND

## SITUATION REPORT

A stark reminder of what fear and the threat of nuclear annihilation did to parts of the world, this Cold War relic has survived largely because it was forgotten. New military powers have restarted the operation and the full might of its diabolical construction can be felt along every lengthy tunnel and dusty alcove. Underground is as mechanically rigid in design as one would expect from Cold War construction, which leads to a level that is almost completely symmetrical and utilitarian as can be.

# SPAWN POINTS (CONFLICT, DECOY, AND SABOTEUR)

Ghosts spawn in a small alcove adjacent to the Offices a militaristic set of closed rooms leading away from the facility proper. The route to the Command Center and other central areas is littered with these little alcoves that make perfect places to hide and let hostiles slip by. Note the side entrances into both the Command Center and upstairs Control Room. These can be used by both teams to make a more roundabout way into some of the objectives.

Flip the entire level and the Ghost spawn in the Offices becomes the Bodark spawn in the Loading Zone. Layout-wise, the approach to any of the central objectives is identical, but mirrored. Try to memorize the side routes to head off attacks by the other team that's attempting the do the same and to cut off any flanking maneuvers.

# POINTS OF INTEREST

## OVERWATCH

The Control Room overlooking the ever-spinning Missile Rack is a great place to hole up even when there isn't an objective nearby. There are only two routes in, and although the windows that look out over the areas below are fodder for grenades of every type, the fact that direct attacks must be funneled up the stairs means it's one of the few areas where you can be certain of enemy routes of entry.

## COMMAND CENTRAL

The Command Center is the home of an objective, but it's also a hardy installation in this base that serves as a great place to fall back to when under fire. By using the side rooms' staircases, it's also possible to take up a position on top of the Command Center, which is a great spot to snipe. So long as the entrances from those adjacent rooms are covered, this is a surprisingly safe place from which to annoy and eradicate hostile forces.

## SIDE SALAD

Both of the other two Points of Interest offer locations that let you and your squad dig in and repel incursions, but they're flanked by rooms that are rife with cover and ready for ambushes or lures away from the main combat zones. The ones next to the Control Room are in fact objective hot spots of their own, so expect plenty of traffic in and out of these rooms across all the various modes found in Underground.

# CONFLICT

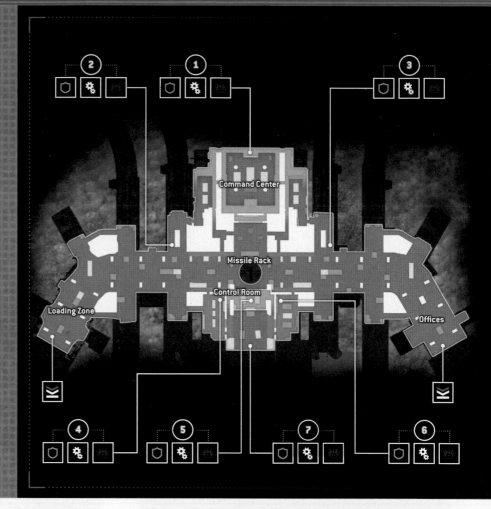

1 HOTSPOT

≡ DEPLOY

🛡 DEFEND

⚙ CONTROL/INTEL

🔥 DEMOLITION

Command Center

Missile Rack

Control Room

Loading Zone

Offices

**1** The Command Center's withering 1960s computer banks and musty shelving aren't much in the way of proper cover. Grenades can be lobbed through the broken window, and the sides are open to attacks from enemies taking cover on just the other side. The key is to keep any attackers back and occupied by the easy cover along the long tables and computers in the center of the room.

**2** Just a few steps outside the offices that flank the Command Center are twin objective hot spots. The first is to the left of the main area, next to a stationary rack of missiles. Cover here is minimal, and directly behind the objective is a long rail car of cover that defenders can attack from. If your squad can get there first, they have a good chance of overwhelming the defenders before they can get to the player capturing the objective. That person capturing should approach from the back of the missiles to give as much side cover as possible.

(3) Second verse, same as the first. Hug the right side of the missiles and capture from the rear to ensure there's a decent amount of flanking cover, and make sure your squad is keeping an eye out for attacks coming from the right and left as defenders try to cut short the capture operation.

(6) Take the same advice offered for objective four and apply it here, and you'll have a pretty good idea of what to expect. The only difference is that the cover in this room is low, and rotated 90 degrees so that it's easier to defend against attacks coming from the north and west. If you and your squad are trying to take the room, try approaching from the eastern entrance, where anyone inside will have to huddle along the shorter ends of cover.

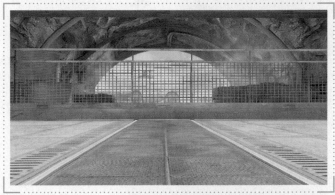

(4) This locker room adjacent to the stairs leading up to the Control Room can be accessed by way of a side tunnel to the west, a raised walkway to the north, and from a doorway facing east out into the center of the map. So long as all three are covered (and a Sensor is thrown out for good measure), this objective shouldn't be too hard to tackle.

(7) The final objective of the level looks out into a snowy field just outside the missile facility. There's absolutely nothing in the way of cover for someone trying to take the objective, so it falls to the captor's allies to repel incoming forces. Keep eyes trained on the Control Room's twin strips of window, as well as the side rooms to the left and right. A frontal assault from below the Control Room isn't unheard of either, though that's slightly easier to hold off, thanks to the forward-facing crates that serve as cover.

## // CAUTION

*The print book was reviewed and approved by Ubisoft, however we're aware that future game updates may result in some inaccuracies. To keep you up to date with these changes please refer to the insert card giving you FREE access to the Prima Official eGuide. The eGuide includes interactive maps for the Adversarial modes as well as Campaign Challenge videos and will update when there's a major change to the game, keeping you prepared for battle.*

(5) The Control Room is one of those areas that just seems to pull activity toward it, and not just because it's such an advantageous place to regroup. When an objective appears here, chances are the first group to get to it is going to be the one that holds it, *unless* the attacking team can, say, toss a Flashbang up into the room right as two teams of attackers charge up the stairs. Even then, the bottlenecks formed by the staircases make this a hard position to retake.

# DECOY

A **OBJECTIVE**

**DEMOLITION**

A Like the second objective in this list, the potential "key" target here is located *underneath* the walkway that leads to the upper perch of the Command Center. Access the room either by way of the entrances from the small stairs leading up from the Command Center, or the tunnel that housed the missile racks seen during Conflict mode. Because of the upper walkway in this room, getting over to the objective can be a little hairy, but there's plenty of cover in here to return fire. If defending, set Stun Mines or Claymores near the entrances and watch the stairs for any sneak attacks.

B Exactly like the first objective, the rooms filled with whirring tape-style hard drives offer just a few routes of entry, so plan accordingly. If working with your team's other squad, you can coordinate an invading first attack team to distract, and a second that launches to take the defenders by surprise.

C No surprise here, the Control Room houses the third possible capture point. By now you should have a fairly good idea of how to proceed: Frag, Flashbangs and firepower are go-to resources when charging up the stairs. Throwing out an EMP and then smoke, in that order, will shut down special scopes that normally see through smoke.

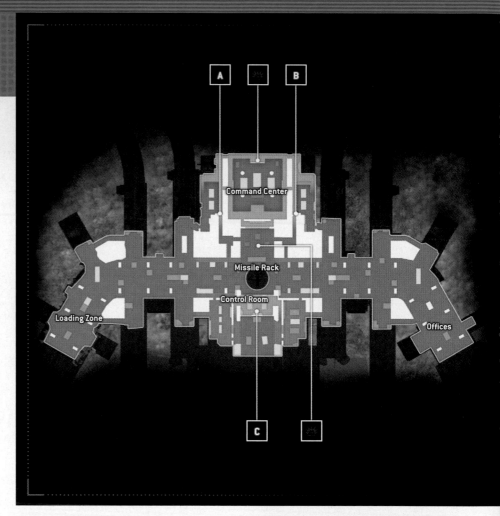

The Command Center awaits! The same reasons that made securing the location difficult during Conflict objectives hold true here: a window just begging for a grenade meal, wide open doors on either side, and plenty of opposition in the Command Center's main room. Sensors can help paint a picture of the defense when you're attacking, and can help warn of incoming attackers when defending. Dig in and get ready for a big firefight.

The open room just outside the Command Center is the second potential bomb site. With flanking doorways looking right toward the bomb plant site, the whole of the complex behind the site, and no doubt plenty of opposition from the Command Center room's twin exits, obscuring the area with smoke may be one of the best ways to halt an advance or slip through to begin planting.

# SABOTEUR

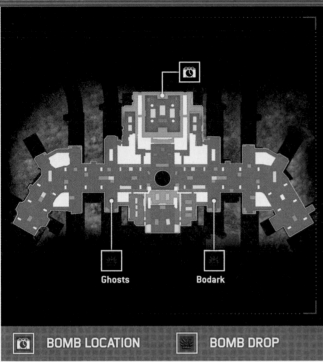

Ghosts          Bodark

| | BOMB LOCATION | | BOMB DROP |

# SIEGE

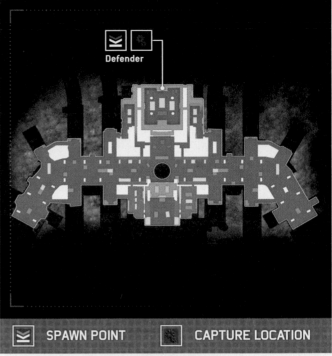

Defender

| | SPAWN POINT | | CAPTURE LOCATION |

It's a long trek from the Command Center where the bomb waits all the way back to the bomb placement location, but just getting to the bomb is a struggle in and of itself. Expect some teams to just hunker down, if they make it into the room, while trying to hold off the first wave of forces from the opposing team. It's a sound strategy, as they can then slip out with the bomb. Sensors and Cameras are big help in pinging the main room of the Command Center before entering, and popping smoke can obscure flanking moves while moving toward the bomb.

The almighty Command Center is once again the place to be for defenders, spawning near the control point at the back of the room. Use the few seconds while the attackers are waiting to spawn in to quickly run up and grab some elevated positions to add a bit more variety and oversight to the room. A UAV parked high up near the ceiling can help light up intruders as they sneak in, and with all the fighting, the attackers may never see it there giving away their position—a valuable means of snuffing out those single enemy lives everyone has in this mode.

Given the near-perfectly symmetrical nature of this map, it shouldn't be a huge surprise that the bomb plant locations for either team are in similar places on opposite ends of the underground bunker. The long tunnels are sniper-friendly, so pick bits of high cover to stick to as the bomb carrier and move slowly from one place to the next, trying to stay out of sight. Remember, if intel pegs you as the bomb carrier, you become an objective, making it that much more likely that you'll get overrun by the entire opposing team.

There's not much that needs to be done differently if you're on the Bodark team, just remember to stick to cover here, avoiding long sight lines where possible and moving as a team, making sure to collect as much intel as possible before leaving cover.

Given the advantage that height has in this room, it's a smart call to try to head off those upper defenders before charging into the room. But that doesn't mean a well-place smoke grenade and small force of a couple of distractions isn't a great way to throw the defense for a loop. Cover is your best friend, and with how close the fighting can be in the close quarters, heavier firepower like LMGs or shotguns can really make quick work of the defenders.

# MILL

## SITUATION REPORT

It's rare that any battlefields end up spilling out into an area so, well, bucolic. The Mill area is an interesting patchwork or rustic, solidly constructed buildings and plenty of heavy woods to mask approaches from the sides. Although there are some rather generous sight lines that would ordinarily be great for snipers, a thick fog has settled over the area, reducing visibility. A small Dam has also limited a river flowing through a creek bed and this allows for covert approaches through the soggy channel.

## SPAWN POINTS (CONFLICT, DECOY, AND SABOTEUR)

A quiet Farm allows Ghosts entry into the Mill, giving them plenty of room to fan out and grab cover next to the various buildings along the way toward the central Mill House and Dam. Cover is plentiful all throughout the map, and should be used whenever possible not just to avoid incoming fire, but to mask approaches on objectives.

Bodark forces slip in near a large Compound. Though cover isn't nearly as plentiful on their end of the map, the wide open spaces are heavily wooded and make for great low-key approaches toward the Dock and Mill House beyond. Closer to the center of the map, cover starts to sprout up , so take up positions that provide maximum sight lines toward the covered bridge and creek bed.

## POINTS OF INTEREST

### THE MILL HOUSE

It may seem old, but this Mill House is more than capable of operating even with the low current of the stream that flows beside it. Central to multiple objectives across the various modes, the Mill House also serves as a strategic location for regrouping and taking cover. Because it has just a few ways in or out, holding the Mill House can help control the flow of combat and set it on your team's terms by coaxing in enemies or directing fire out toward the various paths nearby.

### THE BRIDGE

Because the covered bridge offers cover while traversing from one half of the map to the other, it's often a spot for Sensors and Cameras that serve as an early warning system against enemies approaching from the creek bed and the bridge. The area between the bridge and Dam has trapped many a foolish rookie. While it's certainly possible to jump down from the Dam into the stream below, the two-stage jump is slow and clunky, giving players that set up under the bridge plenty of time to line up shots and take out enemies as they race into the fire to move up the sloping side that forms the only way out.

### CRYPT KEEPERS

The Cemetery area is a hotbed of objective activity, but it's also the easiest way to slip past enemies thanks to high walls and plenty of cover if ambushed. Expect more than a few firefights to go down here, and not just while fighting over an objective. As a gateway to the Church and Well areas, the Cemetery can also serve as a counterpoint to the Mill House, restricting movement and controlling the flow of battle from relative safety.

# CONFLICT

1 HOTSPOT

⊻ DEPLOY

🛡 DEFEND

⚙ CONTROL/INTEL

■ DEMOLITION

**1** A small V-shaped area between a parked SUV and a stack of boats is a frequent objective hot spot. The location's open back means there's very little in the way of cover for defenders, save for a couple of low bits in the building next to the SUV. Beware of attacks coming from the directions of the Dam, the potholed road leading from the bridge, and the Windmills, as plenty of routes funnel down to those directions.

**2** Closer to the nearby Windmills is a lengthy cabin with a fuel truck. Tucked between the abode and its source of fuel is the second objective—one left open to attack from the direction of the nearby covered troop transport. Fire from the main road is also something of a concern, not to mention the crumbling remains of a house on a similarly elevated outcropping on the other side of that main road.

**3** That crumbling building is the source of yet another potential objective. The building's walls of varying heights mean there's plenty of cover, but just as many angles where hostiles can fire in from the other side of what used to be the building's windows. Keep an eye out for attacks from the main road, the elevated forest area, and the direction of the Mill House's small bridge.

**6** Pay close attention to the location of the objective in the Cemetery. There are more spots like it in other modes, but the method for securing the location should be more or less the same: slip in, stay low, and use the headstones for cover. Once the objective is captured, try hopping over the nearby low wall and waiting for enemies to approach, while keeping in mind the Dam as a main route. With luck, you can let enemies get close and begin trying to take the objective for their own, then fire from the cover of the low wall at near point-blank range.

**4** Speaking of bridges, the main covered one plays home to yet another objective, this one between the two legs that hold up the structure in the middle of the creek. There's little here to hide behind when shots come streaking in from what seems like all directions, including the bank leading up toward the Windmills, the bank leading toward the Mill House, a couple of paths that flank the creek, and, of course, the Dam directly overlooking the objective. A full squad is extremely important when trying to occupy this area for any length of time.

**7** A greenhouse near this village's Well is a great place to grab low cover to let enemies pass before ambushing them, but when an objective waits inside, the thin wood and even thinner glass that makes up the walls of the structure offer a pittance in the way of actual protection. The lower concrete parts of the greenhouse are a little better at stopping incoming fire, but as a general rule, it's better to try to find more solid cover if possible.

**// CAUTION**

*The print book was reviewed and approved by Ubisoft, however we're aware that future game updates may result in some inaccuracies. To keep you up to date with these changes please refer to the insert card giving you FREE access to the Prima Official eGuide. The eGuide includes interactive maps for the Adversarial modes as well as Campaign Challenge videos and will update when there's a major change to the game, keeping you prepared for battle.*

**5** Ah, the Mill House—so important to this map, so fraught with potential angles of attack. The most obvious, of course, are the main entrance off the road and from the direction of the large turning wheel. The sandbags near the objective make for good cover from another, more sneaky, route: a back entrance accessible only by scooting around the side of the building. Cameras and Sensors placed nearby are great at spoiling would-be surprises, but it's important to capture the objective and then quickly grab cover around the sandbags to avoid crossfire from outside.

# DECOY

 **A** OBJECTIVE

 **DEMOLITION**

**A** The Cemetery once again plays host to a major objective and source of conflict, this time as one of the potential locations for information leading to the bomb drop location. Use the same techniques you did during Conflict scuffles here to defend the position, and make sure to sweep the perimeter before trying to capture if you're attacking.

**B** Time to head under the bridge again, but just as before in Conflict, there are multiple ways to defend the capture point. There's not a whole lot defenders can do against a combined attacking force, but placing some defenders on reserve nearby to float between the Cemetery and bridge is a great way to respond quickly to incoming threats. Keep an eye out for sharpshooters near the riverbank, and grab what little cover the Bridge supports have if things get too chaotic.

**C** The Mill House's objective is actually rather deviously placed. Sitting behind a railing in the Mill House's second room, the position of this objective is vulnerable to firing angles from the open area just outside, and can mean death to a defender if caught unaware. The open area outside also forces gunmen to step out of cover to take the shot—a perfect opportunity for defenders waiting near the large doors to pop out and finish the attacker off. Sneaking in the back way does allow for cover to fire toward the objective in a pinch, but it's better to use the back way in to take out any defenders looking out toward the road.

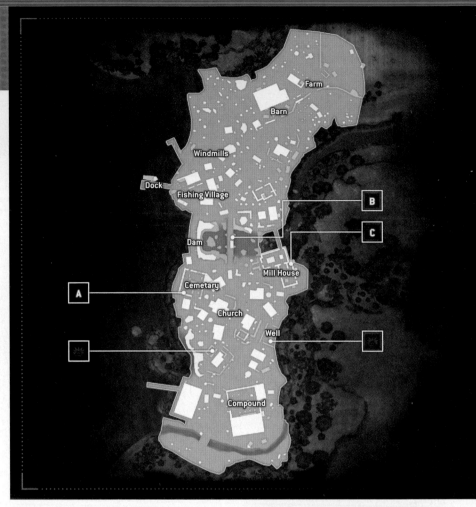

Another perilous greenhouse beckons with the promise of a fresh bomb location (well one of them, anyway). But, as should be obvious by now, it's an extremely hard kind of building to lock down thanks to its flimsy walls and copious windows announcing your presence. Use this to your advantage on defense and douse the building in a hail of gunfire whenever the bomb planter tries to drop his explosive playload. Attackers must weed out any threats before attempting to add a little more heat to the greenhouse.

The Well offers up a second location for a bomb, and there's almost nothing to speak of for cover if you're defending. Baiting an attacker into trying to place the bomb, then lobbing explosives might just work, but it's a risky gamble. Dropping a Camera nearby is a better idea because it allows you to set up a coordinated attack to repel the attackers.

# SABOTEUR

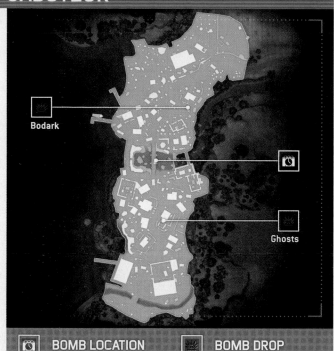

**Bodark**

**Ghosts**

|  BOMB LOCATION |  BOMB DROP |

Given the role that the bridge has played in all the various modes up until now, it should come as no surprise that the central location is right where the bomb waits for both sides. With wide-open flanks, it's going to be a bloodbath trying to sneak in and capture the bomb. Smart players will throw out Sensors or place a Camera above to keep track of the action as the firefights push the momentum back and forth. Just getting to the bomb isn't good enough; your team will need a plan to carry it to its intended destination, so communicate as much as possible before rushing in.

Ghosts are given the unenviable task of carrying the bomb all the way to the greenhouse that served as the grave for so many combatants before. Use the Cemetery and Church as cover while moving, taking the time to thoroughly clear out an area before moving on but keeping a steady pace to avoid respawning enemies from rejoining the battles.

Bodarks must somehow make their way over to a section of lumber and rusting construction equipment to place the bomb. Avoid the main road, as there are far too many locations on either side from which to rain down damage. Instead, try to skirt the outer edges of the map, then sweep in, sticking to cover at all costs.

# SIEGE

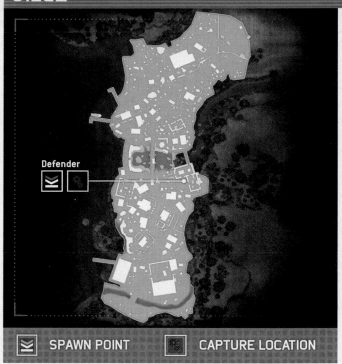

**Defender**

|  SPAWN POINT | CAPTURE LOCATION |

The Defenders' spawn location and the capture point is sandwiched between two buildings facing toward the Mill House. Cramped and narrow, with plenty of opportunities to repel invaders, the capture location is rife with opportunities for sniping from the Mill House itself, as well as protective cover from smoke. Be wary of attackers swooping in from the Dam side of the map or trying to get the drop from behind. A well-placed grenade can end a capture attempt in one fell swoop if the timing is right.

The name of the game for attackers is survival. The more of you there are to coordinate attacks on the Mill House, the better your chances of surviving long enough to finally capture that central location. Under no circumstances should a rush attempt be made to get in. With so many places to grab cover and fire into the objective location from the Mill House, defenders have the upper hand here. UAVs of your own can help with any defenders that might be taking up residence outside the Mill House itself. But a wide, sweeping arc that lets snipers whittle the defenders' numbers are your best bet until you can make a concerted push toward one of the entrances, preferably one that has nearby cover from which to fire.

# 4

# GUERRILLA

Guerrilla mode gives you and up to three friends the chance to fend off wave after wave of enemy troops in a frantic fight for survival. But before you enter a defensive posture, you must first infiltrate and take control of an enemy-controlled HQ, preferably through stealthy means. Once an enemy HQ is secured, get ready for all-out chaos as the enemy counterattack begins. Your team is forced to defend against waves of infantry and even vehicles. Does your team have what it takes to survives 50 waves? The information in this chapter will help prepare you for the battles ahead.

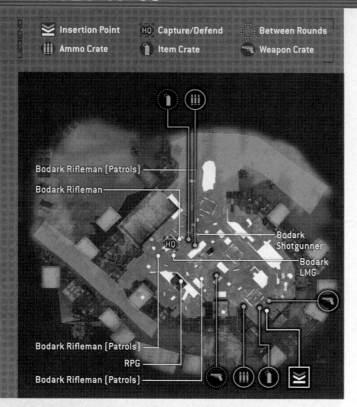

Bodark Rifleman (Patrols)
Bodark Rifleman
Bodark Shotgunner
Bodark LMG
Bodark Rifleman (Patrols)
RPG
Bodark Rifleman (Patrols)

## INFILTRATION

It would appear the enemy has decided normal troops just aren't going to do the trick anymore. To that end, they've called in Bodark units, which won't show up on a sensor sweep due to their optical camouflage and are hard to spot at a distance. Thankfully, they're positioned in exactly the same places as previous infiltrations into this HQ, with one major exception: Instead of a second shotgunner, an RPG-toting grunt sits atop a roof overlooking the HQ. With a few changes, though, even a single Ghost can silently eliminate them all.

Begin by taking the same route used the last two infiltrations. Grab cover near the food stand and wait until the camouflaged patrolling Bodark rifleman turns to head back toward the HQ, then quickly stealth kill him out of the sight of the RPG grunt. Head into the alleyway with the burning vehicle and take cover behind the crates near the HQ. Wait for the second patrolling rifleman to turn and begin moving back toward the HQ, just like the first. Quickly kill him, then head back toward the crates and wait for the stationary Bodark LMG enemy to look away from the RPG goon. With a single precision (suppressed) headshot, take out the RPG-wielder, then wait for the LMG guard to turn back around. Sneak up behind him, stealth kill him, move through the HQ, and then do the same to his buddy. All that remains now is for the patrolling Bodark rifleman to turn and walk away from the clueless Bodark shotgunner so that you can take both out and clear the HQ.

## // Noteworthy Waves

Wave 41—After so many waves of enemies, you and your squad should have a good idea where threats will come from. The Bodark forces don't really mix this up, but they're far more prepared than other troops and will quickly throw out EMP grenades to disable any turrets you set up for cover. Expect them to crash the HQ hard and fast, and with their ability to cloak, it can be harder to spot far-off targets. Gear up for heavy fighting. These enemies are well-armored, and there's no need for a suppressed weapon anymore, so grab a weapon with high penetration and another with a rapid rate of fire to cover your bases. Claymores and incendiary or Frag grenades are a solid investment, but don't forget to stock up again between waves.

Wave 47—Be ready for an absolutely **relentless** assault by a seemingly unending series of shielded enemies. They will slowly move in from all sides, with new ones replacing any that are felled. To make matters worse, RPG and LMG troopers complicate things even further. Wait for the shielded enemies to approach the relative safety of the HQ, then melee them into oblivion. Should an RPG unit spawn in the balcony behind the HQ where his shots are blocked by the HQ itself, leave him until the end; his shots can't get to your team unless you leave the cover of the HQ.

Wave 50—This is it: the last of the waves and the Bodark forces know it. With a whopping 45 hostiles to take down and every combination of heavy-hitting firepower, this one's going to be tough. Coordinate with your fellow Ghosts, adopting a direction to concentrate your fire while your buddies do the same so that between you, all angles are covered. Stay elastic, though, grouping with squadmates to repel multiple attackers as needed, then returning to your primary firing direction. Toward the end of the wave, after you destroy the first APC, a helicopter will glide into the level with another APC, and these should be taken out as quickly as possible with any and all heavy strikes. There's no need to conserve here. Use multiple air strikes and missiles. Judicious use of your Invisibility Wave Streak will make all the difference. Remember that Bodark camo keeps them from being highlighted in night vision, so stick to clear optics unless trying to peer through smoke.

# OFFICE

## SITUATION REPORT

Everyone likes to think they're safe at a simple desk job, but when your high-rise office happens to hold sensitive information in the banks of servers sitting in the middle of the floor, nothing is truly safe. Such was the case in this office complex, now deserted save for hostiles patrolling the floor and the helipad outside. Office furniture makes for lousy cover, so stick to more hardy structures like walls during shoot-outs and keep an eye out for attacks from the skylights dotting the office space.

## PHASES 1-10

**LEGEND**

| | | |
|---|---|---|
| ⊻ Insertion Point | HQ Capture/Defend | ◯ Between Rounds |
| ⦀ Ammo Crate | ⬗ Item Crate | ⬳ Weapon Crate |

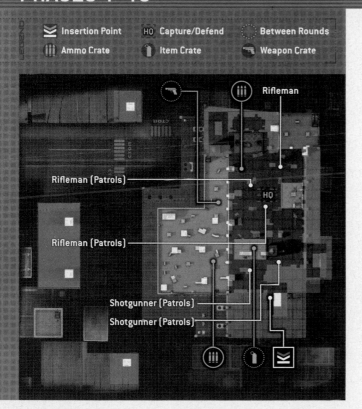

Rifleman

Rifleman (Patrols)

Rifleman (Patrols)

HQ

Shotgunner (Patrols)

Shotgunner (Patrols)

## INFILTRATION

Your squad will begin in an empty stairwell, but it doesn't stay unoccupied for long. If given enough time, a nearby guard will move from his original desk position to another closer to the stairs, then into the room where your squad waits, blowing your cover. Get the drop on him before this can happen by quickly exiting and stealth killing him, and then his buddy, who patrols nearby a set of desks.

## PHASES 21-30

**LEGEND**

⩘ Insertion Point    HQ Capture/Defend    ⬭ Between Rounds

▥ Ammo Crate    🔫 Item Crate    🔫 Weapon Crate

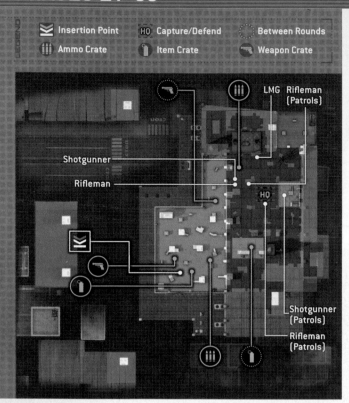

LMG Rifleman (Patrols)

Shotgunner

Rifleman

HQ

Shotgunner (Patrols)

Rifleman (Patrols)

## INFILTRATION

Another group of enemies has taken up residence near the server area HQ, so once again, a stealthy approach is warranted. From the helipad HQ, head directly into the office and grab cover outside of the server room. Wait for the patrolling guard to turn around and begin walking away. Stealth kill him, then look right toward another guard standing near a desk. Hop the low wall of the server room, take out the guard, and then hug that right wall while moving toward the rear of the office.

A shotgunner patrols the perimeter of the server cluster, so let him continue his route walking toward a pair of guards talking to each other. A LMG-wielding guard standing by himself and looking away from the other guards should be taken down next. With him out of the way, move back through the server room quickly to avoid the gaze of the two talking guards, then grab cover and wait for the shotgunner's route to take him back around near your position. Let him pass, then eliminate him from behind before setting up a final sync-shot of the two talking guards with the help of a squadmate to clear the area of all remaining hostiles.

## // Noteworthy Waves

Wave 22—Up until now, there hasn't been a concerted effort by enemies to push into the server area en masse. That changes with this wave, meaning there will be a steady, heavy number of enemies sprinting into the HQ to overwhelm you and your squad. Stick to forward cover near the two entrances and gun down enemies with precision bursts or blind fire. If an enemy slips by, quickly eliminate the hostile with a melee strike and then move back to cover to repel the other forces.

## // CAUTION

### LOOK BEFORE YOU LEAP

*Melee strikes are a great way to eliminate close-range threats, but there's a catch: The camera needs to be pointed in their general direction. In other words, mashing the melee button when near an enemy doesn't guarantee they'll actually be taken out. Ghost Recon: Future Soldier's context-sensitive actions need a bit of guidance, so if you haven't panned the camera toward an enemy, the game will simply think you're trying to reload ... with a hostile in point-blank range.*

Wave 25—A concerted effort to overwhelm the team combines LMG-sporting enemies firing at long range to force suppression while shotgunners rush toward the HQ. It's not just a clever tactic, it's a deadly one; a single shotgun blast at close range is enough to down any Ghost, so assign roles to your squad, letting one or two squadmates concentrate on taking out the LMGs as quickly as possible while the others repel the shotgunners before they can slip into the HQ.

Wave 30—Though there are plenty of familiar threats this wave (including a pesky turret that's quickly remanned when the previous operator is gunned down), the real problem just happens to be a helicopter that buzzes the office. The helicopter only has two areas where it can fire from: the back of the office and the large spread of windows facing out toward the roof. When it does start spraying bullets, the suppression effect can be devastating, so quickly call down a Missile or Airstrike to remove the threat before it ends up chewing through your whole squad.

# PHASES 31–40

⌄ Insertion Point    HQ Capture/Defend    ◎ Between Rounds

▥ Ammo Crate    ❗ Item Crate    ⌐ Weapon Crate

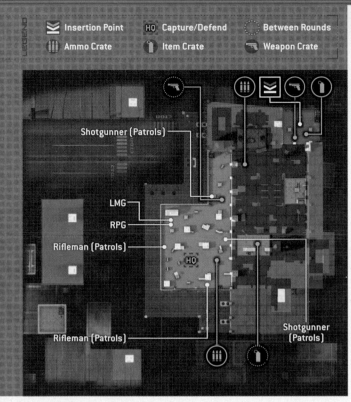

Shotgunner (Patrols)

LMG
RPG
Rifleman (Patrols)

HQ

Rifleman (Patrols)

Shotgunner (Patrols)

## INFILTRATION

Resist the temptation to attack the HQ the same way you did previously. Although there are only six hostiles to deal with, their patrol routes and placement have changed, necessitating a new strategy. Head through the office, back toward the staircase where you first entered the map, then hang a right and grab cover near the windows by the entrance to the rooftops. Let a patrolling rifleman slip by. Once he passes, take him out quietly and move to the nearby air conditioning unit to wait for another patrol.

Two guards crisscross the helipad, so wait for the far guard to approach from the side of the AC unit facing the office. As soon as he draws near enough to perform a stealth kill, pop out of cover and hammer the melee button to take him down before he can raise the alarm. Venture out across the helipad to take out the other patrolling guard, being sure to avoid the pair that are talking somewhat nearby. Leave those two for now, and move back toward the office, grabbing cover by another AC unit until a patrolling guard turns to walk back toward where your squad first spawned in this wave. Take him out quietly, then set up a sync-shot on the last two guards to clean up.

## // Noteworthy Waves

Wave 34—That dangerous combination of LMGs suppressing while scads of shotgunners swarm in is back, and this time, the HQ is much larger, with no real choke points to funnel enemies into. Just as before, designate a couple of your squad members for LMG duty, taking them out before their attacks can cause the screen to shake so violently that the other squad members can't take out the shotgunners. Avoid trying to take cover in the center of the HQ unless it's an emergency, as the small crates offer little in the way of protection.

Wave 35—The disruptive power of LMG troopers will play an even bigger role in the next wave, when their screen-shaking might makes counter-sniping at hostile snipers and RPG troopers on the far-off buildings a huge hassle. Stick to cover to block the incoming shots from afar and deal with the LMGs first. If no one in your squad has picked up a sniper or assault rifle with a serious scope, now would be a good time to do so. Keep it handy; those snipers will be sticking around for a few more rounds.

Wave 39—With dozens of enemies to take down this wave, it probably comes as bad news that they're going to be rushing in as fast as possible. A combination of shielded enemies and shotgunners can make things difficult unless your squad concentrates on taking out encroaching shotgunners first while waiting to deal with the shielded enemies until they're closer. Save grenades until there's fewer than ten enemies remaining; there are far more shielded foes than ever before.

Wave 40—There's no sugarcoating it. This wave is extremely difficult. All of the screen-rattling suppression of an attack helicopter mixes with a rooftop turret, and the pair are overwhelming even *before* you factor in the fact that there are plenty of LMG troopers around. Staying out of range of the turret is a good way to keep it from messing things up, so stick to the helipad as much as possible and let enemies come to you. Snipers on the rooftop will be hard to hit when the helicopter is unloading, so keep moving while in cover to avoid their shots. If things get hectic, use a Invisibility Wave Streak to run for far cover, taking out any LMGs along the way. The sooner the helicopter can be taken out with a lucky Airstrike or a guided Missile, the better.

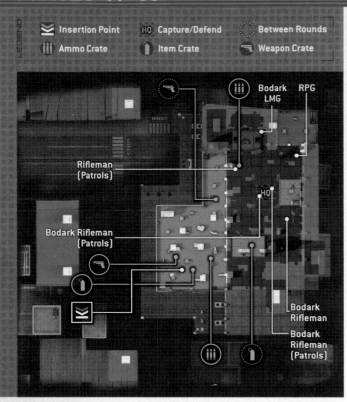

Bodark LMG   RPG

Rifleman (Patrols)

Bodark Rifleman (Patrols)

HQ

Bodark Rifleman

Bodark Rifleman (Patrols)

Grab cover behind the magazine rack, then slip out and take cover behind one of the columns leading outside. Swap to the second column and wait for the RPG hostile's head to turn back toward the front of the office, then sneak up and purge the area of the last threat.

## INFILTRATION

Once again, Bodark squads take over for the final set of waves, adding their Optical Camo to the mix and making targets harder to see at a distance. Thankfully, their numbers during the infiltration round aren't huge; just a half dozen stand between your squad and a clear HQ. Start by slipping into the office through the entrance ahead, keeping some distance from the server area, as two guards now patrol there. Quickly sneak up behind the Bodark trooper and take him out silently, then grab cover along a low wall on the side of the server area.

Wait for the Bodark rifleman to pass, then jump over the cover and perform a stealth kill on him. Wait near that server for the second rifleman to loop around the far server, then quickly sneak up behind him and eliminate the threat. Quickly continue down the path he was traveling and grab cover along the inside of the low cover along the far wall. Wait for an uncloaked rifleman to move to another computer with his back turned to you. Once he's taken out, move toward the back of the office, keeping an eye out for a cloaked Bodark LMG in the corner near the back skylight. That will need to be dispatched before you move on toward a final RPG trooper.

## // Noteworthy Waves

Wave 42—It should become immediately obvious how much more highly trained the Bodark squad is. Instead of relying on sheer numbers, the cloaked hostiles use coordinated attacks, rallying shielded units, lobbing smoke, Flashbangs, and Incendiary Grenades from the windows facing the rooftop, and regularly pushing in from both sides of the server room. Stick to cover at all times, keeping an eye out for the telltale change from blue to orange that signals a hostile has slipped into the server area.

Wave 47—Although an RPG trooper shows up in Wave 45, these units become a serious problem in this wave, particularly because they're paired with numerous shields and even a few LMGs that spray suppressing fire from either end of the office. Stick to targeting the RPGs as quickly as possible; their splash damage can be extremely dangerous and overpower light cover with ease. Let the shielded enemies come to you, and try to flank the LMGs while they're concentrating on your squadmates.

Wave 50—The previous waves have been difficult, sure, but they were nothing compared to the combined onslaught that is Wave 50. Forty-nine enemies turn the office into a hail of gunfire from nearly all directions, most notably heavy spray from no less than three different turrets. The turrets' suppression effect should be dealt with as quickly as possible (a sniper rifle can help by firing through cover if an extreme side angle is too risky. Take out a single turret's gunner (and any replacements that are sure to appear) before moving on to the next. Just when things start to seem a little more calm, a helicopter will drop in, spraying yet more suppression. By now, you should know how effective a Missile Wave Perk is at dealing with airborne threats, but any and all Airstrikes you and your squad have are great for thinning out troop numbers.

# AIRSTRIP

## SITUATION REPORT

A sand-blasted airport overrun with hostiles is enough of a challenge, but when one factors in a looming sandstorm that threatens to destroy any semblance of visibility, things become even more fraught with danger. Nevertheless, your Ghost squad has no choice but to sneak in and secure the HQ, then hold off any rebels that attempt to retake it. The multitiered main structure makes maintaining control an issue, so spread out your squad to cover both routes of entry. Four entrances below and two ladders leading to the upper level mean that there are more points to cover than available Ghosts, but pay close attention to where enemies tend to enter most and prioritize those routes on a per-wave basis.

## PHASES 1-10

**LEGEND**

- ⟨⟨ Insertion Point
- 🅷🅀 Capture/Defend
- ⬭ Between Rounds
- ⫿⫿⫿ Ammo Crate
- ▮ Item Crate
- ⬡ Weapon Crate

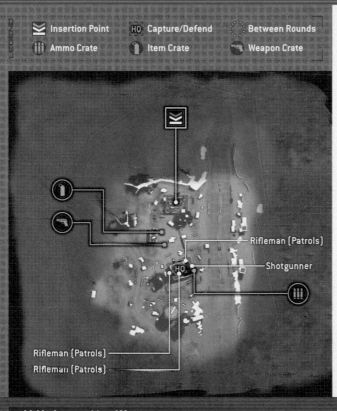

Rifleman (Patrols)
Shotgunner
HQ
Rifleman (Patrols)
Rifleman (Patrols)

## INFILTRATION

With only four hostiles to eliminate, it might seem like this will be the quickest first-round infiltration yet, but the enemies' placement means there's plenty of opportunities for dead bodies to be spotted, so timing is as important as stealth here. Begin by sweeping right and heading toward the HQ. Shadow the rifleman patrolling *outside* the structure first, waiting until he's almost around the corner to make your move. Double back and quickly dispatch the ground-floor rifleman while his buddy walking above heads to a lookout.

Push through the HQ toward the exit ahead, skirting the right side of the doorjamb to avoid being spotted by the shotgunner just on the other side. Take him out, slip up the staircase, hang a right, and dispatch the final guard while he looks out back toward where you began. Alternatively, with only four targets, your whole squad could fan out to attempt a four-way sync-shot, but with three different patrols, the timing will have to be perfect.

## // Noteworthy Waves

Wave 8—Those towers dotting the airfield have been mostly empty until now, but the first repeat appearance of a sniper should be a telltale sign that there will be plenty more in future waves. Note that this is also where RPG troopers take up positions, and the elevation for both sniping and launching rockets is seriously dangerous. Get into the habit of scanning the towers during moments of downtime and if you see someone, even if you're going to take them out, mark them as a target so that your fellow Ghosts know to keep scanning when they have spare moments, too.

Wave 10—Wave 10 brings a pair of APCs to contend with, but also multiple snipers in both the forward and rear towers. The suppressing fire of the vehicles can make lining up a shot on the snipers difficult, so if possible, call in a Missile strike to remove the screen-shaking effect as quickly as possible. When taking out snipers, don't get too greedy; take a couple of quick shots while scoped or in iron sights, then pop back into cover. Aiming for too long is a recipe for a sniper round to the noggin.

**LEGEND**

⟱ Insertion Point      HQ Capture/Defend      ◯ Between Rounds

▥ Ammo Crate           ▮ Item Crate           ▬ Weapon Crate

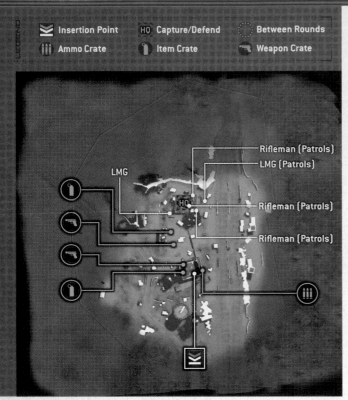

Rifleman (Patrols)
LMG (Patrols)
LMG
HQ
Rifleman (Patrols)
Rifleman (Patrols)

## INFILTRATION

The wind is beginning to pick up a bit, but there's nothing yet in the way of cover from the storm. Because of this, you'll want to give all five guards back near where you first inserted into this map a wide berth. Start by sweeping right, just as before, keeping plenty of distance from the guards patrolling in and out of the HQ. A lone LMG hostile patrols in a wide arc that takes him out near the airstrip. Wait for him to pass by a set of crates, then slip around their left side and take out the heavy gunner to avoid having his lazy patrol wreak havoc on the carefully timed movements to come.

Quickly double back, grabbing cover along the strip of corrugated metal to let the patrolling guard to the left slip back inside, then push forward to the right corner of the wall ahead. A rifleman normally peeks out around this wall, then turns around and heads back into the building, but a quick melee strike when he's near will prevent that. Hang back and wait for another guard to emerge from another doorway, then sneak up behind him and finish the job inside the building. Slip back out, hugging the wall of the HQ, to slip behind and finish off the stationary LMG hostile, then pause and wait for the final patrolling rifleman to emerge before stalking and killing him as he walks away.

## // Noteworthy Waves

Wave 17—It may have taken a while, but the shield troopers are finally out in force. They have a lot of ground to cover but move slowly, which means it's easy for the Ghosts to get distracted by other threats, only to find a shield inches from your face. The same tactics as before hold true here: Waiting for a melee attack is a quick and easy way to get rid of the threat, but don't go charging out of cover just to take one enemy down. Lobbing an Incendiary Grenade just in front can light the shield troopers on fire long before they ever get close.

Wave 18—Snipers have found their roosts and quickly begin taking potshots whenever possible. Counter-sniping isn't going to be easy when there are multiple LMGs throwing fire everywhere. Remember to mark the targets if you're pinned down by incoming fire, and wait for a break in the LMG hail to lob out a grenade. Even if it doesn't hit, having an explosive drop near a gunner will force the enemy to scramble to find a new piece of cover, which gives you time to focus your aim.

Wave 20—It's a familiar combination: a pair of vehicles, some snipers, and a whole lot of bad guys that need shooting. The problem? Some of those bad guys are LMG troopers, which means they have even **more** ways to screw with you and your squad's aim. Spread out to minimize the effect their shots will have, and remember to mark targets. By now, if you haven't used any, your squad should have at least a few Airstrikes on hand. Unleash them to both thin the troop numbers and (with luck) take out one of the APCs for you.

# PHASES 21-30

LEGEND

- ⌄ Insertion Point
- ⫿ Ammo Crate
- HQ Capture/Defend
- ⬚ Item Crate
- ◯ Between Rounds
- ⬒ Weapon Crate

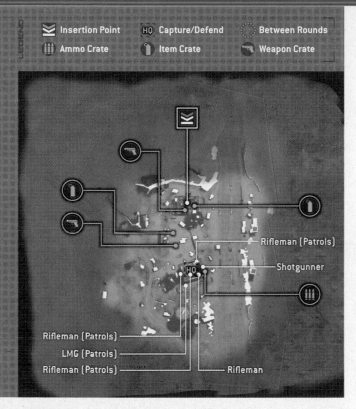

Rifleman (Patrols)

Shotgunner

Rifleman (Patrols)
LMG (Patrols)
Rifleman (Patrols)

Rifleman

## INFILTRATION

Time to head back into the first HQ, and yet more guards are patrolling various parts of the building. Sweep right, keeping a large crate and forklift between you and the HQ for cover. Hug the crate the forklift is holding and wait for the nearby patrol to move left before taking him out, then quickly return to the crate and look to the right corner of the building. Another guard peeks out, pauses, and turns around, while a second guard makes his rounds inside.

Dispatch the guard on the exterior of the building and continue to follow his route to an entrance into the building, pausing as needed to allow the patrolling guard inside to pass and taking care to avoid the gaze of the patrolling guard up above; the grating of his floor offers a glimpse if you're exposed. When the coast is clear, slip through the HQ and dispatch the shotgunner just as before, by veering right past the doorjamb and quickly taking him out.

Head up the stairs and wait for the patrolling guard to start heading back to the right, then slip behind his stationary buddy directly ahead and take him out before sneaking up to kill the guard peering outside. Head down the staircase to the left, slip into the building and dispatch the final patrolling guard to turn that orange floor blue and finish the wave.

## // Noteworthy Waves

Wave 23—If you and your squad have been using copious numbers of Claymores near HQ entrances, you're likely used to the sound of random explosions, but up until now, that's been a good thing. It means an enemy that tried to sneak in has failed. But a new kind of explosion is about to begin, coupled with the unmistakable hiss of a rocket-propelled grenade being flung toward its target. Those sniper towers are now home to RPG troopers, too, so quickly mark and eliminate them as soon as possible.

### // CAUTION

#### ALWAYS BE PREPARED

*You've played enough waves to know that there's always an item and weapon crate dropped between rounds. Great, if you're in need of some Claymores, for instance, but if not, who cares, right? Don't be so quick to dismiss the idea of being able to stock up on literally dozens of explosives. You and your buddies should be hitting the item crate every single round and grabbing as much as possible. Although Drones and Sensors are part of your inventory by default, you can swap them out (such as after Wave 40 when Bodark enemies' Optical Camo make Sensors moot) to carry more useful items. Make the trip out to resupply every time. Trust us.*

Wave 27—Although it's been bad in previous waves, the sandstorm absolutely destroys visibility in this wave, which is a problem considering it's packed with dozens of enemies making a rush toward the HQ, while LMGs make returning fire toward the multiple slow-moving shielded enemies a pain. You do have a secret weapon, however, and it's not just switching to Night Vision Mode (which should be a given anyway since it's impossible to see otherwise). Having saved up the Radar Wave Streak for just such an occasion, your squad should have at least a minute or so of pings that show every single enemy in the level. This is especially useful for exposing the cloaked Bodark enemies in Wave 40 and higher.

Wave 30—The third boss wave offers a different kind of threat, one that hasn't been seen on any previous map: a heavily armored troop transport complete with thumping cannons that can absolutely tear up light cover. In addition, an APC is also part of the attack and snipers are pairing up, two to a tower. Missile strikes are recommended to deal with the vehicles before they can create too much chaos, but the snipers can actually be more deadly. Deal with them before attempting to revive any downed squadmates; remember that even after they've bled out, squadmates can still guide a UAV around to paint targets for the rest of the conscious squad. Having a good picture of all threats is every bit as important as eliminating them.

## PHASES 31-40

**LEGEND**

- ≋ Insertion Point
- ⵘ Ammo Crate
- HQ Capture/Defend
- ⬤ Item Crate
- ◯ Between Rounds
- ⬟ Weapon Crate

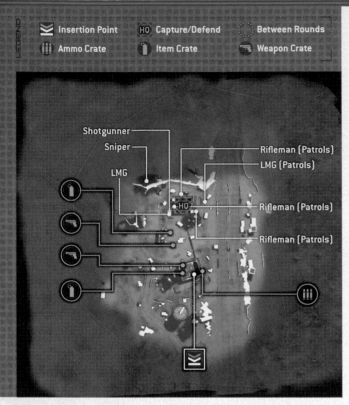

Shotgunner
Sniper
LMG
HQ
Rifleman (Patrols)
LMG (Patrols)
Rifleman (Patrols)
Rifleman (Patrols)

## INFILTRATION

The addition of two more guards means this infiltration will have be adapted a bit. Instead of moving to immediately eliminate the LMG patrol, instead cut in toward the HQ itself to dispatch the guard that's walking near its right side. *Then* go after the LMG and return to the long strip of corrugated metal for cover to avoid the gaze of the soldier that pops out from the corner of the building.

As soon as he turns around, move to cover along the wall he just peeked around and wait for another patrolling rifleman to emerge. Shadow the closest enemy and wait to attack until he stops and starts to turn around to give the rifleman ahead a little more space. Quickly move forward to take out that rifleman, then skulk back through the HQ to emerge from the front-left doorway. Directly to the right is a waiting shotgunner. Take him out, then creep up on and remove his equally stationary LMG friend before looking toward the trees to spot a sniper. Line up a clean headshot and dispose of the not-so-eagle-eyed defender (mark him if the sandstorm has gotten too intense) to capture the HQ.

## // Noteworthy Waves

Wave 33—The rebels start to step things up quite a bit, mounting a rush attack that attempts to overwhelm you and your Ghost squad. Mark far-off targets often, and keep your heads on a swivel to avoid letting one of the numerous hostiles slip in from the rear entrances. Placing Claymores facing toward the smaller entrances can help, but quick reaction and precision attacks are more important.

Wave 35—The sandstorm intensifies in this wave, which only serves to make the double-sniper teams that set up shop in the three towers around the level that much more deadly. Take cover out of range of their shots and concentrate on the LMGs that are trying to mask the approach of multiple shotgunners. The snipers are static; shotgunners enjoy unloading their one-shot kill payloads at close range, so prioritize LMGs, then shotgunners, **then** snipers.

Wave 39—The dangers of Waves 33 and 35 are combined here: with a huge sandstorm cutting into visibility, shielded enemies, shotgunners, and LMGs all mount a concerted rush. Keep on the offensive, targeting LMGs as quickly as possible to avoid their suppressing effect from hitting you and your squad from afar.

Wave 40—Twin snipers dot the towers, LMGs disrupt your view and the hostiles have learned the effectiveness of popping smoke and lobbing Flashbangs. Do your best to thin the herd a bit, but be mindful of the APC that appears over the ridge at the right rear of the HQ. Piloting a Missile into this corner of the map is difficult, so avoid wasting attempts. Instead, stay out of the APC's line of sight and it'll stop firing. A heavier vehicle crashes in from the airstrip, however, and that should most definitely be eliminated with a Missile strike. After reducing the enemies to about a half dozen or so, calling in an Airstrike can remove all the remaining threats in one explosive volley.

# PHASES 41–50

LEGEND
- ⌄ Insertion Point
- HQ Capture/Defend
- ○ Between Rounds
- ⫴ Ammo Crate
- ⬗ Item Crate
- ⬜ Weapon Crate

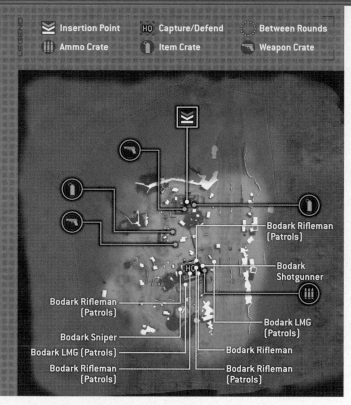

Bodark Rifleman (Patrols)
Bodark Shotgunner
Bodark LMG (Patrols)
Bodark Rifleman (Patrols)
Bodark Sniper
Bodark LMG (Patrols)
Bodark Rifleman (Patrols)
Bodark Rifleman
Bodark Rifleman (Patrols)

## INFILTRATION

Sneaking though the myriad patrol routes of no less than eight cloaked enemies is a tall order, but it can actually be done by a single Ghost if everything is timed right. Begin by moving toward the HQ, but instead of skirting all the way right toward the forklift as before, grab cover behind the strip of concrete that faces toward the building itself. A rifleman patrols inside the building, while another pauses for a moment, then begins walking back toward you and your fellow Ghosts.

Wait until the outside patrol turns back around, then quickly slip out of cover and dispatch him as soon as the Stealth Kill prompt appears. Slip inside behind the patrolling hostile on the ground floor and take him out before slipping underneath the upstairs walkway and toward the entrance leading out to the right. Hang back for a few seconds (a slow five count will do), then pop out and stealth kill the Bodark LMG heading back toward the wide entrance to the HQ. Hold here again and wait for another cloaked LMG enemy to pass on patrol around a set of blue crates, then carefully head back inside through the HQ. When the LMG has his back to the shotgunner you've offed multiple times in the same way already, do it again, and then sneak up behind the LMG guy and take him out.

Head back toward the staircase the shotgunner was guarding, peek inside to make sure the patrolling rifleman is heading back to his outside perch, then kill the stationary guard and that outside threat just as you did the last time you infiltrated this HQ. The final remaining target is actually a cloaked Bodark sniper that is perched on top of the water tower. For a clean shot, head back toward the window that was behind the stationary trooper you just finished off and squeeze off a headshot to end the last infiltration round of the map.

## // Noteworthy Waves

Wave 42—With their Optical Camo, the Bodark LMGs that make up a good portion of this wave are extremely hard to spot, and they're capable of suppressing your team from long range, which makes targeting them a chore. If you or your squad has one available, remember that a Radar Wave Streak (unlike a Sensor) lights up all enemies in the level for a short time. Use it to help lock down those long-range threats to make taking out lesser hostiles a little easier.

Wave 45—Wave 45 may well sport more LMGs than any other wave thus far. It's **teeming** with suppressing fire, and much of which is coming from fairly long range. To complicate things further, snipers also have taken position in the towers. If any of your squad has an especially precise weapon, now is the time to use it, preferably from a high vantage while an LMG gunner of your own can cover the shooter with some suppressing fire on the snipers. Take your time here, picking off the LMG enemies as needed. Going for the snipers early only means more snipers will spawn in their place, so thinning the suppression effect of the LMGs is more important.

Wave 47—As the sandstorm whips up into a frenzy yet again, the Bodark forces decide to use the blinding effect of the storm to mount a heavy push toward the HQ. Expect a concerted rush of shielded enemies and ground troops, plus snipers that use the storm to sneak in pot shots. It can be difficult to deal with both the short- and long-range threats when movement is so important on these rush maps, so don't be afraid to burn an Invisibility Wave Perk to take out the snipers in relative peace from a high position, while keeping the rushing enemies from overwhelming the HQ.

Wave 50—A momentary break in the sandstorm was a tiny respite during the last wave's rush, but for the final wave, it quickly kicks back up again. Amid all that whirling dust is a laundry list of threats: snipers in the towers, shotgunners and shielded enemies pushing in, LMGs creating chaos, and a pair of APCs unloading—and all that's **before** the attack helicopter decides to show up. Airstrikes are a must here to eliminate targets that haven't yet breached the HQ and to thin their overall numbers. Guided Missile strikes are great for taking out the vehicles, but the highest priority should be supporting your fellow Ghosts, as they're likely to go down with so many bullets flying from every direction. Adopt a high-low strategy by planting Claymores in the upper entryways to avoid getting ambushed from above, and keep the ground floor as clear as possible from intrusions with more Claymores and melee strikes on shielded hostiles when they show up. Stay alert, clear the area before reviving a buddy, and make heavy use of those Wave Perks.

# MANSION

## SITUATION REPORT

This Russian mansion has seen better days, but that's not keeping plenty of hostiles from seeing it as a valuable site for occupation. The twin HQs here couldn't be more different; a barn offers plenty of high cover and multiple routes of entry both high and low, while a wide-open space near the mansion itself offers nothing but low cover and plenty of angles of attack. This is going to be one hell of a battle.

# PHASES 1–10

LEGEND

- Insertion Point
- Ammo Crate
- HQ Capture/Defend
- Item Crate
- Between Rounds
- Weapon Crate

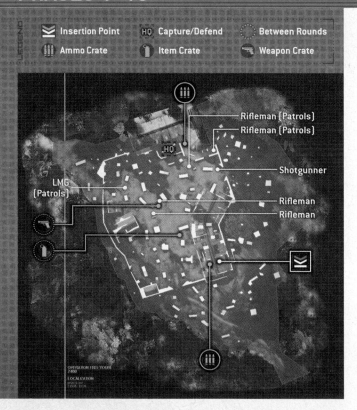

Rifleman (Patrols)
Rifleman (Patrols)
Shotgunner
Rifleman
Rifleman
LMG (Patrols)

OPERATION TREE YOURI
2:00
LOCALIZATION
MOSCOW
CODE: BLUE

## INFILTRATION

Move quickly downstairs and through the barn where your squad deploys to get the drop on a stationary shotgunner. Initially, his back is turned, but he'll turn around right when your squad is upon him. By stealthily killing him as soon as you're in range, you can avoid triggering an alarm. Beyond him patrols a rifleman that should be dispatched as quickly as possible, then double back toward where the shotgunner was and take cover near the truck, allowing another patrolling rifleman to pass before silently dispatching him.

Continue on toward a lone LMG goon smoking a cigarette with his back to the mansion. Deal with him, then double back and move to eliminate a stationary rifleman near a gray car. With him gone, you can take down his friend standing near some low cover to clear the area.

## // Noteworthy Waves

Wave 5—It doesn't take long for the forces here to begin deploying LMG fire. Keep an eye out for where they've taken up position (a Sensor can help with all the little bits of cover), and dispatch them quickly to avoid having their fire wreck your squad's ability to return fire with precision.

Wave 7—Those LMGs were a pain (particularly the one firing from the second floor of the barn in Wave 6), so it shouldn't come as a surprise that shielded enemies decide it's time to make an appearance, too. The usual strategy of waiting for their approach is still sound, but remember that there's precious little high cover in the HQ, so if you have to dispatch them with a close-range melee strike, be sure to pop back into cover as soon as possible.

Wave 8—With LMGs and shielded enemies having shown up, it was only a matter of time before snipers did the same, and they make their presence known right off the bat, firing from both the white house far off in the distance and the closer wooden one to the right of the HQ. LMGs make counter-sniping a pain, so deal with them first to smooth out targeting while your fellow ghosts deal with other threats running around the level.

Wave 9—The first rush of this map happens fairly early compared to others. The enemy makes a concerted effort to lob LMG hostiles that shake up the screen, shielded ones that move in slowly, and plenty of ground troops that attempt to overwhelm the HQ. Maintain cover whenever possible, dispatching targets methodically. Marking LMG gunners so that your fellow Ghosts can concentrate fire in that direction will become a tactic you use all throughout successive waves, so get in the habit of doing it as soon as possible.

Wave 10—Snipers, LMGs, shielded enemies, and shotgunners all show up early—and that's before the steady suppressing fire of two armored vehicles complicate things. Drop in a Missile to remove the vehicular threats when they show up, and deal with LMGs before taking out snipers whenever possible. Keep a clear head and this wave will be over before you know it. Panic, and it could mean defeat before you ever really get started on this level.

### // TIP

**GUIDED GUIDANCE**

*The Missile Wave Perk is an incredibly powerful tool, and one that's absolutely invaluable when it comes to tackling the boss waves' armored vehicles, whether they are on wheels or in the air. Just a single hit will knock out most targets short of tanks, but actually guiding them can take some getting used to. Because the Missile is literally falling toward the end target, guiding it isn't as simple as just pointing where one wants to go. Instead, think of the Missile's movement as operating on a simple vertical trajectory (so up and down should come naturally), but a kind of corkscrew vector for moving laterally. You'll have to "spin" the Missile into position if you're trying to reach, say, a corner of the map by holding left or right in the direction counter to the direction you want to move. In other words, to deliver a Missile strike to the bottom-right of the screen, you'd tilt down, then left to spin the Missile toward its destination. It takes a little getting used to, but once you have it down, you'll never miss a strike.*

# TOM CLANCY'S GHOST RECON FUTURE SOLDIER

## PHASES 11–20

**LEGEND**
- ⩤ Insertion Point
- HQ Capture/Defend
- ⬭ Between Rounds
- ⏍ Ammo Crate
- 🔪 Item Crate
- 🔫 Weapon Crate

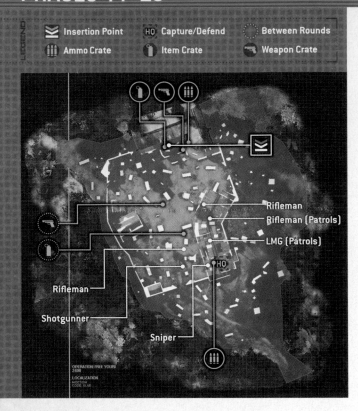

Rifleman
Rifleman (Patrols)
LMG (Patrols)
Rifleman
Shotgunner
Sniper

OPERATION FREE YOURI
2400
LOCALIZATION
MOSCOW
CODE BLUE

## INFILTRATION

Begin by taking a wide sweep of the barn, approaching from beyond the hay bales set up near one of the entrances. Take out the stationary guard as soon as his back is turned, then quickly move to take out the patrolling rifleman when he pauses with his back turned.

Sneak out of the barn and mark the stationary guard near the fuel tank to make sure you and your squad know what direction he's facing, then approach cover near the patrolling LMG, marking the sniper just past him on the floor above. When both of the marked targets have their backs turned, pop out and eliminate the LMG, then exit the barn on the left side, climbing the stairs and grabbing cover to wait for the sniper to look back out across the field.

When his back turns, silently kill him, then jump down and, keeping an eye out for the stationary guard near the fuel tank, eliminate the hostile directly in front of you when the tank guard's back is turned. Sneak up behind that final tank guard and off him to clear the area.

## // Noteworthy Waves

Wave 17—Up until this wave, guarding this HQ has mostly been remarkable only for how unremarkable the enemy threats have been. Most waves have been protracted, long-range battles, but things start getting closer with the appearance of shielded enemies. They are joined by their LMG brethren, which have been sporadic in previous waves. The multiple routes of entry into the upper floor HQ can mean some nasty surprises. Check those stairs often to avoid getting ambushed.

Wave 18—Snipers finally show up for this phase, taking positions in the white house across from the current HQ and the wooden building closer to the previous HQ, and they can be a nightmare to contain, particularly if other enemies have made it to the top floor. Mark the snipers quickly to make all squadmates aware, but don't concentrate solely on the sharpshooters. Shotgunners can sneak in and end things with startling speed.

Wave 19—A unified, rushing attack finally breaks up the languid pace of the previous waves with a vengeance. Expect plenty of shielded troops, shotgunners, and LMGs mixed in with the usual riflemen. And they all push hard toward the three staircases leading to the HQ.

Wave 20—Snipers, LMG fire, shielded foes … what **doesn't** this wave have? Oh, right, a couple of well-armored jeeps. Can't forget that. The key to making it out of this wave intact is controlling the barrels that serve as cover for the HQ. They'll protect your squad from sniper fire and the shots from the armored vehicles, but only if the entrances are covered. Make sure there's always a Ghost trained on the stairs, call down Missiles to eliminate the heavy firepower, and take out the snipers as they appear at either of the usual buildings.

# PHASES 21–30

≥ Insertion Point    HQ Capture/Defend    ○ Between Rounds
Ⅲ Ammo Crate    🔋 Item Crate    🔫 Weapon Crate

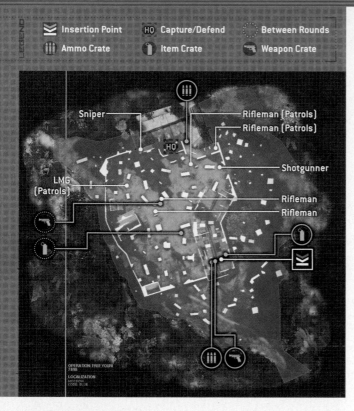

## INFILTRATION

The addition of another patrolling guard means the old route of infiltration isn't as sound, so a new approach is necessary. Start by sweeping out to the left, moving toward the mansion by skirting the left side of some hay bales near the wooden house. Take cover near more hay bales and wait for the patrolling LMG to pass. Take him out, then return to the hay bales and wait for the stationary guard near the car to turn back toward where you started this infiltration phase. Deal with him silently, then move to his nearby friend, and then return to the car to wait for a patrolling rifleman to turn back toward the other patrolling rifleman and his shotgunner buddy.

Take out the rifleman as soon as he has fully turned away from the car you're using for cover, then grab cover near the patrol route of the rifleman by the mansion and wait until the shotgunner turns to look toward the barn. Silence the rifleman, then quickly dispose of the shotgunner while his back is still turned. A final sniper sits stationary, looking out over the whole level. Creep back through the HQ, keeping out of his periphery while heading up the stairs, and finish him off to end this infiltration wave with nary a peep.

## // Noteworthy Waves

Wave 22—This third phase of the map starts with a heavy rush while a few LMGs provide a bit of suppression. Stay nimble here, sticking to the HQ as much as possible and using the elevated area next to the HQ to take out the LMGs while they fire on your fellow Ghosts defending the HQ.

Wave 25—Although you and your squad had to fight off a combination shotgun rush and LMG suppression effort during the last wave, this one keeps some of the shotgunners, adds **more** LMGs, and complicates it further with sniper fire to make things tough. As always, take care of the LMGs as early as possible to allow your team access to the snipers unhampered by a wobbly view.

Wave 28—An absolutely ridiculous number of LMGs pour into the level at the start of this wave, and they don't let up until it's over. Couple that with snipers looking to pick off Ghosts that pop up for too long and shotgunners that rush in, and you have an extremely difficult combination of attacks happening from multiple ranges. A Turret is a great idea to keep rushers at bay, as is going Invisible for a few seconds to sneak around and flank some of the more pesky LMG troopers. Just be sure to mark them first so the Invisible Ghost can make a beeline for them while still under cover, and then head back to cover before it runs out.

Wave 30—A heaping helping of trouble hits hard right from the outset. They're the usual cast of annoyances: Shields, LMGs (two of which set up on the second floor of the barn and should be taken out with precision shots as soon as possible), riflemen, and two snipers per roost are all out in force, and that's before an armored vehicle and APC start spraying their shots. Missile strikes are your friend, of course, but if you've been saving up on Airstrikes, one can help take out a few of the LMGs to stop the screen from shaking for two seconds. So long as the vehicles are taken out early and nobody sticks their head up for too long to be targets for the snipers, this battle will be won with patience and quick shooting.

≥ Insertion Point    HQ Capture/Defend    ◎ Between Rounds

▥ Ammo Crate    ▮ Item Crate    ▭ Weapon Crate

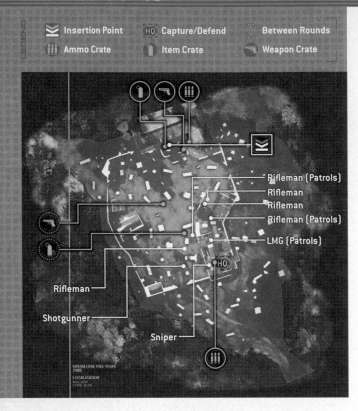

Rifleman (Patrols)
Rifleman
Rifleman
Rifleman (Patrols)
LMG (Patrols)

Rifleman
Shotgunner
Sniper

OPERATION FREE YOURS
2400
LOCALIZATION
MOI: NOW
CORE: BLUE

## INFILTRATION

The days of the one-Ghost show are over; there are simply too many hostiles with crossing lines of sight to allow for a completely covert operation at close range. Instead, a set of sync-shots must be orchestrated and timed properly to overcome the eight different targets that must be taken down with precision. The first group waits just inside the barn: a stationary rifleman on the ground floor, another almost directly above, plus a third patrolling rifleman making a circuit near the first wide entryway out of the barn. Line up a sync-shot and take it with **suppressed** weapons to clear the way for further infiltration.

Sweep outside the barn and wait for a patrolling rifleman to move between the fuel tank and the outside wall of the barn, when he turns to head back, take him out to ensure that the next sync-shot goes off without a hitch. One Ghost should stay in the barn and target the patrolling LMG while the others cross over to the other side of the map and take up a spot to target the two stationary guards below and sniper up above. When the coast is clear, take the combined sync-shot to cleanse this HQ of hostiles.

## // Noteworthy Waves

Wave 36—Be on the lookout for multiple shotgunners and shielded hostiles making a hard push into the HQ from all three staircases. LMGs (particularly ones firing from the other second floor vantage in the barn) will attempt to disrupt from afar, and more than a few riflemen will make it up to your second-floor abode if you don't deal with them quickly, too, so be careful.

Wave 38—The rush on the HQ from Wave 36 makes a return, this time aided by snipers. As always, keep an eye out for LMGs and nip them in the bud before they can mess with your squad's ability to target those snipers. Let one or two Ghosts stick with long-range weapons, while the other two concentrate on repelling the short-range attacks. Shotgunners are going to make a rush toward the HQ, and they can make short work of your team if they get in close. Don't drop your guard once the wave is over, as another rush quickly resumes at the start of the next wave.

Wave 40—The fourth boss wave doesn't skimp on threats. In addition to a more aggressive push by shielded and shotgunner troops making their way up the stairs, the usual complement of snipers and LMGs are there to make things difficult, which leads right up to the appearance of an attack helicopter and armored vehicle ready to rain suppression-causing fire upon the entire team. Make sure the heavier threats are dealt with accordingly, then concentrate on thinning out LMG fire before finally taking out the snipers. As with the last wave, split duties between long-range counter-sniping and dealing with the multitudes of shotguns and shields.

# PHASES 41-50

- ⩘ Insertion Point
- Ⅲ Ammo Crate
- HQ Capture/Defend
- 🛢 Item Crate
- ⬭ Between Rounds
- 🔫 Weapon Crate

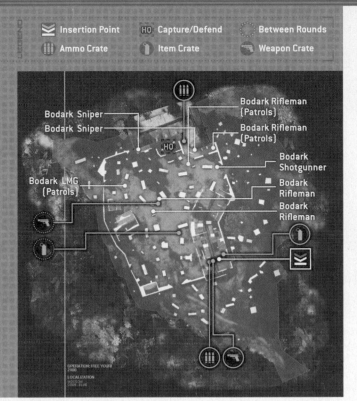

Bodark Sniper
Bodark Sniper
Bodark Rifleman (Patrols)
Bodark Rifleman (Patrols)
Bodark Shotgunner
Bodark LMG (Patrols)
Bodark Rifleman
Bodark Rifleman

## INFILTRATION

An octet of cloaked threats is no small task, but unlike the last infiltration phase, there's a bit more room for picking off enemies one by one—if it's done with stealth and a suppressed weapon. Many of the initial takedowns are done the same way as in the third infiltration. Approach from the far side of the hay bales, wait for the Bodark LMG to pass, take him out and then his buddy by the car, and then another cloaked friend by the low cover. Return to the car and take notice of the Bodark sniper sitting on a balcony overlooking the open area.

Fortunately for your squad, this sniper decides to turn around and stare at the wall from time to time, which gives you room to sneak in and take out both patrolling riflemen. Dispatch the Bodark shotgunner just as you have done in phases before, then grab some cover along the stitch of stone looking toward the sniper. Move to the end, poke out, and, with a silenced weapon, pop him in the head for a silent takedown. Creep up on the sniper at the top of the stairs and get him. You have just completed your last infiltration Mansion had to throw at you. Nice work, Ghosts.

## // Noteworthy Waves

Wave 42—The Bodark forces waste no time in coordinating a pincer attack that has hostiles, including shield enemies and shotgunners, moving in from the left and right simultaneously. Split your forces, keeping one ghost near the front and two on either side, with some overwatch from the top of the stairs to repel the attack. This is the fewest enemies you'll come across this phase, so don't get cocky.

Wave 46—The baleful hiss of an incoming rocket should make it plain that RPGs are going to play a threat in this level, but they're marginally less troublesome than the sheer numbers of LMGs laying down suppressing fire from seemingly every possible angle. The most annoying of those angles is doubtlessly the covered safety of the barn's second floor. Unload as quickly as possible on them (and their low cover, which is vulnerable to heavier weapons fire) to get rid of the annoyance as quickly as possible.

Wave 50—This is it, the final push. An all-out assault begins immediately with an HQ rush from shielded hostiles, shotgunners, riflemen, and the odd LMG providing some choppiness to make fending off the close-range fighters tougher. Break up the HQ into three directions and try to cover them as neatly as possible. Have a fourth Ghost provide overwatch from up the stairs. By now, you and your squad probably have a good idea of what to expect; snipers, armored vehicles, and—wait, is that a tank? Yep, so call down the thunder ASAP or risk being pounded into submission with multiple tank rounds while enemies swarm the HQ. If a squadmate is taken out by a tank round, avoid reviving them until they can crawl to solid safety; it's not worth losing a second Ghost to the same threat. Be accurate, stick to cover, and unleash hell with every Wave Streak you've got. This one's for all the marbles.

# 5

# WEAPONS

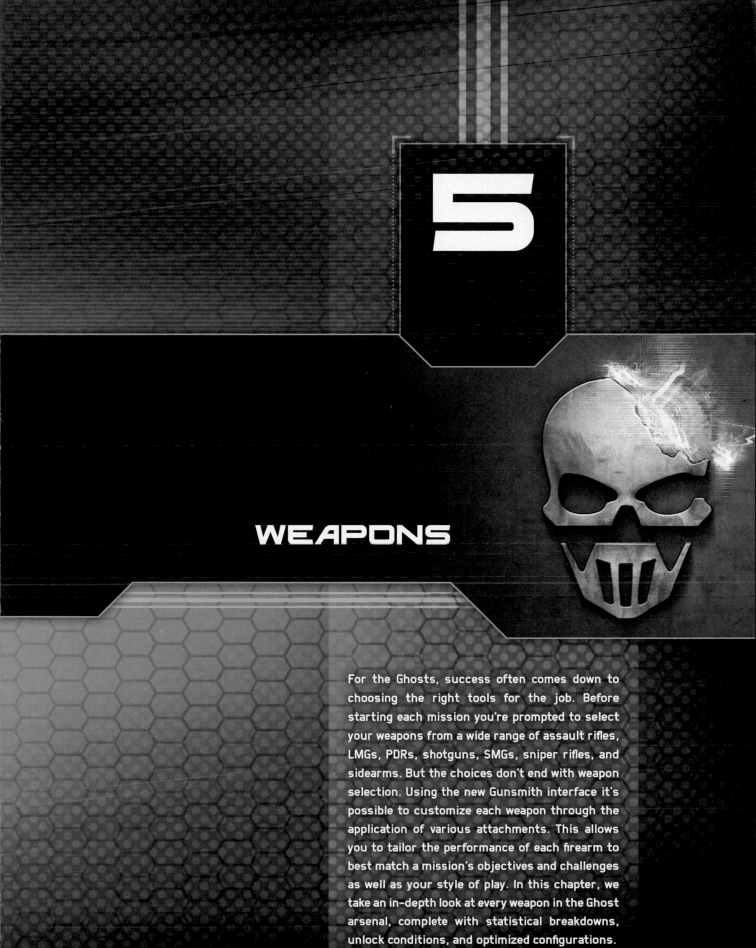

For the Ghosts, success often comes down to choosing the right tools for the job. Before starting each mission you're prompted to select your weapons from a wide range of assault rifles, LMGs, PDRs, shotguns, SMGs, sniper rifles, and sidearms. But the choices don't end with weapon selection. Using the new Gunsmith interface it's possible to customize each weapon through the application of various attachments. This allows you to tailor the performance of each firearm to best match a mission's objectives and challenges as well as your style of play. In this chapter, we take an in-depth look at every weapon in the Ghost arsenal, complete with statistical breakdowns, unlock conditions, and optimized configurations.

# GUNSMITH

*With Gunsmith, you can take a weapon apart and customize it to satisfy the mission parameters and personal preference.*

Gunsmith is a powerful weapon customization tool that allows you to modify any firearm in the game. During the campaign, you can access Gunsmith following each mission briefing. From the Gear Selection screen, select a weapon type and choose the Customize Gear option to open Gunsmith. Once the Gunsmith interface is open, you can cycle through all available weapons within the chosen category, such as assault rifles. Some weapons are not available, as they must first be unlocked by completing missions, weapon challenges, or other tasks. But you can still browse locked weapons and study their unlock conditions. Once you've chosen a weapon in Gunsmith, it's broken into its ten individual components, or modification points. After selecting a weapon's modification point, like it's muzzle, you can then choose from a number of attachments.

## WEAPON STATS

*Monitor the shifting weapon stats as you add and remove certain attachments. Not all attachments improve performance.*

Before modifying a weapon, take into consideration the kind of weapon you want to build. Some (but not all) attachments affect a weapon's core stats: power, range, control, and maneuverability. These four stats determine the weapon's overall performance. Here's a brief description of each stat and how it impacts a weapon's performance.

POWER: This is how much damage a weapon inflicts. The higher the power, the more lethal the weapon. By default, sniper rifles and shotguns are the weapons with the highest power. Armor Piercing Ammo and some underbarrel weapon attachments can improve a weapon's overall power.

RANGE: This rates how effective a weapon is when engaging targets at distance. Weapons with high range ratings are accurate at long range. Snviper rifles and assault rifles are the best ranged weapons. Some optics and a longer barrel can improves a weapon's range.

CONTROL: Both accuracy and recoil are taken into account to determine a weapon's control. A variety of attachments, like grips and Bipods, can be applied to improve a weapon's control.

MANEUVERABILITY: The size of a weapon determines how effective it is in close quarters. Weapon size can be adjusted through the application of different barrels and stocks. Compact weapons, like pistols, SMGs, and PDRs are highly maneuverable and best suited for close-quarters combat (CQC).

## MODIFICATION POINTS

*Monitor the shifting weapon stats as you add and remove certain attachments. Not all attachments improve performance.*

Each weapon has up to ten modification points that allow you to alter both a weapon's performance and appearance. Here's a brief description of each modification point and how alterations to these points can affect performance.

OPTIC: Here you can select from a variety of scopes and sights, usually improving a weapon's range. There is a noticeable difference when peering through each scope. Most scopes have different magnifications and other enhancements that may make it easier to target enemies at long range or during low-light conditions.

STOCK: Some weapons have optional stocks that may affect a weapon's maneuverability and control. In most instances, shorter stocks improve a weapon's maneuverability at the cost of control.

MUZZLE: Muzzle attachments such as Compensators and Flash Hiders affect a weapon's control. Suppressors, on the other hand, always reduce a weapon's power and range, but also significantly reduce the weapon's report, which helps Ghost operatives to remain undetected.

BARREL: Some weapons allow you to swap out barrels, choosing from shorter and longer variants. Shorter barrels benefit by increasing to maneuverability, but they decrease range. Longer barrels affect weapons in the opposite fashion, increasing range at the cost of maneuverability.

SIDE RAIL: Attachments like Aiming Lasers and Heartbeat Sensors can be attached to a weapon's side rail to improve a weapon's performance and enhance its functionality.

GAS SYSTEM: All automatic (and some semi-automatic) weapons have a gas system that affects the weapon's rate of fire and control. Over-gassing a weapon increases the rate of fire, but reduces the control. Under-gassing a weapon reduces the rate of fire, but increases control.

UNDERBARREL: Some weapons have an underbarrel rail to which grips, Bipods , and even weapons-like grenade launchers and shotguns can be attached. Grips are great for improving a weapon's control or maneuverability. Bipods improve a weapon's control while dampening recoil, particularly among LMGs and sniper rifles. Underbarrel grenade launchers and shotguns always reduce a weapon's maneuverability, but sometimes the additional firepower is worth it.

MAGAZINE: With a variety of sizes available, increasing a weapon's magazine capacity means you'll spend less time reloading. But some large magazines may reduce a weapon's maneuverability. Different ammo types are also available and these affect a weapon's power.

TRIGGER GROUP: Choose from a variety of trigger options, including Semi-Auto, Full-Auto and Burst modes. Trigger selection has no impact on a weapon's stats, but more a matter of personal preference.

PAINT: There are a variety of paint schemes and camouflage patterns you can apply to each weapon. These options are purely cosmetic and have no impact on weapon performance or gameplay.

# FIRING RANGE

*Experiment with all weapon functionality while on the Firing Range, including reloads.*

Once you've modified a weapon, you can test fire it by choosing the Firing Range option in Gunsmith. This instantly transports you onto a firing range with silhouette targets placed at various ranges. When hit, the targets on the range turn different colors, indicating how much damage they've absorbed. If a target turns green or orange, it means the damage inflicted was minimal. Red indicates critical damage and black represents lethal damage. Where you hit the target also matters—headshots always inflict the most damage. Practice firing your modified weapon while standing, crouched, and prone. Then move up against cover and then peek around and over the cover and fire the weapon—and don't forget to test the scope view or any other attachments like underbarrel Bipods, grenade launchers, or shotguns. This will help give you an idea of how the weapon will perform in combat. If you're not satisfied with the weapon's performance, return back to Gunsmith and make some adjustments. Make a habit of testing your weapons on the Firing Range before starting a mission. Once you've deployed, there's no way to return to the Gunsmith interface.

# GUNSMITH TIPS

- By making inputs on the directional pad, you can optimize each weapon to maximize its power, range, control, or maneuverability. Gunsmith automatically builds the weapon out of the available attachments, optimizing the configuration to boost the chosen stat. However, these optimized weapon builds are never suppressed. Suppressors reduce a weapon's power and range. Therefore, if you want a suppressed weapon, you'll need to add a Suppressor to the muzzle yourself.
- Some challenges require you to kill a number of enemies without reloading. For these challenges, choose a weapon with a large magazine capacity (like the P90) and consider fitting the weapon with a Semi-Auto trigger to conserve ammo.
- If you've attached a Folded or Collapsed Stock on any weapon, you won't be able to add the Drum Magazine, Dual Magazine, Bipod, or Bipod Grip.
- Bipods provide amazing stability for LMGs; with them, you can fire long bursts with great accuracy and minimal recoil. You can deploy a Bipod while prone or while aiming over low cover, such as a crate or a low wall. But while you're exposed, you're vulnerable to incoming fire—you'll have to retract the Bipod before ducking back behind cover.
- The Aiming Laser side rail attachment is a great addition to any weapon, boosting control. Plus, the red laser looks cool.
- The M110 is very versatile sniper rifle, but you can only attach a Suppressor to the Standard Barrel.
- Always equip a Suppressor on one of your weapons before beginning a mission. If you open fire without a Suppressor attached, you're likely to be detected, giving away your team's position and triggering a firefight.
- Choosing the PDR-C's Angled Foregrip stock prevents the attachment of the underbarrel Vertical Foregrip or Bipod Grip.
- If you select your secondary weapon before interacting with a weapon box, you can swap it for a primary weapon, like an assault rifle, sniper rifle, or LMG. Essentially this allows you to carry around two primary weapons.
- The Backscatter Optic scope doesn't affect a weapon's stats, but it allows you to see enemies hiding behind cover, just like Magnetic view.

## WEAPON PAINT

| Image | Name | Unlock |
|---|---|---|
| | Air Force ABU | Complete the Firefly Rain mission. |
| | Army ACU | Complete the Gallant Thief mission. |
| | ATACS | Complete the Deep Fire mission. |
| | Australian DPCU Urban | Complete the Deep Fire mission. |
| | Brazilian Urban | Complete the Noble Tempest mission. |
| | Canadian Cadpat | Complete the Ember Hunt mission. |
| | Chinese Type 07 Desert | Perform a Ghost Score of 60% in four missions. |
| | Chinese Type 07 Oceanic | Complete the Ember Hunt mission. |
| | Danish T90 | Complete the Valiant Hammer mission. |
| | Estonian | Complete the Gallant Thief mission. |
| | Finnish M05 | Perform a Ghost Score of 60% in five missions. |
| | French Daguet | Complete the Nimble Guardian mission. |
| | Greek | Perform a Ghost Score of 60% in seven missions. |
| | Indian Vertical Lizard | Perform a Ghost Score of 60% in ten missions. |
| | Iranian Special Forces | Perform a Ghost Score of 60% in one missions. |

## WEAPON PAINT

| Image | Name | Unlock |
|---|---|---|
| | Iraqi Urban | Complete the Valiant Hammer mission. |
| | Kuwaiti Special Forces | Perform a Ghost Score of 60% in eight missions. |
| | Libyan | Complete the Subtle Arrow mission. |
| | Marine Marpat | Complete the Invisible Bear mission. |
| | Multicam | — |
| | Navy AOR1 | Complete the Tiger Dust mission. |
| | Navy NWU | Complete the Tiger Dust mission. |
| | Russian Digital | Complete the Silent Talon mission. |
| | Russian MVD | Complete the Shattered Mountain mission. |
| | Solid Black | — |
| | Solid Green | — |
| | Solid Tan | — |
| | Sri Lankan Separatist | Perform a Ghost Score of 60% in two missions. |
| | USSR TTsKO | Perform a Ghost Score of 60% in 11 missions. |
| | USSR TTsKO North Africa | Complete the Nimble Guardian mission. |

# ASSAULT RIFLES

## ASSUALT RIFLE ATTACHMENTS

| Attachment | | Description | Power | Range | Control | Maneuverability | |
|---|---|---|---|---|---|---|---|
| OPTIC | Iron Sights | Standard weapon iron sights that offer quick targeting with a small viewing area. | — | — | — | — | |
| | Red Dot | Non-magnified optic that enables quick target acquisition with little visual interference. | — | — | — | ↑ | |
| | Magnified HWS | 3x magnifier combined with a Holographic Weapon Sight for a good balance between easy targeting and zoom level. | — | — | ↑ | — | |
| | TAC Scope | 4x magnification sight for medium-range engagements. | — | ↑ | — | — | |
| | Backscatter Optic | Backscatter X-ray optic capable of seeing through thin walls at short range. | — | — | — | — | |
| STOCK | Extended | Extended stock provides a good balance between Maneuverability and Control. | — | — | — | — | |
| | Folded | Folded stock that increases Maneuverability, but decreases Control due to lack of stability. | — | — | ↓ | ↑ | |
| | Fixed | Fixed stock that increases Control by reducing the amount of recoil felt. | — | — | ↑ | — | |
| MUZZLE | Standard | Factory muzzle attachment. | — | — | — | — | |
| | Compensator | Compensates for recoil and muzzle climb to increase Control. | — | — | ↑ | — | |
| | Flash Hider | Hides muzzle flash from enemies, but decreases Control. | — | — | ↓ | — | |
| | Suppressor | Hides muzzle flash and reduces the sound produced by firing the weapon, but decreases Power and Range due to the use of subsonic ammunition. | ↓ | ↓ | — | — | |
| BARREL | Standard Barrel | Standard barrel length with a good balance between Maneuverability and Range. | — | — | — | — | |
| | Long Barrel | Longer barrel length increases Range, but the added weight reduces Maneuverability. | — | ↑ | — | ↓ | |
| | Short Barrel | Shorter barrel with decreased weight increases Maneuverability, but decreases Range. | — | ↓ | — | ↑ | |
| SIDE RAIL | Rail Cover | Standard rail cover. | — | — | — | — | |
| | Aiming Laser | Increases Control by providing a visual aid while aiming. | — | — | ↑ | — | |
| | Heartbeat Sensor | Senses nearby enemies and provides Level 1 Intel on their locations. | — | — | — | — | |
| GAS SYSTEM | Standard | Standard gas system with a good balance between Rate of Fire and Control. | — | — | — | — | |
| | Over-Gassed | Gas system that increases Rate of Fire, but decreases Control. | — | — | ↓ | — | |
| | Under-Gassed | Gas system that increases Control, but decreases Rate of Fire. | — | — | ↑ | — | |
| UNDERBARREL | None | Standard underbarrel rail with no effect. | — | — | — | — | |
| | Rail Cover | Standard rail cover. | — | — | — | — | |
| | Vertical Foregrip | Increases Maneuverability by improving stability while moving. | — | — | — | ↑ | |
| | Angled Foregrip | Increases Control by reducing the amount of recoil felt. | — | — | ↑ | — | |
| | Bipod Grip | Increases Maneuverability by improving stability while moving. When ALT-FIRE mode is activated while in cover or prone, a small Bipod deploys to increase Control. | — | — | ↑ | ↑ | |
| | Bipod | When ALT-FIRE mode is activated while in cover or prone, the Bipod deploys and significantly increases Control. | — | — | ↑ | — | |
| | 40mm HEDP Launcher | ALT-FIRE mode: 40mm High Explosive Dual-Purpose grenade launcher intended to wound or kill. Decreases Maneuverability. | ↑ | — | — | ↓ | |
| | 40mm Smoke Launcher | ALT-FIRE mode: 40mm Smoke grenade launcher that creates a smokescreen for concealment. Decreases Maneuverability. | — | — | — | ↓ | |
| | 40mm EMP Launcher | ALT-FIRE mode: 40mm EMP grenade launcher that disrupts equipment and HUDs, or detonates in proximity of an enemy UAV/UCAV. Decreases Maneuverability. | — | — | — | ↓ | |
| | UB Shotgun | 12-gauge buckshot as an ALT-FIRE mode. The added weight decreases Maneuverability. | ↑ | — | — | ↓ | |
| MAGAZINE | Standard Magazine | Standard magazine loaded with FMJ ammunition. | — | — | — | — | |
| | Dual Magazines | Two magazines coupled together, increasing the speed of every other reload. Magazines loaded with FMJ ammunition. | — | — | — | — | |
| | Extended Magazine | Extended magazine loaded with FMJ ammunition. | — | — | — | — | |
| | Drum Magazine | Drum magazine loaded with FMJ ammunition. The added weight decreases Maneuverability. | — | — | — | ↓ | |
| | Armor Piercing Ammo | Standard magazine loaded with AP ammunition capable of dealing more damage to armored targets. | ↑ | — | — | — | |
| TRIGGER GROUP | Full-Auto | Full-Auto trigger group allows for continuous fire while the trigger is pulled. | — | — | — | — | |
| | 2-Stage Trigger | 2-Stage trigger group with dual fire modes. The first stage of the trigger pull fires in Semi-Auto mode. The second stage of the trigger pull fires in Full-Auto mode. | — | — | — | — | |
| | Match Trigger | Match Trigger increases the default trigger sensitivity for increased accuracy and faster follow-up shots. | — | — | — | — | |
| | Semi-Auto | Semi-automatic trigger group allows the weapon to fire one round for every trigger pull. | — | — | — | — | |
| | 2-Round Burst | 2-Round Burst trigger group that fires two rounds for every trigger pull. | — | — | — | — | |
| | 3-Round Burst | 3-Round Burst trigger group that fires three rounds for every trigger pull. | — | — | — | — | |

Assault rifles are standard infantry weapons capable of selective fire. The assault rifles fire high-velocity projectiles from an intermediate cartridge and a detachable magazine. Built to be sturdy and reliable, these weapons are effective in most combat situations, particularly during medium-range engagements.

| Unlock Requirements | ACR | 417 | TAR-21 | AK-200 | AN-94 | A-91 | AK47 | Mk14 |
|---|---|---|---|---|---|---|---|---|
| — | × | × | × | × | × | × | × | × |
| — | × | × | × | × | × | × | × | × |
| Unlocked by completing the Firefly Rain mission. | × | × | × | × | × | × | × | × |
| Unlocked by completing the Nimble Guardian mission. | × | × | × | × | × | × | × | × |
| Unlocked by completing the Ember Hunt mission. | × | × | × | × | × | × | × | × |
| — | × | × | — | × | × | — | × | × |
| — | × | — | — | × | × | — | × | — |
| Unlocked by completing all Shattered Mountain Tactical challenges. | × | × | × | × | — | — | × | × |
| — | × | × | × | × | × | × | × | × |
| Unlocked by completing the Subtle Arrow mission. | × | × | × | × | × | × | × | × |
| Unlocked by completing all Subtle Arrow Tactical challenges. | × | × | × | × | × | × | × | × |
| — | × | × | × | × | × | × | × | × |
| — | × | × | × | × | — | — | × | × |
| — | × | × | × | × | — | — | × | × |
| — | × | × | × | × | — | — | × | × |
| — | × | × | × | × | × | × | × | × |
| Unlocked by completing the Nimble Guardian mission. | × | × | × | × | × | × | × | × |
| Unlocked by completing the Firefly Rain mission. | × | × | × | × | × | × | × | × |
| — | × | × | × | × | × | × | × | × |
| — | × | × | × | × | × | × | × | × |
| — | × | × | × | × | × | × | × | × |
| — | — | — | — | — | — | × | — | — |
| — | × | × | × | × | × | — | × | × |
| — | × | × | × | × | × | × | × | × |
| Unlocked by completing the Nimble Guardian mission. | × | × | × | × | × | — | × | × |
| Unlocked by completing all Gallant Thief Tactical challenges. | × | × | × | × | × | × | × | × |
| Unlocked by completing the Subtle Arrow mission. | × | × | × | × | × | — | × | × |
| Unlocked by completing the Gallant Thief mission. | × | × | × | × | × | × | × | × |
| Unlocked by completing all Firefly Rain Tactical challenges. | × | × | × | × | × | × | × | × |
| Unlocked by completing the Shattered Mountain mission. | × | × | × | × | × | × | × | × |
| Unlocked by completing all Nimble Guardian Tactical challenges. | × | × | × | × | × | — | × | × |
| — | × | × | × | × | × | × | × | × |
| Unlocked by completing all Silent Talon Tactical challenges. | × | × | × | × | × | × | × | × |
| Unlocked by completing all Noble Tempest Tactical challenges. | — | × | — | × | — | — | × | — |
| Unlocked by completing all Noble Tempest Tactical challenges. | × | — | — | — | × | — | — | — |
| Unlocked by completing all Deep Fire Tactical challenges. | × | × | × | × | × | × | × | × |
| — | × | × | × | × | × | × | × | × |
| — | — | — | × | — | — | — | — | — |
| — | × | × | × | × | × | × | × | × |
| — | × | × | × | × | × | × | × | × |
| — | — | — | — | — | × | — | — | — |
| — | × | × | × | — | — | — | — | — |

Denotes ULC Weapon

**417**

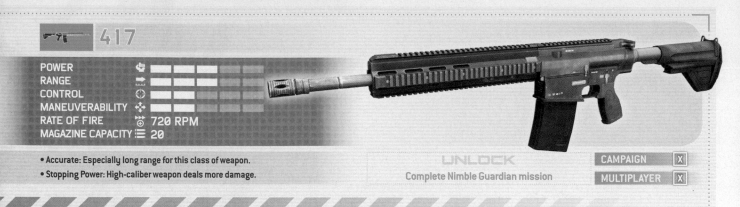

| | |
|---|---|
| POWER | |
| RANGE | |
| CONTROL | |
| MANEUVERABILITY | |
| RATE OF FIRE | 720 RPM |
| MAGAZINE CAPACITY | 20 |

- Accurate: Especially long range for this class of weapon.
- Stopping Power: High-caliber weapon deals more damage.

**UNLOCK**
Complete Nimble Guardian mission

CAMPAIGN [X]
MULTIPLAYER [X]

## OPTIMIZED CONFIGURATIONS

### CONTROL

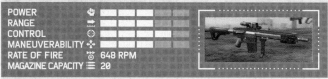

| | |
|---|---|
| POWER | |
| RANGE | |
| CONTROL | |
| MANEUVERABILITY | |
| RATE OF FIRE | 648 RPM |
| MAGAZINE CAPACITY | 20 |

#### CONTROL CONFIGURATION

| Mod. Point | Attachment | 👊 | ➡ | ◎ | ✛ |
|---|---|---|---|---|---|
| Optic | Magnified HWS | — | — | ↑ | — |
| Stock | Fixed | — | — | ↑ | — |
| Muzzle | Compensator | — | — | ↑ | — |
| Barrel | Short Barrel | — | ↓ | — | ↑ |
| Side Rail | Aiming Laser | — | — | ↑ | — |
| Gas System | Under-Gassed | — | — | ↑ | — |
| Underbarrel | Bipod Grip | — | — | ↑ | ↑ |
| Magazine | Armor Piercing Ammo | ↑ | — | — | — |
| Trigger Group | Match Trigger | — | — | — | — |

### MANEUVERABILITY

| | |
|---|---|
| POWER | |
| RANGE | |
| CONTROL | |
| MANEUVERABILITY | |
| RATE OF FIRE | 648 RPM |
| MAGAZINE CAPACITY | 20 |

#### MANEUVERABILITY CONFIGURATION

| Mod. Point | Attachment | 👊 | ➡ | ◎ | ✛ |
|---|---|---|---|---|---|
| Optic | Red Dot | — | — | — | ↑ |
| Stock | Fixed | — | — | ↑ | — |
| Muzzle | Compensator | — | — | ↑ | — |
| Barrel | Short Barrel | — | ↓ | — | ↑ |
| Side Rail | Aiming Laser | — | — | ↑ | — |
| Gas System | Under-Gassed | — | — | ↑ | — |
| Underbarrel | Bipod Grip | — | — | ↑ | ↑ |
| Magazine | Armor Piercing Ammo | ↑ | — | — | — |
| Trigger Group | Semi-Auto | — | — | — | — |

### POWER

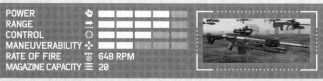

| | |
|---|---|
| POWER | |
| RANGE | |
| CONTROL | |
| MANEUVERABILITY | |
| RATE OF FIRE | 648 RPM |
| MAGAZINE CAPACITY | 20 |

#### POWER CONFIGURATION

| Mod. Point | Attachment | 👊 | ➡ | ◎ | ✛ |
|---|---|---|---|---|---|
| Optic | Tac Scope | — | ↑ | — | — |
| Stock | Fixed | — | — | ↑ | — |
| Muzzle | Compensator | — | — | ↑ | — |
| Barrel | Long Barrel | — | ↑ | — | ↓ |
| Side Rail | Aiming Laser | — | — | ↑ | — |
| Gas System | Under-Gassed | — | — | ↑ | — |
| Underbarrel | UB Shotgun | ↑ | — | — | ↓ |
| Magazine | Armor Piercing Ammo | ↑ | — | — | — |
| Trigger Group | 3-Round Burst | — | — | — | — |

### RANGE

| | |
|---|---|
| POWER | |
| RANGE | |
| CONTROL | |
| MANEUVERABILITY | |
| RATE OF FIRE | 648 RPM |
| MAGAZINE CAPACITY | 20 |

#### RANGE CONFIGURATION

| Mod. Point | Attachment | 👊 | ➡ | ◎ | ✛ |
|---|---|---|---|---|---|
| Optic | Tac Scope | — | ↑ | — | — |
| Stock | Fixed | — | — | ↑ | — |
| Muzzle | Compensator | — | — | ↑ | — |
| Barrel | Long Barrel | — | ↑ | — | ↓ |
| Side Rail | Aiming Laser | — | — | ↑ | — |
| Gas System | Under-Gassed | — | — | ↑ | — |
| Underbarrel | 40mm HEDP Launcher | ↑ | — | — | ↓ |
| Magazine | Armor Piercing Ammo | ↑ | — | — | — |
| Trigger Group | Full-Auto | — | — | — | — |

## A-91

| | | |
|---|---|---|
| POWER | 👊 | |
| RANGE | ➡ | |
| CONTROL | ◎ | |
| MANEUVERABILITY | ✛ | |
| RATE OF FIRE | 🔥 | 858 RPM |
| MAGAZINE CAPACITY | ≡ | 30 |

- **Fast Assault:** Ideal for quickly engaging unexpected targets or firing on the move.
- **Bullpup:** Compact design allows for improved maneuverability.

### UNLOCK
Complete Invisible Bear mission.

| | |
|---|---|
| CAMPAIGN | X |
| MULTIPLAYER | |

---

# OPTIMIZED CONFIGURATIONS

## CONTROL

| | | |
|---|---|---|
| POWER | 👊 | |
| RANGE | ➡ | |
| CONTROL | ◎ | |
| MANEUVERABILITY | ✛ | |
| RATE OF FIRE | 🔥 | 772 RPM |
| MAGAZINE CAPACITY | ≡ | 30 |

### CONTROL CONFIGURATION

| Mod. Point | Attachment | 👊 | ➡ | ◎ | ✛ |
|---|---|---|---|---|---|
| Optic | Magnified HWS | — | — | ↑ | — |
| Stock | — | — | — | — | — |
| Muzzle | Compensator | — | — | ↑ | — |
| Barrel | — | — | — | — | — |
| Side Rail | Aiming Laser | — | — | ↑ | — |
| Gas System | Under-Gassed | — | — | ↑ | — |
| Underbarrel | — | — | — | — | — |
| Magazine | Armor Piercing Ammo | ↑ | — | — | — |
| Trigger Group | Semi-Auto | — | — | — | — |

## MANEUVERABILITY

| | | |
|---|---|---|
| POWER | 👊 | |
| RANGE | ➡ | |
| CONTROL | ◎ | |
| MANEUVERABILITY | ✛ | |
| RATE OF FIRE | 🔥 | 772 RPM |
| MAGAZINE CAPACITY | ≡ | 30 |

### MANEUVERABILITY CONFIGURATION

| Mod. Point | Attachment | 👊 | ➡ | ◎ | ✛ |
|---|---|---|---|---|---|
| Optic | Red Dot | — | — | — | ↑ |
| Stock | — | — | — | — | — |
| Muzzle | Compensator | — | — | ↑ | — |
| Barrel | — | — | — | — | — |
| Side Rail | Aiming Laser | — | — | ↑ | — |
| Gas System | Under-Gassed | — | — | ↑ | — |
| Underbarrel | — | — | — | — | — |
| Magazine | Armor Piercing Ammo | ↑ | — | — | — |
| Trigger Group | Semi-Auto | — | — | — | — |

## POWER

| | | |
|---|---|---|
| POWER | 👊 | |
| RANGE | ➡ | |
| CONTROL | ◎ | |
| MANEUVERABILITY | ✛ | |
| RATE OF FIRE | 🔥 | 772 RPM |
| MAGAZINE CAPACITY | ≡ | 30 |

### POWER CONFIGURATION

| Mod. Point | Attachment | 👊 | ➡ | ◎ | ✛ |
|---|---|---|---|---|---|
| Optic | Tac Scope | — | ↑ | — | — |
| Stock | — | — | — | — | — |
| Muzzle | Compensator | — | — | ↑ | — |
| Barrel | — | — | — | — | — |
| Side Rail | Aiming Laser | — | — | ↑ | — |
| Gas System | Under-Gassed | — | — | ↑ | — |
| Underbarrel | 40mm HEDP Launcher | ↑ | — | — | ↓ |
| Magazine | Armor Piercing Ammo | ↑ | — | — | — |
| Trigger Group | Full-Auto | — | — | — | — |

## RANGE

| | | |
|---|---|---|
| POWER | 👊 | |
| RANGE | ➡ | |
| CONTROL | ◎ | |
| MANEUVERABILITY | ✛ | |
| RATE OF FIRE | 🔥 | 772 RPM |
| MAGAZINE CAPACITY | ≡ | 30 |

### RANGE CONFIGURATION

| Mod. Point | Attachment | 👊 | ➡ | ◎ | ✛ |
|---|---|---|---|---|---|
| Optic | Tac Scope | — | ↑ | — | — |
| Stock | — | — | — | — | — |
| Muzzle | Compensator | — | — | ↑ | — |
| Barrel | — | — | — | — | — |
| Side Rail | Aiming Laser | — | — | ↑ | — |
| Gas System | Under-Gassed | — | — | ↑ | — |
| Underbarrel | 40mm HEDP Launcher | ↑ | — | — | ↓ |
| Magazine | Armor Piercing Ammo | ↑ | — | — | — |
| Trigger Group | Full-Auto | — | — | — | — |

## ACR

| | | |
|---|---|---|
| POWER | ✊ | |
| RANGE | ⇥ | |
| CONTROL | ◎ | |
| MANEUVERABILITY | ✛ | |
| RATE OF FIRE | ⏱ | 915 RPM |
| MAGAZINE CAPACITY | ☰ | 30 |

- **Versatile:** Suitable for a variety of combat scenarios and ranges.
- **Extra Customization:** Weapon features additional attachment points over other weapons.

**UNLOCK**
Complete Firefly Rain mission.

| CAMPAIGN | X |
|---|---|
| MULTIPLAYER | X |

# OPTIMIZED CONFIGURATIONS

## CONTROL

| | | |
|---|---|---|
| POWER | ✊ | |
| RANGE | ⇥ | |
| CONTROL | ◎ | |
| MANEUVERABILITY | ✛ | |
| RATE OF FIRE | ⏱ | 823 RPM |
| MAGAZINE CAPACITY | ☰ | 30 |

### CONTROL CONFIGURATION

| Mod. Point | Attachment | ✊ | ⇥ | ◎ | ✛ |
|---|---|---|---|---|---|
| Optic | Magnified HWS | — | — | ↑ | — |
| Stock | Fixed | — | — | ↑ | — |
| Muzzle | Compensator | — | — | ↑ | — |
| Barrel | Short Barrel | — | ↓ | — | ↑ |
| Side Rail | Aiming Laser | — | — | ↑ | — |
| Gas System | Under-Gassed | — | — | ↑ | — |
| Underbarrel | Bipod Grip | — | — | ↑ | ↑ |
| Magazine | Armor Piercing Ammo | ↑ | — | — | — |
| Trigger Group | 3-Round Burst | — | — | — | — |

## MANEUVERABILITY

| | | |
|---|---|---|
| POWER | ✊ | |
| RANGE | ⇥ | |
| CONTROL | ◎ | |
| MANEUVERABILITY | ✛ | |
| RATE OF FIRE | ⏱ | 823 RPM |
| MAGAZINE CAPACITY | ☰ | 30 |

### MANEUVERABILITY CONFIGURATION

| Mod. Point | Attachment | ✊ | ⇥ | ◎ | ✛ |
|---|---|---|---|---|---|
| Optic | Red Dot | — | — | — | ↑ |
| Stock | Folded | — | — | ↓ | ↑ |
| Muzzle | Compensator | — | — | ↑ | — |
| Barrel | Short Barrel | — | ↓ | — | ↑ |
| Side Rail | Aiming Laser | — | — | ↑ | — |
| Gas System | Under-Gassed | — | — | ↑ | — |
| Underbarrel | Vertical Foregrip | — | — | — | ↑ |
| Magazine | Armor Piercing Ammo | ↑ | — | — | — |
| Trigger Group | 3-Round Burst | — | — | — | — |

## POWER

| | | |
|---|---|---|
| POWER | ✊ | |
| RANGE | ⇥ | |
| CONTROL | ◎ | |
| MANEUVERABILITY | ✛ | |
| RATE OF FIRE | ⏱ | 823 RPM |
| MAGAZINE CAPACITY | ☰ | 30 |

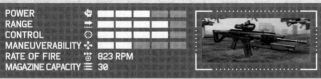

### POWER CONFIGURATION

| Mod. Point | Attachment | ✊ | ⇥ | ◎ | ✛ |
|---|---|---|---|---|---|
| Optic | Tac Scope | — | ↑ | — | — |
| Stock | Fixed | — | — | ↑ | — |
| Muzzle | Compensator | — | — | ↑ | — |
| Barrel | Long Barrel | — | ↑ | — | ↓ |
| Side Rail | Aiming Laser | — | — | ↑ | — |
| Gas System | Under-Gassed | — | — | ↑ | — |
| Underbarrel | UB Shotgun | ↑ | — | — | ↓ |
| Magazine | Armor Piercing Ammo | ↑ | — | — | — |
| Trigger Group | Match Trigger | — | — | — | — |

## RANGE

| | | |
|---|---|---|
| POWER | ✊ | |
| RANGE | ⇥ | |
| CONTROL | ◎ | |
| MANEUVERABILITY | ✛ | |
| RATE OF FIRE | ⏱ | 823 RPM |
| MAGAZINE CAPACITY | ☰ | 30 |

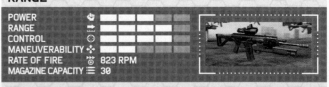

### RANGE CONFIGURATION

| Mod. Point | Attachment | ✊ | ⇥ | ◎ | ✛ |
|---|---|---|---|---|---|
| Optic | Tac Scope | — | ↑ | — | — |
| Stock | Fixed | — | — | ↑ | — |
| Muzzle | Compensator | — | — | ↑ | — |
| Barrel | Long Barrel | — | ↑ | — | ↓ |
| Side Rail | Aiming Laser | — | — | ↑ | — |
| Gas System | Under-Gassed | — | — | ↑ | — |
| Underbarrel | UB Shotgun | ↑ | — | — | ↓ |
| Magazine | Armor Piercing Ammo | ↑ | — | — | — |
| Trigger Group | Semi-Auto | — | — | — | — |

## AK-200

| | | |
|---|---|---|
| POWER | ✊ | ▮▮▮□□ |
| RANGE | ⇒ | ▮▮▮□□ |
| CONTROL | ◎ | ▮▮□□□ |
| MANEUVERABILITY | ✣ | ▮▮□□□ |
| RATE OF FIRE | ⏱ | 750 RPM |
| MAGAZINE CAPACITY | ≣ | 30 |

• **Versatile:** Suitable for a variety of combat scenarios and ranges.
• **Stopping Power:** High-caliber weapon deals more damage.

| CAMPAIGN | X |
|---|---|
| MULTIPLAYER | ☐ |

# OPTIMIZED CONFIGURATIONS

## CONTROL

| | | |
|---|---|---|
| POWER | ✊ | ▮▮▮□□ |
| RANGE | ⇒ | ▮▮▮□□ |
| CONTROL | ◎ | ▮▮▮▮□ |
| MANEUVERABILITY | ✣ | ▮▮□□□ |
| RATE OF FIRE | ⏱ | 675 RPM |
| MAGAZINE CAPACITY | ≣ | 30 |

### CONTROL CONFIGURATION

| Mod. Point | Attachment | ✊ | ⇒ | ◎ | ✣ |
|---|---|---|---|---|---|
| Optic | Magnified HWS | — | — | ↑ | — |
| Stock | Fixed | — | — | ↑ | — |
| Muzzle | Compensator | — | — | ↑ | — |
| Barrel | Short Barrel | — | ↓ | — | ↑ |
| Side Rail | Aiming Laser | — | — | ↑ | — |
| Gas System | Under-Gassed | — | — | ↑ | — |
| Underbarrel | Bipod Grip | — | — | ↑ | ↑ |
| Magazine | Armor Piercing Ammo | ↑ | — | — | — |
| Trigger Group | Full-Auto | — | — | — | — |

## MANEUVERABILITY

| | | |
|---|---|---|
| POWER | ✊ | ▮▮▮□□ |
| RANGE | ⇒ | ▮▮▮□□ |
| CONTROL | ◎ | ▮▮□□□ |
| MANEUVERABILITY | ✣ | ▮▮▮□□ |
| RATE OF FIRE | ⏱ | 675 RPM |
| MAGAZINE CAPACITY | ≣ | 30 |

### MANEUVERABILITY CONFIGURATION

| Mod. Point | Attachment | ✊ | ⇒ | ◎ | ✣ |
|---|---|---|---|---|---|
| Optic | Red Dot | — | — | — | ↑ |
| Stock | Folded | — | — | ↓ | ↑ |
| Muzzle | Compensator | — | — | ↑ | — |
| Barrel | Short Barrel | — | ↓ | — | ↑ |
| Side Rail | Aiming Laser | — | — | ↑ | — |
| Gas System | Under-Gassed | — | — | ↑ | — |
| Underbarrel | Vertical Foregrip | — | — | — | ↑ |
| Magazine | Armor Piercing Ammo | ↑ | — | — | — |
| Trigger Group | Semi-Auto | — | — | — | — |

## POWER

| | | |
|---|---|---|
| POWER | ✊ | ▮▮▮▮□ |
| RANGE | ⇒ | ▮▮▮□□ |
| CONTROL | ◎ | ▮▮▮□□ |
| MANEUVERABILITY | ✣ | ▮□□□□ |
| RATE OF FIRE | ⏱ | 675 RPM |
| MAGAZINE CAPACITY | ≣ | 30 |

### POWER CONFIGURATION

| Mod. Point | Attachment | ✊ | ⇒ | ◎ | ✣ |
|---|---|---|---|---|---|
| Optic | Tac Scope | — | ↑ | — | — |
| Stock | Fixed | — | — | ↑ | — |
| Muzzle | Compensator | — | — | ↑ | — |
| Barrel | Long Barrel | — | ↑ | — | ↓ |
| Side Rail | Aiming Laser | — | — | ↑ | — |
| Gas System | Under-Gassed | — | — | ↑ | — |
| Underbarrel | UB Shotgun | ↑ | — | — | ↓ |
| Magazine | Armor Piercing Ammo | ↑ | — | — | — |
| Trigger Group | Match Trigger | — | — | — | — |

## RANGE

| | | |
|---|---|---|
| POWER | ✊ | ▮▮▮□□ |
| RANGE | ⇒ | ▮▮▮▮□ |
| CONTROL | ◎ | ▮▮▮□□ |
| MANEUVERABILITY | ✣ | ▮□□□□ |
| RATE OF FIRE | ⏱ | 675 RPM |
| MAGAZINE CAPACITY | ≣ | 30 |

### RANGE CONFIGURATION

| Mod. Point | Attachment | ✊ | ⇒ | ◎ | ✣ |
|---|---|---|---|---|---|
| Optic | Tac Scope | — | ↑ | — | — |
| Stock | Fixed | — | — | ↑ | — |
| Muzzle | Compensator | — | — | ↑ | — |
| Barrel | Long Barrel | — | ↑ | — | ↓ |
| Side Rail | Aiming Laser | — | — | ↑ | — |
| Gas System | Under-Gassed | — | — | ↑ | — |
| Underbarrel | UB Shotgun | ↑ | — | — | ↓ |
| Magazine | Armor Piercing Ammo | ↑ | — | — | — |
| Trigger Group | Match Trigger | — | — | — | — |

## AN-94

| | |
|---|---|
| POWER | ■■■□□ □ |
| RANGE | ■■■□□ □ |
| CONTROL | ■■□□□ □ |
| MANEUVERABILITY | ■■□□□ □ |
| RATE OF FIRE | 714 RPM |
| MAGAZINE CAPACITY | 30 |

- Accurate: Especially long range for this class of weapon.
- Rapid-Fire: Weapon features a higher rate of fire than other weapons in its class.

### UNLOCK
Complete Deep Fire weapon challenge.

| CAMPAIGN | X |
|---|---|
| MULTIPLAYER | ☐ |

# OPTIMIZED CONFIGURATIONS

## CONTROL

| | |
|---|---|
| POWER | ■■■□□ □ |
| RANGE | ■■■□□ □ |
| CONTROL | ■■■□□ □ |
| MANEUVERABILITY | ■■□□□ □ |
| RATE OF FIRE | 643 RPM |
| MAGAZINE CAPACITY | 30 |

### CONTROL CONFIGURATION

| Mod. Point | Attachment | ✊ | ➡ | ◎ | ✛ |
|---|---|---|---|---|---|
| Optic | Magnified HWS | — | — | ↑ | — |
| Stock | Extended | — | — | — | — |
| Muzzle | Compensator | — | — | ↑ | — |
| Barrel | — | — | — | — | — |
| Side Rail | Aiming Laser | — | — | ↑ | — |
| Gas System | Under-Gassed | — | — | ↑ | — |
| Underbarrel | Bipod Grip | — | — | ↑ | ↑ |
| Magazine | Armor Piercing Ammo | ↑ | — | — | — |
| Trigger Group | Match Trigger | — | — | — | — |

## MANEUVERABILITY

| | |
|---|---|
| POWER | ■■■□□ □ |
| RANGE | ■■□□□ □ |
| CONTROL | ■■□□□ □ |
| MANEUVERABILITY | ■■■□□ □ |
| RATE OF FIRE | 643 RPM |
| MAGAZINE CAPACITY | 30 |

### MANEUVERABILITY CONFIGURATION

| Mod. Point | Attachment | ✊ | ➡ | ◎ | ✛ |
|---|---|---|---|---|---|
| Optic | Red Dot | — | — | — | ↑ |
| Stock | Folded | — | — | ↓ | ↑ |
| Muzzle | Compensator | — | — | ↑ | — |
| Barrel | — | — | — | — | — |
| Side Rail | Aiming Laser | — | — | ↑ | — |
| Gas System | Under-Gassed | — | — | ↑ | — |
| Underbarrel | Vertical Foregrip | — | — | — | ↑ |
| Magazine | Armor Piercing Ammo | ↑ | — | — | — |
| Trigger Group | Full-Auto | — | — | — | — |

## POWER

| | |
|---|---|
| POWER | ■■■□□ □ |
| RANGE | ■■□□□ □ |
| CONTROL | ■■□□□ □ |
| MANEUVERABILITY | ■□□□□ □ |
| RATE OF FIRE | 643 RPM |
| MAGAZINE CAPACITY | 30 |

### POWER CONFIGURATION

| Mod. Point | Attachment | ✊ | ➡ | ◎ | ✛ |
|---|---|---|---|---|---|
| Optic | Tac Scope | — | ↑ | — | — |
| Stock | Extended | — | — | — | — |
| Muzzle | Compensator | — | — | ↑ | — |
| Barrel | — | — | — | — | — |
| Side Rail | Aiming Laser | — | — | ↑ | — |
| Gas System | Under-Gassed | — | — | ↑ | — |
| Underbarrel | UB Shotgun | ↑ | — | — | ↓ |
| Magazine | Armor Piercing Ammo | ↑ | — | — | — |
| Trigger Group | 2-Round Burst | — | — | — | — |

## RANGE

| | |
|---|---|
| POWER | ■■■□□ □ |
| RANGE | ■■■□□ □ |
| CONTROL | ■■□□□ □ |
| MANEUVERABILITY | ■□□□□ □ |
| RATE OF FIRE | 643 RPM |
| MAGAZINE CAPACITY | 30 |

### RANGE CONFIGURATION

| Mod. Point | Attachment | ✊ | ➡ | ◎ | ✛ |
|---|---|---|---|---|---|
| Optic | Tac Scope | — | ↑ | — | — |
| Stock | Extended | — | — | — | — |
| Muzzle | Compensator | — | — | ↑ | — |
| Barrel | — | — | — | — | — |
| Side Rail | Aiming Laser | — | — | ↑ | — |
| Gas System | Under-Gassed | — | — | ↑ | — |
| Underbarrel | 40mm HEDP Launcher | ↑ | — | — | ↓ |
| Magazine | Armor Piercing Ammo | ↑ | — | — | — |
| Trigger Group | Match Trigger | — | — | — | — |

## TAR-21

| | |
|---|---|
| POWER | ⊘ |
| RANGE | ⇒ |
| CONTROL | ⊙ |
| MANEUVERABILITY | ✛ |
| RATE OF FIRE | 720 RPM |
| MAGAZINE CAPACITY | 30 |

- Fast Assault: Ideal for quickly engaging unexpected targets or firing on the move.
- Bullpup: Compact design allows for improved maneuverability.

UNLOCK
Complete Gallant Thief mission.

| | |
|---|---|
| CAMPAIGN | X |
| MULTIPLAYER | X |

# OPTIMIZED CONFIGURATIONS

## CONTROL

| | |
|---|---|
| POWER | ⊘ |
| RANGE | ⇒ |
| CONTROL | ⊙ |
| MANEUVERABILITY | ✛ |
| RATE OF FIRE | 648 RPM |
| MAGAZINE CAPACITY | 30 |

### CONTROL CONFIGURATION

| Mod. Point | Attachment | ⊘ | ⇒ | ⊙ | ✛ |
|---|---|---|---|---|---|
| Optic | Magnified HWS | — | — | ↑ | — |
| Stock | — | — | — | — | — |
| Muzzle | Compensator | — | — | ↑ | — |
| Barrel | Short Barrel | — | ↓ | — | ↑ |
| Side Rail | Aiming Laser | — | — | ↑ | — |
| Gas System | Under-Gassed | — | — | ↑ | — |
| Underbarrel | Bipod Grip | — | — | ↑ | ↑ |
| Magazine | Armor Piercing Ammo | ↑ | — | — | — |
| Trigger Group | 3-Round Burst | — | — | — | — |

## MANEUVERABILITY

| | |
|---|---|
| POWER | ⊘ |
| RANGE | ⇒ |
| CONTROL | ⊙ |
| MANEUVERABILITY | ✛ |
| RATE OF FIRE | 648 RPM |
| MAGAZINE CAPACITY | 30 |

### MANEUVERABILITY CONFIGURATION

| Mod. Point | Attachment | ⊘ | ⇒ | ⊙ | ✛ |
|---|---|---|---|---|---|
| Optic | Red Dot | — | — | — | ↑ |
| Stock | — | — | — | — | — |
| Muzzle | Compensator | — | — | ↑ | — |
| Barrel | Short Barrel | — | ↓ | — | ↑ |
| Side Rail | Aiming Laser | — | — | ↑ | — |
| Gas System | Under-Gassed | — | — | ↑ | — |
| Underbarrel | Bipod Grip | — | — | ↑ | ↑ |
| Magazine | Armor Piercing Ammo | ↑ | — | — | — |
| Trigger Group | 3-Round Burst | — | — | — | — |

## POWER

| | |
|---|---|
| POWER | ⊘ |
| RANGE | ⇒ |
| CONTROL | ⊙ |
| MANEUVERABILITY | ✛ |
| RATE OF FIRE | 648 RPM |
| MAGAZINE CAPACITY | 30 |

### POWER CONFIGURATION

| Mod. Point | Attachment | ⊘ | ⇒ | ⊙ | ✛ |
|---|---|---|---|---|---|
| Optic | Tac Scope | — | ↑ | — | — |
| Stock | — | — | — | — | — |
| Muzzle | Compensator | — | — | ↑ | — |
| Barrel | Long Barrel | — | ↑ | — | ↓ |
| Side Rail | Aiming Laser | — | — | ↑ | — |
| Gas System | Under-Gassed | — | — | ↑ | — |
| Underbarrel | 40mm HEDP Launcher | ↑ | — | — | ↓ |
| Magazine | Armor Piercing Ammo | ↑ | — | — | — |
| Trigger Group | Full-Auto | — | — | — | — |

## RANGE

| | |
|---|---|
| POWER | ⊘ |
| RANGE | ⇒ |
| CONTROL | ⊙ |
| MANEUVERABILITY | ✛ |
| RATE OF FIRE | 648 RPM |
| MAGAZINE CAPACITY | 30 |

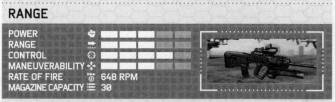

### RANGE CONFIGURATION

| Mod. Point | Attachment | ⊘ | ⇒ | ⊙ | ✛ |
|---|---|---|---|---|---|
| Optic | Tac Scope | — | ↑ | — | — |
| Stock | — | — | — | — | — |
| Muzzle | Compensator | — | — | ↑ | — |
| Barrel | Long Barrel | — | ↑ | — | ↓ |
| Side Rail | Aiming Laser | — | — | ↑ | — |
| Gas System | Under-Gassed | — | — | ↑ | — |
| Underbarrel | 40mm HEDP Launcher | ↑ | — | — | ↓ |
| Magazine | Armor Piercing Ammo | ↑ | — | — | — |
| Trigger Group | Full-Auto | — | — | — | — |

# LIGHT MACHINE GUNS (LMGS)

## LMG ATTACHMENTS

| | Attachment | Description | Power | Range | Control | Maneuverability | |
|---|---|---|:---:|:---:|:---:|:---:|---|
| OPTIC | Iron Sights | Standard weapon iron sights that offer quick targeting with a small viewing area. | — | — | — | — | |
| | Red Dot | Non-magnified optic that enables quick target acquisition with little visual interference. | — | — | — | ↑ | |
| | Magnified HWS | 3x magnifier combined with a Holographic Weapon Sight for a good balance between easy targeting and zoom level. | — | — | ↑ | — | |
| | Tac Scope | 4x magnification sight for medium-range engagements. | — | ↑ | — | — | |
| | Backscatter Optic | Backscatter X-ray optic capable of seeing through thin walls at short range. | — | — | — | — | |
| STOCK | Standard | Standard stock provides a good balance between Maneuverability and Control. | — | — | — | — | |
| | Extended | Extended stock provides a good balance between Maneuverability and Control. | | | — | — | |
| | Folded | Folded stock that increases Maneuverability, but decreases Control due to lack of stability. | — | — | ↓ | ↑ | |
| | Fixed | Fixed stock that increases Control by reducing the amount of recoil felt. | — | — | ↑ | — | |
| MUZZLE | Standard | Factory muzzle attachment. | — | — | — | — | |
| | Compensator | Compensates for recoil and muzzle climb to increase Control. | — | — | ↑ | — | |
| | Flash Hider | Hides muzzle flash from enemies, but decreases Control. | — | — | ↓ | — | |
| BARREL | Standard Barrel | Standard barrel length with a good balance between Maneuverability and Range. | — | — | — | — | |
| | Long Barrel | Longer barrel length increases Range, but the added weight reduces Maneuverability. | — | ↑ | — | ↓ | |
| | Short Barrel | Shorter barrel with decreased weight increases Maneuverability, but decreases Range. | — | ↓ | — | ↑ | |
| SIDE RAIL | Rail Cover | Standard rail cover. | — | — | — | — | |
| | Aiming Laser | Increases Control by providing a visual aid while aiming. | — | — | ↑ | — | |
| | Heartbeat Sensor | Senses nearby enemies and provides Level 1 Intel on their locations. | — | — | — | — | |
| GAS SYSTEM | Standard | Standard gas system with a good balance between Rate of Fire and Control. | — | — | — | — | |
| | Over-Gassed | Gas system that increases Rate of Fire, but decreases Control. | — | — | ↓ | — | |
| | Under-Gassed | Gas system that increases Control, but decreases Rate of Fire. | — | — | ↑ | — | |
| UNDERBARREL | Rail Cover | Standard rail cover. | — | — | — | — | |
| | Vertical Foregrip | Increases Maneuverability by improving stability while moving. | — | — | — | ↑ | |
| | Angled Foregrip | Increases Control by reducing the amount of recoil felt. | — | — | ↑ | — | |
| | Bipod Grip | Increases Maneuverability by improving stability while moving. When ALT-FIRE mode is activated while in cover or prone, a small Bipod deploys to increase Control. | — | — | ↑ | ↑ | |
| | Bipod | When ALT-FIRE mode is activated while in cover or prone, the Bipod deploys and significantly increases Control. | — | — | ↑ | — | |
| MAGAZINE | Standard Magazine | Standard magazine loaded with FMJ ammunition. | — | — | — | — | |
| | Extended Magazine | Extended magazine loaded with FMJ ammunition. | — | — | — | — | |
| | Armor Piercing Ammo | Standard magazine loaded with AP ammunition capable of dealing more damage to armored targets. | ↑ | — | — | — | |
| | Incendiary Ammo | Standard magazine loaded with Incendiary ammunition, dealing splash damage in a small radius. Overall Power is decreased by a lack of penetration. | — | — | — | ↑ | |
| TRIGGER GROUP | Full-Auto | Full-Auto trigger group allows for continuous fire while the trigger is pulled. | — | — | — | — | |
| | Match Trigger | Match Trigger increases the default trigger sensitivity for increased accuracy and faster follow-up shots. | — | — | — | — | |
| | Semi-Auto | Semi-automatic trigger group allows the weapon to fire one round for every trigger pull. | — | — | — | — | |
| | 3-Round Burst | 3-Round Burst trigger group that fires three rounds for every trigger pull. | — | — | — | — | |

Light Machine Guns are fully automatic portable firearms designed to fire several hundred rounds per minute from large-capacity magazines. Forgoing accuracy for a high rate of fire, the main role of these weapons is to lay down cover fire and act as a deterrent. Extremely lethal in short and medium ranges, the LMG performs admirably both as an offensive and defensive weapon.

| Unlock Requirements | Mk48 | Stoner 96 | LSAT | PKP | Type 95 | Ultimax Mk.5 | M60 | RPK |
|---|---|---|---|---|---|---|---|---|
| — | X | X | X | X | X | X | X | X |
| — | X | X | X | X | X | X | X | X |
| Unlocked by completing the Firefly Rain mission. | X | X | X | X | X | X | X | X |
| Unlocked by completing the Nimble Guardian mission. | X | X | X | X | X | X | X | X |
| Unlocked by completing the Ember Hunt mission. | X | X | X | X | X | X | X | X |
| — | — | — | X | — | — | — | X | X |
| — | X | X | — | — | — | X | — | — |
| — | — | — | — | — | — | X | — | X |
| Unlocked by completing all Shattered Mountain Tactical challenges. | — | X | X | — | — | X | — | — |
| — | X | X | X | X | X | X | X | X |
| Unlocked by completing the Subtle Arrow mission. | X | X | X | X | X | X | X | X |
| Unlocked by completing all Subtle Arrow Tactical challenges. | X | X | X | X | X | X | X | X |
| — | X | X | X | X | X | X | X | X |
| — | X | X | X | X | X | X | X | X |
| — | X | X | X | X | X | X | X | X |
| — | X | X | X | X | X | X | X | X |
| Unlocked by completing the Nimble Guardian mission. | X | X | X | X | X | X | X | X |
| Unlocked by completing the Firefly Rain mission. | X | X | X | X | — | X | X | X |
| — | X | X | X | X | X | X | X | X |
| — | X | X | X | X | X | X | X | X |
| — | X | X | X | X | X | X | X | X |
| — | X | X | X | X | X | X | X | X |
| — | X | X | X | X | X | X | X | X |
| Unlocked by completing the Nimble Guardian mission. | X | X | X | X | X | X | X | X |
| Unlocked by completing all Gallant Thief Tactical challenges. | X | X | X | X | X | X | X | X |
| Unlocked by completing the Subtle Arrow mission. | X | X | X | X | X | X | X | — |
| — | X | X | X | X | X | X | X | X |
| Unlocked by completing all Noble Tempest Tactical challenges. | — | — | — | — | — | — | — | X |
| Unlocked by completing all Deep Fire Tactical challenges. | X | X | X | X | X | X | X | X |
| Unlocked by completing the Ember Hunt mission. | X | X | X | X | X | X | X | X |
| — | X | X | X | X | X | X | X | X |
| — | X | X | X | X | X | X | X | X |
| — | | | | | | | | X |
| — | | | | | | X | | |

Denotes ULC Weapon

## LSAT

| | | |
|---|---|---|
| POWER | 👊 | |
| RANGE | ➡ | |
| CONTROL | 🎯 | |
| MANEUVERABILITY | ✥ | |
| RATE OF FIRE | ⏱ | 660 RPM |
| MAGAZINE CAPACITY | ≣ | 150 |

- **Suppressive Fire:** Suppresses targets when continually fired in their direction, especially when user is prone or braced on low cover.
- **Low Recoil:** Weapon recoil compensation system improves stability when firing multiple rounds.

### UNLOCK
Complete Ember Hunt mission.

| CAMPAIGN | X |
|---|---|
| MULTIPLAYER | X |

# OPTIMIZED CONFIGURATIONS

## CONTROL

| | | |
|---|---|---|
| POWER | 👊 | |
| RANGE | ➡ | |
| CONTROL | 🎯 | |
| MANEUVERABILITY | ✥ | |
| RATE OF FIRE | ⏱ | 594 RPM |
| MAGAZINE CAPACITY | ≣ | 150 |

### CONTROL CONFIGURATION

| Mod. Point | Attachment | 👊 | ➡ | 🎯 | ✥ |
|---|---|---|---|---|---|
| Optic | Magnified HWS | — | — | ↑ | — |
| Stock | Fixed | — | — | ↑ | — |
| Muzzle | Compensator | — | — | ↑ | — |
| Barrel | Short Barrel | — | ↓ | — | ↑ |
| Side Rail | Aiming Laser | — | — | ↑ | — |
| Gas System | Under-Gassed | — | — | ↑ | — |
| Underbarrel | Bipod Grip | — | — | ↑ | ↑ |
| Magazine | Armor Piercing Ammo | ↑ | — | — | — |
| Trigger Group | Match Trigger | — | — | — | — |

## MANEUVERABILITY

| | | |
|---|---|---|
| POWER | 👊 | |
| RANGE | ➡ | |
| CONTROL | 🎯 | |
| MANEUVERABILITY | ✥ | |
| RATE OF FIRE | ⏱ | 594 RPM |
| MAGAZINE CAPACITY | ≣ | 150 |

### MANEUVERABILITY CONFIGURATION

| Mod. Point | Attachment | 👊 | ➡ | 🎯 | ✥ |
|---|---|---|---|---|---|
| Optic | Red Dot | — | — | — | ↑ |
| Stock | Fixed | — | — | ↑ | — |
| Muzzle | Compensator | — | — | ↑ | — |
| Barrel | Short Barrel | — | ↓ | — | ↑ |
| Side Rail | Aiming Laser | — | — | ↑ | — |
| Gas System | Under-Gassed | — | — | ↑ | — |
| Underbarrel | Bipod Grip | — | — | ↑ | ↑ |
| Magazine | Armor Piercing Ammo | ↑ | — | — | — |
| Trigger Group | Full-Auto | — | — | — | — |

## POWER

| | | |
|---|---|---|
| POWER | 👊 | |
| RANGE | ➡ | |
| CONTROL | 🎯 | |
| MANEUVERABILITY | ✥ | |
| RATE OF FIRE | ⏱ | 594 RPM |
| MAGAZINE CAPACITY | ≣ | 150 |

### POWER CONFIGURATION

| Mod. Point | Attachment | 👊 | ➡ | 🎯 | ✥ |
|---|---|---|---|---|---|
| Optic | Tac Scope | — | ↑ | — | — |
| Stock | Fixed | — | — | ↑ | — |
| Muzzle | Compensator | — | — | ↑ | — |
| Barrel | Long Barrel | — | ↑ | — | ↓ |
| Side Rail | Aiming Laser | — | — | ↑ | — |
| Gas System | Under-Gassed | — | — | ↑ | — |
| Underbarrel | Bipod Grip | — | — | ↑ | ↑ |
| Magazine | Armor Piercing Ammo | ↑ | — | — | — |
| Trigger Group | Match Trigger | — | — | — | — |

## RANGE

| | | |
|---|---|---|
| POWER | 👊 | |
| RANGE | ➡ | |
| CONTROL | 🎯 | |
| MANEUVERABILITY | ✥ | |
| RATE OF FIRE | ⏱ | 594 RPM |
| MAGAZINE CAPACITY | ≣ | 150 |

### RANGE CONFIGURATION

| Mod. Point | Attachment | 👊 | ➡ | 🎯 | ✥ |
|---|---|---|---|---|---|
| Optic | Tac Scope | — | ↑ | — | — |
| Stock | Fixed | — | — | ↑ | — |
| Muzzle | Compensator | — | — | ↑ | — |
| Barrel | Long Barrel | — | ↑ | — | ↓ |
| Side Rail | Aiming Laser | — | — | ↑ | — |
| Gas System | Under-Gassed | — | — | ↑ | — |
| Underbarrel | Bipod Grip | — | — | ↑ | ↑ |
| Magazine | Armor Piercing Ammo | ↑ | — | — | — |
| Trigger Group | Match Trigger | — | — | — | — |

## MK48

| | |
|---|---|
| POWER ✊ | ▢▢▢□□ |
| RANGE ➡ | ▢▢□□□ |
| CONTROL ✥ | ▢▢□□□ |
| MANEUVERABILITY ✛ | ▢▢□□□ |
| RATE OF FIRE ⏱ | 780 RPM |
| MAGAZINE CAPACITY ☰ | 150 |

- **Suppressive Fire:** Suppresses targets when continually fired in their direction, especially when user is prone or braced on low cover.
- **Heavy Weapon:** Devastating when fired from a stable position: crouched, prone, or braced on low cover.

**UNLOCK**
Complete Campaign Prologue.

| CAMPAIGN | X |
|---|---|
| MULTIPLAYER | X |

## OPTIMIZED CONFIGURATIONS

### CONTROL

| | |
|---|---|
| POWER ✊ | ▢▢▢▢□ |
| RANGE ➡ | ▢▢▢□□ |
| CONTROL ✥ | ▢▢▢▢□ |
| MANEUVERABILITY ✛ | ▢□□□□ |
| RATE OF FIRE ⏱ | 702 RPM |
| MAGAZINE CAPACITY ☰ | 150 |

#### CONTROL CONFIGURATION

| Mod. Point | Attachment | ✊ | ➡ | ✥ | ✛ |
|---|---|---|---|---|---|
| Optic | Magnified HWS | — | — | ↑ | — |
| Stock | Extended | — | — | — | — |
| Muzzle | Compensator | — | — | ↑ | — |
| Barrel | Short Barrel | — | ↓ | — | ↑ |
| Side Rail | Aiming Laser | — | — | ↑ | — |
| Gas System | Under-Gassed | — | — | ↑ | — |
| Underbarrel | Bipod Grip | — | — | ↑ | ↑ |
| Magazine | Armor Piercing Ammo | ↑ | — | — | — |
| Trigger Group | Match Trigger | — | — | — | — |

### MANEUVERABILITY

| | |
|---|---|
| POWER ✊ | ▢▢▢□□ |
| RANGE ➡ | ▢▢□□□ |
| CONTROL ✥ | ▢▢▢□□ |
| MANEUVERABILITY ✛ | ▢▢□□□ |
| RATE OF FIRE ⏱ | 702RPM |
| MAGAZINE CAPACITY ☰ | 150 |

#### MANEUVERABILITY CONFIGURATION

| Mod. Point | Attachment | ✊ | ➡ | ✥ | ✛ |
|---|---|---|---|---|---|
| Optic | Red Dot | — | — | — | ↑ |
| Stock | Collapsed | — | — | ↓ | ↑ |
| Muzzle | Compensator | — | — | ↑ | — |
| Barrel | Short Barrel | — | ↓ | — | ↑ |
| Side Rail | Aiming Laser | — | — | ↑ | — |
| Gas System | Under-Gassed | — | — | ↑ | — |
| Underbarrel | Vertical Foregrip | — | — | — | ↑ |
| Magazine | Armor Piercing Ammo | ↑ | — | — | — |
| Trigger Group | Match Trigger | — | — | — | — |

### POWER

| | |
|---|---|
| POWER ✊ | ▢▢▢□□ |
| RANGE ➡ | ▢▢▢□□ |
| CONTROL ✥ | ▢▢▢□□ |
| MANEUVERABILITY ✛ | ▢□□□□ |
| RATE OF FIRE ⏱ | 702 RPM |
| MAGAZINE CAPACITY ☰ | 150 |

#### POWER CONFIGURATION

| Mod. Point | Attachment | ✊ | ➡ | ✥ | ✛ |
|---|---|---|---|---|---|
| Optic | Tac Scope | — | ↑ | — | — |
| Stock | Extended | — | — | — | — |
| Muzzle | Compensator | — | — | ↑ | — |
| Barrel | Long Barrel | — | ↑ | — | ↓ |
| Side Rail | Aiming Laser | — | — | ↑ | — |
| Gas System | Under-Gassed | — | — | ↑ | — |
| Underbarrel | Bipod Grip | — | — | ↑ | ↑ |
| Magazine | Armor Piercing Ammo | ↑ | — | — | — |
| Trigger Group | Full-Auto | — | — | — | — |

### RANGE

| | |
|---|---|
| POWER ✊ | ▢▢▢□□ |
| RANGE ➡ | ▢▢▢▢□ |
| CONTROL ✥ | ▢▢▢□□ |
| MANEUVERABILITY ✛ | ▢□□□□ |
| RATE OF FIRE ⏱ | 702 RPM |
| MAGAZINE CAPACITY ☰ | 150 |

#### RANGE CONFIGURATION

| Mod. Point | Attachment | ✊ | ➡ | ✥ | ✛ |
|---|---|---|---|---|---|
| Optic | Tac Scope | — | ↑ | — | — |
| Stock | Collapsed | — | — | ↓ | ↑ |
| Muzzle | Compensator | — | — | ↑ | — |
| Barrel | Long Barrel | — | ↑ | — | ↓ |
| Side Rail | Aiming Laser | — | — | ↑ | — |
| Gas System | Under-Gassed | — | — | ↑ | — |
| Underbarrel | Vertical Foregrip | — | — | — | ↑ |
| Magazine | Armor Piercing Ammo | ↑ | — | — | — |
| Trigger Group | Match Trigger | — | — | — | — |

## PKP

| | |
|---|---|
| POWER | ✊ |
| RANGE | ➡ |
| CONTROL | ⊙ |
| MANEUVERABILITY | ✛ |
| RATE OF FIRE | ⊕ 960 RPM |
| MAGAZINE CAPACITY | ≡ 150 |

- **Suppressive Fire:** Suppresses targets when continually fired in their direction, especially when user is prone or braced on low cover.
- **Rapid-Fire:** Weapon features a higher rate of fire than other weapons in its class.

**UNLOCK**

Complete Nimble Guardian weapon challenge.

| CAMPAIGN | X |
|---|---|
| MULTIPLAYER | |

# OPTIMIZED CONFIGURATIONS

## CONTROL

| | |
|---|---|
| POWER | ✊ |
| RANGE | ➡ |
| CONTROL | ⊙ |
| MANEUVERABILITY | ✛ |
| RATE OF FIRE | ⊕ 864 RPM |
| MAGAZINE CAPACITY | ≡ 150 |

### CONTROL CONFIGURATION

| Mod. Point | Attachment | ✊ | ➡ | ⊙ | ✛ |
|---|---|---|---|---|---|
| Optic | Magnified HWS | — | — | ↑ | — |
| Stock | — | — | — | — | — |
| Muzzle | Compensator | — | — | ↑ | — |
| Barrel | Short Barrel | — | ↓ | — | ↑ |
| Side Rail | Aiming Laser | — | — | ↑ | — |
| Gas System | Under-Gassed | — | — | ↑ | — |
| Underbarrel | Bipod Grip | — | — | ↑ | ↑ |
| Magazine | Armor Piercing Ammo | ↑ | — | — | — |
| Trigger Group | Full-Auto | — | — | — | — |

## MANEUVERABILITY

| | |
|---|---|
| POWER | ✊ |
| RANGE | ➡ |
| CONTROL | ⊙ |
| MANEUVERABILITY | ✛ |
| RATE OF FIRE | ⊕ 864 RPM |
| MAGAZINE CAPACITY | ≡ 150 |

### MANEUVERABILITY CONFIGURATION

| Mod. Point | Attachment | ✊ | ➡ | ⊙ | ✛ |
|---|---|---|---|---|---|
| Optic | Red Dot | — | — | — | ↑ |
| Stock | — | — | — | — | — |
| Muzzle | Compensator | — | — | ↑ | — |
| Barrel | Short Barrel | — | ↓ | — | ↑ |
| Side Rail | Aiming Laser | — | — | ↑ | — |
| Gas System | Under-Gassed | — | — | ↑ | — |
| Underbarrel | Bipod Grip | — | — | ↑ | ↑ |
| Magazine | Armor Piercing Ammo | ↑ | — | — | — |
| Trigger Group | Full-Auto | — | — | — | — |

## POWER

| | |
|---|---|
| POWER | ✊ |
| RANGE | ➡ |
| CONTROL | ⊙ |
| MANEUVERABILITY | ✛ |
| RATE OF FIRE | ⊕ 864 RPM |
| MAGAZINE CAPACITY | ≡ 150 |

### POWER CONFIGURATION

| Mod. Point | Attachment | ✊ | ➡ | ⊙ | ✛ |
|---|---|---|---|---|---|
| Optic | Tac Scope | — | ↑ | — | — |
| Stock | — | — | — | — | — |
| Muzzle | Compensator | — | — | ↑ | — |
| Barrel | Long Barrel | — | ↑ | — | ↓ |
| Side Rail | Aiming Laser | — | — | ↑ | — |
| Gas System | Under-Gassed | — | — | ↑ | — |
| Underbarrel | Bipod Grip | — | — | ↑ | ↑ |
| Magazine | Armor Piercing Ammo | ↑ | — | — | — |
| Trigger Group | Match Trigger | — | — | — | — |

## RANGE

| | |
|---|---|
| POWER | ✊ |
| RANGE | ➡ |
| CONTROL | ⊙ |
| MANEUVERABILITY | ✛ |
| RATE OF FIRE | ⊕ 864 RPM |
| MAGAZINE CAPACITY | ≡ 150 |

### RANGE CONFIGURATION

| Mod. Point | Attachment | ✊ | ➡ | ⊙ | ✛ |
|---|---|---|---|---|---|
| Optic | Tac Scope | — | ↑ | — | — |
| Stock | — | — | — | — | — |
| Muzzle | Compensator | — | — | ↑ | — |
| Barrel | Long Barrel | — | ↑ | — | ↓ |
| Side Rail | Aiming Laser | — | — | ↑ | — |
| Gas System | Under-Gassed | — | — | ↑ | — |
| Underbarrel | Bipod Grip | — | — | ↑ | ↑ |
| Magazine | Armor Piercing Ammo | ↑ | — | — | — |
| Trigger Group | Full-Auto | — | — | — | — |

## STONER 96

| | |
|---|---|
| POWER ✊ | |
| RANGE ➡ | |
| CONTROL ⊙ | |
| MANEUVERABILITY ✛ | |
| RATE OF FIRE ⏱ | 960 RPM |
| MAGAZINE CAPACITY ☰ | 150 |

- **Suppressive Fire:** Suppresses targets when continually fired in their direction, especially when user is prone or braced on low cover.
- **Rapid-Fire:** Weapon features a higher rate of fire than other weapons in its class.

**UNLOCK**
Complete Subtle Arrow mission.

| CAMPAIGN | X |
|---|---|
| MULTIPLAYER | X |

# OPTIMIZED CONFIGURATIONS

## CONTROL

| | |
|---|---|
| POWER ✊ | |
| RANGE ➡ | |
| CONTROL ⊙ | |
| MANEUVERABILITY ✛ | |
| RATE OF FIRE ⏱ | 864 RPM |
| MAGAZINE CAPACITY ☰ | 150 |

### CONTROL CONFIGURATION

| Mod. Point | Attachment | ✊ | ➡ | ⊙ | ✛ |
|---|---|---|---|---|---|
| Optic | Magnified HWS | — | — | ↑ | — |
| Stock | Fixed | — | — | ↑ | — |
| Muzzle | Compensator | — | — | ↑ | — |
| Barrel | Short Barrel | — | ↓ | — | ↑ |
| Side Rail | Aiming Laser | — | — | ↑ | — |
| Gas System | Under-Gassed | — | — | ↑ | — |
| Underbarrel | Bipod Grip | — | — | ↑ | ↑ |
| Magazine | Armor Piercing Ammo | ↑ | — | — | — |
| Trigger Group | Match Trigger | — | — | — | — |

## MANEUVERABILITY

| | |
|---|---|
| POWER ✊ | |
| RANGE ➡ | |
| CONTROL ⊙ | |
| MANEUVERABILITY ✛ | |
| RATE OF FIRE ⏱ | 864 RPM |
| MAGAZINE CAPACITY ☰ | 150 |

### MANEUVERABILITY CONFIGURATION

| Mod. Point | Attachment | ✊ | ➡ | ⊙ | ✛ |
|---|---|---|---|---|---|
| Optic | Red Dot | — | — | — | ↑ |
| Stock | Collapsed | — | — | ↓ | ↑ |
| Muzzle | Compensator | — | — | ↑ | — |
| Barrel | Short Barrel | — | ↓ | — | ↑ |
| Side Rail | Aiming Laser | — | — | ↑ | — |
| Gas System | Under-Gassed | — | — | ↑ | — |
| Underbarrel | Vertical Foregrip | — | — | — | ↑ |
| Magazine | Armor Piercing Ammo | ↑ | — | — | — |
| Trigger Group | Full-Auto | — | — | — | — |

## POWER

| | |
|---|---|
| POWER ✊ | |
| RANGE ➡ | |
| CONTROL ⊙ | |
| MANEUVERABILITY ✛ | |
| RATE OF FIRE ⏱ | 864 RPM |
| MAGAZINE CAPACITY ☰ | 150 |

### POWER CONFIGURATION

| Mod. Point | Attachment | ✊ | ➡ | ⊙ | ✛ |
|---|---|---|---|---|---|
| Optic | Tac Scope | — | ↑ | — | — |
| Stock | Fixed | — | — | ↑ | — |
| Muzzle | Compensator | — | — | ↑ | — |
| Barrel | Long Barrel | — | ↑ | — | ↓ |
| Side Rail | Aiming Laser | — | — | ↑ | — |
| Gas System | Under-Gassed | — | — | ↑ | — |
| Underbarrel | Bipod Grip | — | — | ↑ | ↑ |
| Magazine | Armor Piercing Ammo | ↑ | — | — | — |
| Trigger Group | Full-Auto | — | — | — | — |

## RANGE

| | |
|---|---|
| POWER ✊ | |
| RANGE ➡ | |
| CONTROL ⊙ | |
| MANEUVERABILITY ✛ | |
| RATE OF FIRE ⏱ | 864 RPM |
| MAGAZINE CAPACITY ☰ | 150 |

### RANGE CONFIGURATION

| Mod. Point | Attachment | ✊ | ➡ | ⊙ | ✛ |
|---|---|---|---|---|---|
| Optic | Tac Scope | — | ↑ | — | — |
| Stock | Fixed | — | — | ↑ | — |
| Muzzle | Compensator | — | — | ↑ | — |
| Barrel | Long Barrel | — | ↑ | — | ↓ |
| Side Rail | Aiming Laser | — | — | ↑ | — |
| Gas System | Under-Gassed | — | — | ↑ | — |
| Underbarrel | Bipod Grip | — | — | ↑ | ↑ |
| Magazine | Armor Piercing Ammo | ↑ | — | — | — |
| Trigger Group | Match Trigger | — | — | — | — |

# TYPE 95

| | | |
|---|---|---|
| POWER | 👊 | |
| RANGE | ➡ | |
| CONTROL | ⊙ | |
| MANEUVERABILITY | ✛ | |
| RATE OF FIRE | ⏱ | 540 RPM |
| MAGAZINE CAPACITY | ☰ | 80 |

- **Suppressive Fire:** Suppresses targets when continually fired in their direction, especially when user is prone or braced on low cover.
- **Bullpup:** Compact design allows for improved maneuverability.

**UNLOCK**
Complete Ember Hunt weapon challenge.

| | |
|---|---|
| CAMPAIGN | X |
| MULTIPLAYER | ☐ |

---

## OPTIMIZED CONFIGURATIONS

### CONTROL

| | | |
|---|---|---|
| POWER | 👊 | |
| RANGE | ➡ | |
| CONTROL | ⊙ | |
| MANEUVERABILITY | ✛ | |
| RATE OF FIRE | ⏱ | 486 RPM |
| MAGAZINE CAPACITY | ☰ | 80 |

#### CONTROL CONFIGURATION

| Mod. Point | Attachment | 👊 | ➡ | ⊙ | ✛ |
|---|---|---|---|---|---|
| Optic | Magnified HWS | — | — | ↑ | — |
| Stock | — | — | — | — | — |
| Muzzle | Compensator | — | — | ↑ | — |
| Barrel | Short Barrel | — | ↓ | — | ↑ |
| Side Rail | Aiming Laser | — | — | ↑ | — |
| Gas System | Under-Gassed | — | — | ↑ | — |
| Underbarrel | Bipod Grip | — | — | ↑ | ↑ |
| Magazine | Armor Piercing Ammo | ↑ | — | — | — |
| Trigger Group | Full-Auto | — | — | — | — |

### MANEUVERABILITY

| | | |
|---|---|---|
| POWER | 👊 | |
| RANGE | ➡ | |
| CONTROL | ⊙ | |
| MANEUVERABILITY | ✛ | |
| RATE OF FIRE | ⏱ | 486 RPM |
| MAGAZINE CAPACITY | ☰ | 80 |

#### MANEUVERABILITY CONFIGURATION

| Mod. Point | Attachment | 👊 | ➡ | ⊙ | ✛ |
|---|---|---|---|---|---|
| Optic | Red Dot | — | — | — | ↑ |
| Stock | — | — | — | — | — |
| Muzzle | Compensator | — | — | ↑ | — |
| Barrel | Short Barrel | — | ↓ | — | ↑ |
| Side Rail | Aiming Laser | — | — | ↑ | — |
| Gas System | Under-Gassed | — | — | ↑ | — |
| Underbarrel | Bipod Grip | — | — | ↑ | ↑ |
| Magazine | Armor Piercing Ammo | ↑ | — | — | — |
| Trigger Group | Match Trigger | — | — | — | — |

### POWER

| | | |
|---|---|---|
| POWER | 👊 | |
| RANGE | ➡ | |
| CONTROL | ⊙ | |
| MANEUVERABILITY | ✛ | |
| RATE OF FIRE | ⏱ | 486 RPM |
| MAGAZINE CAPACITY | ☰ | 80 |

#### POWER CONFIGURATION

| Mod. Point | Attachment | 👊 | ➡ | ⊙ | ✛ |
|---|---|---|---|---|---|
| Optic | Tac Scope | — | ↑ | — | — |
| Stock | — | — | — | — | — |
| Muzzle | Compensator | — | — | ↑ | — |
| Barrel | Long Barrel | — | ↑ | — | ↓ |
| Side Rail | Aiming Laser | — | — | ↑ | — |
| Gas System | Under-Gassed | — | — | ↑ | — |
| Underbarrel | Bipod Grip | — | — | ↑ | ↑ |
| Magazine | Armor Piercing Ammo | ↑ | — | — | — |
| Trigger Group | Match Trigger | — | — | — | — |

### RANGE

| | | |
|---|---|---|
| POWER | 👊 | |
| RANGE | ➡ | |
| CONTROL | ⊙ | |
| MANEUVERABILITY | ✛ | |
| RATE OF FIRE | ⏱ | 486 RPM |
| MAGAZINE CAPACITY | ☰ | 80 |

#### RANGE CONFIGURATION

| Mod. Point | Attachment | 👊 | ➡ | ⊙ | ✛ |
|---|---|---|---|---|---|
| Optic | Tac Scope | — | ↑ | — | — |
| Stock | — | — | — | — | — |
| Muzzle | Compensator | — | — | ↑ | — |
| Barrel | Long Barrel | — | ↑ | — | ↓ |
| Side Rail | Aiming Laser | — | — | ↑ | — |
| Gas System | Under-Gassed | — | — | ↑ | — |
| Underbarrel | Bipod Grip | — | — | ↑ | ↑ |
| Magazine | Armor Piercing Ammo | ↑ | — | — | — |
| Trigger Group | Full-Auto | — | — | — | — |

## ULTIMAX MK.5

| | |
|---|---|
| POWER ✊ | |
| RANGE ➡ | |
| CONTROL ⊕ | |
| MANEUVERABILITY ✛ | |
| RATE OF FIRE ⏱ | 540 RPM |
| MAGAZINE CAPACITY ☰ | 150 |

- **Suppressive Fire:** Suppresses targets when continually fired in their direction, especially when user is prone or braced on low cover.
- **Quick Reload:** Magazine location allows for quick reloading.

**UNLOCK**

Perform a Ghost Score of 60% in nine missions.

| CAMPAIGN | X |
|---|---|
| MULTIPLAYER | |

## OPTIMIZED CONFIGURATIONS

### CONTROL

| | |
|---|---|
| POWER ✊ | |
| RANGE ➡ | |
| CONTROL ⊕ | |
| MANEUVERABILITY ✛ | |
| RATE OF FIRE ⏱ | 486 RPM |
| MAGAZINE CAPACITY ☰ | 150 |

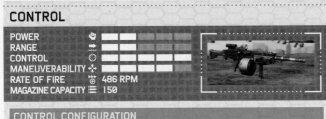

#### CONTROL CONFIGURATION

| Mod. Point | Attachment | ✊ | ➡ | ⊕ | ✛ |
|---|---|---|---|---|---|
| Optic | Magnified HWS | — | — | ↑ | — |
| Stock | Fixed | — | — | ↑ | — |
| Muzzle | Compensator | — | — | ↑ | — |
| Barrel | Short Barrel | — | ↓ | — | ↑ |
| Side Rail | Aiming Laser | — | — | ↑ | — |
| Gas System | Under-Gassed | — | — | ↑ | — |
| Underbarrel | Bipod Grip | — | — | ↑ | ↑ |
| Magazine | Armor Piercing Ammo | ↑ | — | — | — |
| Trigger Group | 3-Round Burst | — | — | — | — |

### MANEUVERABILITY

| | |
|---|---|
| POWER ✊ | |
| RANGE ➡ | |
| CONTROL ⊕ | |
| MANEUVERABILITY ✛ | |
| RATE OF FIRE ⏱ | 486 RPM |
| MAGAZINE CAPACITY ☰ | 150 |

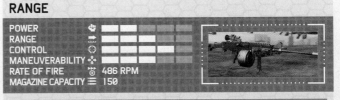

#### MANEUVERABILITY CONFIGURATION

| Mod. Point | Attachment | ✊ | ➡ | ⊕ | ✛ |
|---|---|---|---|---|---|
| Optic | Red Dot | — | — | — | ↑ |
| Stock | Standard | — | — | — | ↑ |
| Muzzle | Compensator | — | — | ↑ | — |
| Barrel | Short Barrel | — | ↓ | — | ↑ |
| Side Rail | Aiming Laser | — | — | ↑ | — |
| Gas System | Under-Gassed | — | — | ↑ | — |
| Underbarrel | Bipod Grip | — | — | ↑ | ↑ |
| Magazine | Armor Piercing Ammo | ↑ | — | — | — |
| Trigger Group | 3-Round Burst | — | — | — | — |

### POWER

| | |
|---|---|
| POWER ✊ | |
| RANGE ➡ | |
| CONTROL ⊕ | |
| MANEUVERABILITY ✛ | |
| RATE OF FIRE ⏱ | 486 RPM |
| MAGAZINE CAPACITY ☰ | 150 |

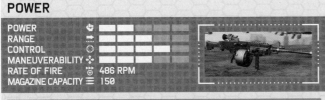

#### POWER CONFIGURATION

| Mod. Point | Attachment | ✊ | ➡ | ⊕ | ✛ |
|---|---|---|---|---|---|
| Optic | Tac Scope | — | ↑ | — | — |
| Stock | Fixed | — | — | ↑ | — |
| Muzzle | Compensator | — | — | ↑ | — |
| Barrel | Long Barrel | — | ↑ | — | ↓ |
| Side Rail | Aiming Laser | — | — | ↑ | — |
| Gas System | Under-Gassed | — | — | ↑ | — |
| Underbarrel | Bipod Grip | — | — | ↑ | ↑ |
| Magazine | Armor Piercing Ammo | ↑ | — | — | — |
| Trigger Group | Match Trigger | — | — | — | — |

### RANGE

| | |
|---|---|
| POWER ✊ | |
| RANGE ➡ | |
| CONTROL ⊕ | |
| MANEUVERABILITY ✛ | |
| RATE OF FIRE ⏱ | 486 RPM |
| MAGAZINE CAPACITY ☰ | 150 |

#### RANGE CONFIGURATION

| Mod. Point | Attachment | ✊ | ➡ | ⊕ | ✛ |
|---|---|---|---|---|---|
| Optic | Tac Scope | — | ↑ | — | — |
| Stock | Standard | — | — | — | ↑ |
| Muzzle | Compensator | — | — | ↑ | — |
| Barrel | Long Barrel | — | ↑ | — | ↓ |
| Side Rail | Aiming Laser | — | — | ↑ | — |
| Gas System | Under-Gassed | — | — | ↑ | — |
| Underbarrel | Bipod Grip | — | — | ↑ | ↑ |
| Magazine | Armor Piercing Ammo | ↑ | — | — | — |
| Trigger Group | 3-Round Burst | — | — | — | — |

# PERSONAL DEFENSE RIFLES (PDRS)

## PDR ATTACHMENTS

| | Attachment | Description | Power | Range | Control | Maneuverability |
|---|---|---|---|---|---|---|
| OPTIC | Iron Sights | Standard weapon iron sights that offer quick targeting with a small viewing area. | — | — | — | — |
| | Red Dot | Non-magnified optic that enables quick target acquisition with little visual interference. | — | — | — | ↑ |
| | Magnified HWS | 3x magnifier combined with a Holographic Weapon Sight for a good balance between easy targeting and zoom level. | — | — | ↑ | — |
| | TAC Scope | 4x magnification sight for medium-range engagements. | — | ↑ | — | — |
| STOCK | Standard | Standard stock provides a good balance between Maneuverability and Control. | — | — | — | — |
| | Extended | Extended stock provides a good balance between Maneuverability and Control. | — | — | — | — |
| | Folded | Folded stock that increases Maneuverability, but decreases Control due to lack of stability. | — | — | ↓ | ↑ |
| | Collapsed | Folded stock that increases Maneuverability, but decreases Control due to lack of stability. | — | — | ↓ | ↑ |
| | Fixed | Fixed stock that increases Control by reducing the amount of recoil felt. | — | — | ↑ | — |
| | Angled Foregrip | Increases Control by reducing the amount of recoil felt. | — | — | ↑ | — |
| MUZZLE | Standard | Factory muzzle attachment. | — | — | — | — |
| | Compensator | Compensates for recoil and muzzle climb to increase Control. | — | — | ↑ | — |
| | Flash Hider | Hides muzzle flash from enemies, but decreases Control. | — | — | ↓ | — |
| | Suppressor | Hides muzzle flash and reduces the sound produced by firing the weapon, but decreases Power and Range due to the use of sub-sonic ammunition. | ↓ | ↓ | — | — |
| SIDE RAIL | Rail Cover | Standard rail cover. | — | — | — | — |
| | Aiming Laser | Increases Control by providing a visual aid while aiming. | — | — | ↑ | — |
| GAS SYSTEM | Standard | Standard gas system with a good balance between Rate of Fire and Control. | — | — | — | — |
| | Over-Gassed | Gas system that increases Rate of Fire, but decreases Control. | — | — | ↓ | — |
| | Under-Gassed | Gas system that increases Control, but decreases Rate of Fire. | — | — | ↑ | — |
| UNDERBARREL | None | Standard underbarrel rail with no effect. | — | — | — | — |
| | Rail Cover | Standard rail cover. | — | — | — | — |
| | Vertical Foregrip | Increases Maneuverability by improving stability while moving. | — | — | — | ↑ |
| | Angled Foregrip | Increases Control by reducing the amount of recoil felt. | — | — | ↑ | — |
| MAGAZINE | Standard Magazine | Standard magazine loaded with FMJ ammunition. | — | — | — | — |
| | Dual Magazines | Two magazines coupled together, increasing the speed of every other reload. Magazines loaded with FMJ ammunition. | — | — | — | — |
| | Extended Magazine | Extended magazine loaded with FMJ ammunition. | — | — | — | — |
| | Armor Piercing Ammo | Standard magazine loaded with AP ammunition capable of dealing more damage to armored targets. | ↑ | — | — | — |
| TRIGGER GROUP | Full-Auto | Full-Auto trigger group allows for continuous fire while the trigger is pulled. | — | — | — | — |
| | 2-Stage Trigger | 2-Stage trigger group with dual fire modes. The first stage of the trigger pull fires in Semi-Auto mode. The second stage of the trigger pull fires in Full-Auto mode. | — | — | — | — |
| | Match Trigger | Match Trigger increases the default trigger sensitivity for increased accuracy and faster follow-up shots. | — | — | — | — |
| | Semi-Auto | Semi-automatic trigger group allows the weapon to fire one round for every trigger pull. | — | — | — | — |
| | 2-Round Burst | 2-Round Burst trigger group that fires two rounds for every trigger pull. | — | — | — | — |
| | 3-Round Burst | 3-Round Burst trigger group that fires three rounds for every trigger pull. | — | — | — | — |

Effective at short and medium range, PDRs are compact versions of assault rifles. Although similar in size to the submachine guns, PDRs are capable of firing armor-piercing rounds, which gives them better range and lethality. As hybrids, they can perform as sidearms, retaining the SMGs compact size and ammo capacity while benefiting from a rifle's stopping power.

| Unlock Requirements | Goblin | AKS-74U | SR-3M | SA58 OSW | PDR-C | L22A2 |
|---|---|---|---|---|---|---|
|  | X | X | X | X | X | X |
|  | X | X | X | X | X | X |
| Unlocked by completing the Firefly Rain mission. | X | X | X | X | X | X |
| Unlocked by completing the Nimble Guardian mission. | X | X | X | X | X | X |
| — | — | — | — | — | X | — |
| — | X | X | X | X | — | — |
| — | X | X | X | X | — | — |
| — | — | X | — | — | — | — |
| Unlocked by completing all Shattered Mountain Tactical challenges. | X | X | — | X | — | — |
| — | — | — | — | — | X | — |
| — | X | X | X | X | X | X |
| Unlocked by completing the Subtle Arrow mission. | X | X | X | X | X | X |
| Unlocked by completing all Subtle Arrow Tactical challenges. | X | X | X | X | X | X |
| — | X | X | X | X | X | X |
| — | X | X | X | X | X | X |
| Unlocked by completing the Nimble Guardian mission. | X | X | X | X | X | X |
| — | X | X | X | X | X | X |
| — | X | X | X | X | X | X |
| — | X | X | X | X | X | X |
| — | — | — | — | — | X | — |
| — | X | X | X | X | — | X |
| — | X | X | X | X | X | X |
| Unlocked by completing the Nimble Guardian mission. | X | X | X | X | — | X |
| — | X | X | X | X | X | X |
| Unlocked by completing all Silent Talon Tactical challenges. | X | X | X | X | — | X |
| Unlocked by completing all Noble Tempest Tactical challenges. | — | — | — | — | X | — |
| Unlocked by completing all Deep Fire Tactical challenges. | X | X | X | X | X | X |
| — | X | X | X | X | X | X |
| — | — | — | X | — | X | — |
| — | X | — | X | X | X | X |
| — | X | X | X | X | X | X |
| — | — | — | — | X | — | — |
| — | X | — | X | — | X | |

## AKS-74U

| | | |
|---|---|---|
| POWER | | |
| RANGE | | |
| CONTROL | | |
| MANEUVERABILITY | | |
| RATE OF FIRE | | 780 RPM |
| MAGAZINE CAPACITY | | 30 |

- **Fast Assault:** Ideal for quickly engaging unexpected targets or firing on the move.
- **Extra Customization:** Weapon features additional attachment points over other weapons.

**UNLOCK**
Perform a Ghost Score of 60% in six missions.

| CAMPAIGN | X |
|---|---|
| MULTIPLAYER | |

# OPTIMIZED CONFIGURATIONS

## CONTROL

| | | |
|---|---|---|
| POWER | | |
| RANGE | | |
| CONTROL | | |
| MANEUVERABILITY | | |
| RATE OF FIRE | | 702 RPM |
| MAGAZINE CAPACITY | | 30 |

### CONTROL CONFIGURATION

| Mod. Point | Attachment | ✊ | ➡ | ⊙ | ✛ |
|---|---|---|---|---|---|
| Optic | Magnified HWS | — | — | ↑ | — |
| Stock | Fixed | — | — | ↑ | — |
| Muzzle | Compensator | — | — | ↑ | — |
| Barrel | — | — | — | — | — |
| Side Rail | Aiming Laser | — | — | ↑ | — |
| Gas System | Under-Gassed | — | — | ↑ | — |
| Underbarrel | Angled Foregrip | — | — | ↑ | — |
| Magazine | Armor Piercing Ammo | ↑ | — | — | — |
| Trigger Group | Semi-Auto | — | — | — | — |

## MANEUVERABILITY

| | | |
|---|---|---|
| POWER | | |
| RANGE | | |
| CONTROL | | |
| MANEUVERABILITY | | |
| RATE OF FIRE | | 702 RPM |
| MAGAZINE CAPACITY | | 30 |

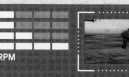

### MANEUVERABILITY CONFIGURATION

| Mod. Point | Attachment | ✊ | ➡ | ⊙ | ✛ |
|---|---|---|---|---|---|
| Optic | Red Dot | — | — | — | ↑ |
| Stock | Folded | — | — | ↓ | ↑ |
| Muzzle | Compensator | — | — | ↑ | — |
| Barrel | — | — | — | — | — |
| Side Rail | Aiming Laser | — | — | ↑ | — |
| Gas System | Under-Gassed | — | — | ↑ | — |
| Underbarrel | Vertical Foregrip | — | — | — | ↑ |
| Magazine | Armor Piercing Ammo | ↑ | — | — | — |
| Trigger Group | Semi-Auto | — | — | — | — |

## POWER

| | | |
|---|---|---|
| POWER | | |
| RANGE | | |
| CONTROL | | |
| MANEUVERABILITY | | |
| RATE OF FIRE | | 702 RPM |
| MAGAZINE CAPACITY | | 30 |

### POWER CONFIGURATION

| Mod. Point | Attachment | ✊ | ➡ | ⊙ | ✛ |
|---|---|---|---|---|---|
| Optic | Tac Scope | — | ↑ | — | — |
| Stock | Fixed | — | — | ↑ | — |
| Muzzle | Compensator | — | — | ↑ | — |
| Barrel | — | — | — | — | — |
| Side Rail | Aiming Laser | — | — | ↑ | — |
| Gas System | Under-Gassed | — | — | ↑ | — |
| Underbarrel | Vertical Foregrip | — | — | — | ↑ |
| Magazine | Armor Piercing Ammo | ↑ | — | — | — |
| Trigger Group | Semi-Auto | — | — | — | — |

## RANGE

| | | |
|---|---|---|
| POWER | | |
| RANGE | | |
| CONTROL | | |
| MANEUVERABILITY | | |
| RATE OF FIRE | | 702 RPM |
| MAGAZINE CAPACITY | | 30 |

### RANGE CONFIGURATION

| Mod. Point | Attachment | ✊ | ➡ | ⊙ | ✛ |
|---|---|---|---|---|---|
| Optic | Tac Scope | — | ↑ | — | — |
| Stock | Fixed | — | — | ↑ | — |
| Muzzle | Compensator | — | — | ↑ | — |
| Barrel | — | — | — | — | — |
| Side Rail | Aiming Laser | — | — | ↑ | — |
| Gas System | Under-Gassed | — | — | ↑ | — |
| Underbarrel | Angled Foregrip | — | — | ↑ | — |
| Magazine | Armor Piercing Ammo | ↑ | — | — | — |
| Trigger Group | Semi-Auto | — | — | — | — |

## GOBLIN

| | |
|---|---|
| POWER | ✊ |
| RANGE | ➡ |
| CONTROL | ◎ |
| MANEUVERABILITY | ✛ |
| RATE OF FIRE | ⏱ 720 RPM |
| MAGAZINE CAPACITY | ☰ 30 |

- Versatile: Suitable for a variety of combat scenarios and ranges.
- Extra Customization: Weapon features additional attachment points over other weapons.

UNLOCK
Complete Campaign Prologue.

| CAMPAIGN | X |
|---|---|
| MULTIPLAYER | X |

# OPTIMIZED CONFIGURATIONS

## CONTROL

| | |
|---|---|
| POWER | ✊ |
| RANGE | ➡ |
| CONTROL | ◎ |
| MANEUVERABILITY | ✛ |
| RATE OF FIRE | ⏱ 648 RPM |
| MAGAZINE CAPACITY | ☰ 30 |

### CONTROL CONFIGURATION

| Mod. Point | Attachment | ✊ | ➡ | ◎ | ✛ |
|---|---|---|---|---|---|
| Optic | Magnified HWS | — | — | ↑ | — |
| Stock | Fixed | — | — | ↑ | — |
| Muzzle | Compensator | — | — | ↑ | — |
| Barrel | — | — | — | — | — |
| Side Rail | Aiming Laser | — | — | ↑ | — |
| Gas System | Under-Gassed | — | — | ↑ | — |
| Underbarrel | Angled Foregrip | — | — | ↑ | — |
| Magazine | Armor Piercing Ammo | ↑ | — | — | — |
| Trigger Group | Semi-Auto | — | — | — | — |

## MANEUVERABILITY

| | |
|---|---|
| POWER | ✊ |
| RANGE | ➡ |
| CONTROL | ◎ |
| MANEUVERABILITY | ✛ |
| RATE OF FIRE | ⏱ 648 RPM |
| MAGAZINE CAPACITY | ☰ 30 |

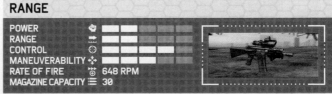

### MANEUVERABILITY CONFIGURATION

| Mod. Point | Attachment | ✊ | ➡ | ◎ | ✛ |
|---|---|---|---|---|---|
| Optic | Red Dot | — | — | — | ↑ |
| Stock | Folded | — | — | ↓ | ↑ |
| Muzzle | Compensator | — | — | ↑ | — |
| Barrel | — | — | — | — | — |
| Side Rail | Aiming Laser | — | — | ↑ | — |
| Gas System | Under-Gassed | — | — | ↑ | — |
| Underbarrel | Vertical Foregrip | — | — | — | ↑ |
| Magazine | Armor Piercing Ammo | ↑ | — | — | — |
| Trigger Group | Match Trigger | — | — | — | — |

## POWER

| | |
|---|---|
| POWER | ✊ |
| RANGE | ➡ |
| CONTROL | ◎ |
| MANEUVERABILITY | ✛ |
| RATE OF FIRE | ⏱ 648 RPM |
| MAGAZINE CAPACITY | ☰ 30 |

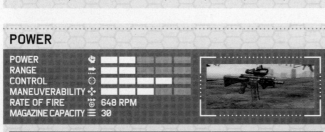

### POWER CONFIGURATION

| Mod. Point | Attachment | ✊ | ➡ | ◎ | ✛ |
|---|---|---|---|---|---|
| Optic | Tac Scope | — | ↑ | — | — |
| Stock | Fixed | — | — | ↑ | — |
| Muzzle | Compensator | — | — | ↑ | — |
| Barrel | — | — | — | — | — |
| Side Rail | Aiming Laser | — | — | ↑ | — |
| Gas System | Under-Gassed | — | — | ↑ | — |
| Underbarrel | Angled Foregrip | — | — | ↑ | — |
| Magazine | Armor Piercing Ammo | ↑ | — | — | — |
| Trigger Group | 3-Round Burst | — | — | — | — |

## RANGE

| | |
|---|---|
| POWER | ✊ |
| RANGE | ➡ |
| CONTROL | ◎ |
| MANEUVERABILITY | ✛ |
| RATE OF FIRE | ⏱ 648 RPM |
| MAGAZINE CAPACITY | ☰ 30 |

### RANGE CONFIGURATION

| Mod. Point | Attachment | ✊ | ➡ | ◎ | ✛ |
|---|---|---|---|---|---|
| Optic | Tac Scope | — | ↑ | — | — |
| Stock | Fixed | — | — | ↑ | — |
| Muzzle | Compensator | — | — | ↑ | — |
| Barrel | — | — | — | — | — |
| Side Rail | Aiming Laser | — | — | ↑ | — |
| Gas System | Under-Gassed | — | — | ↑ | — |
| Underbarrel | Angled Foregrip | — | — | ↑ | — |
| Magazine | Armor Piercing Ammo | ↑ | — | — | — |
| Trigger Group | Semi-Auto | — | — | — | — |

## L22A2

| | |
|---|---|
| POWER | |
| RANGE | |
| CONTROL | |
| MANEUVERABILITY | |
| RATE OF FIRE | 1,020 RPM |
| MAGAZINE CAPACITY | 30 |

- Fast Assault: Ideal for quickly engaging unexpected targets or firing on the move.
- Bullpup: Compact design allows for improved maneuverability.

UNLOCK
Complete Subtle Arrow mission.

| CAMPAIGN | X |
|---|---|
| MULTIPLAYER | X |

# OPTIMIZED CONFIGURATIONS

## CONTROL

| | |
|---|---|
| POWER | |
| RANGE | |
| CONTROL | |
| MANEUVERABILITY | |
| RATE OF FIRE | 918 RPM |
| MAGAZINE CAPACITY | 30 |

### CONTROL CONFIGURATION

| Mod. Point | Attachment | ✊ | ➡ | ◎ | ✛ |
|---|---|---|---|---|---|
| Optic | Magnified HWS | — | — | ↑ | — |
| Stock | — | — | — | — | — |
| Muzzle | Compensator | — | — | ↑ | — |
| Barrel | — | — | — | — | — |
| Side Rail | Aiming Laser | — | — | ↑ | — |
| Gas System | Under-Gassed | — | — | ↑ | — |
| Underbarrel | Angled Foregrip | — | — | ↑ | — |
| Magazine | Armor Piercing Ammo | ↑ | — | — | — |
| Trigger Group | Match Trigger | — | — | — | — |

## MANEUVERABILITY

| | |
|---|---|
| POWER | |
| RANGE | |
| CONTROL | |
| MANEUVERABILITY | |
| RATE OF FIRE | 918 RPM |
| MAGAZINE CAPACITY | 30 |

### MANEUVERABILITY CONFIGURATION

| Mod. Point | Attachment | ✊ | ➡ | ◎ | ✛ |
|---|---|---|---|---|---|
| Optic | Red Dot | — | — | — | ↑ |
| Stock | — | — | — | — | — |
| Muzzle | Compensator | — | — | ↑ | — |
| Barrel | — | — | — | — | — |
| Side Rail | Aiming Laser | — | — | ↑ | — |
| Gas System | Under-Gassed | — | — | ↑ | — |
| Underbarrel | Vertical Foregrip | — | — | — | ↑ |
| Magazine | Armor Piercing Ammo | ↑ | — | — | — |
| Trigger Group | Match Trigger | — | — | — | — |

## POWER

| | |
|---|---|
| POWER | |
| RANGE | |
| CONTROL | |
| MANEUVERABILITY | |
| RATE OF FIRE | 918 RPM |
| MAGAZINE CAPACITY | 30 |

### POWER CONFIGURATION

| Mod. Point | Attachment | ✊ | ➡ | ◎ | ✛ |
|---|---|---|---|---|---|
| Optic | Tac Scope | — | ↑ | — | — |
| Stock | — | — | — | — | — |
| Muzzle | Compensator | — | — | ↑ | — |
| Barrel | — | — | — | — | — |
| Side Rail | Aiming Laser | — | — | ↑ | — |
| Gas System | Under-Gassed | — | — | ↑ | — |
| Underbarrel | Vertical Foregrip | — | — | — | ↑ |
| Magazine | Armor Piercing Ammo | ↑ | — | — | — |
| Trigger Group | Match Trigger | — | — | — | — |

## RANGE

| | |
|---|---|
| POWER | |
| RANGE | |
| CONTROL | |
| MANEUVERABILITY | |
| RATE OF FIRE | 918 RPM |
| MAGAZINE CAPACITY | 30 |

### RANGE CONFIGURATION

| Mod. Point | Attachment | ✊ | ➡ | ◎ | ✛ |
|---|---|---|---|---|---|
| Optic | Tac Scope | — | ↑ | — | — |
| Stock | — | — | — | — | — |
| Muzzle | Compensator | — | — | ↑ | — |
| Barrel | — | — | — | — | — |
| Side Rail | Aiming Laser | — | — | ↑ | — |
| Gas System | Under-Gassed | — | — | ↑ | — |
| Underbarrel | Angled Foregrip | — | — | ↑ | — |
| Magazine | Armor Piercing Ammo | ↑ | — | — | — |
| Trigger Group | Full-Auto | — | — | — | — |

## PDR-C

| | |
|---|---|
| POWER | ✊ ▢▢▢▢▢ |
| RANGE | ➡ ▢▢▢▢▢ |
| CONTROL | ◎ ▢▢▢▢▢ |
| MANEUVERABILITY | ✛ ▢▢▢▢▢ |
| RATE OF FIRE | 🔄 780 RPM |
| MAGAZINE CAPACITY | ☰ 20 |

- **CQC:** Best suited for close-quarters combat engagements.
- **Low Recoil:** Weapon recoil compensation system improves stability when firing multiple rounds.

**UNLOCK**
Complete Tiger Dust mission.

| CAMPAIGN | X |
|---|---|
| MULTIPLAYER | X |

---

# OPTIMIZED CONFIGURATIONS

## CONTROL

| | |
|---|---|
| POWER | ✊ ▢▢▢▢▢ |
| RANGE | ➡ ▢▢▢▢▢ |
| CONTROL | ◎ ▢▢▢▢▢ |
| MANEUVERABILITY | ✛ ▢▢▢▢▢ |
| RATE OF FIRE | 🔄 702 RPM |
| MAGAZINE CAPACITY | ☰ 20 |

### CONTROL CONFIGURATION

| Mod. Point | Attachment | ✊ | ➡ | ◎ | ✛ |
|---|---|---|---|---|---|
| Optic | Magnified HWS | — | — | ↑ | — |
| Stock | Angled Foregrip | — | — | ↑ | — |
| Muzzle | Compensator | — | — | ↑ | — |
| Barrel | — | — | — | — | — |
| Side Rail | Aiming Laser | — | — | ↑ | — |
| Gas System | Under-Gassed | — | — | ↑ | — |
| Underbarrel | None | — | — | — | — |
| Magazine | Armor Piercing Ammo | ↑ | — | — | — |
| Trigger Group | Full-Auto | — | — | — | — |

## MANEUVERABILITY

| | |
|---|---|
| POWER | ✊ ▢▢▢▢▢ |
| RANGE | ➡ ▢▢▢▢▢ |
| CONTROL | ◎ ▢▢▢▢▢ |
| MANEUVERABILITY | ✛ ▢▢▢▢▢ |
| RATE OF FIRE | 🔄 702 RPM |
| MAGAZINE CAPACITY | ☰ 20 |

### MANEUVERABILITY CONFIGURATION

| Mod. Point | Attachment | ✊ | ➡ | ◎ | ✛ |
|---|---|---|---|---|---|
| Optic | Red Dot | — | — | — | ↑ |
| Stock | Angled Foregrip | — | — | ↑ | — |
| Muzzle | Compensator | — | — | ↑ | — |
| Barrel | — | — | — | — | — |
| Side Rail | Aiming Laser | — | — | ↑ | — |
| Gas System | Under-Gassed | — | — | ↑ | — |
| Underbarrel | None | — | — | — | — |
| Magazine | Armor Piercing Ammo | ↑ | — | — | — |
| Trigger Group | Match Trigger | — | — | — | — |

## POWER

| | |
|---|---|
| POWER | ✊ ▢▢▢▢▢ |
| RANGE | ➡ ▢▢▢▢▢ |
| CONTROL | ◎ ▢▢▢▢▢ |
| MANEUVERABILITY | ✛ ▢▢▢▢▢ |
| RATE OF FIRE | 🔄 702 RPM |
| MAGAZINE CAPACITY | ☰ 20 |

### POWER CONFIGURATION

| Mod. Point | Attachment | ✊ | ➡ | ◎ | ✛ |
|---|---|---|---|---|---|
| Optic | Tac Scope | — | ↑ | — | — |
| Stock | Angled Foregrip | — | — | ↑ | — |
| Muzzle | Compensator | — | — | ↑ | — |
| Barrel | — | — | — | — | — |
| Side Rail | Aiming Laser | — | — | ↑ | — |
| Gas System | Under-Gassed | — | — | ↑ | — |
| Underbarrel | None | — | — | — | — |
| Magazine | Armor Piercing Ammo | ↑ | — | — | — |
| Trigger Group | Full-Auto | — | — | — | — |

## RANGE

| | |
|---|---|
| POWER | ✊ ▢▢▢▢▢ |
| RANGE | ➡ ▢▢▢▢▢ |
| CONTROL | ◎ ▢▢▢▢▢ |
| MANEUVERABILITY | ✛ ▢▢▢▢▢ |
| RATE OF FIRE | 🔄 702 RPM |
| MAGAZINE CAPACITY | ☰ 20 |

### RANGE CONFIGURATION

| Mod. Point | Attachment | ✊ | ➡ | ◎ | ✛ |
|---|---|---|---|---|---|
| Optic | Tac Scope | — | ↑ | — | — |
| Stock | Angled Foregrip | — | — | ↑ | — |
| Muzzle | Compensator | — | — | ↑ | — |
| Barrel | — | — | — | — | — |
| Side Rail | Aiming Laser | — | — | ↑ | — |
| Gas System | Under-Gassed | — | — | ↑ | — |
| Underbarrel | None | — | — | — | — |
| Magazine | Armor Piercing Ammo | ↑ | — | — | — |
| Trigger Group | 3-Round Burst | — | — | — | — |

## SA58 OSW

| | |
|---|---|
| POWER | |
| RANGE | |
| CONTROL | |
| MANEUVERABILITY | |
| RATE OF FIRE | 840 RPM |
| MAGAZINE CAPACITY | 20 |

- **Versatile:** Suitable for a variety of combat scenarios and ranges.
- **Stopping Power:** High-caliber weapon deals more damage.

**UNLOCK**
Complete Shattered Mountain weapon challenge.

| CAMPAIGN | X |
|---|---|
| MULTIPLAYER | |

---

# OPTIMIZED CONFIGURATIONS

## CONTROL

| | |
|---|---|
| POWER | |
| RANGE | |
| CONTROL | |
| MANEUVERABILITY | |
| RATE OF FIRE | 756 RPM |
| MAGAZINE CAPACITY | 20 |

### CONTROL CONFIGURATION

| Mod. Point | Attachment | ✊ | ➡ | ◎ | ✣ |
|---|---|---|---|---|---|
| Optic | Magnified HWS | — | — | ↑ | — |
| Stock | Fixed | — | — | ↑ | — |
| Muzzle | Compensator | — | — | ↑ | — |
| Barrel | — | — | — | — | — |
| Side Rail | Aiming Laser | — | — | ↑ | — |
| Gas System | Under-Gassed | — | — | ↑ | — |
| Underbarrel | Angled Foregrip | — | — | ↑ | — |
| Magazine | Armor Piercing Ammo | ↑ | — | — | — |
| Trigger Group | Semi-Auto | — | — | — | — |

## MANEUVERABILITY

| | |
|---|---|
| POWER | |
| RANGE | |
| CONTROL | |
| MANEUVERABILITY | |
| RATE OF FIRE | 756 RPM |
| MAGAZINE CAPACITY | 20 |

### MANEUVERABILITY CONFIGURATION

| Mod. Point | Attachment | ✊ | ➡ | ◎ | ✣ |
|---|---|---|---|---|---|
| Optic | Red Dot | — | — | — | ↑ |
| Stock | Folded | — | — | ↓ | ↑ |
| Muzzle | Compensator | — | — | ↑ | — |
| Barrel | — | — | — | — | — |
| Side Rail | Aiming Laser | — | — | ↑ | — |
| Gas System | Under-Gassed | — | — | ↑ | — |
| Underbarrel | Vertical Foregrip | — | — | — | ↑ |
| Magazine | Armor Piercing Ammo | ↑ | — | — | — |
| Trigger Group | 2-Round Burst | — | — | — | — |

## POWER

| | |
|---|---|
| POWER | |
| RANGE | |
| CONTROL | |
| MANEUVERABILITY | |
| RATE OF FIRE | 756 RPM |
| MAGAZINE CAPACITY | 20 |

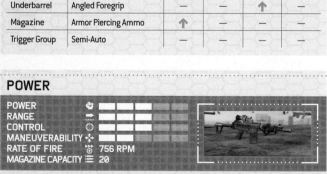

### POWER CONFIGURATION

| Mod. Point | Attachment | ✊ | ➡ | ◎ | ✣ |
|---|---|---|---|---|---|
| Optic | Tac Scope | — | ↑ | — | — |
| Stock | Fixed | — | — | ↑ | — |
| Muzzle | Compensator | — | — | ↑ | — |
| Barrel | — | — | — | — | — |
| Side Rail | Aiming Laser | — | — | ↑ | — |
| Gas System | Under-Gassed | — | — | ↑ | — |
| Underbarrel | Angled Foregrip | — | — | ↑ | — |
| Magazine | Armor Piercing Ammo | ↑ | — | — | — |
| Trigger Group | Match Trigger | — | — | — | — |

## RANGE

| | |
|---|---|
| POWER | |
| RANGE | |
| CONTROL | |
| MANEUVERABILITY | |
| RATE OF FIRE | 756 RPM |
| MAGAZINE CAPACITY | 20 |

### RANGE CONFIGURATION

| Mod. Point | Attachment | ✊ | ➡ | ◎ | ✣ |
|---|---|---|---|---|---|
| Optic | Tac Scope | — | ↑ | — | — |
| Stock | Fixed | — | — | ↑ | — |
| Muzzle | Compensator | — | — | ↑ | — |
| Barrel | — | — | — | — | — |
| Side Rail | Aiming Laser | — | — | ↑ | — |
| Gas System | Under-Gassed | — | — | ↑ | — |
| Underbarrel | Vertical Foregrip | — | — | — | ↑ |
| Magazine | Armor Piercing Ammo | ↑ | — | — | — |
| Trigger Group | Full-Auto | — | — | — | — |

# SR-3M

POWER
RANGE
CONTROL
MANEUVERABILITY
RATE OF FIRE  990 RPM
MAGAZINE CAPACITY  20

- CQC: Best suited for close-quarters combat engagements.
- Rapid-Fire: Weapon features a higher rate of fire than other weapons in its class.

UNLOCK
Complete Noble Tempest weapon challenge.

CAMPAIGN [X]
MULTIPLAYER [ ]

## OPTIMIZED CONFIGURATIONS

### CONTROL

POWER
RANGE
CONTROL
MANEUVERABILITY
RATE OF FIRE  891 RPM
MAGAZINE CAPACITY  20

#### CONTROL CONFIGURATION

| Mod. Point | Attachment | 👊 | ➡ | 🎯 | ✛ |
|---|---|---|---|---|---|
| Optic | Magnified HWS | — | — | ↑ | — |
| Stock | Extended | — | — | — | — |
| Muzzle | Compensator | — | — | ↑ | — |
| Barrel | — | — | — | — | — |
| Side Rail | Aiming Laser | — | — | ↑ | — |
| Gas System | Under-Gassed | — | — | ↑ | — |
| Underbarrel | Angled Foregrip | — | — | ↑ | — |
| Magazine | Armor Piercing Ammo | ↑ | — | — | — |
| Trigger Group | Match Trigger | — | — | — | — |

### MANEUVERABILITY

POWER
RANGE
CONTROL
MANEUVERABILITY
RATE OF FIRE  891 RPM
MAGAZINE CAPACITY  20

#### MANEUVERABILITY CONFIGURATION

| Mod. Point | Attachment | 👊 | ➡ | 🎯 | ✛ |
|---|---|---|---|---|---|
| Optic | Red Dot | — | — | — | ↑ |
| Stock | Folded | — | — | ↓ | ↑ |
| Muzzle | Compensator | — | — | ↑ | — |
| Barrel | — | — | — | — | — |
| Side Rail | Aiming Laser | — | — | ↑ | — |
| Gas System | Under-Gassed | — | — | ↑ | — |
| Underbarrel | Vertical Foregrip | — | — | — | ↑ |
| Magazine | Armor Piercing Ammo | ↑ | — | — | — |
| Trigger Group | 3-Round Burst | — | — | — | — |

### POWER

POWER
RANGE
CONTROL
MANEUVERABILITY
RATE OF FIRE  891 RPM
MAGAZINE CAPACITY  20

#### POWER CONFIGURATION

| Mod. Point | Attachment | 👊 | ➡ | 🎯 | ✛ |
|---|---|---|---|---|---|
| Optic | Tac Scope | — | ↑ | — | — |
| Stock | Extended | — | — | — | — |
| Muzzle | Compensator | — | — | ↑ | — |
| Barrel | — | — | — | — | — |
| Side Rail | Aiming Laser | — | — | ↑ | — |
| Gas System | Under-Gassed | — | — | ↑ | — |
| Underbarrel | Vertical Foregrip | — | — | — | ↑ |
| Magazine | Armor Piercing Ammo | ↑ | — | — | — |
| Trigger Group | Full-Auto | — | — | — | — |

### RANGE

POWER
RANGE
CONTROL
MANEUVERABILITY
RATE OF FIRE  891 RPM
MAGAZINE CAPACITY  20

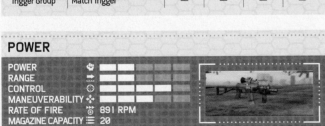

#### RANGE CONFIGURATION

| Mod. Point | Attachment | 👊 | ➡ | 🎯 | ✛ |
|---|---|---|---|---|---|
| Optic | Tac Scope | — | ↑ | — | — |
| Stock | Extended | — | — | — | — |
| Muzzle | Compensator | — | — | ↑ | — |
| Barrel | — | — | — | — | — |
| Side Rail | Aiming Laser | — | — | ↑ | — |
| Gas System | Under-Gassed | — | — | ↑ | — |
| Underbarrel | Vertical Foregrip | — | — | — | ↑ |
| Magazine | Armor Piercing Ammo | ↑ | — | — | — |
| Trigger Group | Full-Auto | — | — | — | — |

# SHOTGUNS

## SHOTGUN ATTACHMENTS

| Attachment | | Description | Power | Range | Control | Maneuverability |
|---|---|---|---|---|---|---|
| OPTIC | Iron Sights | Standard weapon iron sights that offer quick targeting with a small viewing area. | — | — | — | — |
| | Red Dot | Non-magnified optic that enables quick target acquisition with little visual interference. | — | — | — | ↑ |
| | Magnified HWS | 3x magnifier combined with a Holographic Weapon Sight for a good balance between easy targeting and zoom level. | — | — | ↑ | — |
| STOCK | Extended | Extended stock provides a good balance between Maneuverability and Control. | — | — | — | — |
| | Folded | Folded stock that increases Maneuverability, but decreases Control due to lack of stability. | — | — | ↓ | ↑ |
| | Fixed | Fixed stock that increases Control by reducing the amount of recoil felt. | — | — | ↑ | — |
| MUZZLE | Standard | Factory muzzle attachment. | — | — | — | — |
| | Compensator | Compensates for recoil and muzzle climb to increase Control. | — | — | ↑ | — |
| | Flash Hider | Hides muzzle flash from enemies, but decreases Control. | — | — | ↓ | — |
| BARREL | Standard Barrel | Standard barrel length with a good balance between Maneuverability and Range. | — | — | — | — |
| | Long Barrel | Longer barrel length increases Range, but the added weight reduces Maneuverability. | — | ↑ | — | ↓ |
| | Short Barrel | Shorter barrel with decreased weight increases Maneuverability, but decreases Range. | — | ↓ | — | ↑ |
| SIDE RAIL | Rail Cover | Standard rail cover. | — | — | — | — |
| | Aiming Laser | Increases Control by providing a visual aid while aiming. | — | — | ↑ | — |
| GAS SYSTEM | Standard | Standard gas system with a good balance between Rate of Fire and Control. | — | — | — | — |
| | Over-Gassed | Gas system that increases Rate of Fire, but decreases Control. | — | — | ↓ | — |
| | Under-Gassed | Gas system that increases Control, but decreases Rate of Fire. | — | — | ↑ | — |
| UNDERBARREL | Standard Forend | Standard shotgun forend | — | — | — | — |
| | Posted Slide | Increases Maneuverability by improving stability while moving. | — | — | — | ↑ |
| | Rail Cover | Standard rail cover. | — | — | — | — |
| | Vertical Foregrip | Increases Maneuverability by improving stability while moving. | — | — | — | ↑ |
| | Angled Foregrip | Increases Control by reducing the amount of recoil felt. | — | — | ↑ | — |
| MAGAZINE | Buckshot | Standard 12-gauge 00-buckshot shotgun ammunition. | — | — | — | — |
| | Dragon's Breath | Incendiary ammunition capable of burning targets over time. This special ammunition has decreased Range and Power. | ↓ | ↓ | — | — |
| TRIGGER GROUP | Full-Auto | Full-Auto trigger group allows for continuous fire while the trigger is pulled. | — | — | — | — |
| | 2-Stage Trigger | 2-Stage trigger group with dual fire modes. The first stage of the trigger pull fires in Semi-Auto mode. The second stage of the trigger pull fires in Full-Auto mode. | — | — | — | — |
| | Match Trigger | Match Trigger increases the default trigger sensitivity for increased accuracy and faster follow-up shots. | — | — | — | — |
| | Semi-Auto | Semi-automatic trigger group allows the weapon to fire one round for every trigger pull. | — | — | — | — |
| | 2-Round Burst | 2-Round Burst trigger group that fires two rounds for every trigger pull. | — | — | — | — |
| | 3-Round Burst | 3-Round Burst trigger group that fires three rounds for every trigger pull. | — | — | — | — |

This smoothbore firearm fires multiple projectiles in a doughnut spread pattern. Because of the spread and the power of the charge being divided among the pellets, this firearm is particularly lethal in close quarters. During long-range engagements, shotguns are less effective.

| Unlock Requirements | M590A1 | M1014 | M12 | RMB-93 | Saiga 12 | MTs-255 |
|---|---|---|---|---|---|---|
|  | X | X | X | X | X | X |
|  | X | X | X | X | X | X |
| Unlocked by completing the Firefly Rain mission. | X | X | X | X | X | X |
| — | X | X | — | X | X | X |
| — | X | X | — | X | X | X |
| Unlocked by completing all Shattered Mountain Tactical challenges. | X | X | — | X | X | X |
| — | X | X | X | X | X | X |
| Unlocked by completing the Subtle Arrow mission. | X | X | X | X | X | X |
| Unlocked by completing all Subtle Arrow Tactical challenges. | — | — | — | — | — | X |
|  | X | X | X | — | X | X |
|  | X | X | X | — | X | X |
|  | — | X | X | — | X | X |
| — | X | X | X | X | X | X |
| Unlocked by completing the Nimble Guardian mission. | X | X | X | X | X | X |
| — | — | — | X | — | X | — |
| — | — | — | X | — | X | — |
| — | — | — | X | — | X | — |
| — | X | — | — | — | — | — |
| — | X | — | — | — | — | — |
|  | — | X | X | X | X | — |
| — | — | X | X | X | X | — |
| Unlocked by completing the Nimble Guardian mission. | — | — | X | — | X | — |
| — | X | X | X | X | X | X |
| Unlocked by completing all Ember Hunt Tactical challenges. | X | X | X | X | X | X |
| — | — | — | X | — | X | — |
| — | — | — | X | — | — | — |
| — | X | X | X | X | X | X |
| — | X | X | X | X | X | X |
| — | — | — | — | — | X | — |
| — | — | — | X | — | — | — |

## M1014

| | |
|---|---|
| POWER | ✊ |
| RANGE | ➡ |
| CONTROL | ◉ |
| MANEUVERABILITY | ✛ |
| RATE OF FIRE | ⏱ 600 RPM |
| MAGAZINE CAPACITY | ≡ 8 |

- CQC: Best suited for close-quarters combat engagements.
- Single-Shot: Standard weapon trigger fires single-shot.

UNLOCK
Complete Firefly Rain mission.

| CAMPAIGN | X |
|---|---|
| MULTIPLAYER | X |

## OPTIMIZED CONFIGURATIONS

### CONTROL

| | |
|---|---|
| POWER | ✊ |
| RANGE | ➡ |
| CONTROL | ◉ |
| MANEUVERABILITY | ✛ |
| RATE OF FIRE | ⏱ 600 RPM |
| MAGAZINE CAPACITY | ≡ 8 |

#### CONTROL CONFIGURATION

| Mod. Point | Attachment | ✊ | ➡ | ◉ | ✛ |
|---|---|---|---|---|---|
| Optic | Magnified HWS | — | — | ↑ | — |
| Stock | Fixed | — | — | ↑ | — |
| Muzzle | Compensator | — | — | ↑ | — |
| Barrel | Short Barrel | — | ↓ | — | ↑ |
| Side Rail | Aiming Laser | — | — | ↑ | — |
| Gas System | — | | | | |
| Underbarrel | Vertical Foregrip | — | — | — | ↑ |
| Magazine | Buckshot | — | — | — | — |
| Trigger Group | Semi-Auto | — | — | — | — |

### MANEUVERABILITY

| | |
|---|---|
| POWER | ✊ |
| RANGE | ➡ |
| CONTROL | ◉ |
| MANEUVERABILITY | ✛ |
| RATE OF FIRE | ⏱ 600 RPM |
| MAGAZINE CAPACITY | ≡ 8 |

#### MANEUVERABILITY CONFIGURATION

| Mod. Point | Attachment | ✊ | ➡ | ◉ | ✛ |
|---|---|---|---|---|---|
| Optic | Red Dot | — | — | — | ↑ |
| Stock | Folded | — | — | ↓ | ↑ |
| Muzzle | Compensator | — | — | ↑ | — |
| Barrel | Short Barrel | — | ↓ | — | ↑ |
| Side Rail | Aiming Laser | — | — | ↑ | — |
| Gas System | — | | | | |
| Underbarrel | Vertical Foregrip | — | — | — | ↑ |
| Magazine | Buckshot | — | — | — | — |
| Trigger Group | Semi-Auto | — | — | — | — |

### POWER

| | |
|---|---|
| POWER | ✊ |
| RANGE | ➡ |
| CONTROL | ◉ |
| MANEUVERABILITY | ✛ |
| RATE OF FIRE | ⏱ 600 RPM |
| MAGAZINE CAPACITY | ≡ 8 |

#### POWER CONFIGURATION

| Mod. Point | Attachment | ✊ | ➡ | ◉ | ✛ |
|---|---|---|---|---|---|
| Optic | Red Dot | — | — | — | ↑ |
| Stock | Fixed | — | — | ↑ | — |
| Muzzle | Compensator | — | — | ↑ | — |
| Barrel | Long Barrel | — | ↑ | — | — |
| Side Rail | Aiming Laser | — | — | ↑ | — |
| Gas System | — | | | | |
| Underbarrel | Vertical Foregrip | — | — | — | ↑ |
| Magazine | Buckshot | — | — | — | — |
| Trigger Group | Semi-Auto | — | — | — | — |

### RANGE

| | |
|---|---|
| POWER | ✊ |
| RANGE | ➡ |
| CONTROL | ◉ |
| MANEUVERABILITY | ✛ |
| RATE OF FIRE | ⏱ 600 RPM |
| MAGAZINE CAPACITY | ≡ 8 |

#### RANGE CONFIGURATION

| Mod. Point | Attachment | ✊ | ➡ | ◉ | ✛ |
|---|---|---|---|---|---|
| Optic | Red Dot | — | — | — | ↑ |
| Stock | Fixed | — | — | ↑ | — |
| Muzzle | Compensator | — | — | ↑ | — |
| Barrel | Long Barrel | — | ↑ | — | — |
| Side Rail | Aiming Laser | — | — | ↑ | — |
| Gas System | — | | | | |
| Underbarrel | Vertical Foregrip | — | — | — | ↑ |
| Magazine | Buckshot | — | — | — | — |
| Trigger Group | Match Trigger | — | — | — | — |

## M12

| | |
|---|---|
| POWER | |
| RANGE | |
| CONTROL | |
| MANEUVERABILITY | |
| RATE OF FIRE | 360 RPM |
| MAGAZINE CAPACITY | 8 |

- Fast Assault: Ideal for quickly engaging unexpected targets or firing on the move.
- Full Auto: Standard weapon trigger fires fully automatic.

**UNLOCK**
Complete Invisible Bear mission.

| | |
|---|---|
| CAMPAIGN | X |
| MULTIPLAYER | X |

## OPTIMIZED CONFIGURATIONS

### CONTROL

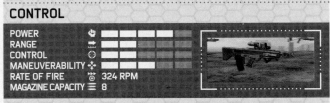

| | |
|---|---|
| POWER | |
| RANGE | |
| CONTROL | |
| MANEUVERABILITY | |
| RATE OF FIRE | 324 RPM |
| MAGAZINE CAPACITY | 8 |

#### CONTROL CONFIGURATION

| Mod. Point | Attachment | ✊ | ➡ | ⊙ | ✣ |
|---|---|---|---|---|---|
| Optic | Magnified HWS | — | — | ↑ | — |
| Stock | — | — | — | — | — |
| Muzzle | Compensator | — | — | ↑ | — |
| Barrel | Short Barrel | — | ↓ | — | ↑ |
| Side Rail | Aiming Laser | — | — | ↑ | — |
| Gas System | Under-Gassed | — | — | ↑ | — |
| Underbarrel | Angled Foregrip | — | — | ↑ | — |
| Magazine | Buckshot | — | — | — | — |
| Trigger Group | Semi-Auto | — | — | — | — |

### MANEUVERABILITY

| | |
|---|---|
| POWER | |
| RANGE | |
| CONTROL | |
| MANEUVERABILITY | |
| RATE OF FIRE | 324 RPM |
| MAGAZINE CAPACITY | 8 |

#### MANEUVERABILITY CONFIGURATION

| Mod. Point | Attachment | ✊ | ➡ | ⊙ | ✣ |
|---|---|---|---|---|---|
| Optic | Red Dot | — | — | — | ↑ |
| Stock | — | — | — | — | — |
| Muzzle | Compensator | — | — | ↑ | — |
| Barrel | Short Barrel | — | ↓ | — | ↑ |
| Side Rail | Aiming Laser | — | — | ↑ | — |
| Gas System | Under-Gassed | — | — | ↑ | — |
| Underbarrel | Vertical Foregrip | — | — | — | ↑ |
| Magazine | Buckshot | — | — | — | — |
| Trigger Group | Match Trigger | — | — | — | — |

### POWER

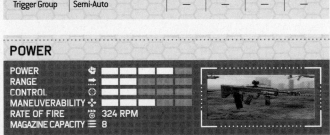

| | |
|---|---|
| POWER | |
| RANGE | |
| CONTROL | |
| MANEUVERABILITY | |
| RATE OF FIRE | 324 RPM |
| MAGAZINE CAPACITY | 8 |

#### POWER CONFIGURATION

| Mod. Point | Attachment | ✊ | ➡ | ⊙ | ✣ |
|---|---|---|---|---|---|
| Optic | Red Dot | — | — | — | ↑ |
| Stock | — | — | — | — | — |
| Muzzle | Compensator | — | — | ↑ | — |
| Barrel | Long Barrel | — | ↑ | — | ↓ |
| Side Rail | Aiming Laser | — | — | ↑ | — |
| Gas System | Under-Gassed | — | — | ↑ | — |
| Underbarrel | Vertical Foregrip | — | — | — | ↑ |
| Magazine | Buckshot | — | — | — | — |
| Trigger Group | 3-Round Burst | — | — | — | — |

### RANGE

| | |
|---|---|
| POWER | |
| RANGE | |
| CONTROL | |
| MANEUVERABILITY | |
| RATE OF FIRE | 324 RPM |
| MAGAZINE CAPACITY | 8 |

#### RANGE CONFIGURATION

| Mod. Point | Attachment | ✊ | ➡ | ⊙ | ✣ |
|---|---|---|---|---|---|
| Optic | Magnified HWS | — | — | ↑ | — |
| Stock | — | — | — | — | — |
| Muzzle | Compensator | — | — | ↑ | — |
| Barrel | Long Barrel | — | ↑ | — | ↓ |
| Side Rail | Aiming Laser | — | — | ↑ | — |
| Gas System | Under-Gassed | — | — | ↑ | — |
| Underbarrel | Angled Foregrip | — | — | ↑ | — |
| Magazine | Buckshot | — | — | — | — |
| Trigger Group | 2-Stage Trigger | — | — | — | — |

# M590A1

| | |
|---|---|
| POWER | |
| RANGE | |
| CONTROL | |
| MANEUVERABILITY | |
| RATE OF FIRE | 180 RPM |
| MAGAZINE CAPACITY | 8 |

- Versatile: Suitable for a variety of combat scenarios and ranges.
- Stopping Power: High-caliber weapon deals more damage.

UNLOCK
Complete Nimble Guardian mission.

CAMPAIGN [X]
MULTIPLAYER [X]

## OPTIMIZED CONFIGURATIONS

### CONTROL

| | |
|---|---|
| POWER | |
| RANGE | |
| CONTROL | |
| MANEUVERABILITY | |
| RATE OF FIRE | 180 RPM |
| MAGAZINE CAPACITY | 8 |

#### CONTROL CONFIGURATION

| Mod. Point | Attachment | 👊 | ➡ | ◎ | ✥ |
|---|---|---|---|---|---|
| Optic | Magnified HWS | — | — | ↑ | — |
| Stock | Fixed | — | — | ↑ | — |
| Muzzle | Compensator | — | — | ↑ | — |
| Barrel | Standard Barrel | — | — | — | — |
| Side Rail | Aiming Laser | — | — | ↑ | — |
| Gas System | — | | | | |
| Underbarrel | Posted Slide | — | — | — | ↑ |
| Magazine | Buckshot | — | — | — | — |
| Trigger Group | Match Trigger | — | — | — | — |

### MANEUVERABILITY

| | |
|---|---|
| POWER | |
| RANGE | |
| CONTROL | |
| MANEUVERABILITY | |
| RATE OF FIRE | 180 RPM |
| MAGAZINE CAPACITY | 8 |

#### MANEUVERABILITY CONFIGURATION

| Mod. Point | Attachment | 👊 | ➡ | ◎ | ✥ |
|---|---|---|---|---|---|
| Optic | Red Dot | — | — | — | ↑ |
| Stock | Folded | — | — | ↓ | ↑ |
| Muzzle | Compensator | — | — | ↑ | — |
| Barrel | Standard Barrel | — | — | — | — |
| Side Rail | Aiming Laser | — | — | ↑ | — |
| Gas System | — | | | | |
| Underbarrel | Posted Slide | — | — | — | ↑ |
| Magazine | Buckshot | — | — | — | — |
| Trigger Group | Semi-Auto | — | — | — | — |

### POWER

| | |
|---|---|
| POWER | |
| RANGE | |
| CONTROL | |
| MANEUVERABILITY | |
| RATE OF FIRE | 180 RPM |
| MAGAZINE CAPACITY | 8 |

#### POWER CONFIGURATION

| Mod. Point | Attachment | 👊 | ➡ | ◎ | ✥ |
|---|---|---|---|---|---|
| Optic | Red Dot | — | — | — | ↑ |
| Stock | Fixed | — | — | ↑ | — |
| Muzzle | Compensator | — | — | ↑ | — |
| Barrel | Long Barrel | — | ↑ | — | ↓ |
| Side Rail | Aiming Laser | — | — | ↑ | — |
| Gas System | — | | | | |
| Underbarrel | Posted Slide | — | — | — | ↑ |
| Magazine | Buckshot | — | — | — | — |
| Trigger Group | Match Trigger | — | — | — | — |

### RANGE

| | |
|---|---|
| POWER | |
| RANGE | |
| CONTROL | |
| MANEUVERABILITY | |
| RATE OF FIRE | 180 RPM |
| MAGAZINE CAPACITY | 8 |

#### RANGE CONFIGURATION

| Mod. Point | Attachment | 👊 | ➡ | ◎ | ✥ |
|---|---|---|---|---|---|
| Optic | Red Dot | — | — | — | ↑ |
| Stock | Fixed | — | — | ↑ | — |
| Muzzle | Compensator | — | — | ↑ | — |
| Barrel | Long Barrel | — | ↑ | — | ↓ |
| Side Rail | Aiming Laser | — | — | ↑ | — |
| Gas System | — | | | | |
| Underbarrel | Posted Slide | — | — | — | ↑ |
| Magazine | Buckshot | — | — | — | — |
| Trigger Group | Semi-Auto | — | — | — | — |

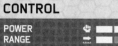

# MTS-255

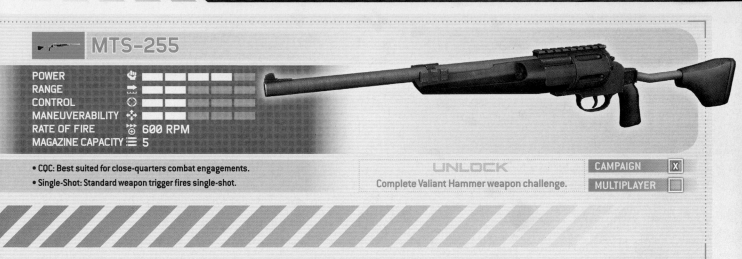

POWER 👊 ▢▢▢▢▢
RANGE 🔜 ▢▢▢▢▢
CONTROL ⊙ ▢▢▢▢▢
MANEUVERABILITY ✛ ▢▢▢▢▢
RATE OF FIRE ⏱ 600 RPM
MAGAZINE CAPACITY ≣ 5

- CQC: Best suited for close-quarters combat engagements.
- Single-Shot: Standard weapon trigger fires single-shot.

UNLOCK
Complete Valiant Hammer weapon challenge.

| | |
|---|---|
| CAMPAIGN | X |
| MULTIPLAYER | ☐ |

# OPTIMIZED CONFIGURATIONS

## CONTROL

POWER 👊 ▢▢▢▢▢
RANGE 🔜 ▢▢▢▢▢
CONTROL ⊙ ▢▢▢▢▢
MANEUVERABILITY ✛ ▢▢▢▢▢
RATE OF FIRE ⏱ 600 RPM
MAGAZINE CAPACITY ≣ 5

### CONTROL CONFIGURATION

| Mod. Point | Attachment | 👊 | 🔜 | ⊙ | ✛ |
|---|---|---|---|---|---|
| Optic | Magnified HWS | — | — | ↑ | — |
| Stock | Fixed | — | — | ↑ | — |
| Muzzle | Compensator | — | — | ↑ | — |
| Barrel | Short Barrel | — | ↓ | — | ↑ |
| Side Rail | Aiming Laser | — | — | ↑ | — |
| Gas System | — | | | | |
| Underbarrel | — | | | | |
| Magazine | Buckshot | — | — | — | — |
| Trigger Group | Match Trigger | — | — | — | — |

## MANEUVERABILITY

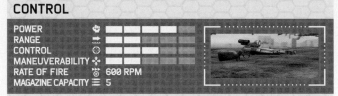

POWER 👊 ▢▢▢▢▢
RANGE 🔜 ▢▢▢▢▢
CONTROL ⊙ ▢▢▢▢▢
MANEUVERABILITY ✛ ▢▢▢▢▢
RATE OF FIRE ⏱ 600 RPM
MAGAZINE CAPACITY ≣ 5

### MANEUVERABILITY CONFIGURATION

| Mod. Point | Attachment | 👊 | 🔜 | ⊙ | ✛ |
|---|---|---|---|---|---|
| Optic | Red Dot | — | — | — | ↑ |
| Stock | Folded | — | — | ↓ | ↑ |
| Muzzle | Compensator | — | — | ↑ | — |
| Barrel | Short Barrel | — | ↓ | — | ↑ |
| Side Rail | Aiming Laser | — | — | ↑ | — |
| Gas System | — | | | | |
| Underbarrel | — | | | | |
| Magazine | Buckshot | — | — | — | — |
| Trigger Group | Match Trigger | — | — | — | — |

## POWER

POWER 👊 ▢▢▢▢▢
RANGE 🔜 ▢▢▢▢▢
CONTROL ⊙ ▢▢▢▢▢
MANEUVERABILITY ✛ ▢▢▢▢▢
RATE OF FIRE ⏱ 600 RPM
MAGAZINE CAPACITY ≣ 5

### POWER CONFIGURATION

| Mod. Point | Attachment | 👊 | 🔜 | ⊙ | ✛ |
|---|---|---|---|---|---|
| Optic | Magnified HWS | — | — | ↑ | — |
| Stock | Fixed | — | — | ↑ | — |
| Muzzle | Compensator | — | — | ↑ | — |
| Barrel | Long Barrel | — | ↑ | — | ↓ |
| Side Rail | Aiming Laser | — | — | ↑ | — |
| Gas System | — | | | | |
| Underbarrel | — | | | | |
| Magazine | Buckshot | — | — | — | — |
| Trigger Group | Semi-Auto | — | — | — | — |

## RANGE

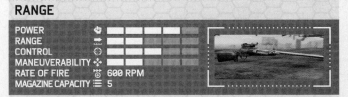

POWER 👊 ▢▢▢▢▢
RANGE 🔜 ▢▢▢▢▢
CONTROL ⊙ ▢▢▢▢▢
MANEUVERABILITY ✛ ▢▢▢▢▢
RATE OF FIRE ⏱ 600 RPM
MAGAZINE CAPACITY ≣ 5

### RANGE CONFIGURATION

| Mod. Point | Attachment | 👊 | 🔜 | ⊙ | ✛ |
|---|---|---|---|---|---|
| Optic | Red Dot | — | — | — | ↑ |
| Stock | Fixed | — | — | ↑ | — |
| Muzzle | Compensator | — | — | ↑ | — |
| Barrel | Long Barrel | — | ↑ | — | ↓ |
| Side Rail | Aiming Laser | — | — | ↑ | — |
| Gas System | — | | | | |
| Underbarrel | — | | | | |
| Magazine | Buckshot | — | — | — | — |
| Trigger Group | Match Trigger | — | — | — | — |

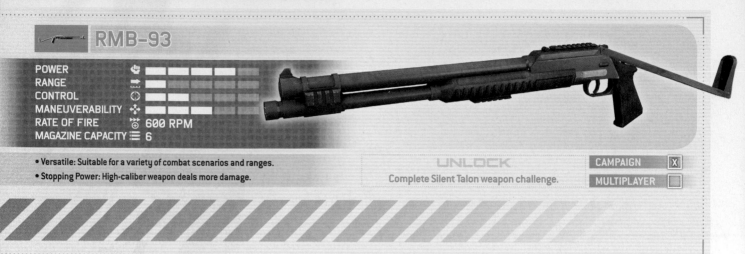

## RMB-93

| | |
|---|---|
| POWER | ✊ |
| RANGE | ➡ |
| CONTROL | ⬡ |
| MANEUVERABILITY | ✛ |
| RATE OF FIRE | 600 RPM |
| MAGAZINE CAPACITY | 6 |

• **Versatile:** Suitable for a variety of combat scenarios and ranges.
• **Stopping Power:** High-caliber weapon deals more damage.

**UNLOCK**
Complete Silent Talon weapon challenge.

| CAMPAIGN | X |
|---|---|
| MULTIPLAYER | |

# OPTIMIZED CONFIGURATIONS

## CONTROL

| | |
|---|---|
| POWER | ✊ |
| RANGE | ➡ |
| CONTROL | ⬡ |
| MANEUVERABILITY | ✛ |
| RATE OF FIRE | 600 RPM |
| MAGAZINE CAPACITY | 6 |

### CONTROL CONFIGURATION

| Mod. Point | Attachment | ✊ | ➡ | ⬡ | ✛ |
|---|---|---|---|---|---|
| Optic | Magnified HWS | — | — | ↑ | — |
| Stock | Fixed | — | — | ↑ | — |
| Muzzle | Compensator | — | — | ↑ | — |
| Barrel | — | — | — | — | — |
| Side Rail | Aiming Laser | — | — | ↑ | — |
| Gas System | — | — | — | — | — |
| Underbarrel | Vertical Foregrip | — | — | — | ↑ |
| Magazine | Buckshot | — | — | — | — |
| Trigger Group | Match Trigger | — | — | — | — |

## MANEUVERABILITY

| | |
|---|---|
| POWER | ✊ |
| RANGE | ➡ |
| CONTROL | ⬡ |
| MANEUVERABILITY | ✛ |
| RATE OF FIRE | 600 RPM |
| MAGAZINE CAPACITY | 6 |

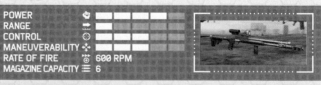

### MANEUVERABILITY CONFIGURATION

| Mod. Point | Attachment | ✊ | ➡ | ⬡ | ✛ |
|---|---|---|---|---|---|
| Optic | Red Dot | — | — | — | ↑ |
| Stock | Folded | — | — | ↓ | ↑ |
| Muzzle | Compensator | — | — | ↑ | — |
| Barrel | — | — | — | — | — |
| Side Rail | Aiming Laser | — | — | ↑ | — |
| Gas System | — | — | — | — | — |
| Underbarrel | Vertical Foregrip | — | — | — | ↑ |
| Magazine | Aiming Laser | — | — | — | — |
| Trigger Group | Semi-Auto | — | — | — | — |

## POWER

| | |
|---|---|
| POWER | ✊ |
| RANGE | ➡ |
| CONTROL | ⬡ |
| MANEUVERABILITY | ✛ |
| RATE OF FIRE | 600 RPM |
| MAGAZINE CAPACITY | 6 |

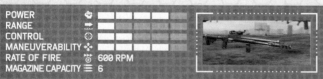

### POWER CONFIGURATION

| Mod. Point | Attachment | ✊ | ➡ | ⬡ | ✛ |
|---|---|---|---|---|---|
| Optic | Red Dot | — | — | — | ↑ |
| Stock | Fixed | — | — | ↑ | — |
| Muzzle | Compensator | — | — | ↑ | — |
| Barrel | — | — | — | — | — |
| Side Rail | Aiming Laser | — | — | ↑ | — |
| Gas System | — | — | — | — | — |
| Underbarrel | Vertical Foregrip | — | — | — | ↑ |
| Magazine | Buckshot | — | — | — | — |
| Trigger Group | Semi-Auto | — | — | — | — |

## RANGE

| | |
|---|---|
| POWER | ✊ |
| RANGE | ➡ |
| CONTROL | ⬡ |
| MANEUVERABILITY | ✛ |
| RATE OF FIRE | 600 RPM |
| MAGAZINE CAPACITY | 6 |

### RANGE CONFIGURATION

| Mod. Point | Attachment | ✊ | ➡ | ⬡ | ✛ |
|---|---|---|---|---|---|
| Optic | Magnified HWS | — | — | ↑ | — |
| Stock | Fixed | — | — | ↑ | — |
| Muzzle | Compensator | — | — | ↑ | — |
| Barrel | — | — | — | — | — |
| Side Rail | Aiming Laser | — | — | ↑ | — |
| Gas System | — | — | — | — | — |
| Underbarrel | Vertical Foregrip | — | — | — | ↑ |
| Magazine | Buckshot | — | — | — | — |
| Trigger Group | Semi-Auto | — | — | — | — |

## SAIGA 12

| | |
|---|---|
| POWER | |
| RANGE | |
| CONTROL | |
| MANEUVERABILITY | |
| RATE OF FIRE | 480 RPM |
| MAGAZINE CAPACITY | 8 |

- Fast Assault: Ideal for quickly engaging unexpected targets or firing on the move.
- Full Auto: Standard weapon trigger fires fully automatic.

UNLOCK
Defeat 50 waves in Guerrilla mode.

| | |
|---|---|
| CAMPAIGN | X |
| MULTIPLAYER | |

## OPTIMIZED CONFIGURATIONS

### CONTROL

| | |
|---|---|
| POWER | |
| RANGE | |
| CONTROL | |
| MANEUVERABILITY | |
| RATE OF FIRE | 432 RPM |
| MAGAZINE CAPACITY | 8 |

#### CONTROL CONFIGURATION

| Mod. Point | Attachment | 👊 | ➡ | 🎯 | ✛ |
|---|---|---|---|---|---|
| Optic | Magnified HWS | — | — | ↑ | — |
| Stock | Fixed | — | — | ↑ | — |
| Muzzle | Compensator | — | — | ↑ | — |
| Barrel | Short Barrel | — | ↓ | — | ↑ |
| Side Rail | Aiming Laser | — | — | ↑ | — |
| Gas System | Under-Gassed | — | — | ↑ | — |
| Underbarrel | Angled Foregrip | — | — | ↑ | — |
| Magazine | Buckshot | — | — | — | — |
| Trigger Group | 2-Round Burst | — | — | — | — |

### MANEUVERABILITY

| | |
|---|---|
| POWER | |
| RANGE | |
| CONTROL | |
| MANEUVERABILITY | |
| RATE OF FIRE | 432 RPM |
| MAGAZINE CAPACITY | 8 |

#### MANEUVERABILITY CONFIGURATION

| Mod. Point | Attachment | 👊 | ➡ | 🎯 | ✛ |
|---|---|---|---|---|---|
| Optic | Red Dot | — | — | — | ↑ |
| Stock | Folded | — | — | ↓ | ↑ |
| Muzzle | Compensator | — | — | ↑ | — |
| Barrel | Short Barrel | — | ↓ | — | ↑ |
| Side Rail | Aiming Laser | — | — | ↑ | — |
| Gas System | Under-Gassed | — | — | ↑ | — |
| Underbarrel | Vertical Foregrip | — | — | — | ↑ |
| Magazine | Buckshot | — | — | — | — |
| Trigger Group | 2-Round Burst | — | — | — | — |

### POWER

| | |
|---|---|
| POWER | |
| RANGE | |
| CONTROL | |
| MANEUVERABILITY | |
| RATE OF FIRE | 432 RPM |
| MAGAZINE CAPACITY | 8 |

#### POWER CONFIGURATION

| Mod. Point | Attachment | 👊 | ➡ | 🎯 | ✛ |
|---|---|---|---|---|---|
| Optic | Red Dot | — | — | — | ↑ |
| Stock | Fixed | — | — | ↑ | — |
| Muzzle | Compensator | — | — | ↑ | — |
| Barrel | Long Barrel | — | ↑ | — | ↓ |
| Side Rail | Aiming Laser | — | — | ↑ | — |
| Gas System | Under-Gassed | — | — | ↑ | — |
| Underbarrel | Vertical Foregrip | — | — | — | ↑ |
| Magazine | Buckshot | — | — | — | — |
| Trigger Group | Match Trigger | — | — | — | — |

### RANGE

| | |
|---|---|
| POWER | |
| RANGE | |
| CONTROL | |
| MANEUVERABILITY | |
| RATE OF FIRE | 432 RPM |
| MAGAZINE CAPACITY | 8 |

#### RANGE CONFIGURATION

| Mod. Point | Attachment | 👊 | ➡ | 🎯 | ✛ |
|---|---|---|---|---|---|
| Optic | Magnified HWS | — | — | ↑ | — |
| Stock | Fixed | — | — | ↑ | — |
| Muzzle | Compensator | — | — | ↑ | — |
| Barrel | Long Barrel | — | ↑ | — | ↓ |
| Side Rail | Aiming Laser | — | — | ↑ | — |
| Gas System | Under-Gassed | — | — | ↑ | — |
| Underbarrel | Angled Foregrip | — | — | ↑ | — |
| Magazine | Buckshot | — | — | — | — |
| Trigger Group | 2-Round Burst | — | — | — | — |

# SUBMACHINE GUNS (SMGS)

## SHOTGUN ATTACHMENTS

| | Attachment | Description | ✊ Power | ➡ Range | ◎ Control | ✛ Maneuverability | |
|---|---|---|---|---|---|---|---|
| **OPTIC** | Iron Sights | Standard weapon iron sights that offer quick targeting with a small viewing area. | — | — | — | — | |
| | Red Dot | Non-magnified optic that enables quick target acquisition with little visual interference. | — | — | — | ↑ | |
| | Magnified HWS | 3x magnifier combined with a Holographic Weapon Sight for a good balance between easy targeting and zoom level. | — | — | ↑ | — | |
| | TAC Scope | 4x magnification sight for medium-range engagements. | — | ↑ | — | — | |
| | Thermal Optic | Thermal imaging optic clearly displays targets and sees through smoke. | — | — | — | ↑ | |
| **STOCK** | Extended | Extended stock provides a good balance between Maneuverability and Control. | — | — | — | — | |
| | Folded | Folded stock that increases Maneuverability, but decreases Control due to lack of stability. | — | — | ↓ | ↑ | |
| | Collapsed | Folded stock that increases Maneuverability, but decreases Control due to lack of stability. | — | — | ↓ | ↑ | |
| **MUZZLE** | Standard | Factory muzzle attachment. | — | — | — | — | |
| | Compensator | Compensates for recoil and muzzle climb to increase Control. | — | — | ↑ | — | |
| | Flash Hider | Hides muzzle flash from enemies, but decreases Control. | — | — | ↓ | — | |
| | Suppressor | Hides muzzle flash and reduces the sound produced by firing the weapon, but decreases FIREPOWER and Range due to the use of sub-sonic ammunition. | ↓ | ↓ | — | — | |
| **SIDE RAIL** | Rail Cover | Standard rail cover. | — | — | — | — | |
| | Aiming Laser | Increases Control by providing a visual aid while aiming. | — | — | ↑ | — | |
| | OTR Scanner | Optical Target Recognition uses Heat detection to find enemies that are visible while aiming or in scope view. | — | — | — | — | |
| **GAS SYSTEM** | Standard | Standard gas system with a good balance between Rate of Fire and Control. | — | — | — | — | |
| | Over-Gassed | Gas system that increases Rate of Fire, but decreases Control. | — | — | ↓ | — | |
| | Under-Gassed | Gas system that increases Control, but decreases Rate of Fire. | — | — | ↑ | — | |
| **UNDERBARREL** | Rail Cover | Standard rail cover. | — | — | — | — | |
| | Vertical Foregrip | Increases Maneuverability by improving stability while moving. | — | — | — | ↑ | |
| | Angled Foregrip | Increases Control by reducing the amount of recoil felt. | — | — | ↑ | — | |
| **MAGAZINE** | Standard Magazine | Standard magazine loaded with FMJ ammunition. | — | — | — | — | |
| | Armor Piercing Ammo | Standard magazine loaded with AP ammunition capable of dealing more damage to armored targets. | ↑ | — | — | — | |
| **TRIGGER GROUP** | Full-Auto | Full-Auto trigger group allows for continuous fire while the trigger is pulled. | — | — | — | — | |
| | 2-Stage Trigger | 2-Stage trigger group with dual fire modes. The first stage of the trigger pull fires in Semi-Auto mode. The second stage of the trigger pull fires in Full-Auto mode. | — | — | — | — | |
| | Match Trigger | Match Trigger increases the default trigger sensitivity for increased accuracy and faster follow-up shots. | — | — | — | — | |
| | Semi-Auto | Semi-automatic trigger group allows the weapon to fire one round for every trigger pull. | — | — | — | — | |
| | 2-Round Burst | 2-Round Burst trigger group that fires two rounds for every trigger pull. | — | — | — | — | |
| | 3-Round Burst | 3-Round Burst trigger group that fires three rounds for every trigger pull. | — | — | — | — | |

Ideal for close-range combat, these weapons have been designed to combine the automatic fire of a machine gun with a cartridge of a pistol. The SMGs are sidearms with increased range and rate of fire, and what they lack in penetration and range, they make up with ease of maneuverability and the ability to fill a nearby target with lead.

| Unlock Requirements | MP7 | P90 | Vector | Skorpion | PP19 | PP2000 |
|---|---|---|---|---|---|---|
| — | X | X | X | X | X | X |
| — | X | X | X | X | X | X |
| Unlocked by completing the Firefly Rain mission. | X | X | X | X | X | X |
| Unlocked by completing the Nimble Guardian mission. | X | X | X | X | X | X |
| Unlocked by completing the Valiant Hammer mission. | X | X | X | X | X | X |
| — | X | — | X | X | X | X |
| — | — | — | X | X | X | X |
| — | X | — | — | — | — | — |
| — | X | X | X | X | X | X |
| Unlocked by completing the Subtle Arrow mission. | X | X | X | X | X | X |
| Unlocked by completing all Subtle Arrow Tactical challenges. | X | X | X | X | X | X |
| — | X | X | X | X | X | X |
| — | X | X | X | X | X | X |
| Unlocked by completing the Nimble Guardian mission. | X | X | X | X | X | X |
| Unlocked by completing the Silent Talon mission. | X | X | X | X | X | X |
| — | X | X | X | X | X | X |
| — | X | X | X | X | X | X |
| — | X | X | X | X | X | X |
| — | X | — | X | X | — | — |
| — | X | — | X | X | — | — |
| Unlocked by completing the Nimble Guardian mission. | — | — | — | X | — | — |
| — | X | X | X | X | X | X |
| Unlocked by completing all Deep Fire Tactical challenges. | X | X | X | X | X | X |
| — | X | X | X | X | X | X |
| — | — | X | — | — | — | X |
| — | X | — | X | X | X | X |
| — | X | X | X | X | X | X |
| — | — | — | X | — | — | — |
| — | X | — | — | X | — | — |

## MP7

| | |
|---|---|
| POWER ✊ | |
| RANGE ➡ | |
| CONTROL ◎ | |
| MANEUVERABILITY ✣ | |
| RATE OF FIRE ⏱ | 1,110 RPM |
| MAGAZINE CAPACITY ☰ | 40 |

- Fast Assault: Ideal for quickly engaging unexpected targets or firing on the move.
- Rapid-Fire: Weapon features a higher rate of fire than other weapons in its class.

### UNLOCK
Complete Nimble Guardian mission.

| | |
|---|---|
| CAMPAIGN | X |
| MULTIPLAYER | X |

---

# OPTIMIZED CONFIGURATIONS

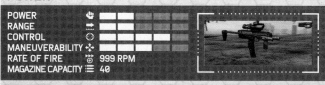

## CONTROL

| | |
|---|---|
| POWER ✊ | |
| RANGE ➡ | |
| CONTROL ◎ | |
| MANEUVERABILITY ✣ | |
| RATE OF FIRE ⏱ | 999 RPM |
| MAGAZINE CAPACITY ☰ | 40 |

### CONTROL CONFIGURATION

| Mod. Point | Attachment | ✊ | ➡ | ◎ | ✣ |
|---|---|---|---|---|---|
| Optic | Magnified HWS | — | — | ↑ | — |
| Stock | Extended | — | — | — | — |
| Muzzle | Compensator | — | — | ↑ | — |
| Barrel | — | — | — | — | — |
| Side Rail | Aiming Laser | — | — | ↑ | — |
| Gas System | Under-Gassed | — | — | ↑ | — |
| Underbarrel | Vertical Foregrip | — | — | — | ↑ |
| Magazine | Armor Piercing Ammo | ↑ | — | — | — |
| Trigger Group | Match Trigger | — | — | — | — |

## MANEUVERABILITY

| | |
|---|---|
| POWER ✊ | |
| RANGE ➡ | |
| CONTROL ◎ | |
| MANEUVERABILITY ✣ | |
| RATE OF FIRE ⏱ | 999 RPM |
| MAGAZINE CAPACITY ☰ | 40 |

### MANEUVERABILITY CONFIGURATION

| Mod. Point | Attachment | ✊ | ➡ | ◎ | ✣ |
|---|---|---|---|---|---|
| Optic | Red Dot | — | — | — | ↑ |
| Stock | Collapsed | — | — | ↓ | ↑ |
| Muzzle | Compensator | — | — | ↑ | — |
| Barrel | — | — | — | — | — |
| Side Rail | Aiming Laser | — | — | ↑ | — |
| Gas System | Under-Gassed | — | — | ↑ | — |
| Underbarrel | Vertical Foregrip | — | — | — | ↑ |
| Magazine | Armor Piercing Ammo | ↑ | — | — | — |
| Trigger Group | 3-Round Burst | — | — | — | — |

## POWER

| | |
|---|---|
| POWER ✊ | |
| RANGE ➡ | |
| CONTROL ◎ | |
| MANEUVERABILITY ✣ | |
| RATE OF FIRE ⏱ | 999 RPM |
| MAGAZINE CAPACITY ☰ | 40 |

### POWER CONFIGURATION

| Mod. Point | Attachment | ✊ | ➡ | ◎ | ✣ |
|---|---|---|---|---|---|
| Optic | Tac Scope | — | ↑ | — | — |
| Stock | Extended | — | — | — | — |
| Muzzle | Compensator | — | — | ↑ | — |
| Barrel | — | — | — | — | — |
| Side Rail | Aiming Laser | — | — | ↑ | — |
| Gas System | Under-Gassed | — | — | ↑ | — |
| Underbarrel | Vertical Foregrip | — | — | — | ↑ |
| Magazine | Armor Piercing Ammo | ↑ | — | — | — |
| Trigger Group | Full-Auto | — | — | — | — |

## RANGE

| | |
|---|---|
| POWER ✊ | |
| RANGE ➡ | |
| CONTROL ◎ | |
| MANEUVERABILITY ✣ | |
| RATE OF FIRE ⏱ | 999 RPM |
| MAGAZINE CAPACITY ☰ | 40 |

### RANGE CONFIGURATION

| Mod. Point | Attachment | ✊ | ➡ | ◎ | ✣ |
|---|---|---|---|---|---|
| Optic | Tac Scope | — | ↑ | — | — |
| Stock | Extended | — | — | — | — |
| Muzzle | Compensator | — | — | ↑ | — |
| Barrel | — | — | — | — | — |
| Side Rail | Aiming Laser | — | — | ↑ | — |
| Gas System | Under-Gassed | — | — | ↑ | — |
| Underbarrel | Vertical Foregrip | — | — | — | ↑ |
| Magazine | Armor Piercing Ammo | ↑ | — | — | — |
| Trigger Group | Match Trigger | — | — | — | — |

**P90**

| | | |
|---|---|---|
| POWER | ✊ | ▯▯▯▯▯ |
| RANGE | ➡ | ▯▯▯▯▯ |
| CONTROL | ⊙ | ▯▯▯▯▯ |
| MANEUVERABILITY | ✛ | ▯▯▯▯▯ |
| RATE OF FIRE | ⏱ | 1,050 RPM |
| MAGAZINE CAPACITY | ☰ | 50 |

- CQC: Best suited for close-quarters combat engagements.
- High-Cap Mag: Base weapon magazine holds more rounds than other weapons of the same class.

**UNLOCK**
Complete Silent Talon mission.

| | |
|---|---|
| CAMPAIGN | X |
| MULTIPLAYER | X |

## OPTIMIZED CONFIGURATIONS

### CONTROL

| | | |
|---|---|---|
| POWER | ✊ | ▯▯▯▯▯ |
| RANGE | ➡ | ▯▯▯▯▯ |
| CONTROL | ⊙ | ▯▯▯▯▯ |
| MANEUVERABILITY | ✛ | ▯▯▯▯▯ |
| RATE OF FIRE | ⏱ | 945 RPM |
| MAGAZINE CAPACITY | ☰ | 50 |

#### CONTROL CONFIGURATION

| Mod. Point | Attachment | ✊ | ➡ | ⊙ | ✛ |
|---|---|---|---|---|---|
| Optic | Magnified HWS | — | — | ↑ | — |
| Stock | — | — | — | — | — |
| Muzzle | Compensator | — | — | ↑ | — |
| Barrel | — | — | — | — | — |
| Side Rail | Aiming Laser | — | — | ↑ | — |
| Gas System | Under-Gassed | — | — | ↑ | — |
| Underbarrel | — | — | — | — | — |
| Magazine | Armor Piercing Ammo | ↑ | — | — | — |
| Trigger Group | 2-Stage Trigger | — | — | — | — |

### MANEUVERABILITY

| | | |
|---|---|---|
| POWER | ✊ | ▯▯▯▯▯ |
| RANGE | ➡ | ▯▯▯▯▯ |
| CONTROL | ⊙ | ▯▯▯▯▯ |
| MANEUVERABILITY | ✛ | ▯▯▯▯▯ |
| RATE OF FIRE | ⏱ | 945 RPM |
| MAGAZINE CAPACITY | ☰ | 50 |

#### MANEUVERABILITY CONFIGURATION

| Mod. Point | Attachment | ✊ | ➡ | ⊙ | ✛ |
|---|---|---|---|---|---|
| Optic | Red Dot | — | — | — | ↑ |
| Stock | — | — | — | — | — |
| Muzzle | Compensator | — | — | ↑ | — |
| Barrel | — | — | — | — | — |
| Side Rail | Aiming Laser | — | — | ↑ | — |
| Gas System | Under-Gassed | — | — | ↑ | — |
| Underbarrel | — | — | — | — | — |
| Magazine | Armor Piercing Ammo | ↑ | — | — | — |
| Trigger Group | 2-Stage Trigger | — | — | — | — |

### POWER

| | | |
|---|---|---|
| POWER | ✊ | ▯▯▯▯▯ |
| RANGE | ⊙ | ▯▯▯▯▯ |
| CONTROL | ⊙ | ▯▯▯▯▯ |
| MANEUVERABILITY | ✛ | ▯▯▯▯▯ |
| RATE OF FIRE | ⏱ | 945 RPM |
| MAGAZINE CAPACITY | ☰ | 50 |

#### POWER CONFIGURATION

| Mod. Point | Attachment | ✊ | ➡ | ⊙ | ✛ |
|---|---|---|---|---|---|
| Optic | Tac Scope | — | ↑ | — | — |
| Stock | — | — | — | — | — |
| Muzzle | Compensator | — | — | ↑ | — |
| Barrel | — | — | — | — | — |
| Side Rail | Aiming Laser | — | — | ↑ | — |
| Gas System | Under-Gassed | — | — | ↑ | — |
| Underbarrel | — | — | — | — | — |
| Magazine | Armor Piercing Ammo | ↑ | — | — | — |
| Trigger Group | Full-Auto | — | — | — | — |

### RANGE

| | | |
|---|---|---|
| POWER | ✊ | ▯▯▯▯▯ |
| RANGE | ⊙ | ▯▯▯▯▯ |
| CONTROL | ⊙ | ▯▯▯▯▯ |
| MANEUVERABILITY | ✛ | ▯▯▯▯▯ |
| RATE OF FIRE | ⏱ | 945 RPM |
| MAGAZINE CAPACITY | ☰ | 50 |

#### RANGE CONFIGURATION

| Mod. Point | Attachment | ✊ | ➡ | ⊙ | ✛ |
|---|---|---|---|---|---|
| Optic | Tac Scope | — | ↑ | — | — |
| Stock | — | — | — | — | — |
| Muzzle | Compensator | — | — | ↑ | — |
| Barrel | — | — | — | — | — |
| Side Rail | Aiming Laser | — | — | ↑ | — |
| Gas System | Under-Gassed | — | — | ↑ | — |
| Underbarrel | — | — | — | — | — |
| Magazine | Armor Piercing Ammo | ↑ | — | — | — |
| Trigger Group | 2-Stage Trigger | — | — | — | — |

## PP19

| | |
|---|---|
| POWER | 👊 |
| RANGE | ➡ |
| CONTROL | ✥ |
| MANEUVERABILITY | ✥ |
| RATE OF FIRE | ⏱ 870 RPM |
| MAGAZINE CAPACITY | ≣ 64 |

- CQC: Best suited for close-quarters combat engagements.
- High-Cap Mag: Base weapon magazine holds more rounds than other weapons of the same class.

**UNLOCK**
Complete Firefly Rain weapon challenge.

| | |
|---|---|
| CAMPAIGN | X |
| MULTIPLAYER | |

# OPTIMIZED CONFIGURATIONS

## CONTROL

| | |
|---|---|
| POWER | 👊 |
| RANGE | ➡ |
| CONTROL | ✥ |
| MANEUVERABILITY | ✥ |
| RATE OF FIRE | ⏱ 783 RPM |
| MAGAZINE CAPACITY | ≣ 64 |

### CONTROL CONFIGURATION

| Mod. Point | Attachment | 👊 | ➡ | ✥ | ✥ |
|---|---|---|---|---|---|
| Optic | Magnified HWS | — | — | ↑ | — |
| Stock | Extended | — | — | — | — |
| Muzzle | Compensator | — | — | ↑ | — |
| Barrel | — | — | — | — | — |
| Side Rail | Aiming Laser | — | — | ↑ | — |
| Gas System | Under-Gassed | — | — | ↑ | — |
| Underbarrel | — | — | — | — | — |
| Magazine | Armor Piercing Ammo | ↑ | — | — | — |
| Trigger Group | Match Trigger | — | — | — | — |

## MANEUVERABILITY

| | |
|---|---|
| POWER | 👊 |
| RANGE | ➡ |
| CONTROL | ✥ |
| MANEUVERABILITY | ✥ |
| RATE OF FIRE | ⏱ 783 RPM |
| MAGAZINE CAPACITY | ≣ 64 |

### MANEUVERABILITY CONFIGURATION

| Mod. Point | Attachment | 👊 | ➡ | ✥ | ✥ |
|---|---|---|---|---|---|
| Optic | Red Dot | — | — | — | ↑ |
| Stock | Folded | — | — | ↓ | ↑ |
| Muzzle | Compensator | — | — | ↑ | — |
| Barrel | — | — | — | — | — |
| Side Rail | Aiming Laser | — | — | ↑ | — |
| Gas System | Under-Gassed | — | — | ↑ | — |
| Underbarrel | — | — | — | — | — |
| Magazine | Armor Piercing Ammo | ↑ | — | — | — |
| Trigger Group | Full-Auto | — | — | — | — |

## POWER

| | |
|---|---|
| POWER | 👊 |
| RANGE | ➡ |
| CONTROL | ✥ |
| MANEUVERABILITY | ✥ |
| RATE OF FIRE | ⏱ 783 RPM |
| MAGAZINE CAPACITY | ≣ 64 |

### POWER CONFIGURATION

| Mod. Point | Attachment | 👊 | ➡ | ✥ | ✥ |
|---|---|---|---|---|---|
| Optic | Tac Scope | — | ↑ | — | — |
| Stock | Extended | — | — | — | — |
| Muzzle | Compensator | — | — | ↑ | — |
| Barrel | — | — | — | — | — |
| Side Rail | Aiming Laser | — | — | ↑ | — |
| Gas System | Under-Gassed | — | — | ↑ | — |
| Underbarrel | — | — | — | — | — |
| Magazine | Armor Piercing Ammo | ↑ | — | — | — |
| Trigger Group | Match Trigger | — | — | — | — |

## RANGE

| | |
|---|---|
| POWER | 👊 |
| RANGE | ➡ |
| CONTROL | ✥ |
| MANEUVERABILITY | ✥ |
| RATE OF FIRE | ⏱ 783 RPM |
| MAGAZINE CAPACITY | ≣ 64 |

### RANGE CONFIGURATION

| Mod. Point | Attachment | 👊 | ➡ | ✥ | ✥ |
|---|---|---|---|---|---|
| Optic | Tac Scope | — | ↑ | — | — |
| Stock | Extended | — | — | — | — |
| Muzzle | Compensator | — | — | ↑ | — |
| Barrel | — | — | — | — | — |
| Side Rail | Aiming Laser | — | — | ↑ | — |
| Gas System | Under-Gassed | — | — | ↑ | — |
| Underbarrel | — | — | — | — | — |
| Magazine | Armor Piercing Ammo | ↑ | — | — | — |
| Trigger Group | Semi-Auto | — | — | — | — |

## PP2000

| | | |
|---|---|---|
| POWER | ✊ | |
| RANGE | ➡ | |
| CONTROL | ⊕ | |
| MANEUVERABILITY | ✛ | |
| RATE OF FIRE | ⏱ | 870 RPM |
| MAGAZINE CAPACITY | ☰ | 44 |

- **Fast Assault:** Ideal for quickly engaging unexpected targets or firing on the move.
- **Low Recoil:** Weapon recoil compensation system improves stability when firing multiple rounds.

UNLO

Complete Gallant Thief weapon challenge.

| CAMPAIGN | X |
|---|---|
| MULTIPLAYER | |

# OPTIMIZED CONFIGURATIONS

## CONTROL

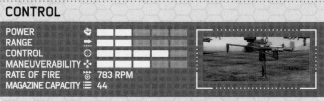

| | | |
|---|---|---|
| POWER | ✊ | |
| RANGE | ➡ | |
| CONTROL | ⊕ | |
| MANEUVERABILITY | ✛ | |
| RATE OF FIRE | ⏱ | 783 RPM |
| MAGAZINE CAPACITY | ☰ | 44 |

### CONTROL CONFIGURATION

| Mod. Point | Attachment | ✊ | ➡ | ⊕ | ✛ |
|---|---|---|---|---|---|
| Optic | Magnified HWS | — | — | ↑ | — |
| Stock | Extended | — | — | — | — |
| Muzzle | Compensator | — | — | ↑ | — |
| Barrel | — | — | — | — | — |
| Side Rail | Aiming Laser | — | — | ↑ | — |
| Gas System | Under-Gassed | — | — | ↑ | — |
| Underbarrel | — | — | — | — | — |
| Magazine | Armor Piercing Ammo | ↑ | — | — | — |
| Trigger Group | Match Trigger | — | — | — | — |

## MANEUVERABILITY

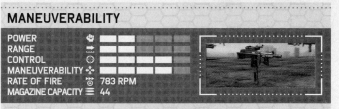

| | | |
|---|---|---|
| POWER | ✊ | |
| RANGE | ➡ | |
| CONTROL | ⊕ | |
| MANEUVERABILITY | ✛ | |
| RATE OF FIRE | ⏱ | 783 RPM |
| MAGAZINE CAPACITY | ☰ | 44 |

### MANEUVERABILITY CONFIGURATION

| Mod. Point | Attachment | ✊ | ➡ | ⊕ | ✛ |
|---|---|---|---|---|---|
| Optic | Red Dot | — | — | — | ↑ |
| Stock | Folded | — | — | ↓ | ↑ |
| Muzzle | Compensator | — | — | ↑ | — |
| Barrel | — | — | — | — | — |
| Side Rail | Aiming Laser | — | — | ↑ | — |
| Gas System | Under-Gassed | — | — | ↑ | — |
| Underbarrel | — | — | — | — | — |
| Magazine | Armor Piercing Ammo | ↑ | — | — | — |
| Trigger Group | Full-Auto | — | — | — | — |

## POWER

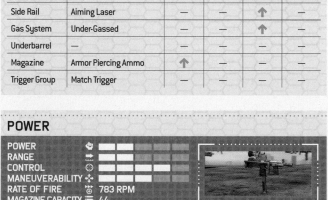

| | | |
|---|---|---|
| POWER | ✊ | |
| RANGE | ➡ | |
| CONTROL | ⊕ | |
| MANEUVERABILITY | ✛ | |
| RATE OF FIRE | ⏱ | 783 RPM |
| MAGAZINE CAPACITY | ☰ | 44 |

### POWER CONFIGURATION

| Mod. Point | Attachment | ✊ | ➡ | ⊕ | ✛ |
|---|---|---|---|---|---|
| Optic | Tac Scope | — | ↑ | — | — |
| Stock | Folded | — | — | ↓ | ↑ |
| Muzzle | Compensator | — | — | ↑ | — |
| Barrel | — | — | — | — | — |
| Side Rail | Aiming Laser | — | — | ↑ | — |
| Gas System | Under-Gassed | — | — | ↑ | — |
| Underbarrel | — | — | — | — | — |
| Magazine | Armor Piercing Ammo | ↑ | — | — | — |
| Trigger Group | Full-Auto | — | — | — | — |

## RANGE

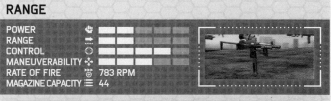

| | | |
|---|---|---|
| POWER | ✊ | |
| RANGE | ➡ | |
| CONTROL | ⊕ | |
| MANEUVERABILITY | ✛ | |
| RATE OF FIRE | ⏱ | 783 RPM |
| MAGAZINE CAPACITY | ☰ | 44 |

### RANGE CONFIGURATION

| Mod. Point | Attachment | ✊ | ➡ | ⊕ | ✛ |
|---|---|---|---|---|---|
| Optic | Tac Scope | — | ↑ | — | — |
| Stock | Extended | — | — | — | — |
| Muzzle | Compensator | — | — | ↑ | — |
| Barrel | — | — | — | — | — |
| Side Rail | Aiming Laser | — | — | ↑ | — |
| Gas System | Under-Gassed | — | — | ↑ | — |
| Underbarrel | — | — | — | — | — |
| Magazine | Armor Piercing Ammo | ↑ | — | — | — |
| Trigger Group | Semi-Auto | — | — | — | — |

## SKORPION

| | |
|---|---|
| POWER | ✊ |
| RANGE | ➡ |
| CONTROL | ◉ |
| MANEUVERABILITY | ✣ |
| RATE OF FIRE | ⏱ 900 RPM |
| MAGAZINE CAPACITY | ▤ 20 |

- CQC: Best suited for close-quarters combat engagements.
- Rapid-Fire: Weapon features a higher rate of fire than other weapons in its class.

| UNLOCK | | |
|---|---|---|
| Complete an infiltration without being detected in Guerrilla mode. | CAMPAIGN | X |
| | MULTIPLAYER | ☐ |

# OPTIMIZED CONFIGURATIONS

## CONTROL

| | |
|---|---|
| POWER | ✊ |
| RANGE | ➡ |
| CONTROL | ◉ |
| MANEUVERABILITY | ✣ |
| RATE OF FIRE | ⏱ 810 RPM |
| MAGAZINE CAPACITY | ▤ 20 |

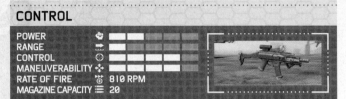

### CONTROL CONFIGURATION

| Mod. Point | Attachment | ✊ | ➡ | ◉ | ✣ |
|---|---|---|---|---|---|
| Optic | Magnified HWS | — | — | ↑ | — |
| Stock | Extended | — | — | — | — |
| Muzzle | Compensator | — | — | ↑ | — |
| Barrel | — | — | — | — | — |
| Side Rail | Aiming Laser | — | — | ↑ | — |
| Gas System | Under-Gassed | — | — | ↑ | — |
| Underbarrel | Angled Foregrip | — | — | ↑ | — |
| Magazine | Armor Piercing Ammo | ↑ | — | — | — |
| Trigger Group | Semi-Auto | — | — | — | — |

## MANEUVERABILITY

| | |
|---|---|
| POWER | ✊ |
| RANGE | ➡ |
| CONTROL | ◉ |
| MANEUVERABILITY | ✣ |
| RATE OF FIRE | ⏱ 810 RPM |
| MAGAZINE CAPACITY | ▤ 20 |

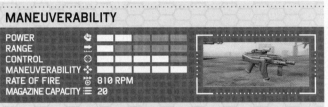

### MANEUVERABILITY CONFIGURATION

| Mod. Point | Attachment | ✊ | ➡ | ◉ | ✣ |
|---|---|---|---|---|---|
| Optic | Red Dot | — | — | — | ↑ |
| Stock | Folded | — | — | ↓ | ↑ |
| Muzzle | Compensator | — | — | ↑ | — |
| Barrel | — | — | — | — | — |
| Side Rail | Aiming Laser | — | — | ↑ | — |
| Gas System | Under-Gassed | — | — | ↑ | — |
| Underbarrel | Vertical Foregrip | — | — | — | ↑ |
| Magazine | Armor Piercing Ammo | ↑ | — | — | — |
| Trigger Group | Match Trigger | — | — | — | — |

## POWER

| | |
|---|---|
| POWER | ✊ |
| RANGE | ➡ |
| CONTROL | ◉ |
| MANEUVERABILITY | ✣ |
| RATE OF FIRE | ⏱ 810 RPM |
| MAGAZINE CAPACITY | ▤ 20 |

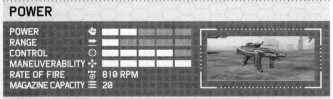

### POWER CONFIGURATION

| Mod. Point | Attachment | ✊ | ➡ | ◉ | ✣ |
|---|---|---|---|---|---|
| Optic | Red Dot | — | — | — | ↑ |
| Stock | Folded | — | — | ↓ | ↑ |
| Muzzle | Compensator | — | — | ↑ | — |
| Barrel | — | — | — | — | — |
| Side Rail | Aiming Laser | — | — | ↑ | — |
| Gas System | Under-Gassed | — | — | ↑ | — |
| Underbarrel | Vertical Foregrip | — | — | — | ↑ |
| Magazine | Armor Piercing Ammo | ↑ | — | — | — |
| Trigger Group | Match Trigger | — | — | — | — |

## RANGE

| | |
|---|---|
| POWER | ✊ |
| RANGE | ➡ |
| CONTROL | ◉ |
| MANEUVERABILITY | ✣ |
| RATE OF FIRE | ⏱ 810 RPM |
| MAGAZINE CAPACITY | ▤ 20 |

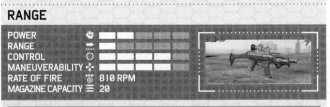

### RANGE CONFIGURATION

| Mod. Point | Attachment | ✊ | ➡ | ◉ | ✣ |
|---|---|---|---|---|---|
| Optic | Tac Scope | — | ↑ | — | — |
| Stock | Extended | — | — | — | — |
| Muzzle | Compensator | — | — | ↑ | — |
| Barrel | — | — | — | — | — |
| Side Rail | Aiming Laser | — | — | ↑ | — |
| Gas System | Under-Gassed | — | — | ↑ | — |
| Underbarrel | Angled Foregrip | — | — | ↑ | — |
| Magazine | Armor Piercing Ammo | ↑ | — | — | — |
| Trigger Group | Semi-Auto | — | — | — | — |

## VECTOR

| | |
|---|---|
| POWER | ☰☰☐☐☐ |
| RANGE | ☰☰☐☐☐ |
| CONTROL | ☰☰☰☐☐ |
| MANEUVERABILITY | ☰☰☰☰☐ |
| RATE OF FIRE | 1,440 RPM |
| MAGAZINE CAPACITY | 28 |

- ast Assault: Ideal for quickly engaging unexpected targets or firing on the move.
- Rapid-Fire: Weapon features a higher rate of fire than other weapons in its class.

**UNLOCK**
Complete Valiant Hammer mission.

| CAMPAIGN | X |
|---|---|
| MULTIPLAYER | X |

## OPTIMIZED CONFIGURATIONS

### CONTROL

| | |
|---|---|
| POWER | ☰☰☐☐☐ |
| RANGE | ☰☰☐☐☐ |
| CONTROL | ☰☰☰☐☐ |
| MANEUVERABILITY | ☰☰☰☐☐ |
| RATE OF FIRE | 1,296 RPM |
| MAGAZINE CAPACITY | 28 |

#### CONTROL CONFIGURATION

| Mod. Point | Attachment | ✊ | ➡ | ◎ | ✛ |
|---|---|---|---|---|---|
| Optic | Magnified HWS | — | — | ↑ | — |
| Stock | Extended | — | — | — | — |
| Muzzle | Compensator | — | — | ↑ | — |
| Barrel | — | — | — | — | — |
| Side Rail | Aiming Laser | — | — | ↑ | — |
| Gas System | Under-Gassed | — | — | ↑ | — |
| Underbarrel | Vertical Foregrip | — | — | — | ↑ |
| Magazine | Armor Piercing Ammo | ↑ | — | — | — |
| Trigger Group | 2-Round Burst | — | — | — | — |

### MANEUVERABILITY

| | |
|---|---|
| POWER | ☰☰☐☐☐ |
| RANGE | ☰☰☐☐☐ |
| CONTROL | ☰☰☰☐☐ |
| MANEUVERABILITY | ☰☰☰☰☐ |
| RATE OF FIRE | 1,296 RPM |
| MAGAZINE CAPACITY | 28 |

#### MANEUVERABILITY CONFIGURATION

| Mod. Point | Attachment | ✊ | ➡ | ◎ | ✛ |
|---|---|---|---|---|---|
| Optic | Red Dot | — | — | — | ↑ |
| Stock | Folded | — | — | ↓ | ↑ |
| Muzzle | Compensator | — | — | ↑ | — |
| Barrel | — | — | — | — | — |
| Side Rail | Aiming Laser | — | — | ↑ | — |
| Gas System | Under-Gassed | — | — | ↑ | — |
| Underbarrel | Vertical Foregrip | — | — | — | ↑ |
| Magazine | Armor Piercing Ammo | ↑ | — | — | — |
| Trigger Group | Semi-Auto | — | — | — | — |

### POWER

| | |
|---|---|
| POWER | ☰☰☐☐☐ |
| RANGE | ☰☰☐☐☐ |
| CONTROL | ☰☰☐☐☐ |
| MANEUVERABILITY | ☰☰☐☐☐ |
| RATE OF FIRE | 1,296 RPM |
| MAGAZINE CAPACITY | 28 |

#### POWER CONFIGURATION

| Mod. Point | Attachment | ✊ | ➡ | ◎ | ✛ |
|---|---|---|---|---|---|
| Optic | Tac Scope | — | ↑ | — | — |
| Stock | Folded | — | — | ↓ | ↑ |
| Muzzle | Compensator | — | — | ↑ | — |
| Barrel | — | — | — | — | — |
| Side Rail | Aiming Laser | — | — | ↑ | — |
| Gas System | Under-Gassed | — | — | ↑ | — |
| Underbarrel | Vertical Foregrip | — | — | — | ↑ |
| Magazine | Armor Piercing Ammo | ↑ | — | — | — |
| Trigger Group | Full-Auto | — | — | — | — |

### RANGE

| | |
|---|---|
| POWER | ☰☰☐☐☐ |
| RANGE | ☰☰☐☐☐ |
| CONTROL | ☰☰☐☐☐ |
| MANEUVERABILITY | ☰☰☐☐☐ |
| RATE OF FIRE | 1,296 RPM |
| MAGAZINE CAPACITY | 28 |

#### RANGE CONFIGURATION

| Mod. Point | Attachment | ✊ | ➡ | ◎ | ✛ |
|---|---|---|---|---|---|
| Optic | Tac Scope | — | ↑ | — | — |
| Stock | Extended | — | — | — | — |
| Muzzle | Compensator | — | — | ↑ | — |
| Barrel | — | — | — | — | — |
| Side Rail | Aiming Laser | — | — | ↑ | — |
| Gas System | Under-Gassed | — | — | ↑ | — |
| Underbarrel | Vertical Foregrip | — | — | — | ↑ |
| Magazine | Armor Piercing Ammo | ↑ | — | — | — |
| Trigger Group | Semi-Auto | — | — | — | — |

# SNIPER RIFLES

## SNIPER RIFLE ATTACHMENTS

| | Attachment | Description | Power | Range | Control | Maneuverability |
|---|---|---|:---:|:---:|:---:|:---:|
| OPTIC | Magnified HWS | 3x magnifier combined with a Holographic Weapon Sight for a good balance between easy targeting and zoom level. | — | — | ↑ | — |
| OPTIC | Tac Scope | 4x magnification sight for medium-range engagements. | — | ↑ | — | — |
| OPTIC | High Power Optic | 8x magnification for medium- to long-range engagements. | — | ↑ | — | — |
| OPTIC | Custom Sniper Optic | 12x magnification for sniping at extreme ranges. | — | ↑ | — | — |
| OPTIC | Thermal Optic | Thermal imaging optic clearly displays targets and sees through smoke. | — | — | — | ↑ |
| STOCK | Standard | Standard stock provides a good balance between Maneuverability and Control. | — | — | — | — |
| STOCK | Extended | Extended stock provides a good balance between Maneuverability and Control. | — | — | — | — |
| STOCK | Folded | Folded stock that increases Maneuverability, but decreases Control due to lack of stability. | — | — | ↓ | ↑ |
| STOCK | Pistol Grip | Pistol grip that increases Maneuverability, but decreases Control due to lack of stability. | — | — | ↓ | ↑ |
| STOCK | Fixed | Fixed stock that increases Control by reducing the amount of recoil felt. | — | — | ↑ | — |
| MUZZLE | Standard | Factory muzzle attachment. | — | — | — | — |
| MUZZLE | Compensator | Compensates for recoil and muzzle climb to increase Control. | — | — | ↑ | — |
| MUZZLE | Flash Hider | Hides muzzle flash from enemies, but decreases Control. | — | — | ↓ | — |
| MUZZLE | Suppressor | Hides muzzle flash and reduces the sound produced by firing the weapon, but decreases Power and Range due to the use of subsonic ammunition. | ↓ | ↓ | — | — |
| BARREL | Standard Barrel | Standard barrel length with a good balance between Maneuverability and Range. | — | — | — | — |
| BARREL | Long Barrel | Longer barrel length increases Range, but the added weight reduces Maneuverability. | — | ↑ | — | ↓ |
| BARREL | Short Barrel | Shorter barrel with decreased weight increases Maneuverability, but decreases Range. | — | ↓ | — | ↑ |
| SIDE RAIL | Rail Cover | Standard rail cover. | — | — | — | — |
| SIDE RAIL | Aiming Laser | Increases Control by providing a visual aid while aiming. | — | — | ↑ | — |
| SIDE RAIL | OTR Scanner | Optical target recognition uses hat detection to find enemies that are visible while aiming or in scope view. | — | — | — | — |
| GAS SYSTEM | Standard | Standard gas system with a good balance between Rate of Fire and Control. | — | — | — | — |
| GAS SYSTEM | Over-Gassed | Gas system that increases Rate of Fire, but decreases Control. | — | — | ↓ | — |
| GAS SYSTEM | Under-Gassed | Gas system that increases Control, but decreases Rate of Fire. | — | — | ↑ | — |
| UNDERBARREL | Rail Cover | Standard rail cover. | — | — | — | — |
| UNDERBARREL | Vertical Foregrip | Increases Maneuverability by improving stability while moving. | — | — | — | ↑ |
| UNDERBARREL | Angled Foregrip | Increases Control by reducing the amount of recoil felt. | — | — | ↑ | — |
| UNDERBARREL | Bipod Grip | Increases Maneuverability by improving stability while moving. When ALT-FIRE mode is activated while in cover or prone, a small Bipod deploys to increase Control. | — | — | ↑ | ↑ |
| UNDERBARREL | Bipod | When ALT-FIRE mode is activated while in cover or prone, the Bipod deploys and significantly increases Control. | — | — | ↑ | — |
| MAGAZINE | Standard Magazine | Standard magazine loaded with FMJ ammunition. | — | — | — | — |
| MAGAZINE | Armor Piercing Ammo | Standard magazine loaded with AP ammunition capable of dealing more damage to armored targets. | ↑ | — | — | — |
| MAGAZINE | Exacto Ammo | Self-guiding projectile capable of locking on to an enemy and adjusting it's trajectory mid-flight. The added guidance system decreases Power. | ↓ | — | — | — |
| MAGAZINE | Raufoss Ammo | Special ammunition that explodes on impact, dealing splash damage in a small radius. Overall Power is decreased by the lack of penetration. | ↓ | — | — | — |
| TRIGGER GROUP | Full-Auto | Full-Auto trigger group allows for continuous fire while the trigger is pulled. | — | — | — | — |
| TRIGGER GROUP | Match Trigger | Match Trigger increases the default trigger sensitivity for increased accuracy and faster follow-up shots. | — | — | — | — |
| TRIGGER GROUP | Semi-Auto | Semi-automatic trigger group allows the weapon to fire one round for every trigger pull. | — | — | — | — |

These high-precision rifles are designed to destroy valuable targets at extended ranges with aimed fire and low ammunition consumption. Forgoing rate of fire in favor of accuracy, these rifles are usually outfitted with telescopic sights and employ high-caliber munitions for long-range engagements.

| Unlock Requirements | M110 | SRR | MSR | PSL-54C | VSS | KSVK | M40A5 | M9130 |
|---|---|---|---|---|---|---|---|---|
| Unlocked by completing the Firefly Rain mission. | ✕ | ✕ | ✕ | ✕ | ✕ | ✕ | ✕ | ✕ |
| Unlocked by completing the Nimble Guardian mission. | ✕ | ✕ | ✕ | ✕ | ✕ | ✕ | ✕ | ✕ |
| Unlocked by completing all Valiant Hammer Tactical challenges. | ✕ | — | ✕ | ✕ | ✕ | ✕ | ✕ | ✕ |
| Unlocked by completing the Noble Tempest mission. | ✕ | — | ✕ | ✕ | ✕ | ✕ | ✕ | ✕ |
| Unlocked by completing the Valiant Hammer mission. | ✕ | ✕ | ✕ | ✕ | ✕ | ✕ | ✕ | ✕ |
| — | — | ✕ | — | — | — | — | ✕ | ✕ |
|  | — | — | — | ✕ | ✕ | — | — | — |
|  | — | — | — | — | ✕ | — | — | — |
| — | — | ✕ | — | — | — | — | — | — |
| Unlocked by completing all Shattered Mountain Tactical challenges. | — | ✕ | — | — | — | — | — | ✕ |
| — | ✕ | — | ✕ | ✕ | — | ✕ | ✕ | ✕ |
| Unlocked by completing the Subtle Arrow mission. | — | — | — | — | — | ✕ | — | — |
| Unlocked by completing all Subtle Arrow Tactical challenges. | ✕ | — | ✕ | ✕ | — | ✕ | ✕ | ✕ |
| — | ✕ | — | ✕ | ✕ | — | ✕ | ✕ | ✕ |
| — | ✕ | — | ✕ | ✕ | — | ✕ | ✕ | ✕ |
| — | ✕ | — | ✕ | ✕ | — | ✕ | ✕ | ✕ |
| — | ✕ | — | ✕ | ✕ | — | ✕ | ✕ | ✕ |
| — | ✕ | ✕ | ✕ | ✕ | ✕ | ✕ | ✕ | ✕ |
| Unlocked by completing the Nimble Guardian mission. | ✕ | ✕ | ✕ | ✕ | ✕ | ✕ | ✕ | ✕ |
| Unlocked by completing the Silent Talon mission. | ✕ | ✕ | ✕ | ✕ | ✕ | ✕ | ✕ | ✕ |
| — | — | — | — | — | ✕ | — | — | — |
| — | — | — | — | — | ✕ | — | — | — |
| — | — | — | — | — | ✕ | — | — | — |
| — | ✕ | ✕ | ✕ | ✕ | ✕ | ✕ | ✕ | ✕ |
| — | — | — | — | — | ✕ | — | ✕ | ✕ |
| Unlocked by completing the Nimble Guardian mission. | ✕ | ✕ | ✕ | ✕ | ✕ | ✕ | ✕ | ✕ |
| Unlocked by completing all Gallant Thief Tactical challenges. | — | — | — | — | ✕ | — | — | — |
| Unlocked by completing the Subtle Arrow mission. | ✕ | ✕ | ✕ | ✕ | ✕ | ✕ | ✕ | ✕ |
| — | ✕ | ✕ | ✕ | ✕ | ✕ | ✕ | ✕ | ✕ |
| Unlocked by completing all Deep Fire Tactical challenges. | ✕ | ✕ | ✕ | ✕ | ✕ | ✕ | ✕ | ✕ |
| Unlocked by completing the Deep Fire mission. | ✕ | ✕ | ✕ | ✕ | ✕ | ✕ | ✕ | ✕ |
| Unlocked by completing all Invisible Bear Tactical challenges. | ✕ | ✕ | ✕ | ✕ | ✕ | ✕ | ✕ | ✕ |
| — | — | — | — | — | ✕ | — | — | — |
| — | ✕ | ✕ | ✕ | ✕ | ✕ | ✕ | ✕ | ✕ |
| — | ✕ | ✕ | ✕ | ✕ | ✕ | ✕ | ✕ | ✕ |

Denotes ULC Weapon

## KSVK

| | |
|---|---|
| POWER | |
| RANGE | |
| CONTROL | |
| MANEUVERABILITY | |
| RATE OF FIRE | 600 RPM |
| MAGAZINE CAPACITY | 5 |

- **Heavy Weapon:** Devastating when fired from a stable position: crouched, prone, or braced on low cover.
- **Stopping Power:** High-caliber weapon deals more damage.

**UNLOCK**
Complete Ember Hunt mission.

| CAMPAIGN | X |
|---|---|
| MULTIPLAYER | |

# OPTIMIZED CONFIGURATIONS

## CONTROL

| | |
|---|---|
| POWER | |
| RANGE | |
| CONTROL | |
| MANEUVERABILITY | |
| RATE OF FIRE | 600 RPM |
| MAGAZINE CAPACITY | 5 |

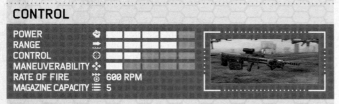

### CONTROL CONFIGURATION

| Mod. Point | Attachment | 👊 | ➡ | ◎ | ✛ |
|---|---|---|---|---|---|
| Optic | Magnified HWS | — | — | ↑ | — |
| Stock | — | — | — | — | — |
| Muzzle | Compensator | — | — | ↑ | — |
| Barrel | Short Barrel | — | ↓ | — | ↑ |
| Side Rail | Aiming Laser | — | — | ↑ | — |
| Gas System | — | — | — | — | — |
| Underbarrel | Angled Foregrip | — | — | ↑ | — |
| Magazine | Armor Piercing Ammo | ↑ | — | — | — |
| Trigger Group | Semi-Auto | — | — | — | — |

## MANEUVERABILITY

| | |
|---|---|
| POWER | |
| RANGE | |
| CONTROL | |
| MANEUVERABILITY | |
| RATE OF FIRE | 600 RPM |
| MAGAZINE CAPACITY | 5 |

### MANEUVERABILITY CONFIGURATION

| Mod. Point | Attachment | 👊 | ➡ | ◎ | ✛ |
|---|---|---|---|---|---|
| Optic | Magnified HWS | — | — | ↑ | — |
| Stock | — | — | — | — | — |
| Muzzle | Compensator | — | — | ↑ | — |
| Barrel | Short Barrel | — | ↓ | — | ↑ |
| Side Rail | Aiming Laser | — | — | ↑ | — |
| Gas System | — | — | — | — | — |
| Underbarrel | Angled Foregrip | — | — | ↑ | — |
| Magazine | Armor Piercing Ammo | ↑ | — | — | — |
| Trigger Group | Semi-Auto | — | — | — | — |

## POWER

| | |
|---|---|
| POWER | |
| RANGE | |
| CONTROL | |
| MANEUVERABILITY | |
| RATE OF FIRE | 600 RPM |
| MAGAZINE CAPACITY | 5 |

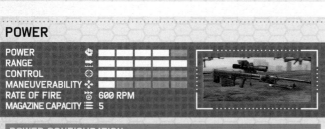

### POWER CONFIGURATION

| Mod. Point | Attachment | 👊 | ➡ | ◎ | ✛ |
|---|---|---|---|---|---|
| Optic | Custom Sniper Optic | — | ↑ | — | — |
| Stock | — | — | — | — | — |
| Muzzle | Compensator | — | — | ↑ | — |
| Barrel | Long Barrel | — | ↑ | — | ↓ |
| Side Rail | Aiming Laser | — | — | ↑ | — |
| Gas System | — | — | — | — | — |
| Underbarrel | Bipod | — | — | ↑ | — |
| Magazine | Armor Piercing Ammo | ↑ | — | — | — |
| Trigger Group | Semi-Auto | — | — | — | — |

## RANGE

| | |
|---|---|
| POWER | |
| RANGE | |
| CONTROL | |
| MANEUVERABILITY | |
| RATE OF FIRE | 600 RPM |
| MAGAZINE CAPACITY | 5 |

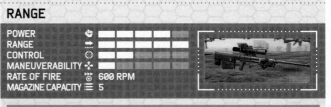

### RANGE CONFIGURATION

| Mod. Point | Attachment | 👊 | ➡ | ◎ | ✛ |
|---|---|---|---|---|---|
| Optic | Custom Sniper Optic | — | ↑ | — | — |
| Stock | — | — | — | — | — |
| Muzzle | Compensator | — | — | ↑ | — |
| Barrel | Long Barrel | — | ↑ | — | ↓ |
| Side Rail | Aiming Laser | — | — | ↑ | — |
| Gas System | — | — | — | — | — |
| Underbarrel | Angled Foregrip | — | — | ↑ | — |
| Magazine | Armor Piercing Ammo | ↑ | — | — | — |
| Trigger Group | Match Trigger | — | — | — | — |

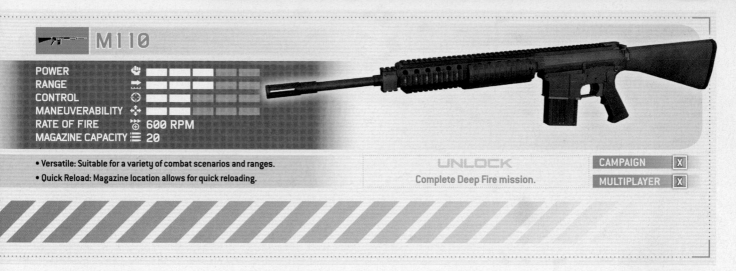

# M110

| | |
|---|---|
| POWER | |
| RANGE | |
| CONTROL | |
| MANEUVERABILITY | |
| RATE OF FIRE | 600 RPM |
| MAGAZINE CAPACITY | 20 |

- Versatile: Suitable for a variety of combat scenarios and ranges.
- Quick Reload: Magazine location allows for quick reloading.

**UNLOCK**
Complete Deep Fire mission.

| | |
|---|---|
| CAMPAIGN | X |
| MULTIPLAYER | X |

## OPTIMIZED CONFIGURATIONS

### CONTROL

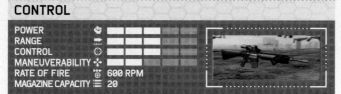

| | |
|---|---|
| POWER | |
| RANGE | |
| CONTROL | |
| MANEUVERABILITY | |
| RATE OF FIRE | 600 RPM |
| MAGAZINE CAPACITY | 20 |

#### CONTROL CONFIGURATION

| Mod. Point | Attachment | 👊 | ➡ | ⊙ | ✛ |
|---|---|---|---|---|---|
| Optic | Magnified HWS | — | — | ↑ | — |
| Stock | — | — | — | — | — |
| Muzzle | Standard | — | — | — | — |
| Barrel | Short Barrel | — | ↓ | — | ↑ |
| Side Rail | Aiming Laser | — | — | ↑ | — |
| Gas System | — | — | — | — | — |
| Underbarrel | Angled Foregrip | — | — | ↑ | — |
| Magazine | Armor Piercing Ammo | ↑ | — | — | — |
| Trigger Group | Match Trigger | — | — | — | — |

### MANEUVERABILITY

| | |
|---|---|
| POWER | |
| RANGE | |
| CONTROL | |
| MANEUVERABILITY | |
| RATE OF FIRE | 600 RPM |
| MAGAZINE CAPACITY | 20 |

#### MANEUVERABILITY CONFIGURATION

| Mod. Point | Attachment | 👊 | ➡ | ⊙ | ✛ |
|---|---|---|---|---|---|
| Optic | Magnified HWS | — | — | ↑ | — |
| Stock | — | — | — | — | — |
| Muzzle | Standard | — | — | — | — |
| Barrel | Short Barrel | — | ↓ | — | ↑ |
| Side Rail | Aiming Laser | — | — | ↑ | — |
| Gas System | — | — | — | — | — |
| Underbarrel | Angled Foregrip | — | — | ↑ | — |
| Magazine | Armor Piercing Ammo | ↑ | — | — | — |
| Trigger Group | Semi-Auto | — | — | — | — |

### POWER

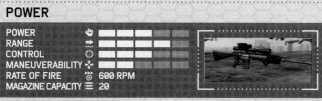

| | |
|---|---|
| POWER | |
| RANGE | |
| CONTROL | |
| MANEUVERABILITY | |
| RATE OF FIRE | 600 RPM |
| MAGAZINE CAPACITY | 20 |

#### POWER CONFIGURATION

| Mod. Point | Attachment | 👊 | ➡ | ⊙ | ✛ |
|---|---|---|---|---|---|
| Optic | Custom Sniper Optic | — | ↑ | — | — |
| Stock | — | — | — | — | — |
| Muzzle | Standard | — | — | — | — |
| Barrel | Long Barrel | — | ↑ | — | ↓ |
| Side Rail | Aiming Laser | — | — | ↑ | — |
| Gas System | — | — | — | — | — |
| Underbarrel | Angled Foregrip | — | — | ↑ | — |
| Magazine | Armor Piercing Ammo | ↑ | — | — | — |
| Trigger Group | Match Trigger | — | — | — | — |

### RANGE

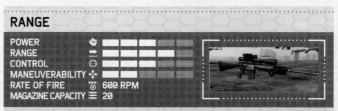

| | |
|---|---|
| POWER | |
| RANGE | |
| CONTROL | |
| MANEUVERABILITY | |
| RATE OF FIRE | 600 RPM |
| MAGAZINE CAPACITY | 20 |

#### RANGE CONFIGURATION

| Mod. Point | Attachment | 👊 | ➡ | ⊙ | ✛ |
|---|---|---|---|---|---|
| Optic | Custom Sniper Optic | — | ↑ | — | — |
| Stock | — | — | — | — | — |
| Muzzle | Standard | — | — | — | — |
| Barrel | Long Barrel | — | ↑ | — | ↓ |
| Side Rail | Aiming Laser | — | — | ↑ | — |
| Gas System | — | — | — | — | — |
| Underbarrel | Angled Foregrip | — | — | ↑ | — |
| Magazine | Armor Piercing Ammo | ↑ | — | — | — |
| Trigger Group | Semi-Auto | — | — | — | — |

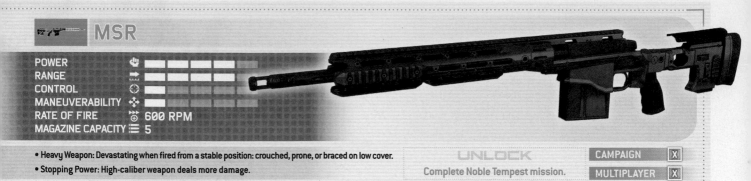

## MSR

| | |
|---|---|
| POWER | |
| RANGE | |
| CONTROL | |
| MANEUVERABILITY | |
| RATE OF FIRE | 600 RPM |
| MAGAZINE CAPACITY | 5 |

- **Heavy Weapon:** Devastating when fired from a stable position: crouched, prone, or braced on low cover.
- **Stopping Power:** High-caliber weapon deals more damage.

**UNLOCK**
Complete Noble Tempest mission.

| CAMPAIGN | X |
|---|---|
| MULTIPLAYER | X |

# OPTIMIZED CONFIGURATIONS

## CONTROL

| | |
|---|---|
| POWER | |
| RANGE | |
| CONTROL | |
| MANEUVERABILITY | |
| RATE OF FIRE | 600 RPM |
| MAGAZINE CAPACITY | 5 |

### CONTROL CONFIGURATION

| Mod. Point | Attachment | ✊ | ➡ | ◎ | ✛ |
|---|---|---|---|---|---|
| Optic | Magnified HWS | — | — | ↑ | — |
| Stock | — | — | — | — | — |
| Muzzle | Standard | — | — | — | — |
| Barrel | Short Barrel | — | ↓ | — | ↑ |
| Side Rail | Aiming Laser | — | — | ↑ | — |
| Gas System | — | — | — | — | — |
| Underbarrel | Bipod | — | — | ↑ | — |
| Magazine | Armor Piercing Ammo | ↑ | — | — | — |
| Trigger Group | Match Trigger | — | — | — | — |

## MANEUVERABILITY

| | |
|---|---|
| POWER | |
| RANGE | |
| CONTROL | |
| MANEUVERABILITY | |
| RATE OF FIRE | 600 RPM |
| MAGAZINE CAPACITY | 5 |

### MANEUVERABILITY CONFIGURATION

| Mod. Point | Attachment | ✊ | ➡ | ◎ | ✛ |
|---|---|---|---|---|---|
| Optic | Magnified HWS | — | — | ↑ | — |
| Stock | — | — | — | — | — |
| Muzzle | Standard | — | — | — | — |
| Barrel | Short Barrel | — | ↓ | — | ↑ |
| Side Rail | Aiming Laser | — | — | ↑ | — |
| Gas System | — | — | — | — | — |
| Underbarrel | Angled Foregrip | — | — | ↑ | — |
| Magazine | Armor Piercing Ammo | ↑ | — | — | — |
| Trigger Group | Match Trigger | — | — | — | — |

## POWER

| | |
|---|---|
| POWER | |
| RANGE | |
| CONTROL | |
| MANEUVERABILITY | |
| RATE OF FIRE | 600 RPM |
| MAGAZINE CAPACITY | 5 |

### POWER CONFIGURATION

| Mod. Point | Attachment | ✊ | ➡ | ◎ | ✛ |
|---|---|---|---|---|---|
| Optic | Custom Sniper Optic | — | ↑ | — | — |
| Stock | — | — | — | — | — |
| Muzzle | Standard | — | — | — | — |
| Barrel | Long Barrel | — | ↑ | — | ↓ |
| Side Rail | Aiming Laser | — | — | ↑ | — |
| Gas System | — | — | — | — | — |
| Underbarrel | Angled Foregrip | — | — | ↑ | — |
| Magazine | Armor Piercing Ammo | ↑ | — | — | — |
| Trigger Group | Match Trigger | — | — | — | — |

## RANGE

| | |
|---|---|
| POWER | |
| RANGE | |
| CONTROL | |
| MANEUVERABILITY | |
| RATE OF FIRE | 600 RPM |
| MAGAZINE CAPACITY | 5 |

### RANGE CONFIGURATION

| Mod. Point | Attachment | ✊ | ➡ | ◎ | ✛ |
|---|---|---|---|---|---|
| Optic | Custom Sniper Optic | — | ↑ | — | — |
| Stock | — | — | — | — | — |
| Muzzle | Standard | — | — | — | — |
| Barrel | Long Barrel | — | ↑ | — | ↓ |
| Side Rail | Aiming Laser | — | — | ↑ | — |
| Gas System | — | — | — | — | — |
| Underbarrel | Bipod | — | — | ↑ | — |
| Magazine | Armor Piercing Ammo | ↑ | — | — | — |
| Trigger Group | Semi-Auto | — | — | — | — |

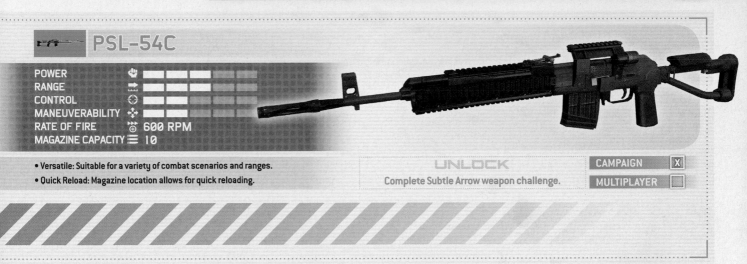

## PSL-54C

| | |
|---|---|
| POWER | ✊ |
| RANGE | ➡ |
| CONTROL | ◎ |
| MANEUVERABILITY | ✛ |
| RATE OF FIRE | ⏱ 600 RPM |
| MAGAZINE CAPACITY | ▤ 10 |

• Versatile: Suitable for a variety of combat scenarios and ranges.
• Quick Reload: Magazine location allows for quick reloading.

UNLOCK
Complete Subtle Arrow weapon challenge.

| CAMPAIGN | X |
|---|---|
| MULTIPLAYER | |

# OPTIMIZED CONFIGURATIONS

## CONTROL

| | |
|---|---|
| POWER | ✊ |
| RANGE | ➡ |
| CONTROL | ◎ |
| MANEUVERABILITY | ✛ |
| RATE OF FIRE | ⏱ 600 RPM |
| MAGAZINE CAPACITY | ▤ 10 |

### CONTROL CONFIGURATION

| Mod. Point | Attachment | ✊ | ➡ | ◎ | ✛ |
|---|---|---|---|---|---|
| Optic | Magnified HWS | — | — | ↑ | — |
| Stock | Fixed | — | — | ↑ | — |
| Muzzle | Standard | — | — | — | — |
| Barrel | Short Barrel | — | ↓ | — | ↑ |
| Side Rail | Aiming Laser | — | — | ↑ | — |
| Gas System | — | | | | |
| Underbarrel | Bipod | — | — | ↑ | — |
| Magazine | Armor Piercing Ammo | ↑ | — | — | — |
| Trigger Group | Match Trigger | — | — | — | — |

## MANEUVERABILITY

| | |
|---|---|
| POWER | ✊ |
| RANGE | ➡ |
| CONTROL | ◎ |
| MANEUVERABILITY | ✛ |
| RATE OF FIRE | ⏱ 600 RPM |
| MAGAZINE CAPACITY | ▤ 10 |

### MANEUVERABILITY CONFIGURATION

| Mod. Point | Attachment | ✊ | ➡ | ◎ | ✛ |
|---|---|---|---|---|---|
| Optic | Magnified HWS | — | — | ↑ | — |
| Stock | Fixed | — | — | ↑ | — |
| Muzzle | Standard | — | — | — | — |
| Barrel | Short Barrel | — | ↓ | — | ↑ |
| Side Rail | Aiming Laser | — | — | ↑ | — |
| Gas System | — | | | | |
| Underbarrel | Bipod | — | — | ↑ | — |
| Magazine | Armor Piercing Ammo | ↑ | — | — | — |
| Trigger Group | Semi-Auto | — | — | — | — |

## POWER

| | |
|---|---|
| POWER | ✊ |
| RANGE | ➡ |
| CONTROL | ◎ |
| MANEUVERABILITY | ✛ |
| RATE OF FIRE | ⏱ 600 RPM |
| MAGAZINE CAPACITY | ▤ 10 |

### POWER CONFIGURATION

| Mod. Point | Attachment | ✊ | ➡ | ◎ | ✛ |
|---|---|---|---|---|---|
| Optic | Custom Sniper Optic | — | ↑ | — | — |
| Stock | Fixed | — | — | ↑ | — |
| Muzzle | Standard | — | — | — | — |
| Barrel | Long Barrel | — | ↑ | — | ↓ |
| Side Rail | Aiming Laser | — | — | ↑ | — |
| Gas System | — | | | | |
| Underbarrel | Bipod | — | — | ↑ | — |
| Magazine | Armor Piercing Ammo | ↑ | — | — | — |
| Trigger Group | Semi-Auto | — | — | — | — |

## RANGE

| | |
|---|---|
| POWER | ✊ |
| RANGE | ➡ |
| CONTROL | ◎ |
| MANEUVERABILITY | ✛ |
| RATE OF FIRE | ⏱ 600 RPM |
| MAGAZINE CAPACITY | ▤ 10 |

### RANGE CONFIGURATION

| Mod. Point | Attachment | ✊ | ➡ | ◎ | ✛ |
|---|---|---|---|---|---|
| Optic | Custom Sniper Optic | — | ↑ | — | — |
| Stock | Fixed | — | — | ↑ | — |
| Muzzle | Standard | — | — | — | — |
| Barrel | Long Barrel | — | ↑ | — | ↓ |
| Side Rail | Aiming Laser | — | — | ↑ | — |
| Gas System | — | | | | |
| Underbarrel | Bipod | — | — | ↑ | — |
| Magazine | Armor Piercing Ammo | ↑ | — | — | — |
| Trigger Group | Semi-Auto | — | — | — | — |

## SRR

| | | |
|---|---|---|
| POWER | ✊ | |
| RANGE | ➡ | |
| CONTROL | ⊙ | |
| MANEUVERABILITY | ✦ | |
| RATE OF FIRE | ⏱ | 600 RPM |
| MAGAZINE CAPACITY | ≡ | 6 |

- **Versatile:** Suitable for a variety of combat scenarios and ranges.
- **Integrated Silencer:** Weapon features an integrated silencer.

**UNLOCK**
Complete Silent Talon mission.

| CAMPAIGN | X |
|---|---|
| MULTIPLAYER | X |

---

# OPTIMIZED CONFIGURATIONS

## CONTROL

| | | |
|---|---|---|
| POWER | ✊ | |
| RANGE | ➡ | |
| CONTROL | ⊙ | |
| MANEUVERABILITY | ✦ | |
| RATE OF FIRE | ⏱ | 600 RPM |
| MAGAZINE CAPACITY | ≡ | 6 |

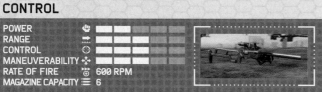

### CONTROL CONFIGURATION

| Mod. Point | Attachment | ✊ | ➡ | ⊙ | ✦ |
|---|---|---|---|---|---|
| Optic | Magnified HWS | — | — | ↑ | — |
| Stock | Fixed | — | — | ↑ | — |
| Muzzle | — | — | — | — | — |
| Barrel | — | — | — | — | — |
| Side Rail | Aiming Laser | — | — | ↑ | — |
| Gas System | — | — | — | — | — |
| Underbarrel | Angled Foregrip | — | — | ↑ | — |
| Magazine | Armor Piercing Ammo | ↑ | — | — | — |
| Trigger Group | Match Trigger | — | — | — | — |

## MANEUVERABILITY

| | | |
|---|---|---|
| POWER | ✊ | |
| RANGE | ➡ | |
| CONTROL | ⊙ | |
| MANEUVERABILITY | ✦ | |
| RATE OF FIRE | ⏱ | 600 RPM |
| MAGAZINE CAPACITY | ≡ | 6 |

### MANEUVERABILITY CONFIGURATION

| Mod. Point | Attachment | ✊ | ➡ | ⊙ | ✦ |
|---|---|---|---|---|---|
| Optic | Magnified HWS | — | — | ↑ | — |
| Stock | Pistol Grip | — | — | ↓ | ↑ |
| Muzzle | — | — | — | — | — |
| Barrel | — | — | — | — | — |
| Side Rail | Aiming Laser | — | — | ↑ | — |
| Gas System | — | — | — | — | — |
| Underbarrel | Angled Foregrip | — | — | ↑ | — |
| Magazine | Armor Piercing Ammo | ↑ | — | — | — |
| Trigger Group | Match Trigger | — | — | — | — |

## POWER

| | | |
|---|---|---|
| POWER | ✊ | |
| RANGE | ➡ | |
| CONTROL | ⊙ | |
| MANEUVERABILITY | ✦ | |
| RATE OF FIRE | ⏱ | 600 RPM |
| MAGAZINE CAPACITY | ≡ | 6 |

### POWER CONFIGURATION

| Mod. Point | Attachment | ✊ | ➡ | ⊙ | ✦ |
|---|---|---|---|---|---|
| Optic | Custom Sniper Optic | — | ↑ | — | — |
| Stock | Fixed | — | — | ↑ | — |
| Muzzle | — | — | — | — | — |
| Barrel | — | — | — | — | — |
| Side Rail | Aiming Laser | — | — | ↑ | — |
| Gas System | — | — | — | — | — |
| Underbarrel | Angled Foregrip | — | — | ↑ | — |
| Magazine | Armor Piercing Ammo | ↑ | — | — | — |
| Trigger Group | Semi-Auto | — | — | — | — |

## RANGE

| | | |
|---|---|---|
| POWER | ✊ | |
| RANGE | ➡ | |
| CONTROL | ⊙ | |
| MANEUVERABILITY | ✦ | |
| RATE OF FIRE | ⏱ | 600 RPM |
| MAGAZINE CAPACITY | ≡ | 6 |

### RANGE CONFIGURATION

| Mod. Point | Attachment | ✊ | ➡ | ⊙ | ✦ |
|---|---|---|---|---|---|
| Optic | Custom Sniper Optic | — | ↑ | — | — |
| Stock | Fixed | — | — | ↑ | — |
| Muzzle | — | — | — | — | — |
| Barrel | — | — | — | — | — |
| Side Rail | Aiming Laser | — | — | ↑ | — |
| Gas System | — | — | — | — | — |
| Underbarrel | Bipod | — | — | ↑ | — |
| Magazine | Armor Piercing Ammo | ↑ | — | — | — |
| Trigger Group | Match Trigger | — | — | — | — |

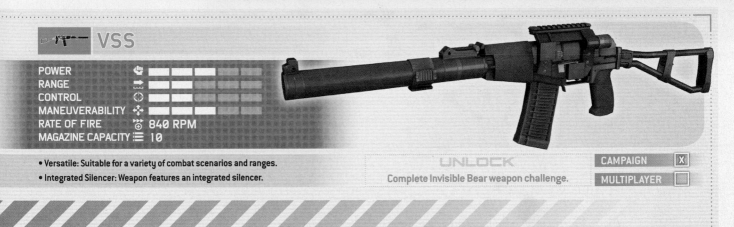

## VSS

| | | |
|---|---|---|
| POWER | ✊ | |
| RANGE | ➡ | |
| CONTROL | ◎ | |
| MANEUVERABILITY | ✛ | |
| RATE OF FIRE | ⏱ | 840 RPM |
| MAGAZINE CAPACITY | ☰ | 10 |

- Versatile: Suitable for a variety of combat scenarios and ranges.
- Integrated Silencer: Weapon features an integrated silencer.

UNLOCK
Complete Invisible Bear weapon challenge.

| CAMPAIGN | X |
|---|---|
| MULTIPLAYER | ☐ |

## OPTIMIZED CONFIGURATIONS

### CONTROL

| | | |
|---|---|---|
| POWER | ✊ | |
| RANGE | ➡ | |
| CONTROL | ◎ | |
| MANEUVERABILITY | ✛ | |
| RATE OF FIRE | ⏱ | 756 RPM |
| MAGAZINE CAPACITY | ☰ | 10 |

#### CONTROL CONFIGURATION

| Mod. Point | Attachment | ✊ | ➡ | ◎ | ✛ |
|---|---|---|---|---|---|
| Optic | Magnified HWS | — | — | ↑ | — |
| Stock | Extended | — | — | — | — |
| Muzzle | — | — | — | — | — |
| Barrel | — | — | — | — | — |
| Side Rail | Aiming Laser | — | — | ↑ | — |
| Gas System | Under-Gassed | — | — | ↑ | — |
| Underbarrel | Bipod Grip | — | — | ↑ | ↑ |
| Magazine | Armor Piercing Ammo | ↑ | — | — | — |
| Trigger Group | Match Trigger | — | — | — | — |

### MANEUVERABILITY

| | | |
|---|---|---|
| POWER | ✊ | |
| RANGE | ➡ | |
| CONTROL | ◎ | |
| MANEUVERABILITY | ✛ | |
| RATE OF FIRE | ⏱ | 756 RPM |
| MAGAZINE CAPACITY | ☰ | 10 |

#### MANEUVERABILITY CONFIGURATION

| Mod. Point | Attachment | ✊ | ➡ | ◎ | ✛ |
|---|---|---|---|---|---|
| Optic | Magnified HWS | — | — | ↑ | — |
| Stock | Folded | — | — | ↓ | ↑ |
| Muzzle | — | — | — | — | — |
| Barrel | — | — | — | — | — |
| Side Rail | Aiming Laser | — | — | ↑ | — |
| Gas System | Under-Gassed | — | — | ↑ | — |
| Underbarrel | Vertical Foregrip | — | — | — | ↑ |
| Magazine | Armor Piercing Ammo | ↑ | — | — | — |
| Trigger Group | Match Trigger | — | — | — | — |

### POWER

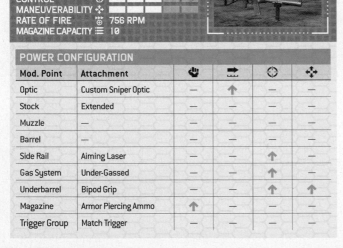

| | | |
|---|---|---|
| POWER | ✊ | |
| RANGE | ➡ | |
| CONTROL | ◎ | |
| MANEUVERABILITY | ✛ | |
| RATE OF FIRE | ⏱ | 756 RPM |
| MAGAZINE CAPACITY | ☰ | 10 |

#### POWER CONFIGURATION

| Mod. Point | Attachment | ✊ | ➡ | ◎ | ✛ |
|---|---|---|---|---|---|
| Optic | Custom Sniper Optic | — | ↑ | — | — |
| Stock | Extended | — | — | — | — |
| Muzzle | — | — | — | — | — |
| Barrel | — | — | — | — | — |
| Side Rail | Aiming Laser | — | — | ↑ | — |
| Gas System | Under-Gassed | — | — | ↑ | — |
| Underbarrel | Bipod Grip | — | — | ↑ | ↑ |
| Magazine | Armor Piercing Ammo | ↑ | — | — | — |
| Trigger Group | Match Trigger | — | — | — | — |

### RANGE

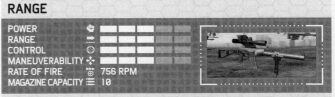

| | | |
|---|---|---|
| POWER | ✊ | |
| RANGE | ➡ | |
| CONTROL | ◎ | |
| MANEUVERABILITY | ✛ | |
| RATE OF FIRE | ⏱ | 756 RPM |
| MAGAZINE CAPACITY | ☰ | 10 |

#### RANGE CONFIGURATION

| Mod. Point | Attachment | ✊ | ➡ | ◎ | ✛ |
|---|---|---|---|---|---|
| Optic | Custom Sniper Optic | — | ↑ | — | — |
| Stock | Extended | — | — | — | — |
| Muzzle | — | — | — | — | — |
| Barrel | — | — | — | — | — |
| Side Rail | Aiming Laser | — | — | ↑ | — |
| Gas System | Under-Gassed | — | — | ↑ | — |
| Underbarrel | Bipod Grip | — | — | ↑ | ↑ |
| Magazine | Armor Piercing Ammo | ↑ | — | — | — |
| Trigger Group | Semi-Auto | — | — | — | — |

# SIDEARMS: PISTOLS

## PISTOL ATTACHMENTS

| | Attachment | Description | Power | Range | Control | Maneuverability | |
|---|---|---|---|---|---|---|---|
| **OPTIC** | Iron Sights | Standard weapon iron sights that offer quick targeting with a small viewing area. | — | — | — | — | |
| | Red Dot | Non-magnified optic that enables quick target acquisition with little visual interference. | — | — | — | ↑ | |
| **MUZZLE** | None | Standard muzzle with no effect | — | — | — | — | |
| | Suppressor | Hides muzzle flash and reduces the sound produced by firing the weapon, but decreases Power and Range due to the use of subsonic ammunition. | ↓ | ↓ | — | — | |
| **GAS SYSTEM** | Standard | Standard gas system with a good balance between Rate of Fire and Control. | — | — | — | — | |
| | Over-Gassed | Gas system that increases Rate of Fire, but decreases Control. | — | — | ↓ | — | |
| | Under-Gassed | Gas system that increases Control, but decreases Rate of Fire. | — | — | ↑ | — | |
| **UNDERBARREL** | None | Standard underbarrel rail with no effect. | — | — | — | — | |
| | Aiming Laser | Increases Control by providing a visual aid while aiming. | — | — | ↑ | — | |
| **MAGAZINE** | Standard Magazine | Standard magazine loaded with FMJ ammunition. | — | — | — | — | |
| | Extended Magazine | Extended magazine loaded with FMJ ammunition. | — | — | — | — | |
| | Armor Piercing Ammo | Standard magazine loaded with AP ammunition capable of dealing more damage to armored targets. | ↑ | — | — | — | |
| **TRIGGER GROUP** | Full-Auto | Full-Auto trigger group allows for continuous fire while the trigger is pulled. | — | — | — | — | |
| | Match Trigger | Match Trigger increases the default trigger sensitivity for increased accuracy and faster follow-up shots. | — | — | — | — | |
| | Semi-Auto | Semi-automatic trigger group allows the weapon to fire one round for every trigger pull. | — | — | — | — | |

The lightest of firearms, these weapons are designed to be operated with one hand and can be used in various scenarios where mobility is key. Their compact design, light weight, and reduced efficiency beyond short-range engagements makes them ideal sidearms.

| Unlock Requirements | 45T | KARD | GSh-18 | OTS-33 | Mk40GL Expl. | G106 Explosive | Defender | Five Seven | MP412 | Wild Boar |
|---|---|---|---|---|---|---|---|---|---|---|
| — | X | X | X | X | — | — | X | X | X | X |
| — | X | X | X | X | — | — | X | X | X | X |
| — | X | X | X | X | — | — | X | X | X | X |
| — | X | X | X | X | — | — | — | — | — | — |
| — | — | — | — | X | — | — | — | — | — | — |
| — | — | — | — | X | — | — | — | — | — | — |
| — | — | — | — | X | — | — | — | — | — | — |
| — | X | X | X | X | — | — | X | X | X | X |
| Unlocked by completing the Nimble Guardian mission. | X | X | X | X | — | — | X | X | X | X |
| — | X | X | X | X | — | — | X | X | X | X |
| Unlocked by completing all Noble Tempest Tactical challenges. | — | — | — | X | — | — | — | — | — | — |
| Unlocked by completing all Deep Fire Tactical challenges. | X | X | X | X | — | — | X | X | X | X |
| — | — | — | — | X | — | — | — | — | — | — |
| — | X | X | X | X | — | — | X | X | X | X |
| — | X | X | X | X | — | — | X | X | X | X |

Denotes ULC Weapon

## 45T

| | | |
|---|---|---|
| POWER | ✊ | ▣▣▢▢▢▢ |
| RANGE | ➡ | ▣▣▣▢▢▢ |
| CONTROL | ◎ | ▣▣▣▢▢▢ |
| MANEUVERABILITY | ✢ | ▣▣▣▢▢▢ |
| RATE OF FIRE | ⏱ | 600 RPM |
| MAGAZINE CAPACITY | ☰ | 15 |

- **Fast Assault:** Ideal for quickly engaging unexpected targets or firing on the move.
- **Extra Customization:** Weapon features additional attachment points over other weapons.

**UNLOCK**
Complete Campaign Prologue.

| CAMPAIGN | X |
|---|---|
| MULTIPLAYER | X |

# OPTIMIZED CONFIGURATIONS

## CONTROL

| | | |
|---|---|---|
| POWER | ✊ | ▣▣▢▢▢▢ |
| RANGE | ➡ | ▣▣▣▢▢▢ |
| CONTROL | ◎ | ▣▣▣▣▢▢ |
| MANEUVERABILITY | ✢ | ▣▣▣▢▢▢ |
| RATE OF FIRE | ⏱ | 600 RPM |
| MAGAZINE CAPACITY | ☰ | 15 |

### CONTROL CONFIGURATION

| Mod. Point | Attachment | ✊ | ➡ | ◎ | ✢ |
|---|---|---|---|---|---|
| Optic | Red Dot | — | — | — | ↑ |
| Stock | — | — | — | — | — |
| Muzzle | None | — | — | — | — |
| Barrel | — | — | — | — | — |
| Side Rail | — | — | — | — | — |
| Gas System | — | — | — | — | — |
| Underbarrel | Aiming Laser | — | — | ↑ | — |
| Magazine | Armor Piercing Ammo | ↑ | — | — | — |
| Trigger Group | Match Trigger | — | — | — | — |

## MANEUVERABILITY

| | | |
|---|---|---|
| POWER | ✊ | ▣▣▢▢▢▢ |
| RANGE | ➡ | ▣▣▣▢▢▢ |
| CONTROL | ◎ | ▣▣▣▢▢▢ |
| MANEUVERABILITY | ✢ | ▣▣▣▣▢▢ |
| RATE OF FIRE | ⏱ | 600 RPM |
| MAGAZINE CAPACITY | ☰ | 15 |

### MANEUVERABILITY CONFIGURATION

| Mod. Point | Attachment | ✊ | ➡ | ◎ | ✢ |
|---|---|---|---|---|---|
| Optic | Red Dot | — | — | — | ↑ |
| Stock | — | — | — | — | — |
| Muzzle | None | — | — | — | — |
| Barrel | — | — | — | — | — |
| Side Rail | — | — | — | — | — |
| Gas System | — | — | — | — | — |
| Underbarrel | Aiming Laser | — | — | ↑ | — |
| Magazine | Armor Piercing Ammo | ↑ | — | — | — |
| Trigger Group | Match Trigger | — | — | — | — |

## POWER

| | | |
|---|---|---|
| POWER | ✊ | ▣▣▣▢▢▢ |
| RANGE | ➡ | ▣▣▣▢▢▢ |
| CONTROL | ◎ | ▣▣▣▢▢▢ |
| MANEUVERABILITY | ✢ | ▣▣▢▢▢▢ |
| RATE OF FIRE | ⏱ | 600 RPM |
| MAGAZINE CAPACITY | ☰ | 15 |

### POWER CONFIGURATION

| Mod. Point | Attachment | ✊ | ➡ | ◎ | ✢ |
|---|---|---|---|---|---|
| Optic | Red Dot | — | — | — | ↑ |
| Stock | — | — | — | — | — |
| Muzzle | None | — | — | — | — |
| Barrel | — | — | — | — | — |
| Side Rail | — | — | — | — | — |
| Gas System | — | — | — | — | — |
| Underbarrel | Aiming Laser | — | — | ↑ | — |
| Magazine | Armor Piercing Ammo | ↑ | — | — | — |
| Trigger Group | Semi-Auto | — | — | — | — |

## RANGE

| | | |
|---|---|---|
| POWER | ✊ | ▣▣▢▢▢▢ |
| RANGE | ➡ | ▣▣▣▣▢▢ |
| CONTROL | ◎ | ▣▣▣▢▢▢ |
| MANEUVERABILITY | ✢ | ▣▣▣▢▢▢ |
| RATE OF FIRE | ⏱ | 600 RPM |
| MAGAZINE CAPACITY | ☰ | 15 |

### RANGE CONFIGURATION

| Mod. Point | Attachment | ✊ | ➡ | ◎ | ✢ |
|---|---|---|---|---|---|
| Optic | Red Dot | — | — | — | ↑ |
| Stock | — | — | — | — | — |
| Muzzle | None | — | — | — | — |
| Barrel | — | — | — | — | — |
| Side Rail | — | — | — | — | — |
| Gas System | — | — | — | — | — |
| Underbarrel | Aiming Laser | — | — | ↑ | — |
| Magazine | Armor Piercing Ammo | ↑ | — | — | — |
| Trigger Group | Semi-Auto | — | — | — | — |

 **GSH-18**

| POWER | ✊ | | | |
|---|---|---|---|---|
| RANGE | ➡ | | | |
| CONTROL | ◇ | | | |
| MANEUVERABILITY | ✛ | | | |
| RATE OF FIRE | ⏱ | 600 RPM | | |
| MAGAZINE CAPACITY | ▤ | 18 | | |

- Fast Assault: Ideal for quickly engaging unexpected targets or firing on the move.
- Armor Piercing: Standard weapon ammunition is armor piercing.

UNLOCK
Score five kills with an air strike in Guerilla mode.

CAMPAIGN [X]
MULTIPLAYER [ ]

## OPTIMIZED CONFIGURATIONS

### CONTROL

| POWER | ✊ | | | |
|---|---|---|---|---|
| RANGE | ➡ | | | |
| CONTROL | ◇ | | | |
| MANEUVERABILITY | ✛ | | | |
| RATE OF FIRE | ⏱ | 600 RPM | | |
| MAGAZINE CAPACITY | ▤ | 18 | | |

#### CONTROL CONFIGURATION

| Mod. Point | Attachment | ✊ | ➡ | ◇ | ✛ |
|---|---|---|---|---|---|
| Optic | Red Dot | — | — | — | ↑ |
| Stock | — | — | — | — | — |
| Muzzle | None | — | — | — | — |
| Barrel | — | — | — | — | — |
| Side Rail | — | — | — | — | — |
| Gas System | — | — | — | — | — |
| Underbarrel | Aiming Laser | — | — | ↑ | — |
| Magazine | Armor Piercing Ammo | ↑ | — | — | — |
| Trigger Group | Semi-Auto | — | — | — | — |

### MANEUVERABILITY

| POWER | ✊ | | | |
|---|---|---|---|---|
| RANGE | ➡ | | | |
| CONTROL | ◇ | | | |
| MANEUVERABILITY | ✛ | | | |
| RATE OF FIRE | ⏱ | 600 RPM | | |
| MAGAZINE CAPACITY | ▤ | 18 | | |

#### MANEUVERABILITY CONFIGURATION

| Mod. Point | Attachment | ✊ | ➡ | ◇ | ✛ |
|---|---|---|---|---|---|
| Optic | Red Dot | — | — | — | ↑ |
| Stock | — | — | — | — | — |
| Muzzle | None | — | — | — | — |
| Barrel | — | — | — | — | — |
| Side Rail | — | — | — | — | — |
| Gas System | — | — | — | — | — |
| Underbarrel | Aiming Laser | — | — | ↑ | — |
| Magazine | Armor Piercing Ammo | ↑ | — | — | — |
| Trigger Group | Semi-Auto | — | — | — | — |

### POWER

| POWER | ✊ | | | |
|---|---|---|---|---|
| RANGE | ➡ | | | |
| CONTROL | ◇ | | | |
| MANEUVERABILITY | ✛ | | | |
| RATE OF FIRE | ⏱ | 600 RPM | | |
| MAGAZINE CAPACITY | ▤ | 18 | | |

#### POWER CONFIGURATION

| Mod. Point | Attachment | ✊ | ➡ | ◇ | ✛ |
|---|---|---|---|---|---|
| Optic | Red Dot | — | — | — | ↑ |
| Stock | — | — | — | — | — |
| Muzzle | None | — | — | — | — |
| Barrel | — | — | — | — | — |
| Side Rail | — | — | — | — | — |
| Gas System | — | — | — | — | — |
| Underbarrel | Aiming Laser | — | — | ↑ | — |
| Magazine | Armor Piercing Ammo | ↑ | — | — | — |
| Trigger Group | Match Trigger | — | — | — | — |

### RANGE

| POWER | ✊ | | | |
|---|---|---|---|---|
| RANGE | ➡ | | | |
| CONTROL | ◇ | | | |
| MANEUVERABILITY | ✛ | | | |
| RATE OF FIRE | ⏱ | 600 RPM | | |
| MAGAZINE CAPACITY | ▤ | 18 | | |

#### RANGE CONFIGURATION

| Mod. Point | Attachment | ✊ | ➡ | ◇ | ✛ |
|---|---|---|---|---|---|
| Optic | Red Dot | — | — | — | ↑ |
| Stock | — | — | — | — | — |
| Muzzle | None | — | — | — | — |
| Barrel | — | — | — | — | — |
| Side Rail | — | — | — | — | — |
| Gas System | — | — | — | — | — |
| Underbarrel | Aiming Laser | — | — | ↑ | — |
| Magazine | Armor Piercing Ammo | ↑ | — | — | — |
| Trigger Group | Semi-Auto | — | — | — | — |

# TOM CLANCY'S GHOST RECON FUTURE SOLDIER

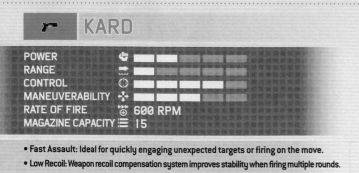

## KARD

| | |
|---|---|
| POWER | |
| RANGE | |
| CONTROL | |
| MANEUVERABILITY | |
| RATE OF FIRE | 600 RPM |
| MAGAZINE CAPACITY | 15 |

- Fast Assault: Ideal for quickly engaging unexpected targets or firing on the move.
- Low Recoil: Weapon recoil compensation system improves stability when firing multiple rounds.

**UNLOCK** — Kill 1,000 enemies in Guerrilla mode.

| CAMPAIGN | X |
| MULTIPLAYER | X |

## OPTIMIZED CONFIGURATIONS

### CONTROL

| | |
|---|---|
| POWER | |
| RANGE | |
| CONTROL | |
| MANEUVERABILITY | |
| RATE OF FIRE | 600 RPM |
| MAGAZINE CAPACITY | 15 |

#### CONTROL CONFIGURATION

| Mod. Point | Attachment | 👊 | ➡ | ◎ | ✜ |
|---|---|---|---|---|---|
| Optic | Red Dot | — | — | — | ↑ |
| Stock | — | — | — | — | — |
| Muzzle | None | — | — | — | — |
| Barrel | — | — | — | — | — |
| Side Rail | — | — | — | — | — |
| Gas System | — | — | — | — | — |
| Underbarrel | Aiming Laser | — | — | ↑ | — |
| Magazine | Armor Piercing Ammo | ↑ | — | — | — |
| Trigger Group | Semi-Auto | — | — | — | — |

### MANEUVERABILITY

| | |
|---|---|
| POWER | |
| RANGE | |
| CONTROL | |
| MANEUVERABILITY | |
| RATE OF FIRE | 600 RPM |
| MAGAZINE CAPACITY | 15 |

#### MANEUVERABILITY CONFIGURATION

| Mod. Point | Attachment | 👊 | ➡ | ◎ | ✜ |
|---|---|---|---|---|---|
| Optic | Red Dot | — | — | — | ↑ |
| Stock | — | — | — | — | — |
| Muzzle | None | — | — | — | — |
| Barrel | — | — | — | — | — |
| Side Rail | — | — | — | — | — |
| Gas System | — | — | — | — | — |
| Underbarrel | Aiming Laser | — | — | ↑ | — |
| Magazine | Armor Piercing Ammo | ↑ | — | — | — |
| Trigger Group | Semi-Auto | — | — | — | — |

### POWER

| | |
|---|---|
| POWER | |
| RANGE | |
| CONTROL | |
| MANEUVERABILITY | |
| RATE OF FIRE | 600 RPM |
| MAGAZINE CAPACITY | 15 |

#### POWER CONFIGURATION

| Mod. Point | Attachment | 👊 | ➡ | ◎ | ✜ |
|---|---|---|---|---|---|
| Optic | Red Dot | — | — | — | ↑ |
| Stock | — | — | — | — | — |
| Muzzle | None | — | — | — | — |
| Barrel | — | — | — | — | — |
| Side Rail | — | — | — | — | — |
| Gas System | — | — | — | — | — |
| Underbarrel | Aiming Laser | — | — | ↑ | — |
| Magazine | Armor Piercing Ammo | ↑ | — | — | — |
| Trigger Group | Match Trigger | — | — | — | — |

### RANGE

| | |
|---|---|
| POWER | |
| RANGE | |
| CONTROL | |
| MANEUVERABILITY | |
| RATE OF FIRE | 600 RPM |
| MAGAZINE CAPACITY | 15 |

#### RANGE CONFIGURATION

| Mod. Point | Attachment | 👊 | ➡ | ◎ | ✜ |
|---|---|---|---|---|---|
| Optic | Red Dot | — | — | — | ↑ |
| Stock | — | — | — | — | — |
| Muzzle | None | — | — | — | — |
| Barrel | — | — | — | — | — |
| Side Rail | — | — | — | — | — |
| Gas System | — | — | — | — | — |
| Underbarrel | Aiming Laser | — | — | ↑ | — |
| Magazine | Armor Piercing Ammo | ↑ | — | — | — |
| Trigger Group | Semi-Auto | — | — | — | — |

## OTS-33

| | | |
|---|---|---|
| POWER | ✊ | |
| RANGE | ➡ | |
| CONTROL | ◎ | |
| MANEUVERABILITY | ✥ | |
| RATE OF FIRE | ⏱ | 900 RPM |
| MAGAZINE CAPACITY | ☰ | 18 |

- CQC: Best suited for close-quarters combat engagements.
- Full Auto: Standard weapon trigger fires fully automatic.

### UNLOCK
Perform a Ghost Score of 60% in three missions.

| | |
|---|---|
| CAMPAIGN | X |
| MULTIPLAYER | ☐ |

## OPTIMIZED CONFIGURATIONS

### CONTROL

| | | |
|---|---|---|
| POWER | ✊ | |
| RANGE | ➡ | |
| CONTROL | ◎ | |
| MANEUVERABILITY | ✥ | |
| RATE OF FIRE | ⏱ | 810 RPM |
| MAGAZINE CAPACITY | ☰ | 18 |

#### CONTROL CONFIGURATION

| Mod. Point | Attachment | ✊ | ➡ | ◎ | ✥ |
|---|---|---|---|---|---|
| Optic | Red Dot | — | — | — | ↑ |
| Stock | — | — | — | — | — |
| Muzzle | None | — | — | — | — |
| Barrel | — | — | — | — | — |
| Side Rail | — | — | — | — | — |
| Gas System | Under-Gassed | — | — | ↑ | — |
| Underbarrel | Aiming Laser | — | — | ↑ | — |
| Magazine | Armor Piercing Ammo | ↑ | — | — | — |
| Trigger Group | Full-Auto | — | — | — | — |

### MANEUVERABILITY

| | | |
|---|---|---|
| POWER | ✊ | |
| RANGE | ➡ | |
| CONTROL | ◎ | |
| MANEUVERABILITY | ✥ | |
| RATE OF FIRE | ⏱ | 810 RPM |
| MAGAZINE CAPACITY | ☰ | 18 |

#### MANEUVERABILITY CONFIGURATION

| Mod. Point | Attachment | ✊ | ➡ | ◎ | ✥ |
|---|---|---|---|---|---|
| Optic | Red Dot | — | — | — | ↑ |
| Stock | — | — | — | — | — |
| Muzzle | None | — | — | — | — |
| Barrel | — | — | — | — | — |
| Side Rail | — | — | — | — | — |
| Gas System | Under-Gassed | — | — | ↑ | — |
| Underbarrel | Aiming Laser | — | — | ↑ | — |
| Magazine | Armor Piercing Ammo | ↑ | — | — | — |
| Trigger Group | Match Trigger | — | — | — | — |

### POWER

| | | |
|---|---|---|
| POWER | ✊ | |
| RANGE | ➡ | |
| CONTROL | ◎ | |
| MANEUVERABILITY | ✥ | |
| RATE OF FIRE | ⏱ | 810 RPM |
| MAGAZINE CAPACITY | ☰ | 18 |

#### POWER CONFIGURATION

| Mod. Point | Attachment | ✊ | ➡ | ◎ | ✥ |
|---|---|---|---|---|---|
| Optic | Red Dot | — | — | — | ↑ |
| Stock | — | — | — | — | — |
| Muzzle | None | — | — | — | — |
| Barrel | — | — | — | — | — |
| Side Rail | — | — | — | — | — |
| Gas System | Under-Gassed | — | — | ↑ | — |
| Underbarrel | Aiming Laser | — | — | ↑ | — |
| Magazine | Armor Piercing Ammo | ↑ | — | — | — |
| Trigger Group | Full-Auto | — | — | — | — |

### RANGE

| | | |
|---|---|---|
| POWER | ✊ | |
| RANGE | ➡ | |
| CONTROL | ◎ | |
| MANEUVERABILITY | ✥ | |
| RATE OF FIRE | ⏱ | 810 RPM |
| MAGAZINE CAPACITY | ☰ | 18 |

#### RANGE CONFIGURATION

| Mod. Point | Attachment | ✊ | ➡ | ◎ | ✥ |
|---|---|---|---|---|---|
| Optic | Red Dot | — | — | — | ↑ |
| Stock | — | — | — | — | — |
| Muzzle | None | — | — | — | — |
| Barrel | — | — | — | — | — |
| Side Rail | — | — | — | — | — |
| Gas System | Under-Gassed | — | — | ↑ | — |
| Underbarrel | Aiming Laser | — | — | ↑ | — |
| Magazine | Armor Piercing Ammo | ↑ | — | — | — |
| Trigger Group | Semi-Auto | — | — | — | — |

# SIDEARMS: GRENADE LAUNCHERS

Grenade launchers are devastating weapons, capable of firing 40mm high-explosive grenades. The high-explosive rounds are the only weapons in the Ghost arsenal capable of damaging armored vehicles. When firing these weapons at long range, aim high to compensate for gravity. Unlike the other weapons, grenade launchers cannot be customized with attachments or camouflage patterns—what you see, is what you get.

## G106 EXPLOSIVE

| | | |
|---|---|---|
| POWER | 👊 | |
| RANGE | ➡ | |
| CONTROL | ◎ | |
| MANEUVERABILITY | ✛ | |
| RATE OF FIRE | ⊕ | 600 RPM |
| MAGAZINE CAPACITY | ≣ | 1 |

- Explosive: Fires a 40mm HEDP round intended to wound or kill.
- Knockdown: 40mm rounds won't arm in close proximity. Unexploded 40mm rounds can temporarily knock down enemies.

UNLOCK
Complete all missions on Elite difficulty.

CAMPAIGN [X]
MULTIPLAYER [ ]

## MK40GL EXPLOSIVE

| | | |
|---|---|---|
| POWER | 👊 | |
| RANGE | ➡ | |
| CONTROL | ◎ | |
| MANEUVERABILITY | ✛ | |
| RATE OF FIRE | ⊕ | 600 RPM |
| MAGAZINE CAPACITY | ≣ | 1 |

- Explosive: Fires a 40mm HEDP round intended to wound or kill.
- Knockdown: 40mm rounds won't arm in close proximity. Unexploded 40mm rounds can temporarily knock down enemies.

UNLOCK
Perform a Ghost Score of 60% in twelve missions.

CAMPAIGN [X]
MULTIPLAYER [X]

## // Mounted Machine Guns

Throughout the course of the campaign you'll encounter several mounted machine guns that can be used to give your team a serious boost in firepower. But go easy on the trigger to prevent overheating. Make sure teammates watch your back while you're manning one of these weapons—if you're not careful, you may get flanked by enemy troops. Some machine guns are fitted with a protective steel plate that helps absorb incoming fire. But if the weapon doesn't have a steel plate, you're extremely vulnerable standing in one spot with no effective cover. In some cases, mounted machine guns are the only way to destroy vehicles such as Mi-24 attack helicopters and BTR-90 Armored Personnel Carriers (APCs).

352

primagames.com

# ITEMS

In addition to a primary and secondary weapon, each Ghost can also carry two items, including a variety of grenades as well as Sensors. Select your items carefully, based on the objectives and area of operations. If civilians are present, think twice about bringing along lethal devices like Frag grenades.

## EMP GRENADE

- Description: Disables equipment and disrupts HUD of any caught in blast.
- Quantity: 3

UNLOCK
Complete Tiger Dust mission.

### FIELD NOTES
These grenades emit an electromagnetic pulse, capable of disabling electronic equipment and vehicles. They're most effective against Bodark spec op units, causing their Optical Camo to malfunction. This makes the enemies much easier to see and target. But the EMP effect won't last long, so neutralize the Bodark units before they recover. EMP grenades can also fry the electronics in automated turrets, rendering them harmless.

## FLASHBANG

- Description: Nonlethal explosive that blinds and disorients anyone in the blast.
- Quantity: 4

UNLOCK
Complete Noble Tempest.

### FIELD NOTES
These nonlethal tactical aids are best deployed in areas where hostiles are operating in close proximity to civilians or hostages. Upon detonation, the device emits a loud sound and bright flash, temporarily blinding and deafening anyone within its blast radius. Affected targets usually rub their eyes and stumble about for a few seconds before eventually recovering.

## FRAG GRENADE

- Description: High-explosive grenade intended to kill or wound.
- Quantity: 3

UNLOCK
Complete Campaign Prologue.

### FIELD NOTES
This is a standard-issue high-explosive fragmentation grenade that is effective against personnel as well as light vehicles. Exercise extreme caution when throwing these grenades to ensure that they don't land near teammates or bounce back toward you. Each grenade has five-second fuse, and you can bank them off walls and around corners. While they're most effective against infantry, in a pinch, they can also be deployed to take out vehicles like the GAZ-66 truck or GAZ-2330 light vehicle.

## INCENDIARY GRENADE

- Description: Sets fire to an area, injuring any who attempt to pass through.
- Quantity: 3

UNLOCK
Complete Silent Talon mission.

### FIELD NOTES
Incendiary grenades are useful during a variety of offensive and defensive situations where you want to limit enemy movement. During firefights, consider deploying these on your flanks to prevent enemy troops from flanking your team. These grenades are also very effective against enemies equipped with ballistic shields. Simply toss a grenade in their path and watch them burn as they step into the fire.

## SENSOR

- Description: Detects nearby enemies, highlighting them on the HUD.
- Quantity: 5

UNLOCK
Complete Campaign Prologue.

### FIELD NOTES
Sensors can detect all enemy contacts within a large radius. The data is automatically relayed to each soldier's HUD through the use of augmented reality. This allows each member of the Ghosts to see all detected threats, even if they're hidden behind cover or within buildings. Threats outside a soldier's line of sight are shown as a silhouette on the HUD. Enemies outlined in yellow are unaware of the Ghosts presence and will not attack. However, enemies outlined in red are on alert and will return fire. By aiming at a contact, you can also see what kind of weapon they're carrying, which is ideal for threat assessment. Make a habit of targeting enemies with sniper rifles, RPGs, or light machine guns (LMGs) first as they pose the biggest threat to your team. Sensors only detect enemies for a limited time, so deploy fresh Sensors as necessary to keep informed of enemy movements. Sensors will not detect Bodark spec ops units unless they have been affected by an EMP grenade.

## SMOKE GRENADE

- Description: Creates a smokescreen, providing concealment.
- Quantity: 4

UNLOCK
Complete Deep Fire mission.

### FIELD NOTES
These grenades emit a thick cloud of gray smoke that is ideal for covering advances or defensive positions. The Ghosts (and Bodark spec ops units) have the ability to see through smoke by activating their Magnetic view or Night Vision Goggles (NVGs). As a result, deploying smoke can give them significant a tactical advantage that allows them to engage while their targets are blind. Smoke from these grenades dissipates after a few seconds, so continue tossing smoke grenades to keep an area obscured.

# ULC WEAPONS

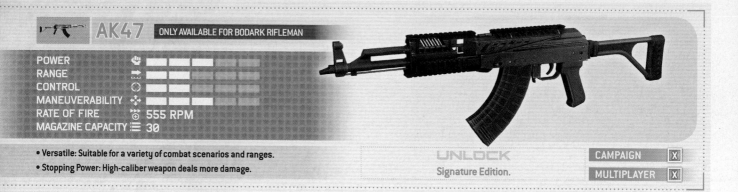

## AK47 — ONLY AVAILABLE FOR BODARK RIFLEMAN

| | |
|---|---|
| POWER | |
| RANGE | |
| CONTROL | |
| MANEUVERABILITY | |
| RATE OF FIRE | 555 RPM |
| MAGAZINE CAPACITY | 30 |

- Versatile: Suitable for a variety of combat scenarios and ranges.
- Stopping Power: High-caliber weapon deals more damage.

UNLOCK
Signature Edition.

| CAMPAIGN | X |
| MULTIPLAYER | X |

## MK14 — ONLY AVAILABLE FOR GHOST RIFLEMAN.

| | |
|---|---|
| POWER | |
| RANGE | |
| CONTROL | |
| MANEUVERABILITY | |
| RATE OF FIRE | 688 RPM |
| MAGAZINE CAPACITY | 20 |

- Accurate: Especially long range for this class of weapon.
- Stopping Power: High-caliber weapon deals more damage.

UNLOCK
Signature Edition.

| CAMPAIGN | X |
| MULTIPLAYER | X |

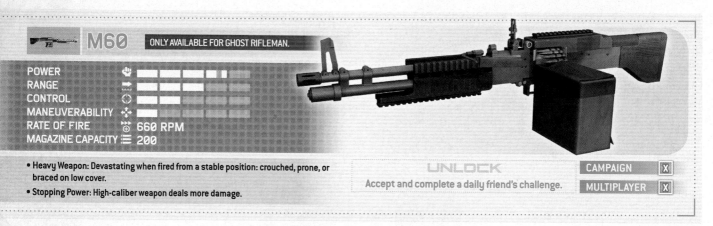

## M60 — ONLY AVAILABLE FOR GHOST RIFLEMAN.

| | |
|---|---|
| POWER | |
| RANGE | |
| CONTROL | |
| MANEUVERABILITY | |
| RATE OF FIRE | 660 RPM |
| MAGAZINE CAPACITY | 200 |

- Heavy Weapon: Devastating when fired from a stable position: crouched, prone, or braced on low cover.
- Stopping Power: High-caliber weapon deals more damage.

UNLOCK
Accept and complete a daily friend's challenge.

| CAMPAIGN | X |
| MULTIPLAYER | X |

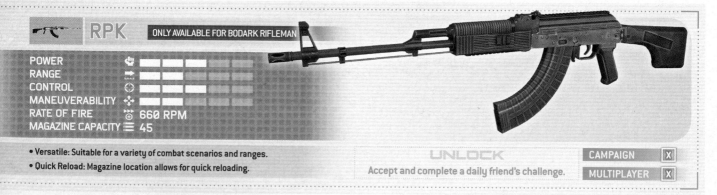

## RPK — ONLY AVAILABLE FOR BODARK RIFLEMAN

| | |
|---|---|
| POWER | |
| RANGE | |
| CONTROL | |
| MANEUVERABILITY | |
| RATE OF FIRE | 660 RPM |
| MAGAZINE CAPACITY | 45 |

- Versatile: Suitable for a variety of combat scenarios and ranges.
- Quick Reload: Magazine location allows for quick reloading.

UNLOCK
Accept and complete a daily friend's challenge.

| CAMPAIGN | X |
| MULTIPLAYER | X |

## M40A5 ONLY AVAILABLE FOR GHOST SCOUT

| | |
|---|---|
| POWER | ✊ |
| RANGE | ➡ |
| CONTROL | ⊙ |
| MANEUVERABILITY | ✛ |
| RATE OF FIRE | ⏱ BOLT–ACTION |
| MAGAZINE CAPACITY | ☰ 5 |

- Accurate: Especially long range for this class of weapon.
- Extra Customization: Weapon features additional attachment points over other weapons.

**UNLOCK**
Best Buy / Pre-order Pack1.

| CAMPAIGN | X |
|---|---|
| MULTIPLAYER | X |

## M9130 ONLY AVAILABLE FOR BODARK SCOUT

| | |
|---|---|
| POWER | ✊ |
| RANGE | ➡ |
| CONTROL | ⊙ |
| MANEUVERABILITY | ✛ |
| RATE OF FIRE | ⏱ BOLT–ACTION |
| MAGAZINE CAPACITY | ☰ 5 |

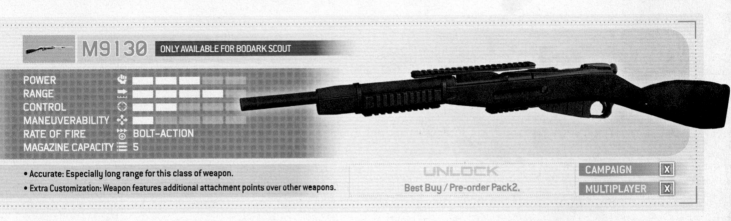

- Accurate: Especially long range for this class of weapon.
- Extra Customization: Weapon features additional attachment points over other weapons.

**UNLOCK**
Best Buy / Pre-order Pack2.

| CAMPAIGN | X |
|---|---|
| MULTIPLAYER | X |

## DEFENDER ONLY AVAILABLE FOR GHOST FACTION.

| | |
|---|---|
| POWER | ✊ |
| RANGE | ➡ |
| CONTROL | ⊙ |
| MANEUVERABILITY | ✛ |
| RATE OF FIRE | ⏱ 600 RPM |
| MAGAZINE CAPACITY | ☰ 5 |

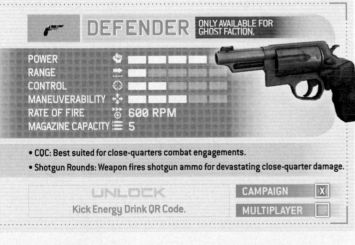

- CQC: Best suited for close-quarters combat engagements.
- Shotgun Rounds: Weapon fires shotgun ammo for devastating close-quarter damage.

**UNLOCK**
Kick Energy Drink QR Code.

| CAMPAIGN | X |
|---|---|
| MULTIPLAYER | |

## 5.7 USG ONLY AVAILABLE FOR GHOST FACTION.

| | |
|---|---|
| POWER | ✊ |
| RANGE | ➡ |
| CONTROL | ⊙ |
| MANEUVERABILITY | ✛ |
| RATE OF FIRE | ⏱ 600 RPM |
| MAGAZINE CAPACITY | ☰ 18 |

- Fast Assault: Ideal for quickly engaging unexpected targets or firing on the move.
- Extra Customization: Weapon features additional attachment points over other weapons.

**UNLOCK**
Watch the Alpha movie for hidden code.

| CAMPAIGN | X |
|---|---|
| MULTIPLAYER | |

## MP412 ONLY AVAILABLE FOR BODARK FACTION.

| | |
|---|---|
| POWER | ✊ |
| RANGE | ➡ |
| CONTROL | ⊙ |
| MANEUVERABILITY | ✛ |
| RATE OF FIRE | ⏱ 600 RPM |
| MAGAZINE CAPACITY | ☰ 6 |

- Versatile: Suitable for a variety of combat scenarios and ranges.
- Stopping Power: High-caliber weapon deals more damage.

**UNLOCK**
Facebook Game.

| CAMPAIGN | X |
|---|---|
| MULTIPLAYER | |

## WILD BOAR ONLY AVAILABLE FOR BODARK FACTION.

| | |
|---|---|
| POWER | ✊ |
| RANGE | ➡ |
| CONTROL | ⊙ |
| MANEUVERABILITY | ✛ |
| RATE OF FIRE | ⏱ 600 RPM |
| MAGAZINE CAPACITY | ☰ 6 |

- Versatile: Suitable for a variety of combat scenarios and ranges.
- Stopping Power: High-caliber weapon deals more damage.

**UNLOCK**
Get the code from Warmongersinc.net.

| CAMPAIGN | X |
|---|---|
| MULTIPLAYER | |

# 6

## COMPENDIUM

Looking for details on each Campaign challenge? The Compendium contains all the quick reference information you need, including the criteria and unlocks associated with each Campaign challenge, every Uplay activity and reward, and a full listing of every achievement and trophy for the Campaign, multiplayer, and Guerilla mode.

PAKISTAN

TIGE

WEAP

DIFFICU
UNLOCK

- Kill

SIL

WEA

DIFFIC
UNLO

- WI
in

FIR

WEA

DIFR
UNL

-

PRIM

## EMBER HUNT

### WEAPON CHALLENGE: TIGHT BURST

**DIFFICULTY:** ★☆☆☆☆
**UNLOCK:** TYPE 95

- Take down five enemies with an LMG while firing nonstop

### TACTICAL CHALLENGES

**DIFFICULTY:** ★★★★☆
**UNLOCK:** DRAGON'S BREATH

- No Safe Distance: Stealthy kill all Russian riflemen assaulting the house
- Neck Breaker: Kill 40 enemies by snapping their necks
- Countersniper: Kill all Bodark snipers during your escape

## DEEP FIRE

NORWEGIAN SEA

### WEAPON CHALLENGE: RIFLE MASTER

**DIFFICULTY:** ★★☆☆☆
**UNLOCK:** AN-94

- Kill eight enemies in under 30 seconds using an assault rifle

### TACTICAL CHALLENGES

**DIFFICULTY:** ★★★★★
**UNLOCK:** ARMOR PIERCING AMMO

- Undetected: Reach the drilling ship entrance without killing any guards
- Roger Dodger: Once the timer has started, make it to the control room in under 2 minutes
- Wrecker: Destroy all enemy vehicles during the gunride

RUSSIA

## VALIANT HAMMER

### WEAPON CHALLENGE: SHOTGUN MASTER

**DIFFICULTY:** ★★☆☆☆
**UNLOCK:** MTS-255

- With a shotgun, take out three enemies using exactly three cartridges in three seconds max

### TACTICAL CHALLENGES

**DIFFICULTY:** ★★★☆☆
**UNLOCK:** HIGH POWER SCOPE

- Ghostly Recon: On Veteran difficulty, reach the observation point without alerting any enemies
- Engraved: Rack up kills on all enemy snipers in the cemetery without being shot
- Innovative Diversity: Your squad must kill enemies with at least 15 different weapons

SIBERIA

# GALLANT THIEF

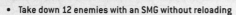

## WEAPON CHALLENGE: UP THE ANTE

DIFFICULTY: ★★☆☆☆
UNLOCK: PP2000

- Take down 12 enemies with an SMG without reloading

## TACTICAL CHALLENGES

DIFFICULTY: ★★★★★
UNLOCK: GRIPOD

- Quigley: Kill two enemies with a single bullet
- Hands On: Reach the canteen without firing a weapon
- Secret Service: On Elite difficulty, find President Volodin inside the prison in under two minutes

# INVISIBLE BEAR

## WEAPON CHALLENGE: MASTER SNIPER

DIFFICULTY: ★★☆☆☆
UNLOCK: VSS

- Using a sniper rifle, kill 15 consecutive enemies without any misses

## TACTICAL CHALLENGES

DIFFICULTY: ★★★☆☆
UNLOCK: RAUFOSS AMMO

- Dodge the Dot: Avoid being taken out by a sniper during the mission
- Clean Sweep: Clear General Bukharov's room in under 20 seconds
- Disruptor: Kill at least 10 Bodark while they are still under the effects of an EMP

# SHATTERED MOUNTAIN

## WEAPON CHALLENGE: PERSONAL OFFENSE

DIFFICULTY: ★★☆☆☆
UNLOCK: SA58 OSW

- Make five consecutive kills on unalerted enemies using a PDR

## TACTICAL CHALLENGES

DIFFICULTY: ★★★★★
UNLOCK: FIXED STOCK

- Swamp Fox: On Elite difficulty, reach the swamp without being detected
- Countdown: Kill all high value targets in the farm area in three seconds
- HVT: Intercept the two fleeing HVTs in under six minutes

## GHOST CHALLENGES

| Challenge | Reward |
|---|---|
| Perform a Ghost Score of 60% in one mission | Iranian Special Forces weapon paint |
| Perform a Ghost Score of 60% in two missions | Sri Lankan Separatist weapon paint |
| Perform a Ghost Score of 60% in three missions | OTs-33 pistol |
| Perform a Ghost Score of 60% in four missions | Chinese Type 07 Desert weapon paint |
| Perform a Ghost Score of 60% in five missions | Finnish M05 weapon paint |
| Perform a Ghost Score of 60% in six missions | AKS-74U PDR |
| Perform a Ghost Score of 60% in seven missions | Greek weapon paint |
| Perform a Ghost Score of 60% in eight missions | Kuwaiti Special Forces weapon paint |
| Perform a Ghost Score of 60% in nine missions | Ultimax Mk.5 LMG |
| Perform a Ghost Score of 60% in ten missions | Indian Vertical Lizard weapon paint |
| Perform a Ghost Score of 60% in eleven missions | USSR TTsKO weapon paint |
| Perform a Ghost Score of 60% in twelve missions | MK40GL grenade launcher |

| Elite Challenge | Reward |
|---|---|
| Complete all missions on Elite difficulty | G106 grenade launcher |

## UPLAY ACTIVITIES

| Name | Description | Units Earned |
|---|---|---|
| First Strike | Complete the first Campaign mission | 10 |
| Mission Accomplished | Complete the entire Campaign | 20 |
| Brothers in Arms | Complete a Friend Challenge | 30 |
| One Man Army | Reach Level 10 on one Rifleman, one Scout, and one Engineer character | 40 |

## UPLAY REWARDS

| Reward | Description | Cost |
|---|---|---|
| TC's Ghost Recon FS Theme | A *Tom Clancy's Ghost Recon Future Soldier* Theme | 10 |
| Double Time | This reward can unlock both weapons at a decision point. Valid for one decision on one MP character | 20 |
| Rock and Roll | Receive the M60 and RPK light machine guns | 30 |
| Rooftops Map | Receive the Rooftops map to play in Guerrilla mode | 40 |

# CAMPAIGN COMPLETION UNLOCKS

## PROLOGUE: COMPLETION UNLOCKS

| Type | Category | Item |
|---|---|---|
| Weapon | PDR | Goblin |
| Weapon | LMG | Mk48 |
| Weapon | Sidearm | 45T |
| Attachment | Optics | Iron Sight |
| Attachment | Optics | Red Dot |
| Attachment | Underbarrel | Vertical Foregrip |
| Attachment | Underbarrel | Rail Cover |
| Attachment | Magazine | Standard |
| Attachment | Stock | Standard |
| Attachment | Muzzle | Suppressor |
| Items | Grenades | Frag Grenades |
| Items | Grenades | Sensors |
| Paint | Weapon paint | Solid Black |
| Paint | Weapon paint | Solid Green |
| Paint | Weapon paint | Solid Tan |
| Paint | Weapon paint | Multicam |

## NIMBLE GUARDIAN: COMPLETION UNLOCKS

| Type | Category | Item |
|---|---|---|
| Weapon | Assault Rifle | 417 |
| Weapon | SMG | MP7 |
| Weapon | Shotgun | M590A1 |
| Attachment | Optic | Tac Scope |
| Attachment | Underbarrel | Angled Foregrip |
| Attachment | Side Rail | Aiming Laser |
| Attachment | Stock | Folded |
| Items | Camo | Optical Camo |
| Items | View | Magnetic |
| Paint | Weapon paint | USSR TTsKO North Africa |
| Paint | Weapon paint | French Daguet |

## SUBTLE ARROW: COMPLETION UNLOCKS

| Type | Category | Item |
|---|---|---|
| Weapon | PDR | L22A2 |
| Weapon | LMG | Stoner 96 |
| Attachment | Muzzle | Compensator |
| Attachment | Underbarrel | Bipod |
| Items | Drone | UAV |
| Paint | Weapon paint | Libyan |

## NOBLE TEMPEST: COMPLETION UNLOCKS

| Type | Category | Item |
|---|---|---|
| Weapon | Sniper Rifle | MSR |
| Attachment | Optics | Custom Sniper Optic |
| Items | Grenade | Flashbang |
| Items | Drone | UAV + Crawler |
| Paint | Weapon paint | Brazilian Urban |

## TIGER DUST: COMPLETION UNLOCKS

| Type | Category | Item |
|---|---|---|
| Weapon | PDR | PDR-C |
| Items | Grenades | EMP |
| Items | Drone | Warhound |
| Paint | Weapon paint | Navy NWU |
| Paint | Weapon paint | Navy AOR1 |

## SILENT TALON: COMPLETION UNLOCKS

| Type | Category | Item |
|---|---|---|
| Weapon | Sniper Rifle | SRR |
| Weapon | SMG | P90 |
| Attachment | Side Rail | OTR Scanner |
| Items | Grenades | Incendiary |
| Items | Goggles | Night Vision |
| Paint | Weapon paint | Russian Digital |

## FIREFLY RAIN: COMPLETION UNLOCKS

| Type | Category | Item |
|---|---|---|
| Weapon | Assault Rifle | ACR |
| Weapon | Shotgun | M1014 |
| Attachment | Optic | Magnified HWS |
| Paint | Weapon paint | Air Force ABU |

## EMBER HUNT: COMPLETION UNLOCKS

| Type | Category | Item |
|---|---|---|
| Weapon | Sniper Rifle | KSVK |
| Weapon | LMG | LSAT |
| Attachment | Magazine | Incendiary Ammo |
| Attachment | Optic | Backscatter Optic |
| Paint | Weapon paint | Chinese Type 07 Oceanic |
| Paint | Weapon paint | Canadian Cadpat |

## DEEP FIRE: COMPLETION UNLOCKS

| Type | Category | Item |
|---|---|---|
| Weapon | Sniper Rifle | M110 |
| Attachment | Magazine | EXACTO Ammo |
| Items | Grenades | Smoke |
| Paint | Weapon paint | ATACS |
| Paint | Weapon paint | Australian DPCU Urban |

## VALIANT HAMMER: COMPLETION UNLOCKS

| Type | Category | Item |
|---|---|---|
| Weapon | SMG | Vector |
| Weapon | LMG | Ultimax Mk.5 |
| Attachment | Optic | Thermal Optic |
| Paint | Weapon paint | Danish T90 |
| Paint | Weapon paint | Iraqi Urban |

## GALLANT THIEF: COMPLETION UNLOCKS

| Type | Category | Item |
|---|---|---|
| Weapon | Assault Rifle | TAR-21 |
| Attachment | Underbarrel | 40mm HEDP Launcher |
| Paint | Weapon paint | Army ACU |
| Paint | Weapon paint | Estonian |

## INVISIBLE BEAR: COMPLETION UNLOCKS

| Type | Category | Item |
|---|---|---|
| Weapon | Shotgun | M12 |
| Weapon | Assault Rifle | A-91 |
| Paint | Weapon paint | Marine Marpat |

## SHATTERED MOUNTAIN: COMPLETION UNLOCKS

| Type | Category | Item |
|---|---|---|
| Paint | Weapon paint | Russian MVD |

## GHOST SCOUT PROGRESSION

| Level | Reward |
|-------|--------|
| 4 | NVT Scope OR Decoy Grenade |
| 6 | Watch Cap V2 |
| 8 | Med Kit |
| 12 | BLD-3 Flash Bulb |
| 14 | CW Mask V1 |
| 16 | EXACTO Rounds OR OTR Scanner |
| 20 | SRR OR P90 |
| 22 | CW Mask V2 |
| 24 | KARD |
| 28 | Stun Mine OR Augmented Camo |
| 30 | CBRN V1 |
| 32 | MSR OR Vector |
| 36 | Armor Piercing Ammo |
| 38 | CBRN V2 |
| 40 | Claymore OR RAUFOSS Rounds |
| 44 | Hood V1 |
| 50 | Hood V2 |

## BODARK SCOUT PROGRESSION

| Level | Reward |
|-------|--------|
| 4 | NVT Scope OR Decoy Grenade |
| 6 | CWH-1 V2 |
| 8 | Med Kit |
| 12 | BLD-3 Flash Bulb |
| 14 | CWM-1 V1 |
| 16 | EXACTO Rounds OR OTR Scanner |
| 20 | VSS OR PP19 |
| 22 | CWM-1 V2 |
| 24 | OTS-33 |
| 28 | Stun Mine OR Augmented Camo |
| 30 | MTM-1 V1 |
| 32 | KSVK OR Skorpion |
| 36 | Armor Piercing Ammo |
| 38 | MTM-1 V2 |
| 40 | Claymore OR RAUFOSS Rounds |
| 44 | CWH-2 V1 |
| 50 | CWH-2 V2 |

## GHOST ENGINEER PROGRESSION

| Level | Reward |
|-------|--------|
| 4 | UAV OR Field Computer |
| 6 | Tac Cap Opt A V2 |
| 8 | Med Kit |
| 12 | BLD-3 Flash Bulb |
| 14 | Tac Cap Opt B V1 |
| 16 | Smoke Grenade OR Dragon's Breath |
| 20 | M1014 OR PDR-C |
| 22 | Tac Cap Opt B V2 |
| 24 | KARD |
| 28 | Slugs OR Jammer |
| 30 | Tac Cap Opt C V1 |
| 32 | M12 OR L22A2 |
| 36 | Armor Piercing Ammo |
| 38 | Tac Cap Opt C V2 |
| 40 | Sentry Turret OR UCAV |
| 44 | Watch Cap V1 |
| 50 | Watch Cap V2 |

## BODARK ENGINEER PROGRESSION

| Level | Reward |
|-------|--------|
| 4 | UAV OR Field Computer |
| 6 | GFC-1 V2 |
| 8 | Med Kit |
| 12 | BLD-3 Flash Bulb |
| 14 | CWC-1 V1 |
| 16 | Smoke Grenade OR Dragon's Breath |
| 20 | MTs-255 OR SR-3M |
| 22 | CWC-1 V2 |
| 24 | OTS-33 |
| 28 | Slugs OR Jammer |
| 30 | GWC-1 V1 |
| 32 | Saiga 12 OR SA58 OSW |
| 36 | Armor Piercing Ammo |
| 38 | GWC-1 V2 |
| 40 | Sentry Turret OR UCAV |
| 44 | GFC-2 V1 |
| 50 | GFC-2 V2 |

## GHOST RIFLEMAN PROGRESSION

| Level | Reward |
|-------|--------|
| 4 | 40mm Smoke Launcher OR UB Stun Gun |
| 6 | MICH 2015 V2 |
| 8 | Med Kit |
| 12 | BLD-3 Flash Bulb |
| 14 | FAST-B Opt A V1 |
| 16 | Ammo Box OR 40mm EMP Launcher |
| 20 | 417 OR Stoner 96 |
| 22 | FAST-B Opt A V2 |
| 24 | KARD |
| 28 | Incendiary Grenade OR 40mm HEDP Launcher |
| 30 | FAST-B Opt B V1 |
| 32 | TAR-21 OR LSAT |
| 36 | Armor Piercing Ammo |
| 38 | FAST-B Opt B V2 |
| 40 | Incendiary Ammo OR Backscatter Optic |
| 44 | IWH-2014 V1 |
| 50 | IWH-2014 V2 |

## BODARK RIFLEMAN PROGRESSION

| Level | Reward |
|-------|--------|
| 4 | 40mm Smoke Launcher OR UB Stun Gun |
| 6 | GPH-3A V2 |
| 8 | Med Kit |
| 12 | BLD-3 Flash Bulb |
| 14 | GPH-1A V1 |
| 16 | Ammo Box OR 40mm EMP Launcher |
| 20 | AN-94 OR Type 95 |
| 22 | GPH-1A V2 |
| 24 | OTS-33 |
| 28 | Incendiary Grenade OR 40mm HEDP Launcher |
| 30 | GPH-2A V1 |
| 32 | A-91 OR Ultimax Mk.5 |
| 36 | Armor Piercing Ammo |
| 38 | GPH-2A V2 |
| 40 | Incendiary Ammo OR Backscatter Optic |
| 44 | GPH-3B V1 |
| 50 | GPH-3B V2 |

primagames.com

# TOM CLANCY'S GHOST RECON FUTURE SOLDIER™

## PRIMA Official Game Guide

**Written by David Knight and Sam Bishop**

## PRIMA GAMES

**An Imprint of Random House, Inc.**

3000 Lava Ridge Road, St. 100
Roseville, CA 95661

www.primagames.com

**Product Managers:** Paul Giacomotto, James Knight
**Digital Product Manager:** James Knight
**Design & Layout:** Marc W. Riegel
**Copyeditor:** Sara Wilson

ISBN: 978-0-307-46967-0
Printed in the United States of America

## SPECIAL THANKS

Special thanks from David Knight and Sam Bishop: Thanks to Ubisoft for their support...particularly the testers and Theodor Diea. Additionally, Paul Bernardo stepped up big time to help with data mining and capturing gameplay footage.

Special thanks from Prima Games: Huge thanks to all the supporting Ubisoft team! Specifically—Alexandre Nicq, Adrian Lacey, Sebastien Signoret, Alex Banks, Danielle Lajoie, Lindsay Cohen, Martial Potron, Tara Manasse, Theodor Diea, and Trey Williamson. Also very important to the creation of this guide—Donato Tica, Paul Bernardo, Greg Off, Stacy Burt, Jeremy Chan, Josh Richardson, and David Brothers. Last but not least—the authors, David Knight and Sam Bishop, for their dedication and drive to make something good...even through sickness. Thank you all!

The following development team also contributed to the making of this guide:

Jean-Marc Geffroy, Creative Director
Eric Couzian, Game Director
Xavier Marquis, Art Director
Laurent Fischer, Technical Art Director
Roman Campos Oriola, Lead Game Designer
Martial Potron, Game Designer
Elie Benhamou, Game Designer
Matthieu Crepaux, Lead Level Designer
Vincent Hamache, Lead Level Designer

Florent Guillaume, Level Designer
Sirada Jensen, Level Designer
Thibaut Machin, Level Designer
Frederick Gaveau, Level Designer
Olivier Conorton, Level Designer
Matthieu Chane, Level Designer
Mathieu Purzycki, Senior UI Artist
Lionel Ledain, Project Assistant
David Grivel, Game Designer

### Adversarial Mode contributors:

Tommy Jacob, Creative Director
David Self, Art Director
Kevin Sizer, Game Designer
Tray Epperly, Game Designer

Vinson Johnson , Game Designer
Evan Champlin, Level Design Lead
Michael Climer, Vehicles and Weapons Artist
JD Cragg, Vehicles & Weapons Artist

# GHOST RECON
## FUTURE SOLDIER

## ACHIEVEMENTS AND TROPHIES

| Image | Name | Description | Gamerscore | Trophy |
|---|---|---|---|---|
| **Campaign** | | | | |
| | Loose Thread | Secure Gabriel Paez | 20 | Bronze |
| | What goes up ... | Shoot down the cargo plane | 20 | Bronze |
| | Precious Cargo | Secure the VIP and transfer him to the exfiltration team | 20 | Bronze |
| | Source Control | Secure the VIPs and transfer them to the exfiltration team | 20 | Bronze |
| | EOD | Destroy the Russian weapons transfer station | 20 | Bronze |
| | ... must come down. | Destroy the plane with the weapons system on board while it is in flight | 20 | Bronze |
| | Blood Brother | Rescue the Georgian Spec Ops | 20 | Bronze |
| | Fuel for the Fire | Secure the drilling ships and complete the mission | 20 | Bronze |
| | Breathing Room | Destroy the second piece of enemy artillery | 20 | Bronze |
| | Special Election | Rescue Russian President Volodin from the prison camp | 20 | Bronze |
| | Relieved of Command | Kill the general commanding the Moscow defenses | 20 | Bronze |
| | No Loose Ends | Eliminate the leader of the Raven's Rock faction | 20 | Bronze |
| | Just Another Day at the Office | Complete the Campaign | 30 | Silver |
| | Future Soldier | Complete the Campaign on Regular difficulty | 40 | Silver |
| | Advanced Warfighter | Complete the Campaign on Elite difficulty | 50 | Gold |
| | Battle Buddies | Complete the Campaign in Co-op | 30 | Bronze |
| | Tactician | Complete 50% of the tactical challenges | 10 | Bronze |
| | Master Tactician | Complete 100% of the tactical challenges | 25 | Silver |
| | Qualified | Have a Ghost score of 90% for a single mission | 25 | Bronze |
| | Good Enough for Government Work | Have a Ghost Skill of 80% for all missions | 10 | Bronze |
| **Guerrilla Mode** | | | | |
| N/A | Just a Box | Complete an infiltration sequence without being detected | 10 | Bronze |
| | Good Effect on Target | Kill more than five enemies with an airstrike | 10 | Bronze |
| | Quality Beats Quantity | Defeat 50 enemy waves | 30 | Silver |
| | Doing Work | Kill 1000 enemies while in Guerrilla mode | 10 | Bronze |